Born in Boston in 1803, Ralph Waldo Emerson early knew adversity. His father died when he was eight; his widowed mother was forced to become a landlady to support her five sons. After working his way through Harvard, the author suffered first from temporary loss of vision in one eye, then from a lung disease; later he was to experience the early deaths of his first wife, two of his brothers, and his first son. As a schoolteacher he was dissatisfied; as pastor he was forced to resign his position because of doctrinal differences with his Church. He persevered, however, to become one of his country's most vital voices: an immensely influential lecturer, essayist and poet and a fierce foe of slavery and political immorality. On his trips abroad, he came in contact with such figures as Wordsworth, Tennyson, and Dickens, and formed a deep friendship with Thomas Carlyle. At home his circle of friends included Margaret Fuller, Bronson Alcott, Hawthorne, and Thoreau. His death in 1882 was mourned not only by the village of Concord—where he had lived most of his life—but by the nation whose highest ideals he had so nobly represented.

SELECTED WRITINGS OF

Ralph Waldo Emerson

EDITED AND WITH A FOREWORD BY
WILLIAM H. GILMAN

Revised and Updated Bibliography

A SIGNET CLASSIC

NEW AMERICAN LIBRARY

NEW YORK AND SCARBOROUGH, ONTARIO

SIGNET, SIGNET CLASSIC, MENTOR, PLUME, MERIDIAN AND NAL
BOOKS are published *in the United States* by
New American Library,
1633 Broadway, New York, New York 10019,
in Canada by The New American Library of Canada Limited,
81 Mack Avenue, Scarborough, Ontario M1L 1M8

First Printing, November, 1965

10   11   12   13   14   15   16   17   18

PRINTED IN THE UNITED STATES OF AMERICA

Table of Contents

III. Poems

FOREWORD

Like Bottom, Emerson once confessed, he wanted to play all the parts. When he read Scott he wanted to be a novelist; if he saw a verse or two, even in a newspaper, he would be a poet; in his daydreams he yearned to be a painter; after reading Herschel on the study of the physical sciences, he wanted to buy a telescope and a laboratory and be a natural scientist; if he heard boys reciting their mathematics, he thought of being a mathematician. "There is almost no walk of the muse," he wrote, "& more almost no way of life but at some time or other, I have caught the romance of it—farmer, stageman, merchant, editor, but far far above all the herb & berry woman." Except for Whitman, perhaps no American in the nineteenth century was so responsive to all experience, all occupations, all interests and powers of the body, soul, and mind. Harold Laski describes the prototypical American as a man trying to be a specialist in omnicompetence. If he was thinking more of practical men like Jefferson and Franklin, he was also describing Emerson, at least in his aspirations. Emerson wanted to be the universal sensibility, the one man who stood for all men. When he warned Bronson Alcott against a too narrowly personal mode of allusion, he defined his own ideal of an author: "The author's Ego must be the human Ego, & not that of his name & town." This cosmic ego was to include every mode of experience, every kind of knowledge, every aesthetic, ethical, or metaphysical perception which could be metamorphosed into versions of the truth. Notably, it included the feminine sensibility: it is the "herb & berry woman" who climaxes Emerson's list of occupations or roles. He meant, of course, the tough yet perceptive, the patient, knowing, docile woman who has extracted by experience and observation the secrets of nature and who serves them up to man to heal and nourish him.

It is no surprise that Emerson found a parallel to himself in a Shakespearean character whose achieved ideal would have been the dramatic rendering of all roles. Emerson's entire life, personal, intellectual, and social, is best read as a drama, a permanent agon, a struggle with elusive or menacing forces, in which no permanent victory was possible. His journals are sometimes a "soliloquy," sometimes a running dialogue between his various selves. His essays and lectures are frequently dramatic engagements between himself and his audience—congregation, lecture crowd, readers. Emerson was a multiple personality trying to be single. Every history in the world was his history, he said; he would find himself in Atrides, the Vedas, the New Testament, and the Declaration of Independence. His doctrine of $\dot{\epsilon}\nu$ $\kappa\alpha\dot{\iota}$ $\pi\hat{\alpha}\nu$—the one and the many—embraces the world outside but also himself. "Write always to yourself," he said, "& you write to an eternal public." Like his own poet, he would stand "among partial men for the complete man." He struggled to embrace and reconcile all that was various, diverse, and individual, and live a life for once that illustrated the most a man could be. He was or tried to be the ideal son, nephew, friend, teacher, preacher, traveler, lover, husband, father, gardener, farmer, letter writer, thinker, knower, and doer. Most of all, he tried to be the active soul, with a sensibility so fine that no experience could possibly be empty of meaning. For most of his early years—to 1840, say—Emerson expressed an almost compulsive ambition to be everything that he could be, to think all the great thoughts, have visions of divine and unalterable truth, be a human personality so apparently without limit as to challenge the very gods. Pleased by tokens of divinity which implied that man could escape limitation if only he listened to the God within and rejected every thought, custom and attitude that lacked the sanction of his own intuition of the truth, Emerson seemed to ascend year by year on a trajectory that was pointed toward the infinite. At times almost nothing seemed too intractable, too impervious, to be brought under benign laws, if only one were, as Emerson described himself, "an endless seeker, with no Past at my back." Nothing in the universe, not war, nor sin, nor pleasure, nor insanity, nor sleep, nor death seemed beyond the reach of Emerson's enveloping empathy. Everything had a life, a role to be enacted; everything required the right actor to voice its own proper being. Like Bottom, Emerson would play all the parts.

Emerson gave various names to the one actor who could play all the parts—the scholar, the poet, the transcendentalist, the active soul. Whatever his name, his occupation was always the same—to feel what he thought—to fuse passion, intellect, imagination, understanding, reason, and soul; to open doors everywhere, to the darkest realm of the unconscious as well as to the sublime; to experiment, to try out ideas, to unsettle everything; to be like nature itself, always creating, always growing, always becoming something else, never standing still, because the penalty for standing still was death.

In many ways Emerson was the most ambitious man in America, in an age when the climate of political and economic opportunity encouraged unlimited ambition and the hope of attaining freedom without limit, or limitation. But whereas most of his countrymen pursued their ambitions in the material sphere of political and economic freedom, Emerson followed his in the sphere of the soul, of man's total organic being. He sometimes complained about the limitations of the body, in the manner of Byron or Shelley, and the dichotomy between soul and body bewildered him at times, but in his earlier years at least he seemed able to resolve the problem by appeal to the power of spirit. Hence it was once believed that Emerson maintained a continual state of equanimity or equilibrium where conflicts between the ideal and the actual were only minor and ephemeral. The opposite is the truth. The law of Emerson's life, like the psychological law of most creative lives, was the law of simultaneous ebb and flow, of continuous conflict and tension between what Emerson early called, in Johnson's phrase, "opposite probabilities." He thought he had a double consciousness; in fact he had a multiple consciousness; not one angle of vision, but several angles of vision, and he regularly saw things not only from different angles of vision at different times but from different angles of vision at the same time. It is now conventional to describe Emerson's way of seeing in linear and sequential terms—as in successive if interrupted perceptions of subtended arcs of meaning, the totals of which formed a completed circle or set of circles. The theory accounts for

only a part of Emerson's intellectual behavior. The evidence
is that Emerson's vision was just as much the product of
concurrent tensions, of a bipolarity which found him simultaneously attracted to and repelled by opposed ideas. This
pattern is necessarily not apparent in his essays, where
the need of ordering thought in discrete units denies expression to the psychological reality. That reality is clearer in
the journals, especially in passages where Emerson is ex-
plicit. To understand that psychological reality is to have the
foundation for understanding Emerson.

The Emerson of changing moods—of alternating angles of
vision—is well-known. Emerson admitted this part of his condition in the much-quoted phrase, "I am always insincere, as
always knowing there are other moods." In a curious metaphor, he described this puzzling phenomenon of shifts in the
power of knowing things in some moods which we do not
know in others by invoking hypnosis (for which he had mostly contempt): we are like "mesmerized patients who are
clairvoyant at night & in the day know nothing of that which
they told." He wrote the poem "Days" in 1851; a year later
he could not remember composing or correcting it, knew he
could not write its like again, concluded again that "one
state of mind does not remember or conceive of another
state."

But Emerson had also the capacity for doubled and contrary vision. At 21 he saw that if knowledge was power it
was also pain. At 22 he saw that if the evil principle created
the soul then good could come from evil, but that if the
good principle created the soul, then evil could come from
good. He saw that improvement carried with it the seeds of
corruption, and that good could be promoted by the worst,
like "the scavenger bustard that removes carrion. . . ." At 23,
at 24, he couldn't be certain that God existed or certain that
He did not. Life itself was a contradictory progress toward
death. As late as December, 1834, even while he was composing *Nature*, he could ask in his journal, "a lockjaw which
bended a man's head backward to his heels, and that beastly
hydrophobia which makes him bark at his wife & children,
—what explains these?" By 1835 he could write that the
lover of truth would "recognize all the opposite negations
between which as walls his being is swung," and would submit himself "to the inconvenience of suspense & imperfect
opinion. . . ." The image is original and compelling, and it

tells us far more of Emerson's real and permanent state of mind than the image of the ecstatic mystic in *Nature* with his head lifted into infinite space, a transparent eyeball which sees all and becomes "part or particle of God." It interprets, for example, the baffled Emerson of 1850, who admitted he couldn't reconcile his views—melioration and the unchanging power of mind through the ages; the sacredness of individuals and the plausibility of communities; the divinity of man and his dependence on creature comforts. His term for this was "bi-polarity"; later he spelled it out— the whole world was "a series of balanced antagonisms."

The eternal conflict, swinging between opposite negations —and opposite affirmations, too—Emerson summarized briefly in 1842: "I am *Defeated* all the time; yet to Victory I am born." Thus as omnicompetent actor he had to be simultaneously the hero both of a tragedy and a comedy, bound always to be losing but destined to be winning. In 1862, when most of his best work had been done, he provided from Newtonian calculus a helpful metaphor to describe the contrary yet progressive movements of his mind: "Fluxions, I believe, treat of flowing numbers, as, for example, the path through space of a point on the rim of a cart-wheel. Flowing or varying." He went on to say that his own values were variable—his estimates of America, now low, now ideal; of his own mental resources, "all or nothing"; of literature, sometimes all-sufficient, sometimes poor experimenting. The flowing figure is truer to the whole Emerson than the static illustrations, if the wheel represents the activity of the whole mind as holding simultaneously opposed views, as having both top and bottom, and as being constantly active, moving both up and down, and forward. And a comment Emerson made six months later, in a grim mood, is also helpful: "I defend myself against failure in my main design by making every inch of the road to it pleasant."

He was reasserting, of course, what he had believed for years, the primacy of process over product, the fascination with the ways and the effects of thought rather than thought itself. "Not so much matter *what* as *how* men do and speak," he wrote in 1823. "Style not matter gives immortality." Having a great thought, when the eyes of his eyes were opened, sometimes sent Emerson bolt upright to his feet and striding around the room like a tiger in a cage, thrilling him so much that he couldn't find the composure and concentration to write the thought down, yet leaving him satisfied with the unverbalized experience of intellectual rapture. But he was an artist before he was a mystic. In theory the unverbalized thought, "the wise silence," as he called it, was the highest experience, the reach beyond the finitude of words. In practice, Emerson verbalized his experiences at all levels, from moments of inspired insight into the heart of being and truth down to moments when he merely observed or reported the external facts. He was always busy and always fascinated by what he was doing and how he was doing it. "The one thing in the world, of value," he wrote, "is the active soul." The word, degraded in modern times, had a host of inherited meanings for Emerson; to these he added his own, and as time went on, particularly after 1840, he modified the meanings of soul to correspond with his deepened view of reality. The old meanings included that by virtue of which a thing was alive, the immaterial essence of a thing, the spiritual entity which is independent of the body and directly related to God, and that in man which survives after death and makes him immortal. Among Emerson's major synonyms for soul, insofar as they refer to the individual, were life, energy, sensibility, creativity, love, sentiment, conscience, identity, intellect, and genius. The soul was an organic composite of powers in the person, a hypersensitive power of response, like a spontaneous reflex, to all forms of experience, the power of creating something out of the response, emotional power, moral power, and the power of mind. It was the simultaneous power of instinctive perception and passionate feeling and thinking about the perception. It was the whole person. By its power the ideal individual could assimilate all experience and phenomena into himself and become one with nature and God, and since it was common to all men it could unite man with mankind. And "the soul's emphasis," thought Emerson, "is always right."

That Emerson's sense of the soul should have developed was inevitable, and a testimonial to the vitality and authenticity of his concept. Briefly, after his fortieth year, Emerson came to recognize two principal truths: that the soul's powers were not unlimited, and that nature's power, exhibited through the development of races and of nations, tended to envelop the individual soul and assimilate it into its program of progressive development. Not that the soul lost its identity or freedom: in "Fate" (1860) Emerson gave full recognition to the external powers which man cannot control. Even so, no other power could ultimately prevail over the power of thought: "Intellect," said Emerson, with a flash of his early confidence, "annuls Fate. So far as a man thinks, he is free."

To summarize these clues to the understanding of Emerson, he was a dramatic personality himself, and he wrote mostly as a dramatist of ideas. He tried, that is, to give all experiences and all ideas the expression and vent which was proper to them. He tried to assume himself into the human condition and the human condition into himself, so that what was subjective at firsthand would become objective. Thus his journals—the place to begin the study of Emerson—are loaded with records of highly personal experiences and observations; deliberately, it is clear, he re-formed or recast them into generalized and dramatic experiences before uttering them in a lecture or publishing them in an essay.

It is indispensable in reading to bear in mind that unlike most essays almost all of Emerson's were originally written to be delivered to a public audience, and that Emerson deliberately practiced the arts of rhetoric and eloquence. The relation between writer (or speaker) and audience required a dramatic rendition of ideas. In the later twentieth century we have virtually lost the sense of relation between the written and the spoken word. For Emerson and his generation the relation was taken for granted, and the rhythms and tones of speech in writing were supposed to be those that would be most effective in an address. Poetry too was written to be spoken or even declaimed. In Emerson's prose as in his poetry, we must listen for what Frost describes as "the speaking tone of voice somehow entangled in the words and fastened to the page for the ear of the imagination." And while the voice will frequently be that which sounds out Emerson's own belief, it will not necessarily be so. It is just as likely to be the dramatic Emerson's statement of what he called *"the other side."* Emerson affirms a credo—not consistent, but a credo—and he does it with the traditional techniques of eloquence: the flat statement, the homely illustration, hyperbole, epigram, wit, whatever rhetorical device seems necessary to get the public empathetically involved in the affirmation. But he will state the other side, the side he doesn't believe or only partly believes, with equal eloquence. In Emerson the careful listener will find the voices of most of the opposing forces that attracted men's minds in the nineteenth century—the transcendentalist, the skeptic, the patrician, the democrat, the conservative and the liberal, Napoleon and Christ or Plato, the chauvinistic American and the civilized European contemptuous of American greed and barbarism, the mystic and the pragmatist, the reformer and the antireformer, the abolitionist and the antiabolitionist, the hardheaded businessman, the idealist and antimaterialist, the self-reliant individual and the devotee of communal action, the immigrant and the old New Englander, the rich man and the poor man, the scientist and the symbolist, the latter-day Puritan, the city man and the villager. Expecting Emerson to be consistent, then, is like expecting every character in Shakespeare to agree with every other character.

Emerson's intellectual and imaginative life was in some ways the eternal romantic's pursuit of the unattainable, the pursuit of a beauty which would immediately escape you if you tried to lay your hands on it. "Strange," he noticed, "that what I have not is always more excellent than what I have. . . ." It was also the pursuit of truth which could come only in brief glimpses, so that the sense of truth was never a permanent possession. He saw himself, he saw man, as having a certain amount of truth lodged in the soul, "a certain perception of absolute being, as justice, love, & the like, natures which must be the God of God," and which make up "our centripetal force." But "on the other side, all is to seek. We understand nothing; our ignorance is abysmal; . . . whither we go, what we do, who we are, we cannot even so much as guess. We stagger & grope." He saw himself, he saw man, as a being imbedded in God, as a form of God, and he could say "with a mountainous aspiring" that he himself was God when he transferred his inmost self out of his body, fortunes, and private will, and retired into total justice and love. "But why not always so?" he painfully asked. Why did the individual "kill the divine life?" "Into that dim problem," he had to confess, "I cannot enter. A believer in Unity, a seer of Unity, I yet behold two." The uncertain stance between the sense of full knowledge of his being and of constantly discovering what he didn't know tormented him into asking, "Cannot I conceive the Universe without a Contradiction?"

But a universe without a contradiction would have meant a system and Emerson had no system, as he wisely realized

by 1839. In his twenties he set out to compile an encyclo-
pedia of "definitions" which would add up to a complete description of the universe. Soon he realized it was impossible; more important, for the purposes of understanding him,
he discovered that the curve on which he plotted his perceptions of truth was "a parabola whose arcs would never
meet. . . ." One has only to visualize an upward parabola, with
its components of focus, axis, fixed line or directrix, and moving point to see how near it comes as a model to Emerson's
method and results. It encompasses his hostility to closed
systems, the openness of his mind, the endlessness of his
search, the bipolarities and oppositions that mark his passing observations, and withal the ultimate stability of his over-
all vision. It is a far better model than the set of circles upon
circles which he develops later, for while the circle's figure
suggests radiance and expansion, it also suggests perimeters,
the measurable, the finite, the conclusive and the exclusive.
However one wants to think about Emerson, the important
thing is constantly to see that it is tension between oppositions that is behind his writing. And it is just this creative
tension that should be one of the major recommendations to
the reader in the later twentieth century. We are bewildered
by other specific conflicts than those which puzzled and discouraged Emerson, and most of us lack his conviction that
if the truth-seeker continues to report his impressions as they
really are he need not worry about the proportion or congruency of the aggregate. But perhaps we are shackled by
our theories of knowledge. Emerson's epistemology was not
that of the scientist or the philosopher; it was that of the
poet and the prophet. "The faith," he wrote, "is the evidence."

I have said that the study of Emerson is best begun in
the journals. Lest this seem to encourage the biographical
fallacy—the critical approach which explains works of art
in terms of the events of a man's life—we need to know that
the journals are preponderantly the record of Emerson thinking and feeling rather than recalling physical experiences.
Emerson didn't exclude these; many of the best passages record walks in Concord, alone or with Thoreau or Ellery
Channing, or Emerson's travels in Rome or Paris or the
American Midwest. Many of his notebooks indeed are thoroughly mundane; they include at least eleven ledgers of accounts, thirty-one pocket diaries, and half a dozen careful

indexes to his journals—the means by which he found what
he had written on a multitude of topics so he could use it.
Many separate entries, mostly unprinted, expose a constant
curiosity about clock-time, the size and cost of things, and
the facts of growth. Emerson noted the exact value of property in Boston and New York, in the hundreds of millions;
the fastest time for the ten-mile run and for various boat
races; the fact that 40 percent of the English were illiterate
but only one-half of 1 percent in Massachusetts; that a ribbon
factory always kept a £20,000 stock on hand; that a gun
could be fired about one thousand times before it burst; that a
young ass's seed in one month would fill a hat; that the Bunker Hill Monument cost $101,688; that Prince Esterhazy's in-
come was £400,000; that Jenny Lind got $176,675.09 for
ninety-three concerts. He noted the cost of a Stuart portrait,
the price of land in Illinois, the population of Italy and England, the birth dates of Copernicus, Shakespeare, Newton,
Cervantes, and scores of others, the exact time it took a ship
to sail to Canton and himself to travel by sulky from Boston
to Watertown or Cambridge, the value of his own invest-
ments, and many other most untranscendental matters.

But more typically the journals give us the truth and the
intellectual or moral excitement which Emerson found only
in his response to the experience of the passing moment. It
is in the journals that one can see the organic instinct, the
raw, unmediated, unqualified thought, the thought that shot
out spontaneously like a living and growing thing. To study
the journals is to discover and understand the complexities
of Emerson's thought. And the journals are the more valuable to the extent that even Emerson himself, daring as he
was, never published some of the things he really felt and
thought. Unfortunately, the whole story of Emerson in the
journals will not be available until the new edition is in print.
But they are still the best way of coming to know Emerson.

A familiar image in Emerson is that of force, power,
energy—the ideal essence that lies behind all phenomena—
taking shape in a tree or a vegetable and sending itself out in
the shape of buds, leaves, and fruits. The journals record the
process of birth and growth; the lectures, essays, and poems
are the products. At least one critic of Emerson insists that
only the product matters, only the product deserves study.
But there is both fascination and a deeper understanding in
watching the process, as though one could see the way in

which a seed sends out roots, could actually *see* how any natural thing is really made. Emerson's method was to write down in the heat of inspired vision the truth as it seemed to him at the moment, regardless of contrary perceptions he might have had at other moments. The thought might be a single sentence; it might be a paragraph, even an incomplete one; it might be three or four pages. It might be authentic, it might not. Emerson tended to believe that it was. The value of a journal to him was that each individual act of composition arose from experience, immediate or remote, felt at the moment or recalled from the past. Sentences could be written at any time, without seeming to have any relation to each other. Eventually some question would pose itself, and show that the sentences all belonged together, were parts of a whole. The process was like crystallization, as he noted long before he began to create his formal compositions. He would think of "a particular fact of singular beauty & interest." This would lead him to more thoughts, seen first partially, then more fully, but in the aggregate he could see no order. If left alone, domesticated in the mind, they would take their own order, and this order was divine. It was "God's architecture."

It is this organic theory of the way thought took on necessitated form that explains much of Emerson's fascination as a man and persuasiveness as a writer. As an organic being he absorbed into his active soul everything in the earth and in the lower and upper atmospheres—everything produced in the self, in nature, in society. As an artist he liked to think that all assimilated experience formed itself naturally, and in passive obedience to innate law, into beautiful entities, like those in nature itself. And it is true that hundreds of passages in his journals have this effect—that both the words and the form are spontaneous and inspired. When these passages go unmodified into lectures or essays, as they frequently do, the effect goes with them. Yet if one looks closely at hundreds of other passages, one sees that, like most artists, Emerson combined inspiration with craft, spontaneity with deliberate workmanship. Like a gardener, he pruned and wired the trees of his thought. In his theory nature was superior to art; in his practice art shaped nature where nature could not shape itself.

Of the thousands of illustrations that might be given, a

few must suffice. On March 2, 1834, Emerson wrote in his journal:

> It is very seldom that a man is truly alone. He needs to retire as much from his solitude as he does from society into very loneliness. While I am reading & writing in my chamber I am not alone though there is nobody there. There is one means of procuring solitude which to me & I apprehend to all men is effectual, & that is to go to the window & look at the stars. If they do not startle you & call you off from vulgar matters I know not what will. I sometimes think that the atmosphere was made transparent with this design to give man in the heavenly bodies a perpetual admonition of God & superior destiny. Seen in the streets of cities, how great they are! When I spoke of this to G.A.S[ampson]. he said, that he had sought in his chamber a place for prayer & could not find one till he cast his eye upon the stars.—

Over two years later he reshaped and pruned these burning thoughts, illustrative, he would have maintained, of God's architecture, into a far better passage—the opening passage in the second section of *Nature*:

> To go into solitude, a man needs to retire as much from his chamber as from society. I am not solitary whilst I read and write, though nobody is with me. But if a man would be alone, let him look at the stars. The rays that come from those heavenly worlds will separate between him and what he touches. One might think the atmosphere was made transparent with this design, to give man, in the heavenly bodies, the perpetual presence of the sublime. Seen in the streets of cities, how great they are! . . .

On August 15, 1834, Emerson wrote the following in his journal (angle brackets show cancellations, arrows show insertions or additions, square brackets show guesses at the words he left out, probably in his haste):

↑For the Lecture on Nat. Hist.↓

> Natural history by itself has no value; it is like a single sex. But marry it to human history, & it is poetry. < at once. > Whole Floras, all Linnaeus' & Buffon's volumes contain not one line of poetry, but the meanest natural fact, the habit of a plant, the < noise > ↑organs,↓ or work, ↑or noise↓ of an insect applied to ↑the interpretation [of] or even associated↓ [with] a fact in human nature is beauty, is poetry, is truth at once.

In 1836, in the chapter "Language," in *Nature*, he said it this way:

> . . . All the facts in natural history taken by themselves have no value, but are barren like a single sex. But marry it to human history, and it is full of life. Whole Floras, all Linnaeus's and Buffon's volumes, are dry catalogues of facts; but the most trivial of these facts, the habit of a plant, the organs, or work, or noise of an insect, applied to the illustration of a fact in intellectual philosophy, or, in any way, associated to human nature, affects us in the most lively and agreeable manner. . . .

The process of refinement, of adjustment of the raw nature in the original utterance, did not stop when the journal passages went into lectures or essays (note that Emerson went back to the second passage when he needed something for an 1835 lecture); Emerson refined his thought when new editions of his works were called for. In *Nature* (1836) he wrote that man could become "part or particle of God"; in 1849 he apparently changed it to "part or parcel"; his revised edition of 1870 reads "particle" again. In 1847 he made some five hundred substantive changes in *Essays* (1841). He cut out directional links, redundant illustrations, blurred images; he worked for more conciseness and lucidity, concreteness, and color; he changed meanings to reflect his own changes of opinion about man's limitations (which now seemed greater than in 1836) and about the nature of God and the nature of the soul. And in several journals of the late 1850's and 1860's he regretfully noted things that should have gone into his later essays.

The generalizations we may derive from passages and practices such as these embrace most though not all of Emerson's typical techniques: (1) write the perception down when you have it; make no bones about getting it precisely right; don't stop to reflect—write to no particular purpose, but in the belief that the truth will find its own way to the surface, and in the natural form it ought to take; (2) when rewriting, recomposing, for a particular purpose, keep the original content and form where they seem unexceptionably authentic; (3) condense, be precise, choose the exact word; (4) expand, if the original is cryptic; (5) eliminate the personal or transform the personal into the universal, Emerson the person into Emerson the speaker for all men; (6) shift units about till they appear in their best order; (7) change things from the concrete to the abstract or the abstract to the concrete, whichever best serves the purpose; (8) write for the audience outside as well as the private ear.

Emerson liked to pretend, according to the romantic mode, that art was of the unconscious. In fact, his art was characteristically conscious and deliberate. *Thought* might be spontaneous, and the images that accompanied it, through which it was expressed, were typically spontaneous for Emerson. But composition was not. Composition had laws "as strict as those of sculpture & architecture," wrote Emerson in 1831. "No man can write well who thinks there is any choice of words for him," he said; "there is always a right word, & every other than that is wrong." Sometimes the right word came out of the passion which accompanied the thought; sometimes it had to be consciously sought. The message of Emerson to the writer of today or any day is clear: "look in thy heart & write," (he quoted this from Sidney); then purify what you have written, recompose it, work at it to produce the *illusion* that it is spontaneous, natural, and necessitated. Despite Emerson's onetime theory that the intuition would take one directly to the truth, he knew the pursuit of that truth and its appropriate expression had to be constant. In his ideal theory, all things were always flowing, the artist must always remain in the rear of his object, and his work could never be complete. Emerson followed "happy guides," he says in "Forerunners," but never could he "reach their sides." And in "The World-Soul," he complained:

> Alas! the Sprite that haunts us
> Deceives our rash desire;
> It whispers of the glorious gods,
> And leaves us in the mire.

One may well ask, if Emerson felt this way, why he ever bothered to try grasping the ideal. Perhaps the answer to all the problems raised by both his thought and his theory and practice of art is that he could only *hope,* deeply, instinctively, that what he saw and reported was true, in essence and in form.

It is time now to consider the obvious problems which

Emerson's theory and practice of perception and execution raise. To put them crudely—and this has been done before —why should anyone expect to find durable truth in a man whose perceptions alter so much from day to day or year to year? Why isn't the most ignorant citizen or the young adolescent as much an authority as Emerson, if truth-telling means merely looking into one's heart and writing, if the instincts can always be trusted to yield the truth? Doesn't Emerson preach and practice relativism and indifferentism? And since Emerson's cast of mind, however much he recognizes tragedy, evil, all that divides and frustrates, is predominantly optimistic, isn't he just thinking what he wants to think, regardless of the opposing evidence? If so, how can he have any value to modern man, who lives in fear of destruction from without and from within—by nuclear war, overpopulation, and racial strife, or by the gradual crumbling of his mind and psyche under the stress of mounting fear?

Perhaps there are no final answers to these questions. But the understanding of Emerson requires recognition of some facts which the questions ignore. First of all, Emerson wrote out of wide knowledge of all that had been thought and said in the past. He knew Greek, Latin, French, German, and Italian. All his adult life he continued to read voraciously in the developing thought of his times, in science, as in philosophy, poetry, history, biography, and even fiction. The man who said books are for the scholar's idle times had a large personal library, borrowed thousands of books from libraries, athenaeums, and friends, and read hundreds of magazines and newspapers (as late as 1871 he took twelve different papers and periodicals; in 1865 he was reading experimental poetry). His "instinctive" perceptions were habitually influenced by and sometimes derived from the thinking of other men, from Plato to Bell, from the Indian scriptures to Herschel, from Swedenborg to Lyell to Oken, from the Bible to Hume to Carlyle. As late as 1868 he was accepting the challenges of nineteenth-century astronomy, geology, and zoology, and the challenge to old concepts of history which he had found in the work of Mommsen, Max Müller, and Lepsius. It is true that he had little use for logical systems *per se,* and he denied the scientific affirmation that knowledge can arise only from observation and experimental verification at the empirical level. But it is not literally true that he trusted solely in the uninstructed intuition as a means of knowing. He followed the guidelines furnished by collective human wisdom. No one who knows less than Emerson can furnish as authentic a vision.

As we have seen, his multiple vision frequently left him totally bewildered as to certainty. Safety for Emerson, as for his intelligent followers, lay in the constant subjection of intuited perceptions to the test of experience. If an idea didn't work, it was to be thrown out. Perhaps Emerson never said anything more telling than his statement in "Fate": "Once we thought positive power was all. Now we learn, that negative power, or circumstance, is half." It is equally telling that he went on in the essay to confront the new perception and to find a means of dealing with it. The parabola of the mind's movements had no conceivable termini, but every point in the arc related to directrix and axis, the actual as well as the ideal. The role of experience in Emerson's philosophy—and the philosophy itself—has been shrewdly summed up by Professor Frederic I. Carpenter as "pragmatic mysticism":

> [His philosophy] is idealistic in that it puts the mystical experience first. It is dualistic in that it looks both ways from its position on the bridge between the soul and nature. It is monistic in that it maintains that this bridge is the only reality. But it is pragmatic in that it tests all truths (including the mystical belief in the value of life) by experience.

This still may not satisfy the skeptic who holds that Emerson's criteria of experience were faulty. But it may represent more than any other mode of thought that which was and still is characteristically American, in its belief in the power of the mind to reach beyond the immediate actuality to some kind of hopeful vision, in its distrust of abstractions and systems of thought, in its demand that ideas prove themselves, make sense in terms of the individual's experience, and in its capacity for dynamic adaptation without the sacrifice of abiding principles. Most of all, the philosophy, and the psychology behind it, postulated a rapacious zest for experience, for being fully alive, for enduring and transcending the defeats of the impeded vision. Emerson took constant risks in following the bent of his thought wherever it might go: the risk of self-contempt, of distrust of his chosen roles of scholar and poet, of being self-satisfied, isolated and alienated, or deceived by his own enthusiasms, and of spirit-

ual disaster; the risks of orthodoxy and the risks of heter-
odoxy; the risk of being wrong and the risk of being right—
all the risks a man can take when he grimly determines to
abandon repose and seek the truth. The example to the
twentieth century is obvious. A man or woman today might
not want to imitate Emerson, but if he did at least he would
know what it meant to be fully alive.

There are other ways in which Emerson will either challenge or satisfy modern man. Take everything he said about
slavery and the Negro, from his early journals through his
"Speech on Emancipation in the West Indies" in 1844, his
denunciation of the Fugitive Slave Act of 1850, his speeches
on slavery in the 1850's, and his later observations on the
condition of the Negro; subtract the theory of racial inferiority and superiority which was merely the overwhelming
theory of the times, accepted even by learned men; substitute "segregation" for "slavery" and "segregationist" for
"slave owner"; and Emerson belongs to the most enlightened
thinking of our times. For Emerson, slavery was above all
a moral wrong, an inhuman and groundless deprivation of
rights. The Negro was "nearest to geology" only because he
had been kept down by an immoral civilization. The slave
owner put himself in the power of the slave by the very fe-
rociousness of his dedication to slavery. Negroes would become strong when they changed the image imposed upon
them, saw themselves as strong, and began to act accordingly.
Southerners were honest about the Negro, Northerners were
hypocritical and selfish, especially in their churches and Sunday schools. Well before the Fourteenth Amendment Emerson argued—or perhaps accepted another's argument—that
the United States henceforth "knows no color, no race, in its
law, but legislates for all alike,—one law for all men. . . ."
He accepted universal suffrage, for white and Negro alike.
He saw with horror how the violence engendered by the
proslavery people in the South stifled all dissent, so that not
even a moderate Southerner dared to voice a contrary opinion. He verbally mauled the system of justice begotten by
slavery whereby the courts were staffed by judges who corrupted the law to further slavery. In the privacy of his
journal, at least, he said the Negro should tell the government in effect that its taxation of him was unjust, since it
denied him the protection the taxes were supposed to pay for.
And in 1867 he compressed all his feeling, including a drastic

change in his concept of race, into a blunt indictment of the segregationist: "You complain that the Negroes are a base class. Who makes & keeps the Jew or the Negro base, who but you, who exclude them from the rights which others enjoy?"

Many a random view of Emerson's is also close to twentieth-century reactions. The government, he thought, should learn how to check the population, so that every person would be essential. It should not subsidize people directly, but Emerson saw no reason why it shouldn't give every citizen who reached voting age a couple of acres from the holdings of deceased persons or from its public lands. Though depressed by swarms of anonymous people in the cities, he stood for the melting-pot theory and castigated the American nativist movement. He deplored the rage and hate of the Chartists but sympathized with their efforts to achieve social justice, as he did with the French revolutionists of 1848. He understood poverty better than riches and generally found himself on the side of the poor. Inevitably he believed in the higher law and refused to obey the Fugitive Slave Law because it required men to violate their innate moral sense. He learned that a man could not separate himself from the political questions of his age. He derided dry formalism in religion and education, and thought college professors should be elected after a competition for the attention of boys on the street; they should then teach the boys to think for themselves. In art he defended private symbolism and the urge to experiment. Like the "lost" and the "forgotten" generations, he was disillusioned by the postwar decay of idealism and the regression to mere moneymaking and venality. He resisted "the Establishment"—"the party of the Past"; he supported "the Movement"—"the party of the Future."

And despite his prevailing optimism, he could feel a very modern sense of loneliness and terror. An introvert, he early deplored what seemed to him a nature so cold and cautious that he couldn't speak a hearty word to anyone despite his desire and need for warm friendship. The death of his first wife may have removed the only person with whom he could have shared his deepest self. His effort in 1840 to justify the distance at which he had to keep his friends sometimes seems desperate. The sad knowledge that true intellectual union of human beings was impossible came to him in conversations with Thoreau; they both stated "the eternal loneliness" of the human condition, and Emerson added, "how insular & pathetically solitary, are all the people we know!" And deep inside he knew terror in some of the forms we consider modern. Once he said that we fly to Beauty from the terrors of finite nature. Contrariwise, he was thankful for the terror of dreams, since so much terror had departed from the waking life. As for the outside world, people, he noted, had lost their forefathers' terror of sin and judgment, but the ironic replacement was the torment of uncertainty as to proper action; it was "distrust of the value of what we do. . . ."

Still, however much the dark underside of Emerson may attract the modern reader, it is not the side that prevails. What prevails, and what endures, is the seeker. Emerson sought explanations of the lines of force in society, the mind, science, and the universe as earnestly in his day as did Henry Adams a generation later. Perhaps his nearest parallel in our age is Teilhard de Chardin, who also believes that life is continual movement and discovery, that evolution is working in the spiritual as well as the material sphere, and that the pursuit and enlargement of knowledge must lead finally to total unity of man with the universe and then with God. And Emerson would probably have shared a much older seeker's paradoxical defense of eternal inquiry. St. Augustine once wrote that the inquiry "concerning the incomprehensible is justified, and the inquirer has found something, if he has succeeded in finding how far what he sought passes comprehension. Comprehending the incomprehensibility of what he seeks, yet he will go on seeking, because he cannot slacken his pursuit so long as progress is made in the actual inquiry into things incomprehensible: so long as he is continually bettered by the search after so great a good— both sought that it may be found, and found that it may be sought: still sought that the finding may be sweeter, still found that the seeking may be more eager." As a seeker, Emerson carried on a human activity we have always had and will always need. The main business of a seeker is to think. And as Emerson put it, "Life consists of what a man is thinking of all day."

WILLIAM H. GILMAN

AN EMERSON CHRONOLOGY

1803   Emerson is born in Boston, May 25.

1811ff.   His father dies, and for years his mother takes
            in boarders to provide for him and his four
            brothers, William, Edward, Charles (later all
            lawyers), and Bulkeley, who is mentally re-
            tarded, and whom Emerson helps care for till his
            death in 1859.

1817–1821   He attends Harvard College, where he waits on
            table; belongs to a literary society; wins two
            prizes for essays and one for oratory; writes
            poetry; and starts keeping a journal (1820). In
            the summers he teaches in secondary schools.

1822–1831   He maintains himself by teaching school, which
            he dislikes; loses vision in one eye for several
            months; pursues theological studies at Harvard;
            is ordained to preach (1826); develops lung trou-
            ble and travels to Charleston and St. Augustine
            to recover his health; becomes junior pastor at the
            Second Church (Unitarian) in Boston; marries
            Ellen Tucker (1829) and loses her in death from
            tuberculosis (1831).

1832–1836   He resigns his pastorate; suffers from weak
            health; travels to Italy, France, England, and
            Scotland; meets Landor, Coleridge, Carlyle, and
            Wordsworth; returns home to preach, lecture,
            and write; lives at the Old Manse in Concord;
            learns of the death of his brother Edward in
            Puerto Rico; formulates a Transcendentalist phi-

losophy; marries Lydia Jackson (1835); inherits over $22,000 from his first wife; buys the spacious Coolidge house in Concord for $3500; suffers the death of Charles from tuberculosis; publishes *Nature* (September, 1836); meets Bronson Alcott and Margaret Fuller; rejoices in the birth of his first son, Waldo (1836); and helps form the "Transcendental Club."

1837–1841   He lectures regularly every year, mostly in Boston and New England towns but also in New York; enjoys working in his garden; delivers the Phi Beta Kappa Address at Harvard ("The American Scholar," 1837); forms friendships with Thoreau, Margaret Fuller, Elizabeth Hoar, Caroline Sturgis, Anna Barker, and Samuel Gray Ward —later her husband; acts as Carlyle's American agent; addresses the graduates of Harvard Divinity School ("The Divinity School Address," 1838); is attacked by conservative Congregational and Unitarian clergymen; refuses to join Brook Farm, a Utopian community; helps to found and later edits *The Dial*; rejoices in the birth of two daughters, Ellen (1839) and Edith (1841); publishes *Essays* (March, 1841); and invites Thoreau to live in his home.

1842–1846   He continues lecturing, adding Philadelphia and Baltimore to his tours; feels bitter grief at the death of Waldo (January 27, 1842); meets Hawthorne, who lives in the Old Manse; enlarges his land holdings; translates Dante's *Vita Nuova*; welcomes the birth of a new son, Edward Waldo (1844); publicly attacks slavery in "Emancipation in the British West Indies"; publishes *Essays: Second Series* (October, 1844); allows Thoreau to build a hut on his land near Walden Pond; contributes heavily to the support of Alcott; and publishes *Poems* (December, 1846).

1847–1854   He sets out two acres of pear trees; goes to England to lecture on "Representative Men" and other subjects; visits Carlyle and Wordsworth again; meets Tennyson, Clough, Dickens, and others; visits Paris; gives another lecture series in London; returns to Concord (July, 1848); resumes lecturing in New England; acquires more land; begins smoking cigars; publishes *Nature; Addresses, and Lectures* (1849) and *Representative Men* (1850); extends his annual lecture tours to western New York, Ohio, Illinois, and Missouri; and denounces Webster and the Fugitive Slave Law of 1850 in major speeches in 1851 and 1854.

1855–1860 He lectures in New England, New York, Canada, Ohio, Illinois, Wisconsin, Michigan, Washington, D.C., and Indiana; congratulates Whitman on *Leaves of Grass* (July, 1855); speaks out for Charles Sumner after the attack by Preston Brooks and for Kansas relief (1856); publishes *English Traits* (August, 1856); addresses a Concord Cattle Show (1858); speaks in defense of John Brown (November, 1859); urges Whitman to alter the sex poems in *Leaves of Grass*; and publishes *The Conduct of Life* (1860).

1861–1865 He continues to lecture, from Boston to Milwaukee; is silenced by a noisy mob when he attempts to address the Massachusetts Anti-slavery Society; helps arm Concord soldiers (1861); talks with Sumner, Seward, and Lincoln in Washington (February, 1862); reads a funeral speech for Thoreau (May, 1862); fervently supports the Emancipation Proclamation (January, 1863); visits West Point as an official inspector; is elected to the American Academy of Arts and Sciences (1864); and eulogizes Lincoln (1865).

1866–1871 He lectures in New England and the Middle West; receives a Doctor of Laws degree from Harvard; publishes more poems in *May-Day and Other Pieces* (1867); revises his first six volumes of prose (published as *The Prose Works*, 1870); publishes new essays in *Society and Solitude* (1870); lectures on the Intellect at Harvard (1870); writes an introduction to Plutarch's *Morals* (1870); goes on a railroad trip to the

Far West; lectures in San Francisco; and visits Salt Lake City and Yosemite (1871).

1872–1882   His house burns in July, 1872; his health declines, and he virtually gives up lecturing and writing. He travels to England, France, Italy, and Egypt (1872–1873); returns to a triumphant welcome in Concord, where his house has been restored; allows James Elliott Cabot and Ellen to compose essays from his lectures, which were published as *Letters and Social Aims* (1875); and collaborates with them in *Selected Poems* (1876).

1882   Emerson dies from pneumonia, April 27.

TEXTUAL NOTE

Most of the texts of the journals after 1834 are taken from microfilms of the original manuscripts in Houghton Library and are published by permission of the Ralph Waldo Emerson Memorial Association and by arrangement with Houghton Mifflin Company and The Belknap Press of Harvard University Press. The texts of the journal passages from 1820 through 1834 are reprinted by permission of the publishers from William H. Gilman *et al.*, Editors, *The Journals and Miscellaneous Notebooks of Ralph Waldo Emerson,* Cambridge, Mass., The Belknap Press of Harvard University Press, Copyright 1960, 1961, 1963, 1964, by The President and Fellows of Harvard College. A few passages in 1852 (?) and 1854 (?) come from Emerson's journal WO Liberty, recently discovered in the Library of Congress. The texts of the letters are reprinted by permission from Ralph L. Rusk, Editor, *The Letters of Ralph Waldo Emerson,* New York, Columbia University Press, 1939; from *Letters from Ralph Waldo Emerson to a Friend*, Boston, Houghton Mifflin, 1899; from *The Correspondence of Thomas Carlyle and Ralph Waldo Emerson*, Boston, Houghton Mifflin, 1884; and from the photocopy of the letter to Whitman in *The Bookman*, VI (1898), and in Horace Traubel, *With Walt Whitman in Camden*, ed. Sculley Bradley, Philadelphia, University of Pennsylvania, 1953. I have altered or supplied some punctuation and capitalization in both journals and letters, and I have made a few emendations in the journals.

The text of the essays (except "Thoreau" and "Education") is that of *The Prose Works of Ralph Waldo Emerson, New and Revised Edition*, 2 vols., Boston, Fields, Osgood, 1870 (Copyright 1869). Where I have suspected this text I have sometimes made corrections after collation with one or more of the following editions: *Nature* (1836); *Essays* (1841); *Essays: First Series* (1850, copyright 1847); *Essays: Second Series* (1844, 1850); *Nature; Addresses, and Lectures* (1849); *Miscellanies: Embracing Nature, Addresses, and Lectures* (1857, copyright 1855, 1860, copyright 1856, and 1876); *Representative Men* (1850); and *The Conduct of Life* (1860). I have made a few emendations of my own, notably "boasts and repudiations" for "boats and repudiations" in "The Poet" (see p. 324 below). "Thoreau" is reprinted from *The Atlantic Monthly* X (August, 1862) with two corrections. "Education" is excerpted from *The Works of Ralph Waldo Emerson*, Riverside Edition, ed. James Elliot Cabot, 1883, vol. X. The poems are also taken from the Riverside Edition, with some corrections from *Poems* (1847, copyright 1846) the so-called "Sixth Edition" of 1857, and *May-Day and Other Pieces* (1867). I have been unable to collate either of these with the *Selected Poems, New and Revised Edition* of 1876, but this was prepared after the decline of Emerson's memory and other faculties and after he had become heavily dependent upon his daughter Ellen and his friend James Elliot Cabot for literary judgment. For the dating of most of the poems I have relied on Edward Waldo Emerson's notes in the Centenary Edition and upon the work of Carl F. Strauch and Stephen E. Whicher, but I have ventured some conjectures based on my own research.

Despite frequent reprintings from Edward Emerson's Centenary Edition of his father's works, the edition has no authority by modern bibliographical standards. Edward Emerson made hundreds of changes, mainly in punctuation; in so doing he sacrificed Emerson's intention to the supposed improvements of early twentieth-century punctuation. A new edition edited according to the principles of the 1903 edition would require that the punctuation be modernized again according to whatever norms an editor chose to impose sixty or more years later. Such an edition might be consistent, as the 1903 edition is not, but it would be even further away from Emerson's intention. To determine that intention in all instances will be the aim of the new edition of Emerson's works, now in its planning stage, but not due for completion for several years. Since no single scholar can hope to match the efforts of the numerous editors committed to this edition, I have made the best possible compromise by choosing for most of my selections what was almost certainly the last revised edition to which Emerson was able to give serious attention. On July 26, 1869, Emerson wrote in his journal NY, "This morning sent my six prose volumes, revised & corrected, to Fields & Co. for their new Edition in two volumes." The six volumes were *Nature; Addresses, and Lectures, Essays: First and Second Series, Representative Men, English Traits,* and *Conduct of Life*—all of Emerson's major publications in prose through 1860. Another set of his works, some described as "New and Revised," was published in 1876 in a Little Classic Edition. On May 21, 1876, Emerson wrote to Titus Coan that he was "correcting proof every other day" for this "new edition of all his old books." But it is very much to be doubted if Emerson made any significant changes in this edition. And at present there is no evidence that he actually revised and corrected a previous edition in 1876 as he did in 1869. Pending the full-scale scholarly collation of all editions and issues of his works and examination of his numerous errata lists in journals and marked copies of his own works, the 1870 edition collated with earlier editions would seem to come the nearest to what Emerson finally wanted his readers to see.

The principal features of this edition, as compared with the Centenary Edition, are Emerson's use of a single comma between subject and verb, commas around restrictive as well as nonrestrictive clauses, a comma between a verb and a noun clause introduced by *that,* and a comma after a coordinating conjunction, like *and,* or *for.* The same features appear in *Nature; Addresses, and Lectures* (1849) and *Essays* (1841, 1847) and *Essays: Second Series* (1844, 1850). That these practices were not tyrannies forced on Emerson by printing-house stylists is clear from their frequent appearance in both the manuscript journals and in Rusk's edition of the letters, where the punctuation is undisturbed. Obviously they reflect Emerson's sense of the proper rhythm of his sentences, of the kinds of pauses and emphases he felt as he wrote, or as he read what he had written. He was not always consistent, but his inconsistencies are better borne than the interferences of the Centenary Edition. Emerson's style cannot be studied with a confidence from an edition he did not create. With a little adjustment the modern reader should have no trouble reading Emerson.

In editing the journals I have taken pains to show whether

passages have been excised and whether they are continuous. Three dots (. . .) before a passage indicate that something precedes it in the paragraph of which it is a part. Four dots at the end of a passage indicate that matter at the end of a paragraph is omitted. Five dots between passages (. . . . .) indicate that intervening matter has not been printed. The dating, which is my own, assigns passages to specific dates when the manuscript source does so; places passages between dates when the manuscript source shows the dates within a reasonable number of pages before and after the passage; and queries dates with a question mark where the manuscript provides no grounds for exactness. The reader needs to know that in his later journals, from the 1850's on, Emerson frequently supplied very few dates, and he sometimes made entries months or years after he began a journal. Thus much of the dating in this as in all other editions must remain conjectural until the Belknap Press edition of the journals offers more assurance.

I have printed the journals and letters in such a way as to indicate as much as possible their informality, but only in a few instances, as with the passage on p. 167, have I shown cancellations (< >) and insertions (↑ ↓). The passage mentioned shows the first effort, which lapses into prose, to write what became the poem "Two Rivers" (see p. 472). Readers who want to see the original form of other passages which Emerson later published will find them on p. 64 ("October, 1836"), used in "The Over-soul," pp. 282–3, and on p. 99 ("October 23, 1840"), used in "Circles," p. 304.

Dates at the end of the essays show the year of first publication, except for "Education," where the dates are those of the original lectures used by Cabot for the essay. The date at left after a poem is that of known or conjectured composition; the date at the right is that of first publication. "1846 (1847)" means the first edition of *Poems,* dated 1847 on the title page, but actually issued in 1846.

I. JOURNALS AND LETTERS

January 25, 1820. Mixing with the thousand pursuits & passions & objects of the world as personified by Imagination is profitable & entertaining. These pages are intended at this their commencement to contain a record of new thoughts (when they occur); for a receptacle of all the old ideas that partial but peculiar peepings at antiquity can furnish or furbish; for tablet to save the wear & tear of weak Memory & in short for all the various purposes & utility real or imaginary which are usually comprehended under that comprehensive title *Common Place book.* . . .

June 7, 1820. . . . People prate of the dignity of human nature. Look over the whole history of its degradation & find what odious vice, what sottish & debasing enormity the degenerate naughtiness of man has never crouched unto & adored. To things animate & things inanimate, to the ghosts of dead men whose lives were bloody & cruel, lewd & foul, —to beasts & grovelling reptiles, dogs, serpents & crocodiles —they have bowed down & adored—. . . . But it is a joyful change to see human nature unshackling herself & asserting her divine origin;—employed in encountering prejudices & detecting frauds; checking & chastising profane abuse; subjecting to legitimate controul those fiery passions which corrode & fret the soul; & woe to those whose malignity would fright her from her pursuit. . . . The soul hath appetites & capacities by which when well guided she soars & climbs continually towards perfection & is backed by omnipotence in her magnificent career. . . .

June 19, 1820. . . . I love the picturesque glitter of a summer morning's landscape; it kindles this burning admiration of nature & enthusiasm of mind.

We feel at these times that eternal analogy which subsists between the external changes of nature & scenes of good & ill that chequer human life. . . .

October 25, 1820. I find myself often idle, vagrant, stupid, & hollow. This is somewhat appalling & if I do not discipline myself with diligent care I shall suffer severely from remorse & the sense of inferiority hereafter. All around me are industrious & will be great, I am indolent & shall be insignificant. Avert it heaven! avert it virtue! I need excitement.

March 25, 1821. I am sick—if I should die what would become of me? We forget ourselves & our destinies in health, & the chief use of temporary sickness is to remind us of these concerns. I must improve my time better. I must prepare myself for the great profession I have purposed to undertake. I am to give my soul to God & withdraw from sin & the world the idle or vicious time & thoughts I have sacrificed to them; & let me consider this as a resolution by which I pledge myself to act in all variety of circumstances & to which I must recur often in times of carelessness and temptation—to measure my conduct by the rule of conscience.

January(?), 1822. This fact that the seeds of corruption are buried in the causes of improvement strikes us everywhere in the political, moral, & natural history of the world. It seems to indicate the intentions of Providence to limit human perfectibility and to bind together good and evil like life and death by indissoluble connection.

February 23, 1822. What is evil? There is an answer from every corner of this globe—from every mountain and valley and sea. The enslaved, the sick, the disappointed, the poor, the unfortunate, the dying, the surviving, cry out It is here. . . .

What is its origin? The sin which Adam brought into the world and entailed upon his children.

37

1822. I have a nasty appetite which I will not

13, 1822. In twelve days I shall be nineteen years old; which I count a miserable thing. Has any other educated person lived so many years and lost so many days? . . .

Look next from the history of my intellect to the history of my heart. A blank, my lord. I have not the kind affections of a pigeon. Ungenerous & selfish, cautious & cold, I yet wish to be romantic. Have not sufficient feeling to speak a natural hearty welcome to a friend or stranger and yet send abroad wishes & fancies of a friendship with a man I never knew. There is not in the whole wide Universe of God (my relations to Himself I do not understand) one being to whom I am attached with warm & entire devotion,—not a being to whom I have joined fate for weal or wo, not one whose interests I have nearly & dearly at heart;—and this I say at the most susceptible age of man.

November, 1822. To establish by whatever specious argumentation the perfect expediency of the worst institution on earth is *prima facie* an assault upon Reason and Common sense. No ingenious sophistry can ever reconcile the unperverted mind to the pardon of *Slavery*; nothing but tremendous familiarity, and the bias of private *interest*. . . .

1823. Not so much matter *what* as *how* men do & speak. . . . Style not matter gives immortality.

April 8, 1823. . . . There *is* a huge & disproportionate abundance of *evil* on earth. Indeed the good that is here, is but a little island of light, amidst the unbounded ocean. . . .

April–May, 1823. The great illusion by which men suffer themselves to be mocked is the idea of their independence. . . .
. . . There is no other separate ultimate resource, for, God is within [man], God about him, he is a part of God himself. . . .

December 21, 1823. Who is he that shall controul me? Why may not I act & speak & write & think with entire freedom? What am I to the Universe, or, the Universe, what is it to me? Who hath forged the chains of Wrong & Right, of Opinion & Custom? And must I wear them? Is Society my anointed King? Or is there any mightier community or any man or more than man, whose slave I am? I am solitary in the vast society of beings; I consort with no species; I indulge no sympathies. I see the world, human, brute & inanimate nature; I am in the midst of them, but not *of* them; I hear the song of the storm,—the Winds & warring Elements sweep by me—but they mix not with my being. I see cities & nations & witness passions,—the roar of their laughter,—but I partake it not;—the yell of their grief,—it touches no chord in me; their fellowships & fashions, lusts & virtues, the words & deeds they call glory & shame,—I disclaim them all. I say to the Universe, Mighty one! thou art not my mother; Return to chaos, if thou wilt, I shall still exist. I live. If I owe my being, it is to a destiny greater than thine. Star by Star, world by world, system by system shall be crushed,—but I shall live.

February 22, 1824. . . . Thus ever the Mind is enlightened by Misery. If Knowledge be power, it is also Pain.

April 18, 1824. I am beginning my professional studies. In a month I shall be *legally* a man. And I deliberately dedicate my time, my talents, & my hopes to the Church. . . .

I cannot dissemble that my abilities are below my ambition. . . . I have or had a strong imagination & consequently a keen relish for the beauties of poetry. . . . My reasoning faculty is proportionately weak, nor can I ever hope to write a Butler's Analogy or an Essay of Hume. Nor is it strange that with this confession I should choose theology, which is from everlasting to everlasting 'debateable Ground.' For, the highest species of reasoning upon divine subjects is rather the fruit of a sort of moral imagination, than of the 'Reasoning Machines' such as Locke & Clarke & David Hume.

July–August, 1824. Why has my motley diary no jokes? Because it is a soliloquy & every man is grave alone. . . .

October 8, 1824. It is a striking feature in our condition that we so hardly arrive at truth. There are very few things of which we can wisely be certain tho' we often let unfounded prejudices grow into bigoted faith. We are immersed in opposite probabilities whenever we turn our thoughts to any of those speculations that are the proper exercise of our understandings. . . .

October–November, 1824. The best thing one can do in this world is to sidle quietly along without any inflexible philosophy. . . .

January, 1825. It is my own humor to despise pedigree. . . . The dead sleep in their moonless night; my business is with the living. . . .

March 1, 1825. . . . There is no doubt much metaphysical difficulty too hard & high for our faculties concerning the origin of evil. But the question is as perplexing to the Manichee as to his antagonist, Whether the soul that does a good action was created by the good principle or by the evil? If by the evil it follows that good may arise from the fountain of all evil. If it was created by the good principle it follows that evil may rise from the fountain of all good.

1826(?) . . . There is no thought which is not seed as well as fruit. . . .

January 8, 1826. Since I wrote before, I know something more of the grounds of hope & fear for what is to come. But if my knowledge is greater so is my courage. I know that I *know* next to nothing but I know too that the amount of probabilities is vast, both in mind & in morals. It is not certain that God exists but that he does not is a most bewildering & improbable chimera.

. . . . .

All things are double one against another said Solomon. The whole of what we know is a system of Compensations. Every defect in one manner is made up in another. Every suffering is rewarded; every sacrifice is made up; every debt is paid.

March 16, 1826. My external condition may to many seem comfortable, to some enviable but I think that few men ever suffered[1] more genuine misery than I have suffered. . . .

---

[1] In degree not in amount. [Emerson's note.]

March 27, 1826. My years are passing away. Infirmities are already stealing on me that may be the deadly enemies that are to dissolve me to dirt and little is yet done to establish my consideration among my contemporaries & less to get a memory when I am gone. . . .

May 28(?), 1826. I please myself with contemplating & nourishing my own independence—the invincibility of thought; with imagining a firmness of purpose, or if that be not philosophically tenable, a 'fixedness of opinion which opinion is the growth of the Deity's laws indeed but over which even Omnipotence has no controul.

July 28, 1826. . . . Satisfaction with our lot is not consistent with the intentions of God & with our nature. It is our duty to aim at change, at improvement, at perfection. It is our duty to be discontented, with the measure we have of knowledge & of virtue, to forget the things behind & press toward those before.

September–October, 1826. . . . The doctrine of Immortality, the grand revelation of Christianity, illuminates and ennobles the existence of man. This solves the question concerning the existence of evil, for if man is immortal, this world is his place of discipline & the value of pain is then disclosed.

January 15, 1827. And what is the amount of all that is called religion in the world? Who is he that has seen God of whom so much is known or where is one that has risen from the dead? Satisfy me beyond the possibility of doubt of the certainty of all that is told me concerning the other world and I will fulfil the conditions on which my salvation is suspended. The believer tells me he has an evidence historical & internal which make the presumption so strong that it is almost a certainty that it rests on the highest of probabilities. Yes; but change that imperfect to perfect evidence & I too will be a Christian. But now it must be admitted I am not certain that any of these things are true. The nature of God may be different from what he is represented. I never beheld him. I do not know that he exists. This good which invites me now is visible & specific. I will at least embrace it this time by way of experiment, & if it is wrong certainly

God can in some manner signify his will in future. Moreover I will guard against evil consequences resulting to others by the vigilance with which I conceal it.

February 16, 1827. My weight is lb. 141½.

February 27, 1827. [St. Augustine, Fla.] A fortnight since I attended a meeting of the Bible Society. The Treasurer of this institution is Marshal of the district & by a somewhat unfortunate arrangement had appointed a special meeting of the Society & a Slave Auction at the same time & place, one being in the Government house & the other in the adjoining yard. One ear therefore heard the glad tidings of great joy whilst the other was regaled with "Going gentlemen, Going!" And almost without changing our position we might aid in sending the scriptures into Africa or bid for "four children without the mother who had been kidnapped therefrom. . . ."

March 11, 1827. To believe too much is dangerous because it is the near neighbour of unbelief. Pantheism leads to Atheism.

September–October, 1827. A few days hence an unforeseen exposure to a storm or to cold, will shut you up in your chamber, will heat your blood to fever and stretch you on your bed. A few days more and idle eyes will run over your obituary in the newspaper. The selfish world will soon forget you. The sun will shine on your funeral as bright as he did at your bridal day & for one word that is spoken of your character ten, twenty will be spoken of the settlement of your estate. When two or three weeks of decent grief are gone those of your own household will quote the day of your death as a convenient date, & not an occasion of grief; so rapidly in men's hearts are the strongest passages of the past, swallowed up in interests & din of the present. . . .

January–February, 1828. It is not enough considered by us how much it is the fault of each of us that there is so much sin & evil in the world. . . .

To William Emerson

Concord, 30 April. 1828.

My dear brother,

I am very much disturbed, & so is my mother, at the idea of your Sickness, and the more, because we have no confidence that you have recovered. Since you did not tell us when you were seriously sick, it may be that you are so now. You naughty boy how dare you work so hard? Have you forgotten that all the Emersons overdo themselves? Dont you die of the leprosy of your race—ill weaved ambition. Pah how it smells, I'll none of it. Why here am I lounging on a system for these many months writing something less than a sermon a month for my main business,—all the rest of the time being devoted to needful recreation after such unparalleled exertions. And the consequence is—I begin to mend, and am said to look less like a monument & more like a man. I cant persuade that wilful brother Edward of mine to use the same sovereign nostrum. If I have written but five lines & find a silly uneasiness in my chest or in my narvous system to use the genuine anile word . . . I escape from the writing desk as from a snake & go straight to quarter myself on the first person I can think of in Divinity Hall who can afford to entertain me, i. e. on the person whose time is worth the least. Especially do I court laughing persons; and after a merry or only a gossipping hour where the talk has been mere soap bubbles I have lost all sense of the mouse in my chest, am at ease, & can take my pen or book. I always take as much exercise as my hip can bear and always at intervals & not in a mass. Norton says tis certain this climate will not admit of the sedentary habits that scholars in Europe have always indulged. Clear I am that he who would *act* must *lounge*. . . .

Most affectionately yours

Waldo

June 25, 1828. What is the matter with the world that it is so out of joint? Simply that men do not rule themselves but let circumstances rule them. . . .

September 11, 1828. . . . Let it be felt that the mind is all, & then it will follow in irresistible logic as it does in actual truth that the only reasonable efforts to increase human happiness must be aimed at the mind & not at the body. . . .

November 11, 1828. I would write a sermon upon the text men are made a law unto themselves to advise them to fear & honour themselves. . . .

November, 1828. Don't you see you are the Universe to yourself. You carry your fortunes in your own hand. . . .

December 21, 1828. I have now been four days engaged to Ellen Louisa Tucker. Will my Father in Heaven regard us with kindness, and as he hath, as we trust, made us for each other, will he be pleased to strengthen & purify & prosper & eternize our affection!

January 17, 1829. She has the purity & confiding religion of an angel. Are the words common? the words are true. Will God forgive me my sins & aid me to deserve this gift of his mercy.

July–September, 1829. Oh Ellen, I do dearly love you—

November 3(?), 1830. No man addicted to chemistry ever discovered a salt, or an acid, which he thought divine, never discovered a law which he thought God. No man devoted to literary criticism ever imagined that any of the thoughts that formed his study was God. But the man who cultivated the moral powers, ascended to a thought, & said *This is God*. The faith is the evidence.

November, 1830. . . . God finds his perfection in himself; so must man.

December 29, 1830. Every science is the record or account of the dissolution of the objects it considers. All history is an epitaph. All life a progress toward death. . . . In the decays of time we flee to the gospel. We are driven to Truth by the decays of the Universe. Near 5000 die in two hours. So that almost every pulse is a knell. . . .

January 17(?), 1831. The greatest man is he that is not man at all but merges his human will in the divine & is merely an image of God.

February 13, 1831. Ellen Tucker Emerson died 8th February. Tuesday morning 9 o'clock.

Five days are wasted since Ellen went to heaven to see, to know, to worship, to love, to intercede. God be merciful to me a sinner & repair this miserable debility in which her death has left my soul. Two nights since, I have again heard her breathing, seen her dying. O willingly, my wife, I would lie down in your tomb. But I have no deserts like yours, no such purity, or singleness of heart. Pray for me Ellen & raise the friend you so truly loved, to be what you thought him. When your friends or mine cross me, I comfort myself by saying, you would not have done so. Dear Ellen (for that is your name in heaven) shall we not be united even now more & more, as I more steadfastly persist in the love of truth & virtue which you loved? Spirits are not deceived & now you know the sins & selfishness which the husband would fain have concealed from the confiding wife—help me to be rid of them; suggest good thoughts as you promised me, & show me truth. Not for the world, would I have left you here alone; stay by me & lead me upward. Reunite us, O thou Father of our Spirits.

There is that which passes away & never returns. This miserable apathy, I know, may wear off. I almost fear when it will. Old duties will present themselves with no more repulsive face. I shall go again among my friends with a tranquil countenance. Again I shall be amused, I shall stoop again to little hopes & little fears & forget the graveyard. But will the dead be restored to me? Will the eye that was closed on Tuesday ever beam again in the fulness of love on me? Shall I ever again be able to connect the face of outward nature, the mists of the morn, the star of eve, the flowers, & all poetry, with the heart & life of an enchanting friend? No. There is one birth & one baptism & one first love and the affections cannot keep their youth any more than men.

March 4, 1831. . . . The Religion that is afraid of science dishonours God & commits suicide. It acknowledges that it is not equal to the whole of truth, that it legislates, tyrannizes over a village of God's empire but is not the immutable universal law. Every influx of atheism, of skepticism is thus made useful as a mercury pill assaulting & removing a diseased religion & making way for truth, & itself is presently purged into the draught. . . .

March 4(?), 1831. Whole zeal of opposers of one uniform, spiritual influence proceeds from inattention to the strictly divine character of ordinary phenomena. All is miracle, & the mind revolts at representations of 2 kinds of miracle.

July 8, 1831. No man can write well who thinks there is any choice of words for him. The laws of composition are as strict as those of sculpture & architecture. There is always one line that ought to be drawn or one proportion that should be kept & every other line or proportion is wrong, & so far wrong as it deviates from this. So in writing, there is always a right word, & every other than that is wrong. There is no beauty in words except in their collocation. The effect of a fanciful word misplaced, is like that of a horn of exquisite polish growing on a human head.

July 15(?), 1831. The things taught in schools & colleges are not an education but the means of education.

July 29, 1831. Suicidal is this distrust of reason; this fear to think; this doctrine that 'tis pious to believe on others' words, impious to trust entirely to yourself. To think is to receive. Is a man afraid that the faculties which God made can outsee God—can find more than he made or different —can bring any report hostile to himself? To reflect is to receive truth immediately from God without any medium. . . .

September 14, 1831. The first questions still remain to be asked after all the progress of Science. What an abyss is my ignorance.

July–October, 1831.
> I write the things that are
> Not what appears;
> Of things as they are in the eye of God
> Not in the eye of Man.

October 27, 1831. . . . In good writing every word means something. In good writing words become one with things. . . .

December 28(?), 1831. In my study my faith is perfect. It breaks, scatters, becomes confounded in converse with men. Hume doubted in his study & believed in the world.—

January 7, 1832. There is a process in the mind very analogous to crystallization in the mineral kingdom. I think of a particular fact of singular beauty & interest. In thinking of it I am led to many more thoughts which show themselves first partially and afterwards more fully. But in the multitude of them I see no order. When I would present them to others they have no beginning. There is no method. Leave them now, & return to them again. Domesticate them in your mind, do not force them into arrangement too hastily & presently you shall find they will take their own order. And the order they assume is divine. It is God's architecture.

January 10, 1832. It is the best part of the man, I sometimes think, that revolts most against his being the minister. His good revolts from official goodness. If he never spoke or acted but with the full consent of his understanding, if the whole man acted always, how powerful would be every act & every word. Well then or ill then how much power he sacrifices by conforming himself to say & do in other folks' time instead of in his own! The difficulty is that we do not make a world of our own but fall into institutions already made & have to accommodate ourselves to them to be useful at all. . . .

May 23(?), 1832. Every form is a history of the thing. The comparative anatomist can tell at sight whether a skeleton belonged to a carnivorous or herbivorous animal. A climber, a jumper, a runner, a digger, a builder. The Conchologist can tell at sight whether the shell covered an animal that fed on animals or on vegetables, whether it were a river or a sea shell, whether it dwelt in still or in turbid waters. Every thing is a monster till we know what it is for . . . A lobster is monstrous but when we have been shown the reason of the case & the color & the tentacula & the proportion of the claws & seen that he has not a scale nor a bristle nor any quality but fits to some habit & condition of the creature he then seems as perfect & suitable to his sea house as a glove to a hand. A man in the rocks under the sea would be a monster but a lobster is a most handy & happy fellow there.

June 2, 1832. A man's style is his mind's voice. Wooden minds have wooden voices. Truth is shrill as a fife, various as a panharmonicon.

August 11, 1832. A stomach ache will make a man as contemptible as a palsy. Under the diarrhoea have I suffered now one fortnight & weak am as a reed. Still the truth is not injured, not touched though thousands of them that love it fall by the way. Serene, adorable, eternal it lives, though Goethe, Mackintosh, Cuvier, Bentham, Hegel die in their places which no living men can fill.

August 12(?), 1832. What we say however trifling must have its roots in ourselves or it will not move others. No speech should be separate from our being like a plume or a nosegay, but like a leaf or a flower or a bud though the topmost & remotest, yet joined by a continuous line of life to the trunk & the seed.

October 17, 1832. If it be agreed that I am always to express my thought, what forbids me to tell the company that a flea bites me or that my occasions call me behind the house? Plainly this, that my thoughts being rightly ordered, these will appear to myself insignificant compared with those that engage my attention.

1832(?) Still the objection to these speculations remains that the most important part of Rhetoric is that which cannot be taught, which every one must learn by himself, & which cannot part from his consciousness. Certain moods of mind arise in me which lead me at once to my pen & paper, but which are quite indescribable: and these attend me through every sentence of my writing, & determine the form of every clause, yet are these muses quite too subtle & evanescent to sit for their portraits.

January 15, 1833. [At sea] I learn in the sunshine to get an altitude & the latitude but am a dull scholar as ever in real figures. Seldom I suppose was a more inapt learner of arithmetic, astronomy, geography, political economy than I am as I daily find to my cost. It were to brag much if I should there end the catalogue of my defects. My memory of history—put me to the pinch of a precise question—is as bad; my comprehension of a question in technical metaphysics very slow, & in all arts practick, in driving a bargain, or hiding emotion, or carrying myself in company as a man for an hour, I have no skill. . . .

January 16, 1833. The inconvenience of living in a cabin is that people become all eye. 'Tis a great part of wellbeing to ignorize a good deal of your fellowman's history & not count his warts nor expect the hour when he shall wash his teeth.

January 25, 1833. . . . Honour evermore aboard ship to the man of action,—to the brain in the hand. Here is our stout master worth a thousand philosophers—a man who can strike a porpoise, & make oil out of his blubber, & steak out of his meat; who can thump a mutineer into obedience in two minutes; who can bleed his sick sailor, & mend the box of his pump; who can ride out the roughest storm on the American coast, &, more than all, with the sun & a three cornered bit of wood, & a chart, can find his way from Boston across 3000 miles of stormy water into a little gut of inland sea 9 miles wide with as much precision as if led by a clue.

April 7, 1833. [Rome] I love St Peter's Church. It grieves me that after a few days I shall see it no more. It has a peculiar smell from the quantity of incense burned in it. The music that is heard in it is always good & the eye is always charmed. It is an ornament of the earth. It is not grand, it is so rich & pleasing; it should rather be called the sublime of the beautiful.

July, 1833. [Paris] It is a pleasant thing to walk along the Boulevards & see how men live in Paris. One man has live snakes crawling about him & sells soap & essences. Another sells books which lie upon the ground. Another under my window all day offers a gold chain. Half a dozen walk up & down with some dozen walking sticks under the arm. A little further, one sells cane tassels at 5 sous. Here sits Boots brandishing his brush at every dirty shoe. Then you pass several tubs of gold fish. Then a man sitting at his table cleaning gold & silver spoons with emery & haranguing the passengers on its virtues. Then a person who cuts profiles with scissors—"Shall be happy to take yours, Sir." Then a table of card puppets which are made to crawl. Then a hand organ. Then a wooden figure . . . which can put an apple in its mouth whenever a child buys a plum. Then a flower merchant. Then a bird-shop with 20 parrots, 4 swans, hawks, & nightingales. Then the show of the boy with four legs &c &c without end. All these are the mere boutiques on the sidewalk, moved about from place to place as the sun or rain or the crowd may lead them.

July 13, 1833. I carried my ticket from Mr Warden to the Cabinet of Natural History in the Garden of Plants. How much finer things are in composition than alone. 'Tis wise in man to make Cabinets. When I was come into the Ornithological Chambers, I wished I had come only there. The fancy-coloured vests of these elegant beings make me as pensive as the hues & forms of a cabinet of shells, formerly. It is a beautiful collection & makes the visitor as calm & genial as a bridegroom. The limits of the possible are enlarged, & the real is stranger than the imaginary. Some of the birds have a fabulous beauty. One parrot of a fellow, called *Psittacus erythropterus* from New Holland, deserves as special mention as a picture of Raphael in a Gallery. He is the beau of all birds. Then the hummingbirds little & gay. Least of all is the Trochilus Niger. I have seen beetles larger. The *Trochilus pella* hath such a neck of gold & silver & fire! Trochilus Delalandi from Brazil is a glorious little tot—la mouche magnifique.

• • • • •

I saw black swans & white peacocks, the ibis, the sacred & the rosy; the flamingo, with a neck like a snake, the Toucan rightly called *rhinoceros;* & a vulture whom to meet in the wilderness would make your flesh quiver, so like an executioner he looked.

In the other rooms I saw amber containing perfect musquitoes, grand blocks of quartz, native gold in all its forms of crystallization, threads, plates, crystals, dust; & silver black as from fire. Ah said I this is philanthropy, wisdom, taste—to form a Cabinet of natural history. Many students were there with grammar & note book & a class of boys with their tutor from some school. Here we are impressed with the inexhaustible riches of nature. The Universe is a more amazing puzzle than ever as you glance along this bewildering series of animated forms,—the hazy butterflies, the carved shells, the birds, beasts, fishes, insects, snakes,—& the upheaving principle of life everywhere incipient in the very rock aping organized forms. Not a form so grotesque, so savage nor so beautiful but is an ex-

pression of some property inherent in man the observer,—
an occult relation between the very scorpions and man. I
feel the centipede in me—cayman, carp, eagle, & fox. I am
moved by strange sympathies, I say continually "I will be
a naturalist."

September 2, 1833. . . . Glad I bid adieu to England, the
old, the rich, the strong nation, full of arts & men & memories; nor can I feel any regret in the presence of the best
of its sons that I was not born here. I am thankful that I
am an American as I am thankful that I am a man. . . .

September 11, 1833. Wednesday. I have been nihilizing
as usual & just now posting my Italian journal. Admirable
story of Grizel Cochrane in Chambers' Magazine. Never was
a regular dinner with all scientific accompaniments so philo-
sophic a thing as at sea. I tipple with all my heart here. May
I not?

November–December, 1833. This Book is my Savings Bank.
I grow richer because I have somewhere to deposit my
earnings; and fractions are worth more to me because corresponding fractions are waiting here that shall be made
integers by their addition.

April 22, 1834. There are people who read Shakspear for
his obscenity as the glaucous gull is said to follow the
walrus for his excrement. I would be as great a geographer
as an eagle—& every winter like a bird or member of congress go south.

April 26, 1834. Good is promoted by the worst. Don't
despise even the Kneelands & Andrew Jacksons. In the great
cycle they find their place & like the insect that fertilizes
the soil with worm casts or the scavenger bustard that removes carrion they perform a beneficence they know not
of, & cannot hinder if they would.

May 16, 1834. I remember when I was a boy going upon
the beach & being charmed with the colors & forms of the
shells. I picked up many & put them in my pocket. When I
got home I could find nothing that I gathered—nothing
but some dry ugly mussel & snail shells. Thence I learned

that Composition was more important than the beauty of individual forms to effect. On the shore they lay wet & social by the sea & under the sky.

June 10(?), 1834. Webster's speeches seem to be the utmost that the unpoetic West has accomplished or can. We all lean on England, scarce a verse, a page, a newspaper but is writ in imitation of English forms, our very manners & conversation are traditional & sometimes the life seems dying out of all literature & this enormous paper currency of Words is accepted instead. I suppose the evil may be cured by this rank rabble party, the Jacksonism of the country, heedless of English & of all literature—a stone cut out of the ground without hands—they may root out the hollow dilettantism of our cultivation in the coarsest way & the newborn may begin again to frame their own world with greater advantage. Meantime Webster is no imitator but a true genius for his work if that is not the highest. But every true man stands on the top of the world. He has a majestic understanding, which is in its right place the servant of the reason, & employed ever to bridge over the gulf between the revelations of his Reason, his Vision, & the facts within in the microscopic optics of the calculators that surround him. Long may he live.

November 15, 1834. Hail to the quiet fields of my fathers! Not wholly unattended by supernatural friendship & favor let me come hither. . . . And be it so. Henceforth I design not to utter any speech, poem, or book that is not entirely & peculiarly my work. I will say at Public Lectures & the like, those things which I have meditated for their own sake & not for the first time with a view to that occasion. If otherwise you select a new subject & labor to make a good appearance on the appointed day, it is so much lost time to you & lost time to your hearer. It is a parenthesis in your genuine life. You are your own dupe, & for the sake of conciliating your audience you have failed to edify them & winning their ear you have really lost their love & gratitude.

November 23, 1834. The root & seed of democracy is the doctrine Judge for yourself. Reverence thyself. It is the inevitable effect of that doctrine where it has any effect (which is rare) to insulate the partizan, to make each man a state. . . .

December 2, 1834. Concord. The age of puberty is a crisis in the life of the man worth studying. It is the passage from the Unconscious to the Conscious; from the sleep of the Passions to their rage; from careless receiving to cunning providing; from beauty to use; from omnivorous curiosity to anxious stewardship; from faith to doubt; from maternal Reason to hard short-sighted Understanding; from Unity to disunion; the progressive influences of poetry, eloquence, love, regeneration, character, truth, sorrow, and of search for an Aim, & the contest for Property.

. . . . .

A lockjaw which bended a man's head backward to his heels, and that beastly hydrophobia which makes him bark at his wife & children,—what explains these?

December 21, 1834. Blessed is the day when the youth discovers that Within and Above are synonyms.

December 21(?), 1834. If I were more in love with life & as afraid of dying as you seem to insinuate I would go to a Jackson Caucus or to the Julien Hall & I doubt not the unmixed malignity, the withering selfishness, the impudent vulgarity that mark those meetings would speedily cure me of my appetite for longevity. In the hush of these woods I find no Jackson placards affixed to the trees.

December 29(?), 1834. Extremes meet. Misfortunes even may be so accumulated as to be ludicrous. To be shipwrecked is bad; to be shipwrecked on an iceberg is horrible; to be shipwrecked on an iceberg in a snowstorm, confounds us; to be shipwrecked on an iceberg in a storm and to find a bear on the snow bank to dispute the sailor's landing which is not driven away till he has bitten off a sailor's arm, is rueful to laughter.

To Lydia Jackson

Concord, 1 February—[1835]

One of my wise masters, Edmund Burke, said, 'A wise man will speak the truth with temperance that he may speak it the longer.' In this new sentiment that you awaken in me, my Lydian Queen, what might scare others pleases me, its quietness, which I accept as a pledge of permanence. I delighted myself on Friday with my quite domesticated position & the good understanding that grew all the time, yet I went & came without one vehement word—or one passionate sign. In this was nothing of design, I merely surrendered myself to the hour & to the facts. I find a sort of grandeur in the modulated expressions of a love in which the individuals, & what might seem even reasonable personal expectations, are steadily postponed to a regard for truth & the universal love. Do not think me a metaphysical lover. I am a man & hate & suspect the over refiners, & do sympathize with the homeliest pleasures & attractions by which our good foster mother Nature draws her children together. Yet am I well pleased that between us the most permanent ties should be the first formed & thereon should grow whatever others human nature will. . . .

Under this morning's severe but beautiful light I thought dear friend that hardly should I get away from Concord. I must win you to love it. I am born a poet, of a low class without doubt yet a poet. That is my nature & vocation. My singing be sure is very 'husky,' & is for the most part in prose. Still am I a poet in the sense of a perceiver & dear lover of the harmonies that are in the soul & in matter, & specially of the correspondences between these & those. A sunset, a forest, a snow storm, a certain river-view, are more to me than many friends & do ordinarily divide my day with my books. Wherever I go therefore I guard & study my rambling propensities with a care that is ridiculous to people, but to me is the care of my high calling. Now Concord is only one of a hundred towns in which I could find these necessary objects but Plymouth I fear is not one. Plymouth is streets; I live in the wide champaign.

Time enough for this however. If I succeed in preparing my lecture on Michel Angelo Buonaroti this week for Thursday, I will come to Plymouth on Friday. If I do not succeed—do not attain unto the Idea of that man—I shall read of Luther, Thursday & then I know not when I shall steal a visit.—

Dearest forgive the egotism of all this letter. Say they not 'The more love the more egotism'? Repay it by as much & more. Write, write to me. And please dear Lidian take that same low counsel & leave thinking for the present & let the winds of heaven blow away your dyspepsia.

                                        Waldo E.

February 2, 1835. Let Christianity speak ever for the poor & the low. Though the voice of society should demand a defence of slavery from all its organs that service can never be expected from me. My opinion is of no worth, but I have not a syllable of all the language I have learned, to utter for the planter. If by opposing slavery I go to undermine institutions I confess I do not wish to live in a nation where slavery exists. . . .

February 25, 1835. I looked upon trades, politics, & domestic life, as games to keep men amused & hinder them from asking *cui bono,* until their eyes & minds are grown. . . .

March 23, 1835. . . . He who approaches a woman unlawfully [and] thinks he has overcome her . . . will shortly discover that he has put himself wholly in the power of that worthless slut. . . .

March 23(?), 1835. Sects fatten on each other's faults. . . .

March 27, 1835. He who writes should seek not to say what may be said but what has not been said that is yet true. . . .

March 28, 1835. Saturn, they say, devoured his children, thereby presignifying the man who thought & instantly turned round to see how his thoughts were made. The hen that eats the egg.

April 12(?), 1835. Language of Nature. No man ever grew so learned as to exhaust the significance of any part of nature. Nature never became a toy to a wise spirit. The flowers, the animals, the mountains reflected all the wisdom of his best hour as much as they had delighted the simplicity of his childhood. The Germans believed in this necessary Trinity of God,—the Infinite; the finite; & the passage from Infinite into Finite; or, the Creation. It is typified in the act of thinking. Whilst we contemplate we are infinite; the thought we express is partial & finite; the expression is the third part & is equivalent to the act of Creation. . . .

May 10(?), 1835. Hard Times. In this contradictory world of Truth the hard times come when the good times are in the world of commerce; namely, sleep, fulleating, plenty of money, care of it, & leisure; these are the hard times. Nothing is doing & we lose every day.

. . . . .

The young preacher is discouraged by learning the motives that brought his great congregation to church. Scarcely ten came to hear his sermon. . . . Never mind how they came, my friend, never mind who or what brought them any more than you do who or what set you down in Boston in 1835. Here they are real men & women, fools I grant but potentially divine, every one of them convertible. Every ear is yours to gain. Every heart will be glad & proud & thankful for a master. There where you are, serve them & they must serve you. They care nothing for you but be to them a Plato, be to them a Christ & they shall all be Platos & all be Christs.

May 14, 1835. There is hardly a surer way to incur the censure of infidelity & irreligion than sincere faith and an entire devotion. For to the common eye, pews, vestries, family prayer, sanctimonious looks & words constitute religion, which the devout man would find hindrances. And so we go, trying always to weld the finite & infinite, the absolute & the seeming, together. On the contrary the manner in which religion is most positively affirmed by men of the world is barefaced skepticism.

When I write a book on spiritual things I think I will advertise the reader that I am a very wicked man, & that consistency is nowise to be expected of me.

June 4(?), 1835. The clouds are our water carriers,—and do you see that hand-breadth of greener grass where the cattle have dropped dung? That was the first lecturer on Agriculture.

June, 1835. By the First Philosophy, is meant the original laws of the mind. It is the science of what *is* in distinction from what *appears*. It is one mark of them that their enunciation awakens the feeling of the Moral Sublime, and *great men* are they who believe in them. They resemble great circles in astronomy, each of which, in what direction soever it be drawn, contains the whole sphere. So each of these implies all the truth. These laws are Ideas of the

Reason, and so are obeyed easier than expressed. They astonish the Understanding and seem to it gleams of a world in which we do not live.

. . . Our compound nature differences us from God, but our Reason is not to be distinguished from the divine Essence. We have yet devised no words to designate the attributes of God which can adequately stand for the Universality & perfection of our own intuitions. To call the Reason 'ours', or 'human', seems an impertinence, so absolute & unconfined it is. The best we can say of God, we mean of the mind as it is known to us. . . .

Man is conscious of a twofold nature which manifests itself in perpetual self-contradiction. Our English philosophers to denote this duality, distinguish the Reason and the Understanding. Reason is the superior principle. Its attributes are Eternity & Intuition. We belong to it, not it to us. Human individuality is an upstart just now added to this Eternal Beatitude.

Time & Space are below its sphere. It considers things according to more intimate properties. It beholds their essence wherein is seen what they can produce. It is in all men, even in the worst, & constitutes them men. In bad men it is dormant; in the good, efficient. But it is perfect and identical in all, underneath the peculiarities, the vices, & the errors of the individual. A man feels that his fortune, friendships, opinions, yea, all the parts of his individual existence, are merely superficial to the principle of Right. Compared with the self existence of the laws of Truth & Right whereof he is conscious, his personality is a parasitic deciduous atom. Hence the doctrine of Cosmism, that the Soul which was, shall be, but that our private life which was created, may be dissipated.

The authority of Reason cannot be separated from its vision. They are not two acts, but one. The sight commands, & the command sees.

The Understanding is the executive faculty, the hand of the mind. It mediates between the soul & inert matter. It works in time & space, & therefore successively. It divides, compares, reasons, invents. It lives from the Reason, yet disobeys it. It commands the material world, yet often for the pleasure of the sense.

The Ideas of the Reason assume a new appearance as they descend into the Understanding. Invested with space & time they walk in masquerade. It incarnates the Ideas of Reason. Thus the gods of the ancient Greeks are all Ideas (as Cupid, Apollo, the Muse, &c or Love, Poesy, Wisdom, &c) but make an awkward appearance joined with the appetites of beasts. Reason, seeing in objects their remote effects, affirms the effect as the permanent Character. The Understanding listening to Reason, on one side, which saith *It is*, & to the senses, on the other side, which say *It is not*, takes middle ground & declares *It will be*. Heaven is the projection of the Ideas of Reason on the plane of the Understanding. The mind reveals that Virtue is happiness; that good spirits associate; that the only Rank is Character; that Virtue is the key to the secrets of the world. The Understanding accepts the oracle, but, with its short sight not apprehending the truth, declares that in Futurity it is so, & adds all manner of fables of its own.

. . . . .

What a benefit if a rule could be given whereby the mind dreaming amidst the gross fogs of matter, could, at any moment east itself, and find the sun. But the common life is an endless succession of phantasms. And long after we have deemed ourselves recovered & sound, light breaks in upon us & we find we have yet had no sane hour. Another morn rises on mid-noon.

July 27, 1835. Every body leads two or three lives, has two or three consciousnesses which he nimbly alternates. Here am I daily lending my voice & that with heat often to opinions & practices opposite to my own. . . .

July 30, 1835. You affirm that the moral development contains all the intellectual & that Jesus was the perfect man. I bow in reverence unfeigned before that benign man. I know more, hope more, am more because he has lived. But if you tell me that in your opinion he has fulfilled all the conditions of man's existence, carried out to the utmost at least by implication, all man's powers, I suspend my assent. I do not see in him cheerfulness; I do not see in him the love of Natural Science; I see in him no kindness for Art; I see in him nothing of Socrates, of Laplace, of Shakspeare. The perfect man should remind us of all great men. Do you ask me if I would rather resemble Jesus than any other man? If I should say Yes, I should suspect myself of superstition.

August 1, 1835. The distinction of fancy & imagination seems to me a distinction in kind. The fancy aggregates; the Imagination animates. The Fancy takes the world as it stands & selects pleasing groups by apparent relations. The Imagination is Vision, regards the world as symbolical, sees all external objects as types & pierces the emblem for the real sense. . . .

After thirty a man wakes up sad every morning excepting perhaps five or six until the day of his death. . . .

August 2, 1835. Charles wonders that I don't become sick at the stomach over my poor journal yet is obdurate habit callous even to contempt.—I must scribble on if it were only to say in confirmation of Oegger's doctrine that I believe I never take a step in thought when engaged in conversation without some material symbol of my proposition figuring itself incipiently at the same time. My sentence often ends in babble from a vain effort to represent that picture in words. How much has a figure, an illustration availed every sect. As when the reabsorption of the soul into God was figured by a phial of water broken in the sea. This morning I would have said that a man sees in the gross of the acts of his life the domination of his instincts or genius over all other causes. His wilfulness may determine the character of moments but his will determines that of years. While I thus talked I *saw* some crude *symbols* of the thought with the mind's eye, as it were, a mass of grass or weeds in a stream of which the spears or blades shot out from the mass in every direction but were immediately curved round to float all in one direction. When presently the conversation changed to the subject of Thomas à Kempis's popularity & how Aristotle & Plato come safely down as if God brought them in his hand (tho' at no time are there more than five or six men who read them) & of the Natural Academy by which the exact value of every book is determined maugre all hindrance or furtherance, then saw I as I spoke the old pail in the Summer Street kitchen with potatoes swimming in it, some at the top, some in the midst & some lying at the bottom; & I spoiled my fine thought by saying that books take their place according to their specific gravity "as surely as potatoes in a tub." And I suppose that any man who will watch his intellectual process will find a material image cotemporaneous with every thought & furnishing the garment of the thought.

. . . . .

We have little control of our thoughts. We are pensioners upon Ideas. They catch us up for moments into their heavens & so fully possess us that we take no thought for the morrow, gaze like children without an effort to make them our own. By & by we fall out of that rapture & then bethink us where we have been & what we have seen & go painfully gleaning up the grains that have fallen from the sheaf.

When I see the doors by which God entereth into the mind that there is no sot nor fop nor ruffian nor pedant into whom thoughts do not enter by passages which the individual ever left open I can expect any revolution.

September 14, 1835. I was married to Lydia Jackson.

October, 1835. We all know how life is made up; that a door is to be painted; a lock to be repaired; a cord of wood is wanted; the house smokes; or I have a diarrhea; then the tax; & a hopeless visitor; & the stinging recollection of an injurious or a very awkward word, these eat up the hours. How then is any acquisition, how is any great deed or wise & beautiful work possible? Let it enhance the praise of Milton, Shakspear & Laplace. These oppress & spitefully tyrannize over me because I am an Idealist.

December 26, 1835. There are two objects between which the mind vibrates like a pendulum; one, the desire of truth; the other, the desire of Repose. He in whom the love of Repose predominates, will accept the first creed he meets, Arianism, Calvinism, Socinianism; he gets rest & reputation; but he shuts the door of Truth. He in whom the love of Truth predominates will keep himself aloof from all moorings & afloat. He will abstain from dogmatism & recognize all the opposite negations between which as walls his being is swung. On one side he will feel that God is impersonal. On the other, that the Universe is his work.

He submits to the inconvenience of suspense & imperfect opinion but he is a candidate for truth & respects the highest law of his being.

To Lidian Emerson

New York, Thursday 12 May [1836]

.Dear Lidian,

Yesterday afternoon we attended Charles's funeral. Mother & Elizabeth heard the prayers but did not go out. The remains are deposited for a time in a tomb of Mr Griswold, a friend & connexion of Susan's.—Mother is very well & bears her sorrow like one made to bear it & to comfort others. Elizabeth is well and the strength & truth of her character appears under this bitter calamity. . . .

And so, Lidian, I can never bring you back my noble friend who was my ornament, my wisdom & my pride.—A soul is gone so costly & so rare that few persons were capable of knowing its price and I shall have my sorrow to myself for if I speak of him I shall be thought a fond exaggerator. He had the fourfold perfection of good sense, of genius, of grace, & of virtue, as I have never seen them combined. I determined to live in Concord, as you know, because he was there, and now that the immense promise of his maturity is destroyed, I feel not only unfastened there and adrift but a sort of shame at living at all.

I am thankful, dear Lidian, that you have seen & known him to that degree you have,—I should not have known how to forgive you an ignorance of him, had he been out of your sight. Thanks thanks for your kindest sympathy & appreciation of him. And you must be content henceforth with only a piece of your husband; for the best of his strength lay in the soul with which he must no more on earth take counsel. How much I saw through his eyes. I feel as if my own were very dim.

Yours affectionately

Waldo E.

May 16, 1836. And here I am again at home but I have come alone. My brother, my friend, my ornament, my joy & pride has fallen by the wayside, or rather has risen out of this dust. Charles died at New York Monday afternoon, 9 May. His prayer that he might not be sick was granted him. He was never confined to a bed. He rode out on Monday afternoon with Mother, promising himself to begin his journey with me on my arrival, the next day; on reaching home, he stepped out of the carriage alone, walked up the steps & into the house without assistance, sat down on the stairs, fainted, & never recovered. Beautiful without any parallel in my experience of young men, was his life, happiest his death. Miserable is my own prospect from whom my friend is taken. Clean & Sweet was his life, untempted almost, and his action on others all-healing, uplifting & fragrant. I read now his pages, I remember all his words & motions without any pang, so healthy & humane a life it was, & not like Edward's, a tragedy of poverty & sickness tearing genius. His virtues were like the victories of Timoleon, & Homer's verses, they were so easy & natural. I cannot understand why his mss. journal should have so bitter a strain of penitence & deprecation. I mourn that in losing him I have lost his all, for he was born an orator, not a writer. His written pages do him no justice, and as he felt the immense disparity between his power of conversation & his blotted paper, it was easy for him to speak with scorn of written composition.

Now commences a new & gloomy epoch of my life. I have used his society so fondly & solidly. It was pleasant to unfold my thought to so wise a hearer. It opened itself genially to his warm & bright light, and borrowed color & sometimes form from him. Besides my direct debt to him of how many valued thoughts,—through what orbits of speculation have we not travelled together, so that it would not be possible for either of us to say, This is my thought, That is yours.

May 19, 1836. I find myself slowly, after this helpless mourning. I remember states of mind that perhaps I had long lost before this grief, the native mountains whose tops reappear after we have traversed many a mile of weary region from home. Them shall I ever revisit? . . .

June 3(?), 1836. We are always learning that duration & magnitude are of no account to the soul. In the eternity of nature centuries are lost as moments are. In the immensity of matter, there is no great & no small. The grass & foliage that covers the whole globe from the snow that caps the north pole to the snow that caps the south pole cost no more design or effort, than went to the opening the bell of one lily, or to the germination of a grain of wheat. Time is nothing to laws. The ocean is a large drop; a drop is a small ocean.

June 7, 1836. Many letters from friends who loved or honored Charles. I know not why it is, but a letter is scarcely welcome to me. I expect to be lacerated by it & if I come safe to the end of it, I feel like one escaped.

September 20, 1836. A rail road, State Street, Bunker Hill monument are genuine productions of the age but no art.

The reason is manifest. They are not wanted. The statue of Jove was to be worshipped. The Virgin of Titian was to be worshipped. Jesus, Luther were reformers; Moses, David did something, the builders of cathedrals feared. Love & fear laid the stones in their own order.

What interest has Greenough to make a good statue? Who cares whether it is good? a few prosperous gentlemen & ladies, but the Universal Yankee nation roaring in the Capitol to approve or condemn would make his eye & hand go to a new tune.

September 20(?), 1836. Our admiration of the Antique is not admiration of the Old but of the Natural. . . .

.   .   .   .   .

A man's wife has more power over him than the State has.

September 23, 1836. When I spoke or speak of the democratic element I do not mean that ill thing vain & loud which writes lying newspapers, spouts at caucuses, & sells its lies for gold, but that spirit of love for the General good whose name this assumes. There is nothing of the true democratic element in what is called Democracy; it must fall, being wholly commercial. I beg I may not be understood to praise anything which the soul in you does not honor, however grateful may be names to your ear & your pocket.

September 28(?), 1836. A very good discourse on Marriage might be written by him who would preach the nature of things. Let him teach how fast the frivolous external fancying fades out of the mind. Let him teach both husband & wife to mourn for the rapid ebb of inclination not one moment, to yield it no tear. As this fancy picture, these fata-Morgana, this cloud scenery fades forever the solid mountain chains whereupon the sky rests in the far perspective of the soul begin to appear. The parties discover every day the deep & permanent character each of the other as a rock foundation on which they may safely build their nuptial bower. They learn slowly that all other affection than that which rests upon what they are is superstitious & evanescent, that all concealment, all pretension is wholly vain, that to the amiable & useful & heroic qualities which inhere in the other belong a certain portion of love, of pleasure, of veneration which is as exactly measured as the attraction of a pound of iron, that there is no luck nor witchcraft nor destiny nor divinity in marriage that can produce affection but only those qualities that by their nature extort it, that all love is mathematical.

October 19, 1836. The individual is always dying. The Universal is life. As much truth & goodness as enters into me so much I live. As much error & sin so much death is in me.

October 23, 1836. I wrote to Warren Burton thus;
In the newness of bereavement we are deaf to consolation, the spirit being occupied with exploring the facts, acquainting itself with the length & breadth of its disaster when a beloved person quits our society.—What we are slow to learn we learn at last, that this affliction has no acme & truly speaking no end. A passion of sorrow even though we seek it does not exhaust it but there stands the irreparable fact more grievous when all the mourners are gone than before that our being is henceforward the poorer by the loss of all the talents & affections of another soul. We may find many friends & other & noble gifts but this loss is never the less. My own faith teaches me that when one of these losses befals me it is because the hour is struck in my own constitution, a crisis has there taken place which makes it best for my whole being, makes it necessary for my whole being that this influence be withdrawn. A purer vision, an advanced state of the faculties shall hereafter inform you & me I doubt not of all those reasons & necessities which now transcend our faculties.

October 24(?), 1836. Malthus revolts us by looking at a man as an animal. So do those views of genius semi-medical which I spit at.

October, 1836. And what is God? We cannot say but we see clearly enough. We cannot say, because he is the unspeakable, the immeasureable, the perfect—but we see plain enough in what direction it lies. First we see plainly that the All is in Man, that as the proverb says, "God comes to see us without bell." That is, as there is no screen or ceiling between our heads & the infinity of space, so is there no bar or wall in the Soul where man the effect ceases & God the cause begins. The walls are taken away; we lie open on one side to all the deeps of spiritual nature, to all the attributes of God. Justice we see & know; that is of God. Truth we see & know, that is of God. Love, Freedom, Power, these are of God. For all these & much more there is a general nature in which they inhere or of which they are phases and this is Spirit. It is essentially vital. The love that is in me, the justice, the truth can never die & that is all of me that will not die. All the rest of me is so much death, my ignorance, my vice, my corporeal pleasure. But I am nothing else than a capacity for justice, truth, love, freedom, power. I can inhale, imbibe them forevermore. They shall be so much to me that I am nothing, they all. Then shall God be all in all. Herein is my Immortality. . . .

October 31, 1836. Last night at 11 o'clock, a son was born to me. Blessed child! a lovely wonder to me, and which makes the Universe look friendly to me. How remote from my knowledge, how alien, yet how kind does it make the Cause of Causes appear! The stimulated curiosity of the father sees the graces & instincts which exist, indeed, in every babe, but unnoticed in others; the right to see all, know all, to examine nearly, distinguishes this relation, & endears this sweet child. Otherwise I see nothing in it of mine; I am no conscious party to any feature, any function, any perfection I behold in it. I seem to be merely a brute occasion of its being & nowise attaining to the dignity even of a second cause no more than I taught it to suck the breast. Please God, that "he, like a tree of generous kind,

> By living waters set,"

may draw endless nourishment from the fountains of Wisdom & Virtue!

Now am I Pygmalion.

November 3(?), 1836. This age will be characterized as the era of Trade, for every thing is made subservient to that agency. The very savage on the shores of the N. W. America, holds up his shell & cries, 'a dollar!' Government at home is conducted on such principles. Superstition gives way; Patriotism; Martial Ardor; Romance in the people; but avarice does not.

Meantime, it is also a Social era, the age of associations, the powers of Combination are discovered & hence of course the age of Constitutions, of Universal suffrage, of schools, of revision of laws, abolition of imprisonment, of railroads.

November, 1836. The sublime enters into everything even into a baker's score or a school boy's multiplication table, as the Light beams into privies & garrets. . . .

November 8, 1836. I dislike to hear the patronizing tone in which the self sufficient young men of the day talk of ministers "adapting their preaching to the great mass." Was the sermon good? "O yes, good for you & me, but not understood by the great mass." Don't you deceive yourself, say I, the great mass understand what's what, as well as the little mass. The self-conceit of this tone is not more provoking than the profound ignorance it argues is pitiable.

November 19, 1836. I said to Alcott that I thought that the great Man should occupy the whole space between God and the mob. He must draw from the infinite source on the one side & he must penetrate into the heart & mind of the rabble on the other. From one, he must draw his strength; to the other, he must owe his Aim. Thus did Jesus, dwelling in mind with pure God & dwelling in social position & hearty love with fishers & women. Thus did Shakspear the great English man, drawing direct from the soul at one end, & piercing into the play-going populace at the other. The one yokes him to the real, the other to the apparent; at one pole, is Reason; at the other, common sense. Plotinus united with God is not united with the world; Napoleon, Rothschild, Falstaff, united with the world have no communion with the Divine.

December 10, 1836. Pleasant walk yesterday, the most pleasant of days. At Walden pond, I found a new musical instrument which I call the ice-harp. A thin coat of ice covered a part of the pond but melted around the edge of the shore. I threw a stone upon the ice which rebounded with a shrill sound, & falling again & again, repeated the note with pleasing modulation. I thought at first it was the 'peep' 'peep' of a bird I had scared. I was so taken with the music that I threw down my stick & spent twenty minutes in throwing stones single or in handfuls on this crystal drum.

March 29(?), 1837. I rode well. My horse took hold of the road as if he loved it.

April 8, 1837. Ah! my darling boy, so lately received out of heaven leave me not now! Please God, this sweet symbol of love & wisdom may be spared to rejoice, teach, & accompany me.

April 10, 1837. Slavery is an institution for converting men into monkeys.

April 22, 1837. Polarity is a law of all being. Superinduce the magnetism at one end of a needle, the opposite magnetism takes place at the other end. If the south attracts, the north repels.——To empty here, you must condense there. Light, shade; heat, cold; centrifugal, centripetal; action, reaction; if the mind idealizes at one end perfect goodness into God coexistently it abhors at the other end a Devil.

May 6, 1837. Sad is this continual postponement of life. I refuse sympathy & intimacy with people as if in view of some better sympathy & intimacy to come. But whence & when? I am already thirty four years old. Already my friends & fellow workers are dying from me. Scarcely can I say that I see any new men or women approaching me; I am too old to regard fashion; too old to expect patronage of any greater or more powerful. Let me suck the sweetness of those affections & consuetudes that grow near me,—that the Divine Providence offers me. These old shoes are easy to the feet. But no, not for mine, if they have an ill savor. I was made a hermit & am content with my lot. I pluck golden fruit from rare meetings with wise men. I can well abide alone in the intervals, and the fruit of my own tree shall have a better flavor.

May 7, 1837. The Sabbath reminds me of an advantage which education may give namely a normal piety, a certain levitical education which only rarely devout genius could countervail. I cannot hear the young men whose theological instruction is exclusively owed to Cambridge & to public institution, without feeling how much happier was my star which rained on me influences of ancestral religion. The depth of the religious sentiment which I knew in my Aunt Mary imbuing all her genius & derived to her from such hoarded family traditions, from so many godly lives & godly deaths of sainted kindred at Concord, Malden, York, was itself a culture, an education. . . . In my childhood Aunt Mary herself wrote the prayers which first my brother William & when he went to college I read aloud morning & evening at the family devotions, & they still sound in my ear with their prophetic & apocalyptic ejaculations. Religion was her occupation, and when years after, I came to write sermons for my own church I could not find any examples or treasuries of piety so hightoned, so profound or promising such rich influence as my remembrances of her conversation & letters.

May 20, 1837. The man of strong Understanding always acts unfavorably upon the man of Reason, disconcerts, and makes him less than he is.

May 26, 1837. Who shall define to me an Individual? I behold with awe & delight many illustrations of the One Universal Mind. I see my being imbedded in it. As a plant in the earth so I grow in God. I am only a form of him. He is the soul of me. I can even with a mountainous aspiring say, *I am God*, by transferring my *Me* out of the flimsy & unclean precincts of my body, my fortunes, my private will, & meekly retiring upon the holy austerities of the Just & the Loving—upon the secret fountains of Nature. That thin & difficult ether, I also can breathe. The mortal lungs & nostrils burst & shrivel, but the soul itself needeth no organs, it is all element & all organ. Yet why not always so? How came the Individual thus armed & impassioned to parricide, thus murderously inclined ever to traverse & kill the divine life. Ah wicked Manichee! Into that dim problem I cannot enter. A believer in Unity, a seer of Unity, I yet behold two. Whilst I feel myself in sympathy with Nature & rejoice with greatly beating heart in the course of Justice & Benevolence overpowering me, I yet find little access to this Me of Me. I fear what shall befal; I am not enough a party to the Great Order to be tranquil. I hope & I fear. I do not see. At one time, I am a Doer. A divine life, I create scenes & persons around & for me & unfold my thought by a perpetual successive projection. At least I so say, I so feel. But presently I return to the habitual attitude of suffering.

I behold; I bask in beauty; I await; I wonder; Where is my Godhead now? This is the Male & Female principle in nature. One man, male & female created he him. Hard as it is to describe God, it is harder to describe the Individual.

A certain wandering light comes to me which I instantly perceive to be the Cause of Causes. It transcends all proving. It is itself the ground of being; and I see that it is not one & I another, but this is the life of my life. That is one fact then; that in certain moments I have known that I existed directly from God, and am, as it were, his organ. And in my ultimate consciousness Am He. Then, secondly, the contradictory fact is familiar, that I am a surprised spectator & learner of all my life. This is the habitual posture of the mind —beholding. But whenever the day dawns, the great day of truth on the soul, it comes with awful invitation to me to accept it, to blend with its aurora.

Cannot I conceive the Universe without a Contradiction?

May 31, 1837. We have had two peerless summer days after all our cold winds & rains. I have weeded corn & strawberries, intent on being fat & have forborne study. The Maryland yellow-throat pipes to me all day long seeming to say extacy! Extacy! and the Bobo'lincoln flies & sings.

June 29, 1837. Almost one month lost to study by bodily weakness & disease.

July 29, 1837. . . . Pope and Johnson and Addison write as if they had never seen the face of the Country but had only read of trees & rivers in books. The striped fly that eats our squash & melon vines, the rosebug, the cornworm, the red old-leaf of the vines that entices the eye to new search for the lurking strawberry, the thicket and little bowers of the pea vine, the signs of ripeness and all the hints of the garden, these grave city writers never knew. The towers of white blossoms which the chestnut tree uplifts in the landscape in July; the angle of strength (almost a right angle) at which the oak puts out its iron arms; the botany of the meadows & watersides—what had Queen Ann's wits to do with these creatures? Did they ever prick their fingers with the thorn of a gooseberry? Did they ever hear the squeak of a bat, or see his flitting?

September 19, 1837. On the 29 August, I received a letter from the Salem Lyceum signed I. F. Worcester, requesting me to lecture before the institution next winter and adding "The subject is of course discretionary with yourself provided no allusions are made to religious controversy, or other exciting topics upon which the public mind is honestly divided." I replied on the same day to Mr. W. by quoting these words & adding "I am really sorry that any person in Salem should think me capable of accepting an invitation so encumbered."

October 6, 1837. . . . If you don't like the world, make it to suit you. All true men have done so before you. . . .

October 8, 1837. The young Southerner comes here a spoiled child with graceful manners, excellent self command, very good to be spoiled more, but good for nothing else, a mere parader. He has conversed so much with rifles, horses & dogs that he is become himself a rifle, a horse & a dog and in civil educated company where anything human is going forward he is dumb & unhappy; like an Indian in a church. Treat them with great deference as we often do, and they accept it all as their due without misgiving. Give them an inch & they take a mile. They are mere bladders of conceit. Each snippersnapper of them all undertakes to speak for the entire Southern states. "At the South, the reputation of Cambridge" &c. &c. which being interpreted, is, "In my negro village of Tuscaloosa or Cheraw or St Marks I supposed so & so." "We, at the South," forsooth. They are more civilized than the Seminoles, however, in my opinion; a little more. Their question respecting any man is like a Seminole's, How can he fight? In this country, we ask, What can he do? His pugnacity is all they prize in man, dog, or turkey. The proper way of treating them is not deference but to say as Mr Ripley does "Fiddle faddle" in answer to each solemn remark about "The South." "It must be confessed" said the young man, "that in Alabama, we are dead to every thing, as respects politics." "Very true," replied Mr Ripley, "leaving out the last clause."

October 16, 1837. A lovely afternoon and I went to Walden Water & read Goethe on the bank.

October 28, 1837. The event of death is always astounding; our philosophy never reaches, never possesses it; we are always at the beginning of our catechism; always the definition is yet to be made, What is Death? I see nothing to help beyond observing what the mind's habit is in regard to that crisis. Simply, I have nothing to do with it. It is nothing to me. After I have made my will & set my house in order, I shall do in the immediate expectation of death the same things I should do without it. But more difficult is it to know the death of another. . . .

November 24, 1837. When a zealot comes to me & represents the importance of this Temperance Reform my hands drop—I have no excuse—I honor him with shame at my own inaction.

Then a friend of the slave shows me the horrors of Southern slavery—I cry guilty guilty! Then a philanthropist tells me the shameful neglect of the Schools by the Citizens. I feel guilty again.

Then I hear of Byron or Milton who drank soda water & ate a crust whilst others fed fat & I take the confessional anew.

Then I hear that my friend has finished Aristophanes, Plato, Cicero & Grotius, and I take shame to myself.

Then I hear of the generous Morton who offers a thousand dollars to the cause of Socialism, and I applaud & envy.

Then of a brave man who resists a wrong to the death and I sacrifice anew.

I cannot do all these things but these my shames are illustrious tokens that I have strict relations to them all. None of these causes are foreigners to me. My Universal Nature is thus marked. These accusations are parts of me too. They are not for nothing.

November 26, 1837. How can such a question as the Slave Trade be agitated for forty years by the most enlightened nations of the world without throwing great light on ethics into the general mind? The fury with which the slaveholder & the slavetrader defend every inch of their plunder, of their bloody deck, & howling Auction, only serves as a Trump of

Doom to alarum the ear of Mankind, to wake the sleepers & drag all neutrals to take sides & listen to the argument & to the Verdict which justice shall finally pronounce. The loathsome details of the kidnapping; of the middle passage; six hundred living bodies sit for thirty days betwixt death & life in a posture of stone & when brought on deck for air, cast themselves into the sea—were these details merely produced to harrow the nerves of the susceptible & humane or for the purpose of engraving the question on the memory that it should not be dodged or obliterated & securing to it the concentration of the whole Conscience of Christendom?

February 19, 1838. Solitude is fearsome & heavy hearted. I have never known a man who had so much good accumulated upon him as I have. Reason, health, wife, child, friends, competence, reputation, the power to inspire, & the power to please. Yet leave me alone a few days, & I creep about as if in expectation of a calamity. My mother, my brother are at New York. A little farther,—across the sea, —is my friend Thomas Carlyle. In the islands I have another friend, it seems. I will love you all & be happy in your love. My gentle wife has an angel's heart; & for my boy, his grief is more beautiful than other people's joy. . . .

May 4, 1838. Walter Scott says, that, "at night, the kind are savage. . . ."

June 8, 1838. A good deal of character in our abused age. The rights of woman, the antislavery-, temperance-, peace-, health-, and money movements; female speakers, mobs & martyrs, the paradoxes, the antagonism of old & new, the anomalous church, the daring mysticism & the plain prose, the uneasy relation of domestics, the struggling toward better household arrangements—all indicate life at the heart not yet justly organized at the surface.

June 9, 1838. Why do we seek this lurking beauty, in skies, in poems, in drawings? Ah because there we are safe, there we neither sicken nor die. I think we fly to Beauty as an asylum from the terrors of finite nature. We are made immortal by this kiss, by the contemplation of beauty. Strange, strange that the door to it should thus perversely be through the prudent, the punctual, the frugal, the careful;

& that the adorers of beauty, musicians, painters, Byrons, Shelleys, Keatses, & such like men, should turn themselves out of doors, & out of sympathies, & out of themselves. Whilst I behold the holy lights of the June sunset last evening or tonight I am raised instantly out of fear & out of time, & care not for the knell of this coughing body.—Strange the succession of humors that pass through this human spirit. Sometimes I am the organ of the Holy Ghost & sometimes of a vixen petulance. . . .

June 12, 1838. Do not be an unwise churl & rail at society nor so worldly wise as to condemn solitude. But use them as conditions. Be their master, not their slave. Make circumstance,—all circumstance, conform to the law of your mind. Be always a king, & not they, & nothing shall hurt you.

June 16, 1838. The Unbelief of the Age is attested by the loud condemnation of trifles. Look at our silly religious papers. Let a minister wear a cane, or a white hat, go to a theatre, or avoid a Sunday school, let a school book with a Calvinistic sentence or a Sunday schoolbook without one, be heard of, & instantly all the old grannies squeak & gibber & do what they call sounding an alarm, from Bangor to Mobile. Alike nice & squeamish is its ear; you must on no account say "stink" or "damn."

June 18, 1838. The art of writing consists in putting two things together that are unlike and that belong together like a horse & cart. Then have we somewhat far more goodly & efficient than either.

. . . . .

Ah my country! In thee is the reasonable hope of mankind not fulfilled. It should be that when all feudal straps & bandages were taken off an unfolding of the Titans had followed & they had laughed & leaped young giants along the continent & ran up the mountains of the West with the errand of Genius & of love. But the utmost thou hast yet produced, is a puny love of beauty in Allston, in Greenough; in Bryant; in Everett; in Channing; in Irving; an imitative love of grace. . . . Ah me! the cause is one; the diffidence of Ages in the Soul has crept over thee too, America. No man here believeth in the soul of Man but only in some name or person old & departed. . . .

June 23, 1838. I hate goodies. I hate goodness that preaches. Goodness that preaches undoes itself. A little electricity of virtue lurks here & there in kitchens & among the obscure—chiefly women, that flashes out occasional light & makes the existence of the thing still credible. But one had as lief curse & swear as be guilty of this odious religion that watches the beef & watches the cider in the pitcher at the table, that shuts the mouth hard at any remark it cannot twist nor wrench into a sermon, & preaches as long as itself & its hearer is awake. Goodies make us very bad. We should, if the race should increase, be scarce restrained from calling for bowl & dagger. We will almost sin to spite them. Better indulge yourself, feed fat, drink liquors, than go straight laced for such cattle as these.

To Amos Bronson Alcott

Concord, 28 June, 1838

My dear Sir,

I have read Psyche twice through some pages thrice; and yet am scarcely able to make up my mind on the main question submitted to me—Shall it be published? It is good and it is bad; it is great, & it is little. If the book were mine, I would on no account print it; and the book being yours, I do not know but it behoves you to print it in defiance of all the critics.

The general design of the book as an affirmation of the spiritual nature to an unbelieving age, is good; the topics good; the form excellent, & of great convenience divided into natural chapters by the topics that arise. The ideas out of which the book originates are commanding; the book holy. There are in it happy & valuable thoughts; some good sentences; some happy expressions. It is the work of a man who has a more simple & steadfast belief in the soul, than any other man; and so it tends to inspire faith.

Yet with these merits, I read the book with a certain perplexity, arising, I think, from a want of unity of design in the book itself.

Is it a Gospel—a book of exhortation, & popular devotion?

Or, is it a book of thought addressed to cultivated men? Which of these two?

1. Is it a Gospel? It evinces on every page great elevation

of character, & often assumes, in the thought & expression, the tone of a prophet. Well; let it preach, then, to the chidden world. There is sin & sorrow enough to make a call; & the preacher believes in his heart. And, in this view, I certainly would not criticise this scroll any more than that of Habbakuk or Jeremy; but would sit & take with docility my portion of reproof.—But, as I read, it departs from that character. To the prophetic tone belongs simplicity, not variety, not taste, not criticism. As a book of practical holiness, this seems to me not effective. This is fanciful, playful, ambitious, has a periphrastic style & masquerades in the language of Scripture, *Thee & Thou, Hath & Doth*. The prophet should speak a clear discourse straight home to the conscience in the language of earnest conversation.

Such portions of the book, however, as are written in this vein, lead me to say, that, you only can be the judge whether the publication may be suspended.

But, as I have intimated, other passages come, & make the book amenable to other laws.

2. Is it a book of thought addressed to literary men? I looked for this; for the writing of a philosopher seeing things under a scientific point of view, & not for a book of popular ethics. But this it is not. In the first place, the degree in which the former element is introduced vitiates it for a scientific book; the condition of which, is, that an observer quite passionless & detached—a mere eye & pen—sees & records, without praise, without blame, without personal relation— like a god. But there runs throughout this book, as already intimated, a tone of scarcely less than prophetic pretension; which, howeve[r] allowable in a gospel, is wholly out of place in philosophy, where truth, not duty, is the question. Or, in the second place, if such a tone is ever admissible, one thing only can justify it, to wit, the actual contributing a large amount of unknown truths, say, as Kepler, as Newton did. But this is not your object. The book neither abounds in new propositions nor writes out applications of old truth in systematic detail to existing abuses. This, you know, is my old song. I demand your propositions; your definitions; your thoughts (in the stricter use of that term, i. e. a new quality or relation abstracted); your facts observed in nature; as in solid blocks. But your method is the reverse of this. Your page is a series of touches. You play. You play with the thought: never strip off your coat,

& dig, & strain, & drive into the root & heart of the matter.
I wish you would, with this my complaint before you, open
at a few pages of Psyche at random & see what a style this
is to baulk & disappoint expectation. To use a coarse word—
tis all stir & no go.—There is no progress. I become nervous at the patience with which my author husbands his
thought—plays about it with a variety of fine phrases, each
of which alone were elegant & welcome, but together, are
superfluity. Meantime, the present Ideas of Truth, of Love, of
the Infinite, give, I allow, a certain grandeur to the whole. I
thought, as I read, of the Indian jungles, vast & flowering,
where the sky & stars are visible alway, but no house, no
mountain, no man, no definite objects whatever, & no
change, or progress; & so, one acre in it is like another,
& I can sleep in it for centuries. But mortal man must save
his time, & see a new thing at every step. Moreover, I think
it carries to an extreme the aphoristic style which is only
good if dense with thought, but we must not multiply into
many sentences what could better be condensed into one.
It is graceful when intermingled with a freer speech, but by
itself is short & chopping like a cord of chips for a cord of
wood.

If, therefore, the book is to be addressed to men of study,
I think it demands;

1. The most resolute compression almost to a numbering of
the sentences 1, 2, 3, 4, as they are *things,* & casting out the
rest. Of course, enrich it by any additional pertinent matter,
withholding nothing because it is a *pearl,* which seems to be
intimated p. 289.

2. The omission of all passages conveying this prophetic
pretension, of which I have spoken; and shading or modifying
all passages that are too obvious personal allusions, until
they speak to the condition of all, or at least of a class.
The author's Ego must be the human Ego, & not that of his
name & town. (Some of these personal allusions seem to be
in pp. 198, 212, 259, 260, 289, &c)

3. The dropping of the Scriptural termination, as in do*eth,*
work*eth*; of thou & thine; and the earnest adoption of the
language you speak in your own house; and the more sparing
use of several words which, through the MS., recur too
frequently; such as, *Ideal,* image, ministry; genius; worthy,
worthier, worthily; belie; mission; &c.

Thus far, my dear sir, go my axe & knife. You will see in

the accompanying sheets a few verbal or local criticisms that occurred as I went along. I have also made an experiment or two at a condensation of one of your paragraphs to see if it would not gain thereby. I have indicated some passages that struck me more favorably. There are many such which I have not indicated. The book of Innocence, I esteem least valuable. I think the second & fourth books the best.

And now having said all these things in the relentless use of my critical bludgeon, I frankly tell you that I doubt entirely my jurisdiction in the matter; I may do great harm by inducing you to with hold the volume; & if you feel any promptings to print it as it stands, I will immediately & cheerfully make my contract as I proposed with Messrs Metcalf & Co. In the circumstances, if you should feel undecided, I should think it best that some third person should be selected by you who should read it & decide.

Or if you would like to make trial of the public pulse, why would it not do to print one or two or three chapters successively & anonymously in one of the magazines, & if they drew such attention as you liked, then you would print the book with more confidence.

Your friend,
R. W. Emerson.

July 1, 1838. There is a limit to the effect of written eloquence. It may do much, but the miracles of eloquence can only be expected from the man who thinks on his legs. . . .

August 17, 1838. Life is a pretty tragedy especially for women. On comes a gay dame of manners & tone so fine & haughty that all defer to her as to a countess, & she seems the dictator of society. Sit down by her, & talk of her own life in earnest, & she is some stricken soul with care & sorrow at her vitals, & wisdom or charity cannot see any way of escape for her from remediless evils. She envies her companion in return, until she also disburdens into her ear the story of *her* misery, as deep & hopeless as her own.

August 22, 1838. I decline invitations to evening parties chiefly because besides the time spent, commonly ill, in the party, the hours preceding & succeeding the visit, are lost for any solid use, as I am put out of tune for writing or reading. That makes my objection to many employments that seem trifles to a bystander as packing a trunk, or any small handiwork, or correcting proof sheets, that they put me out of tune.

August 25, 1838. How expressive is form! I see by night the shadow of a poor woman against a window curtain that instantly tells a story of so much meekness, affection, & labor, as almost to draw tears.

August 25(?), 1838. The Whole History of the negro is tragedy. By what accursed violation did they first exist that they should suffer always. . . . I think they are more pitiable when rich than when poor. Of what use are riches to them? They never go out without being insulted. Yesterday I saw a family of negroes riding in a Coach. How pathetic!

August 28, 1838. It is very grateful to my feelings to go into a Roman Cathedral, yet I look as my countrymen do at the Roman priesthood. It is very grateful to me to go into an English Church & hear the liturgy read. Yet nothing would induce me to be the English priest. I find an unpleasant dilemma in this, nearer home. I dislike to be a clergyman & refuse to be one. Yet how rich a music would be to me a holy clergyman in my town. It seems to me he cannot be a man, quite & whole; yet how plain is the need of one, & how high yes highest is the function. Here is Division of labor that I like not. A man must sacrifice his manhood for the social good. Something is wrong, I see not what.

September 1, 1838. Looked over S.G. Ward's portfolio of drawings & prints. In landscapes it ought to be that the painter should give us not surely the enjoyment of a real landscape;—for, air, light, motion, life, dampness, heat, & actual infinite space, he cannot give us,—but the suggestion of a better, fairer creation than we know; he should crowd a greater number of beautiful effects into his picture than co-exist in any real landscape. All the details, all the prose of nature, he should omit, & give us only the spirit & splendor. So that we should find his landscape more exalting to the inner man than is Walden Pond or the Pays de Vaud. All spiritual activity is abridgment, selection.

September 12, 1838. Yesterday the Middlesex Association

met here with two or three old friends beside. Yet talking this morning in detail with two friends of the proposition often made of a journal to meet the wants of the time, it seemed melancholy as soon as it came to the details. It is strange how painful is the actual world, the painful kingdom of time & place. There dwells care & canker & fear. With thought, with the ideal is immortal hilarity, the rose of joy. All the muses sing, but with names, & persons, & today's interests, is grief. . . .

September 18, 1838. Housekeeping. If my garden had only made me acquainted with the muckworm, the bugs, the grasses & the swamp of plenty in August, I should willingly pay a free tuition. But every process is lucrative to me far beyond its economy. For the like reason keep house. Whoso does, opens a shop in the heart of all trades, professions & arts so that upon him these shall all play. By keeping house I go to a universal school where all knowledges are taught me & the price of tuition is *my annual expense*. Thus I want my stove set up. I only want a piece of sheet iron 31 inches by 33. But that want entitles me to call on the professors of tin & iron in the village, Messrs Wilson & Dean & inquire of them the kinds of iron they have or can procure, the cost of production of a pound of cast or wrought metal, & any other related information they possess, & furthermore to lead the conversation to the practical experiment of the use of their apparatus for the benefit of my funnel & blower, all which they courteously do for a small fee. In like manner, I play the chemist with ashes, soap, beer, vinegar, manure, medicines; the naturalist with trees, shrubs, hens, pigs, cows, horses, fishes, bees, cankerworms, wood, & coal; the politician with the selectmen, the assessors, the Probate Court, the town-meeting.

October 5, 1838. Once I thought it a defect peculiar to me, that I was confounded by interrogatories & when put on my wits for a definition was unable to reply without injuring my own truth: but now, I believe it proper to man to be unable to answer in terms the great problems put by his fellow: it is enough if he can live his own definitions. A problem appears to me. I cannot solve it with all my wits: but leave it there; let it lie awhile: I can by patient faithful truth live at last its uttermost darkness into light.

To Henry Ware, Jr.[1]

Concord, Oct. 8, 1838.

My dear Sir,

I ought sooner to have acknowledged your kind letter of last week & the sermon it accompanied. The Letter was right manly & noble. The sermon I have read with attention. If it assails any statements of mine perhaps I am not as quick to see it as most writers—certainly I felt no disposition to depart from my habitual contentment that you should speak your thought whilst I speak mine. I believe I must tell you what I think of my new position. It strikes me very oddly & even a little ludicrously that the good & great men of Cambridge should think of raising me into an object of criticism. I have always been from my very incapacity of methodical writing a chartered libertine, free to worship & free to rail, lucky when I was understood but never esteemed near enough to the institutions & mind of society to deserve the notice of the masters of literature & religion. I have appreciated fully the advantage of my position for I well knew that there was no scholar less willing or less able to be a polemic. I could not give account of myself if challenged. I could not possibly give you one of the "arguments" on which as you cruelly hint any position of mine stands. For I do not know, I confess, what arguments mean in reference to any expression of a thought. I delight in telling what I think but if you ask me how I dare say so or why it is so I am the most helpless of mortal men; I see not even that either of these questions admits of an answer. So that in the present droll posture of my affairs when I see myself suddenly raised into the importance of a heretic, I am very uneasy if I advert to the supposed duties of such a personage who is expected to make good his thesis against all comers. I therefore tell you plainly I shall do no such thing. I shall read what you & other good men write as I have always done, glad when you speak my thought & skipping the page that has nothing for me. I shall go on just as before, seeing whatever I can & telling what I see and I suppose with the same fortune as has hitherto attended me, the joy of finding that my abler & better brothers who work with the

[1] The letter is an answer to Reverend Mr. Ware's criticism of Emerson's Divinity School Address. The text is Emerson's first draft, with cancellations omitted and some punctuation added.

sympathy of society & love it, unexpectedly confirm my perceptions, & find my nonsense is only their own thought in motley.

And so I am
Your affectionate servant,
R. W. Emerson

October 12, 1838. Succession, division, parts, particles—this is the condition, this the tragedy of man. All things cohere & unite. Man studies the parts, strives to tear the part from its connexion, to magnify it, & make it a whole. He sides with the Part against other Parts; & fights for parts, fights for lies. & his whole mind becomes an *inflamed Part*, an amputated member, a wound, an offence. Meantime within him is the Soul of the Whole, the Wise Silence, the Universal Beauty to which every part & particle is equally related, the eternal One. Speech is the sign of partiality, difference, ignorance, and the more perfect the understanding between men, the less need of words. And when I know all, I shall cease to commend any part. An ignorant man thinks the divine wisdom is conspicuously shown in some fact or creature: a wise man sees that every fact contains the same. I should think Water the best invention, if I were not acquainted with Fire & Earth & Air. But as we advance, every proposition, every action, every feeling, runs out into the infinite. If we go to affirm anything we are checked in our speech by the need of recognizing all other things until speech presently becomes rambling, general, indefinite & merely tautology. The only speech will at last be action such as Confucius describes the Speech of God.

October 31, 1838. Yesterday eve. Lidian's soirée. As soon as the party is broken up, I shrink, & wince, & try to forget it. There is no refuge but in oblivion of such misdemeanors.

November 8, 1838. Let me never fall into the vulgar mistake of dreaming that I am persecuted whenever I am contradicted. No man, I think, had ever a greater well-being with a less desert than I. I can very well afford to be accounted bad or foolish by a few dozen or a few hundred persons,—I who see myself greeted by the good expectation of so many friends far beyond any power of thought or communication of thought residing in me. Besides, I own, I am often inclined to take part with those who say I am bad or foolish, for I fear I am both. I believe & know there must be a perfect compensation. I know too well my own dark spots. Not having myself attained, not satisfied myself, far from a holy obedience,—how can I expect to satisfy others, to command their love? A few sour faces, a few biting paragraphs, —is but a cheap expiation for all these shortcomings of mine.

November 10(?), 1838. Shakspear fills us with wonder the first time we approach him. We go away, & work, & think, for years, & come again, he astonishes us anew. Then having drank deeply & saturated us with his genius, we lose sight of him for another period of years. By & by we return, & there he stands immeasureable as at first. We have grown wiser, but only that we should see him wiser than ever. He resembles a high mountain which the traveller sees in the morning & thinks he shall quickly near it & pass it & leave it behind. But he journeys all day till noon, till night. There still is the dim mountain close by him, having scarce altered its bearings since the morning light.

November 14, 1838. What is the hardest task in the World? To think. I would put myself where I have so often been in the attitude of meeting as it were face to face an abstract truth,—& I cannot; I blench; I withdraw on this side, on that. I seem to know what he meant who said, "No man can see God face to face & live."

Musical Eyes. I think sometimes that my lack of Musical ear, is made good to me through my eyes. That which others hear, I *see.* All the soothing plaintive brisk or romantic moods which corresponding melodies waken in them, I find in the carpet of the wood, in the margin of the pond, in the shade of the hemlock grove, or in the infinite variety & rapid dance of the treetops as I hurry along.

November 27, 1838. I have no less disgust than any other at the cant of Spiritualism. I had rather hear a round volley of Ann Street oaths than the affectation of that which is divine on the foolish lips of coxcombs.

February 22(?), 1839. The pathetic lies usually not in miseries but petty losses & disappointments as when the poor family have spent their little utmost upon a wedding or a christening festival, & their feast is dishonored by some insult or petty disaster,—the falling of the salver, or the spoiling of a carpet. When I was a boy, I was sent by my mother with a dollar bill to buy me a pair of shoes at Mr Baxter's Shop, & I lost the bill; & remember being sent out by my disappointed mother to look among the fallen leaves under the poplar trees opposite the house for the lost bank note.

May 19(?), 1839. At Church today I felt how unequal is this match of words against things. Cease, o thou unauthorized talker, to prate of consolation, & resignation, and spiritual joys, in neat & balanced sentences. For I know these men who sit below, & on the hearing of these words look up. Hush quickly; for care & calamity are things to them. There is Mr Tolman the shoemaker, whose daughter is gone mad. And he is looking up through his spectacles to hear what you can offer for his case. Here is my friend, whose scholars are all leaving him, & he knows not what to turn his hand to, next. Here is my wife who has come to church in hope of being soothed & strengthened after being wounded by the sharp tongue of a slut in her house. Here is the stage driver who has the jaundice, & cannot get well. Here is B who failed last week, and he is looking up. O speak things, then, or hold thy tongue.

May 26, 1839. If as Hedge thinks I overlook great facts in stating the absolute laws of the soul; if as he seems to represent it the world is not a dualism, is not a bipolar Unity, but is *two*, is Me and It, then is there the Alien, the Unknown, and all we have believed & chanted out of our deep instinctive hope is a pretty dream.

May 28, 1839. How can I hope for a friend to me who have never been one?

June 12, 1839. I know no means of calming the fret & perturbation into which too much sitting, too much talking, brings me so perfect as labor. I have no animal spirits, therefore when surprised by company & kept in a chair for many hours, my heart sinks, my brow is clouded & I think I will run for Acton woods, & live with the squirrels henceforward.

But my garden is nearer, and my good hoe as it bites the ground revenges my wrongs & I have less lust to bite my enemies. I confess I work at first with a little venom, lay to a little unnecessary strength. But by smoothing the rough hillocks, I smooth my temper; by extracting the long roots of the piper grass, I draw out my own splinters; & in a short time I can hear the Bobalink's song & see the blessed deluge of light & colour that rolls around me.

August 27, 1839. . . . On Sunday we heard sulphurous Calvinism. The Preacher railed at Lord Byron. I thought Lord Byron's vice better than Rev. Mr M's virtue. . . .

September 14, 1839. Education. . . . We all are involved in the condemnation of words, an Age of words. We are shut up in schools & college recitation rooms for ten or fifteen years & come out at last with a bellyfull of words & do not know a thing. We cannot use our hands or our legs or our eyes or our arms. We do not know an edible root in the woods. We cannot tell our course by the stars nor the hour of the day by the sun. It is well if we can swim & skate. We are afraid of a horse, of a cow, of a dog, of a cat, of a spider. Far better was the Roman rule to teach a boy nothing that he could not learn standing. Now here are my wise young neighbors who instead of getting like the wordmen into a railroad-car, where they have not even the activity of holding the reins, have got into a boat which they have built with their own hands with sails which they have contrived to serve as a tent by night, & gone up the river Merrimack to live by their wits on the fish of the stream & the berries of the wood. . . . The farm the farm is the right school. . . . The farm by training the physical rectifies & invigorates the metaphysical & moral nature.

Now so bad we are that the world is stripped of love & of terror. Here came the other night an Aurora so wonderful, a curtain of red & blue & silver glory, that in any other age or nation it would have moved the awe & wonder of men & mingled with the profoundest sentiments of religion & love & we all saw it with cold arithmetical eyes, we knew how many colours shone, how many degrees it extended, how many hours it lasted, & of this heavenly flower we beheld nothing more: a primrose by the brim of the river of time. . . .

I lament that I find in me no enthusiasm, no resources

for the instruction & guidance of the people when they shall discover that their present guides are blind. This convention of Education is cold, but I should perhaps affect a hope I do not feel if I were bidden to counsel it. I hate preaching whether in pulpits or Teachers' meetings. Preaching is a pledge & I wish to say that I think & feel today with the proviso that tomorrow perhaps I shall contradict it all. Freedom boundless I wish. I will not pledge myself not to drink wine, not to drink ink, not to lie, & not to commit adultery lest I hanker tomorrow to do these very things by reason of my having tied my hands. Besides Man is so poor he cannot afford to part with any advantages or bereave himself of the functions even of one hair. I do not like to speak to the Peace society if so I am to restrain me in so extreme a privilege as the use of the sword & bullet. For the peace of the man who has forsworn the use of the bullet seems to me not quite peace, but a canting impotence: but with knife & pistol in my hands, if I, from greater bravery & honor, cast them aside, then I know the glory of Peace.

September 14(?), 1839. The mob are always interesting. We hate editors, preachers, & all manner of scholars, and fashionists. A blacksmith, a truckman, a farmer we follow into the barroom & watch with eagerness what they shall say, for such as they, do not speak because they are expected to, but because they have somewhat to say.

October 18, 1839. *Lectures.* In these golden days it behooves me once more to make my annual inventory of the world. For the five last years I have read each winter a new Course of lectures in Boston, and each was my creed & confession of faith. Each told all I thought of the past, the present & the future. Once more I must renew my work and I think only once in the same form though I see that he who thinks he does something for the last time ought not to do it at all. Yet my objection is not to the thing but to the form; & the concatenation of errors called *society* to which I still consent, until my plumes be grown, makes even a duty of this concession also. So I submit to sell tickets again. But the form is neither here nor there. What shall be the substance of my shrift? Adam in the garden, I am to new name all the beasts in the field & all the gods in the sky. I am to invite men drenched in time to recover themselves & come out of

time, & taste their native immortal air. I am to fire with
what skill I can the artillery & sympathy & emotion. I am to
indicate constantly, though all unworthy, the Ideal and Holy
Life, the life within life,—the Forgotten Good, the Unknown
Cause in which we sprawl & sin. I am to try the magic of
sincerity, that luxury permitted only to kings & poets. I am
to celebrate the spiritual powers in their infinite contrast to
the magical powers & the mechanical philosophy of this
time. I am to console the brave sufferers under evils whose
end they cannot see by appeals to the great optimism self-
affirmed in all bosoms.

October 19, 1839. Who can blame men for seeking excitement. They are polar & would you have them sleep in a dull
eternity of equilibrium? Religion, love, ambition, money, war,
brandy, some fierce antagonism must break the round of perfect circulation or no spark, no joy, no event can be. As good
not be.

In the country the lover of nature dreaming through the
wood would never awake to thought if the scream of an
eagle, the cries of a crow or a curlew near his head did not
break the continuity. Nay if the truth must out the finest
lyrics of the poet come of this coarse parentage, the imps of
matter beget such child on the soul, fair daughter of God.

October 21(?), 1839. A part of the protest we are called to
make is to the popular mode of virtuous endeavor. "Will
you not come to this convention & nominate a Temperance
ticket? Let me show you the immense importance of the
step." Nay, my friend, I do not work with those tools. The
principles on which your church & state are built are false
& a portion of this virus vitiates the smallest detail even of
your charity & religion. Though I own I sympathize with
your desire & abhor your adversaries yet I shall persist in
wearing this robe all loose & unbecoming as it is of inaction,
this wise passiveness, until my hour comes when I can see
how to act with truth as well as to refuse.

November 13, 1839. Do something, it matters little or not
at all whether it be in the way of what you call your profession or not, so it be in the plane or coincident with the axis
of your character. The reaction is always proportioned to the
action, and it is the reaction that we want. Strike the hardest

blow you can, & you can always do this by work which is agreeable to your nature. This is economy.

November 14, 1839. *Systems.* I need hardly say to any one acquainted with my thoughts that I have no System. When I was quite young I fancied that by keeping a Manuscript Journal by me, over whose pages I wrote a list of the great topics of human study, as *Religion, Poetry, Politics, Love,* &c in the course of a few years I should be able to complete a sort of Encyclopaedia containing the net value of all the definitions at which the world had yet arrived. But at the end of a couple of years my Cabinet Cyclopaedia though much enlarged was no nearer to a completeness than on its first day. Nay somehow the whole plan of it needed alteration nor did the following months promise any speedier term to it than the foregoing. At last I discovered that my curve was a parabola whose arcs would never meet, and came to acquiesce in the perception that although no diligence can rebuild the Universe in a model by the best accumulation or disposition of details, yet does the World reproduce itself in miniature in every event that transpires, so that all the laws of nature may be read in the smallest fact. So that the truth speaker may dismiss all solicitude as to the proportion & congruency of the aggregate of his thoughts so long as he is a faithful reporter of particular impressions.

November 17, 1839. Why should they call me goodnatured? I too like puss have a retractile claw.

. . . . .

Men kill themselves. And run the risk of great absurdity; for our faculties fail us here to say what is the amount of this freedom, this only door left open in all the padlocked secrets of nature, this single door ajar, this main entry & royal staircase admitting apparently to the Presence-Chamber, yet so designedly it seems left wide. It may be that he who sheathes his knife in his own heart does an act of grand issues, & it may be a preposterous one. I think I would not try it until I had first satisfied myself that I did not baulk & fool myself. The question is whether it is the way *out*, or the way *in*.

December 22(?), 1839. *Treat things poetically.* Every thing should be treated poetically—law, politics, housekeeping, money. A judge and a banker must drive their craft poetically as well as a dancer or a scribe. That is, they must exert that higher vision which causes the object to become fluid & plastic. Then they are inventive, they detect its capabilities. If they do not this they have nothing that can be called success, but the work & the workman become blockish & near the point of everlasting congelation. All human affairs need the perpetual intervention of this elastic principle to preserve them supple & alive as the earth needs the presence of caloric thro' its pores to resist the tendency to absolute solidity. If you would write a code or logarithms or a cookbook you cannot spare the poetic impulse. We must not only have hydrogen in balloons and steel springs under coaches but we must have fire under the Andes at the core of the world. No one will doubt that battles must be fought poetically who reads Plutarch or Las Casas. Economy must be poetical, inventive, alive: that is its essence, and therein is it distinguished from mere parsimony, which is a poor, dead, base thing: but economy inspires respect,—is clean & accomplishes much.

February 19, 1840. I closed last Wednesday, 12th instant, my Course of Lectures in Boston, On the Present Age. . . .

These lectures give me little pleasure. I have not done what I hoped when I said, I will try it once more. I have not once transcended the coldest selfpossession. I said I will agitate others, being agitated myself. I dared to hope for extacy & eloquence. A new theatre, a new art, I said, is mine. Let us see if philosophy, if ethics, if chiromancy, if the discovery of the divine in the house & the barn, in all works & all plays, cannot make the cheek blush, the lip quiver, & the tear start. I will not waste myself. On the strength of Things I will be borne, and try if Folly, Custom, Convention, & Phlegm cannot be made to hear our sharp artillery. Alas! alas! I have not the recollection of one strong moment. A cold mechanical preparation for a delivery as decorous,—fine things, pretty things, wise things,—but no arrows, no axes, no nectar, no growling, no transpiercing, no loving, no enchantment.

And why?

I seem to lack constitutional vigor to attempt each topic as I ought. I ought to seek to lay myself out utterly,—large, enormous, prodigal, upon the subject of the week. But a hateful experience has taught me that I can only expend, say, twenty one hours on each lecture, if I would also be ready & able for the next. Of course, I spend myself prudently: I economize; I cheapen: whereof nothing grand ever grew. Could I spend sixty hours on each, or what is better, had I such Energy that I could rally the lights & mights of sixty hours into twenty, I should hate myself less, I should help my friend.

February 21, 1840. The aim of art is always at somewhat better than nature, but the work of art is always inferior to nature.

April 7(?), 1840. In all my lectures, I have taught one doctrine, namely, the infinitude of the private man. This, the people accept readily enough, & even with loud commendation, as long as I call the lecture, Art; or Politics; or Literature; or the Household; but the moment I call it Religion,—they are shocked, though it be only the application of the same truth which they receive elsewhere, to a new class of facts.

April 9, 1840. We walked this P.M. to Edmund Hosmer's & Walden Pond.—The south wind blew & filled with bland & warm light the dry sunny woods. The last year's leaves flew like birds through the air. As I sat on the bank of the Drop or God's Pond & saw the amplitude of the little water, what space, what verge, the little scudding fleets of ripples found to scatter & spread from side to side & take so much time to cross the pond, & saw how the water seemed made for the wind, & the wind for the water, dear playfellows for each other,—I said to my companion, I declare this world is so beautiful that I can hardly believe it exists. . . .

April 27(?), 1840. True Criticism is inexhaustible. Every new thought supersedes all foregone thought & makes a new light on the whole world.

June 19, 1840. We see the river glide below us but we see not the river that glides over us & envelopes us in its floods. A month ago I met myself as I was speeding away from some trifle to chase a new one & knew that I had eaten lotus & been a stranger from my home all this time.

And now I see that with that word & thought in my mind another wave took me & washed my remembrance away & only now I regain myself a little & turn in my sleep.

June 24(?), 1840. The language of the street is always strong. What can describe the folly & emptiness of scolding like the word *jawing?* I feel too the force of the double negative, though clean contrary to our grammar rules. And I confess to some pleasure from the stinging rhetoric of a rattling oath in the mouth of truckmen & teamsters. How laconic & brisk it is by the side of a page of the North American Review. Cut these words & they would bleed; they are vascular & alive; they walk & run. Moreover they who speak them have this elegancy, that they do not trip in their speech. It is a shower of bullets, whilst Cambridge men & Yale men correct themselves & begin again at every half sentence. . . .

. . . . .

How am I touched & gladly surprised by hearing the chemist propounding the theory of heat viz that every particle of matter is in constant revolution round its own axis, slower or faster, alike in a column of smoke, or a stone jug. Increase the heat, & you accelerate the revolution by separating the atoms; increase the heat again & the particles acquire such freedom that the form is changed to liquid; increase the heat again & they gyrate in larger circles & become gas & (as we call it) die, or enter into the universe again. Shall we not apply the moral for our consolation to these men of fire & these men of stone that sit around us? The dullest lump is yet amenable to this law of fire. Warm him with love & he too must begin to feel new freedom & presently to become luminous with thought & glowing with affection.

Now for near five years I have been indulged by the gracious Heaven in my long holiday in this godly house of mine entertaining & entertained by so many worthy & gifted friends and all this time poor Nancy Barron the madwoman has been screaming herself hoarse at the poorhouse across the brook & I still hear her whenever I open my window.

June–August, 1840. What is so bewitching as the experiments of young children on grammar & language? The purity of their grammar corrects all the anomalies of our irregular verbs & anomalous nouns. They carry the analogy thorough. *Bite* makes *bited,* and *eat eated* in their preterite. Waldo says there is no "telling" on my microscope meaning no name of the maker as he has seen on knifeblades, &c. "Where is the wafer that *lives* in this box?" &c. They use the strong double negative which we English have lost from our books, though we keep it in the street.

To Samuel G. Ward

CONCORD, *July 18th, 1840.*

The reason why I am curious about you is that with tastes which I also have, you have tastes and powers and corresponding circumstances which I have not and perhaps cannot divine. Certainly we will not quarrel with our companion that he has more roots subterranean or aerial sent out into the great universe to draw his nourishment withal. The secret of virtue is to know that the richer another is, the richer am I;—how much more if that other is my friend. If you are a mighty hunter, if you are a Mohawk Indian with a string of equivocal, nay truculent-looking hair-tufts at your belt, if we agree well enough to draw together, those wild experiences of yours will add vivacity to the covenant. So good luck to your fishing! . . .

What can I tell you? Not the smallest event enlivens our little sandy village; we have not even rigged out a hay cart for a whortleberry party. If I look out of the window there is perhaps a cow; if I go into the garden there are cucumbers; if I look into the brook there is a mud turtle. In the sleep of the great heats there was nothing for me but to read the Vedas, the bible of the tropics, which I find I come back upon every three or four years. It is sublime as heat and night and a breathless ocean. It contains every religious sentiment, all the grand ethics which visit in turn each noble and poetic mind, and nothing is easier than to separate what must have been the primeval inspiration from the endless ceremonial nonsense which caricatures and contradicts it through every chapter. It is of no use to put away the book: if I trust myself in the woods or in a boat upon the pond, nature makes a Bramin of me presently: eternal necessity, eternal compensation, unfathomable power, unbroken silence,—this is her creed. Peace, she saith to me, and purity

and absolute abandonment—these penances expiate all sin
and bring you to the beatitude of the "Eight Gods."

R. W. E.

July 31(?), 1840. Every history in the world is my history.
I can as readily find myself in the tragedy of the Atrides as
in the Saxon Chronicle, in the Vedas as in the New Testament, in Aesop as in the Cambridge Platform or the Declaration of Independence. The good eye, the good ear, can
translate fast enough the slight varieties of dialect in these
cognate tongues. The wildest fable, the bloodiest tragedy is
all too true.

To Margaret Fuller

Concord, Aug. 4, 1840

. . . I begin to wish to see a different Dial from that which I
first imagined. I would not have it too purely literary. I wish
we might make a Journal so broad & great in its survey that
it should lead the opinion of this generation on every great
interest & read the law on property, government, education,
as well as on art, letters, & religion. A great Journal people
must read. And it does not seem worth our while to work
with any other than sovereign aims. So I wish we might
court some of the good fanatics and publish chapters on
every head in the whole Art of Living. I am just now turning my pen to scribble & copy on the subjects of 'Labor,'
'Farm,' 'Reform,' 'Domestic Life,' etc. and I asked myself
why should not the Dial present this homely & most grave
subject to the men & women of the land. If it could be well
& profoundly discussed, no youth in the country could sleep
on it. And the best conceivable paper on such a topic would
of course be a sort of fruitful Cybele, mother of a hundred
gods and godlike papers. That papyrus reed should become
a fatal arrow. I know the danger of such latitude of plan in
any but the best conducted Journal. It becomes friendly to
special modes of reform, partisan, bigoted, perhaps whimsical; not universal & poetic. But our round table is not,
I fancy, in imminent peril of party & bigotry, & we shall
bruise each the other's whims by the collision. Literature
seems to me great when it is the ornament & entertainment
of a soul which proposes to itself the most extensive the most

kind, the most solemn action whereof man is capable. Do not imagine that I am preparing to bestow my growing chapter on Reforms on your innocent readers. Quite otherwise; as you know my present design is to compile a miscellany of my own. . . .

August 16, 1840. After seeing A.B. [Anna Barker] I rode with M F [Margaret Fuller] to the Plains. She taxed me as often before so now more explicitly with inhospitality of soul. She & C. [Caroline Sturgis] would gladly be my friends, yet our intercourse is not friendship, but literary gossip. I count & weigh but do not love. They make no progress with me, but however often we have met, we still meet as strangers. They feel wronged in such relation, & do not wish to be catechised & criticised. I thought of my experience with several persons which resembled this: and confessed that I would not converse with the divinest person more than one week. M. [Margaret] insisted that it was no friendship which was so soon exhausted, & that I ought to know how to be silent & companionable at the same moment. She would surprise me,—she would have me say & do what surprised myself. I confess to all this charge with humility unfeigned. I can better converse with G.B. [George Bradford?] than with any other. E.H. [Elizabeth Hoar] & I have a beautiful relation not however quite free from the same hardness & fences. Yet would nothing be so grateful to me as to melt once for all these icy barriers, & unite with these lovers. But great is the law. . . .

But this survey of my experience taught me anew that no friend I have surprises, none exalts me. This then is to be set down, is it not? to the requirements we make of the friend, that he shall constrain us to sincerity, & put under contribution all our faculties.

To Caroline Sturgis

CONCORD? AUGUST 16(?), 1840

My dear friend, I should gladly make this fine style a fact, but a friend is not made in a day nor by our will. You & I should only be friends on imperial terms. We are both too proud to be fond & too true to feign. But I dare not engage my peace so far as to make you necessary to me as I can easily see any establishment of habitual intercourse would do, when the first news I may hear is that you have found in some heaven foreign to me your mate, & my beautiful castle is exploded to shivers. Then I take the other part & say, Shall I not trust this chosen child that not possibly will she deceive a noble expectation or content herself with less than greatness. When she gives herself away it will be only to an equal virtue, then will I gain a new friend without utter loss of that which now is. But that which set me on this writing was the talk with Margaret F last Friday who taxed me on both your parts with a certain inhospitality of soul inasmuch as you were both willing to be my friends in the full & sacred sense & I remained apart, critical, & after many interviews still a stranger. I count & weigh, but do not love.—I heard the charge, I own, with great humility & sadness. I confess to the fact of cold & imperfect intercourse, but not to the impeachment of my will, and not to the deficiency of my affection. If I count & weigh, I love also. I cannot tell you how warm & glad the naming of your names makes my solitude. You give me more joy than I could trust my tongue to tell you. Perhaps it is ungrateful never to testify by word to those whom we love, how much they are our benefactors. But to my thought this is better to remain a secret from the lips to soften only the behaviour.

But I do not get nearer to you. Whose fault is that? With all my heart I would live in your society. I would gladly spend the remainder of my days in the holy society of the best the wisest & the most beautiful. Come & live near me whenever it suits your pleasure & if you will confide in me so far I will engage to be as true a brother to you as ever blood made. But I thank you for saying that you were sure of me, in reply to M's wish. The ejaculation & the reply were both delicious to me.[1]

To Caroline Sturgis

CONCORD? AUGUST? *c.* 20? 1840?

I hate every thing frugal and cowardly in friendship. *That,* at least should be brave and generous. When we fear the withdrawal of love from ourselves by the new relations which

---

[1] The unsigned letter is apparently a rough draft.

our companions must form, it is mere infidelity. We believe in our eyes and not in the Creator. We do not see any equal pretender in the field, and we conclude that Beauty and Virtue must vail their high top, and buy their Eden by the loss of that which makes them ours. But we are wiser with the next sun, and know that a true and *native* friend is only the extension of our own being and perceiving into other skies and societies, there learning wisdom, there discerning spirits, and attracting our own for us, as truly as we had done hitherto in our strait enclosure. I wish you to go out an adventurous missionary, into all the nations of happy souls, and by all whom you can greatly, and by any whom you can wholly love, I see that I too must be immeasurably enriched. . . .

August–September, 1840. Do not *say* things. What you *are* stands over you the while & thunders so that I cannot hear what you say to the contrary.

September 16(?), 1840. "He can toil terribly," said Cecil of Sir Walter Raleigh. Is there any sermon on Industry that will exhort me like these few words. These sting & bite & kick me. I will get out of the way of their blows by making them true of myself.

September 17, 1840. I am only an experimenter. Do not, I pray you, set the least value on what I do, or the least discredit on what I do not, as if I had settled anything as true or false. I unsettle all things. No facts are to me sacred, none are profane; I simply experiment, an endless seeker, with no Past at my back.

To Margaret Fuller

Concord, 25, September, 1840.

My dear friend,

The day is so fine that I must try to draw out of its azure magazines some ray to celebrate our friendship, and yet nature does rarely say her best words to us out of serene and splendid weather. Twilight, night, winter, & storm, the muses love, & not the halcyon hours. You must always awaken my wonder: our understanding is never perfect: so was it in this last interview, so is it ever. And yet there is progress. Ever friendly your star beams now more friendly & benign on me. I once fancied your nature & aims so eccentric that I had a foreboding that certain crises must impend in your history that would be painful to me to witness in the conviction that I could not aid even by sympathy. I said, it is so long before we can quite meet that perhaps it is better to part now, & leave our return to the Power that orders the periods of the planets. But you have your own methods of equipoise & recovery, without event, without convulsion, and I understand now your language better, I hear my native tongue, though still I see not into you & have not arrived at your law. Absent from you I am very likely to deny you, and say that you lack this & that. The next time we meet you say with emphasis that very word. I pray you to astonish me still, & I will learn to make no rash sentences upon you.—Now in your last letter, you, O divine mermaid or fisher of men, to whom all gods have given the witch-hazel-wand, or caduceus, or spirit-discerner which detects an Immortal under every disguise in every lurking place, (and with this you have already unearthed & associated to yourself a whole college of such,) do say, [for I am willing & resolute for the sake of an instance to fix one quarrel on you,] that I am yours & yours shall be, let me dally how long soever in this or that other temporary relation. I on the contrary do constantly aver that you & I are not inhabitants of one thought of the Divine Mind, but of two thoughts, that we meet & treat like foreign states, one maritime, one inland, whose trade & laws are essentially unlike. I find or fancy in your theory a certain wilfulness and not pure acquiescence which seems to me the only authentic mode. Our friend is part of our fate; those who dwell in the same truth are friends; those who are exercised on different thoughts are not, & must puzzle each other, for the time. For the time! But who dare say how quickly the old eternity shall swallow up the Time, or how ripe is already in either soul the augury of the dissolution of the barriers of difference in the glimpse of ultimate unity?—I am willing to see how unskilfully I make out a case of difference & will open all my doors to your sunshine & morning air. Nothing is to me more welcome nor to my recent speculation more familiar than the Protean energy by which the brute horns of Io become the crescent moon of Isis, and nature lifts itself through everlasting transition to the higher & the highest. Whoever lives must rise & grow. Life like the nimble Tartar still overleaps the Chinese wall of distinctions that had made an eternal boundary in our geography—and I who have taxed your exclusion in friendship, find you—last Wednesday, the meekest & most loving of the lovers of mankind. I thought you a great court lady with a Louis Quatorze taste for diamonds & splendor, and I find you with a "Bible in your hand," faithful to the new Ideas, beholding undaunted their tendency, & making ready your friend "to die a beggar." Honor & love to you ever from all gentle hearts,— a wreath of laurel, &, far better, the wreath of olive & of palm. My little boy for whom you promised good fortune was dressed & on his feet when I came home & is recovering his good health. All things go smoothly with me in these days but myself who am much of the time but a fat weed on the lazy wharf. Lidian sends her love to you & is overjoyed to hear of "the Bible."

Yours affectionately,
R. W. E.

September 26, 1840. You would have me love you. What shall I love? Your body? The supposition disgusts you. What you have thought & said? Well, whilst you were thinking & saying them, but not now. I see no possibility of loving anything but what now is, & is becoming; your courage, your enterprize, your budding affection, your opening thought, your prayer, I can love,—but what else?

October 7, 1840. . . . Do not accuse me of sloth. Do not ask me to your philanthropies, charities, & duties, as you term them;—mere circumstances;—flakes of the snow cloud, leaves of the tree;—I sit at home with the cause grim or glad. I think I may never do anything that you shall call a deed again. I have been writing with some pains Essays on various matters as a sort of apology to my country for my apparent idleness. But the poor work has looked poorer daily as I strove to end it. My genius seemed to quit me in such a mechanical work, a seeming wise,—a cold exhibition of dead thoughts. When I write a letter to any one whom I love, I have no lack of words or thoughts: I am wiser than myself & read my paper with the pleasure of one who receives a letter, but what I write to fill up the gaps of a chapter is hard & cold, is grammar & logic; there is no magic in it; I do

not wish to see it again. Settle with yourself your accusations
of me. If I do not please you, ask me not to please you, but
please your self. What you call my indolence, nature does
not accuse; the twinkling leaves, the sailing fleets of water-
flies, the deep sky like me well enough and know me for
their own. With them I have no embarrassments, diffidences,
or compunctions: with them I mean to stay. You think it is
because I have an income which exempts me from your day-
labor, that I waste, (as you call it,) my time in sungazing &
stargazing. You do not know me. If my debts, as they
threaten, should consume what money I have, I should live
just as I do now: I should eat worse food & wear a coarser
coat and should wonder in a potato patch instead of in a
wood—but it is I & not my Twelve Hundred dollars a year,
that love God.

October 17, 1840. Yesterday George & Sophia Ripley,
Margaret Fuller & Alcott discussed here the new Social Plans.
I wished to be convinced, to be thawed, to be made nobly
mad by the kindlings before my eye of a new dawn of
human piety. But this scheme was arithmetic & comfort;
this was a hint borrowed from the Tremont House & U.S.
Hotel; a rage in our poverty & politics to live rich & gentle-
manlike, an anchor to leeward against a change of weather;
a prudent forecast on the probable issue of the great questions of Pauperism & property. And not once could I be
inflamed,—but sat aloof & thoughtless, my voice faltered &
fell. It was not the cave of persecution which is the palace of
spiritual power, but only a room in the Astor House hired
for the Transcendentalists. I do not wish to remove from my
present prison to a prison a little larger. I wish to break all
prisons. I have not yet conquered my own house. It irks &
repents me. Shall I raise the siege of this hencoop & march
baffled away to a pretended siege of Babylon? It seems to me
that so to do were to dodge the problem I am set to solve, &
to hide my impotency in the thick of a crowd. I can see too,
afar, that I should not find myself more than now,—no,
not so much, in that select, but not by me selected, frater-
nity. Moreover to join this body would be to traverse all my
long trumpeted theory, and the instinct which spoke from it,
that one man is a counterpoise to a city,—that a man is
stronger than a city, that his solitude is more prevalent &
beneficent than the concert of crowds.

October 18(?), 1840. The acquirer of riches seems to me a man of energy good or bad; the inheritor of riches to be a man lamed by his shoes, crippled by his crutches. The respect I pay to a poet I understand; the respect I pay to a ship-master, to a farmer, and to every other conqueror of men or things; but the deference I pay to wealth is opaque, & not transparent, is a superstition.

October 23, 1840. And must I go & do somewhat if I would learn new secrets of self reliance? for my chapter is not finished. But self reliance is precisely that secret,—to make your supposed deficiency redundancy. If I am true, the theory is, the very want of action, my very impotency shall become a greater excellency than all skill & toil.

And thus, o Circular philosopher, you have arrived at a fine Pyrrhonism, at an equivalence & indifference of all actions & would fain teach us that *if we are true,* forsooth, our crimes may be lively stones out of which we shall construct the temple of the true God.

October 24, 1840. Out of doors, in the snow, in the fields, death looks not funereal, but natural, elemental, even fair. In doors it looks disagreeable; I think who will have my coats. I do not wish to know that my body will be the subject of a funeral.

October 25, 1840. What a pity that we cannot curse & swear in good society. Cannot the stinging dialect of the Sailors be domesticated? It is the best rhetoric and for a hundred occasions those forbidden words are the only good ones. My page about "Consistency" would be better written thus; Damn Consistency. . . .

October 26(?), 1840. When I go into my garden with the spade & dig a bed, I feel such an exhilaration & health from the work that I discover that I have been defrauding myself all this time in letting others do for me what I should have done with my own hands. . . .

. . . . .

Our little romances into which we fling ourselves with so much eagerness, end suddenly, & we are almost sad to find how easily we can brook the loss. Let us learn at least that the tragedy of other men, of the sufferers in the old world, was as slight & medicable. We are made for joy & not for pain. We are full of outlets; full of resources; made of means, as the infusories are said to be the genetical atoms of which we are made.

December 20(?), 1840. A droll dream last night, whereat I ghastly laughed. A congregation assembled, like some of our late Conventions, to debate the Institution of Marriage; & grave & alarming objections stated on all hands to the usage; when one speaker at last rose & began to reply to the arguments, but suddenly extended his hand & turned on the audience the spout of an engine which was copiously supplied from within the wall with water & whisking it vigorously about, up, down, right, & left, he drove all the company in crowds hither & thither & out of the house. Whilst I stood watching, astonished & amused at the malice & vigor of the orator, I saw the spout lengthened by a supply of hose behind, & the man suddenly brought it round a corner & drenched me as I gazed. I woke up relieved to find myself quite dry, and well convinced that the Institution of Marriage was safe for tonight.

January 31(?), 1841. All my thoughts are foresters. I have scarce a day-dream on which the breath of the pines has not blown, & their shadows waved. Shall I not then call my little book Forest Essays?

April 20, 1841. Would it not be well to write for the young men at Waterville a history of our present literary & philosophical crisis, a portrait of the parties, & read the augury of the coming hours? In England ethics & philosophy have died out. How solitary is Coleridge & how conspicuous, not so much from his force as from his solitude. In this country a throng of eager persons read & hear every divine word. Yet for the most part there is great monotony in the history of our young men of the liberal or reforming class. They have only got as far as rejection, not as far as affirmation. They seem therefore angry & railers: they have nothing new or memorable to offer; & that is the vice of their writings—profuse declamation but no new matter. After a very short time, this becomes to the reader insufferably wearisome, and the fine young men & women who looked but the other day in that direction with eyes of hope like the first rays of morning, are turning away with a kind of bitterness from the saturation of talk, of promise, & of preaching. Silence, personal prowess, cheerfulness, solid doing seem to be the natural cures.

We are a puny & fickle folk. Hesitation & following are our diseases. The rapid wealth which hundreds in the community acquire in trade or by the incessant expansions of our population & arts, enchants the eyes of all the rest, the luck of one is the hope of thousands, & the whole generation is discontented with the tardy rate of growth which contents every European community. America is therefore the country of small adventures, of short plans, of daring risks, not of patience, not of great combinations, not of long, persistent, closewoven schemes, demanding the utmost fortitude, temper, faith, & poverty. . . .

April 23, 1841. . . . Or, when I wish, it is permitted me to say, these hands, this body, this history of Waldo Emerson are profane & wearisome, but I, I descend not to mix myself with that or with any man. Above his life, above all creatures I flow down forever a sea of benefit into races of individuals. Nor can the stream ever roll backward, or the sin or death of a man taint the immutable energy which distributes itself into men as the sun into rays or the sea into drops.

April 24(?), 1841. I frequently find the best part of my ride in the Concord Coach from my house to Winthrop Place to be in Prince Street, Charter Street, Ann Street & the like places at the North End of Boston. The dishabille of both men & women, their unrestrained attitudes & manners make pictures greatly more interesting than the cleanshaved & silkrobed procession in Washington & Tremont Streets. I often see that the attitudes of both men & women engaged in hard work are more picturesque than any which art & study could contrive, for the Heart is in these first. I say *picturesque;* because when I pass these groups, I instantly know whence all the fine pictures I have seen had their origin: I feel the painter in me; these are the traits which make us feel the force & eloquence of *form* & the sting of color. But the painter is only *in* me; it does not come to the fingers' ends. But whilst I see a true painting, I feel how it was made; I feel that genius organizes, or it is lost. It is as impossible for the aspirant to paint a right picture, as for grass to bear apples. But when the genius comes, it makes fingers, it is pliancy & the power of translating the circumstance in the street into oils & colors. Raphael must be born & Salvator must be born. It is the gift of God, as Fanny Elssler can dance & Braham can sing, when many a worthy citizen & his wife however disposed can by no culture either paint, dance, or sing.

Do not let them be so ridiculous as to try, but know thou, know all, that no citizen, or citizen's wife, no soul, is without organ. Each soul is a soul or an individual in virtue of its having or I may say being a power to translate the universe into some particular language of its own; if not into a picture, a statue, or a dance, why then, into a trade, or an art, or a science or a mode of living, or a conversation, or a character, or an influence—into something great, human, & adequate which, if it do not contain in itself all the dancing, painting, & poetry that ever was, it is because the man is faint hearted & untrue.

June–July, 1841. I value my welfare too much to pay you any longer the compliment of attentions. I shall not draw the thinnest veil over my defects, but if you are here, you shall see me as I am. You will then see that though I am full of tenderness, and born with as large hunger to love & to be loved as any man can be, yet its demonstrations are not active & bold, but are passive & tenacious. My love has no flood & no ebb, but is always there under my silence, under displeasure, under cold, arid, and even weak behaviour.

. . . . .

I think that only is real which men love & rejoice in—not the things which starve & freeze & terrify them.

To Thomas Carlyle

CONCORD, 31 July, 1841.

MY DEAR CARLYLE,—Eight days ago—when I had gone to Nantasket Beach, to sit by the sea and inhale its air and refresh this puny body of mine—came to me your letter, all bounteous as all your letters are, generous to a fault, generous to the shaming of me, cold, fastidious, ebbing person that I am. Already in a former letter you had said too much good of my poor little arid book,—which is as sand to my eyes,—and now in this you tell me it shall be printed in London, and graced with a preface from the man of men. I can only say that I heartily wish the book were better, and I must try and deserve so much favor from the kind gods by a bolder and truer living in the months to come; such as may perchance one day relax and invigorate this cramp hand of mine, and teach it to draw some grand and adequate strokes, which other men may find their own account and not their good-nature in repeating. Yet I think I shall never be killed by my ambition. I behold my failures and shortcomings there in writing, wherein it would give me much joy to thrive, with an equanimity which my worst enemy might be glad to see. And yet it is not that I am occupied with better things. One could well leave to others the record, who was absorbed in the life. But I have done nothing. I think the branch of the "tree of life" which headed to a bud in me, curtailed me somehow of a drop or two of sap, and so dwarfed all my florets and drupes. Yet as I tell you I am very easy in my mind, and never dream of suicide. My whole philosophy— which is very real—teaches acquiescence and optimism. Only when I see how much work is to be done, what room for a poet—for any spiritualist—in this great, intelligent, sensual, and avaricious America, I lament my fumbling fingers and stammering tongue. I have sometimes fancied I was to catch sympathetic activity from contact with noble persons; that you would come and see me; that I should form stricter habits of love and conversation with some men and women here who are already dear to me,—and at some rate get off the numb palsy, and feel the new blood sting and tingle in my fingers' ends. Well, sure I am that the right word will be spoken though I cut out my tongue. Thanks, too, to your munificent Fraser for his liberal intention to divide the profits of the *Essays*. I wish, for the encouragement of such a bookseller, there were to be profits to divide. But I have no faith in your public for their heed to a *mere* book like mine. There are things I should like to say to them, in a lecture-room or in a "steeple house," if I were there. Seven hundred and fifty copies! Ah no!

And so my dear brother has quitted the roaring city, and gone back in peace to his own land,—not the man he left it, but richer every way, chiefly in the sense of having done something valiantly and well, which the land, and the lands, and all that wide elastic English race in all their dispersion, will know and thank him for. The holy gifts of nature and solitude be showered upon you! Do you not believe that the fields and woods have their proper virtue, and that there are good and great things which will not be spoken in the city? I give you joy in your new and rightful home, and the same greetings to Jane Carlyle! with thanks and hopes and loves to you both.

R. W. EMERSON.

As usual at this season of the year, I, incorrigible spouting Yankee, am writing an oration to deliver to the boys in one of our little country colleges, nine days hence. You will say I do not deserve the aid of any Muse. O but if you knew how natural it is to me to run to these places! Besides, I always am lured on by the hope of saying something which shall stick by the good boys. I hope Brown did not fail to find you, with thirty-eight sovereigns (I believe) which he should carry you.

July–August, 1841. Rich, say you? Are you rich? how rich? rich enough to help any body? rich enough to succor the friendless, the unfashionable, the eccentric, rich enough to make the Canadian in his wagon, the itinerant travelling with his written paper which recommends him to the Charitable, the Italian foreigner with his few broken words of English, the ugly lame pauper hunted by overseers from town to town, even the poor insane or half insane wreck of man or woman feel the noble exception of your presence & your house from the general bleakness & stoniness;—to make such feel that they were greeted with a voice that made them both remember & hope. What is vulgar but to refuse the claim? what is gentle but to allow it?

August 22, 1841. I expect from good Whigs put into office by the respectability of the country much less skill to deal with Texas or Britain than from some strong sinner like Jackson or Kendall who first conquered his own government & may then use the same genius to conquer a foreign government.

August 22(?), 1841. I remember when a child in the pew on Sundays amusing myself with saying over common words as "black," "white," "board," &c, twenty or thirty times, until the word lost all meaning & fixedness, & I began to doubt which was the right name for the thing, when I saw that neither had any natural relation, but all were arbitrary. It was a child's first lesson in Idealism.

August 27(?), 1841. Our forefathers walked in the world & went to their graves tormented with the fear of sin & the terror of the Day of Judgment. We are happily rid of those terrors, and our torment is the utter uncertainty & perplexity of what we ought to do; the distrust of the value of what we do; and the distrust that the Necessity which we all at last believe in, is Fair.

To Mary Moody Emerson

Concord, Sept 21, 1841
Tuesday P. M.

My dear Aunt

Dr. Ripley died this morning soon after four o'clock. . . . The fall of this oak makes some sensation in the forest, old & doomed as it was, and on many accounts I could wish you had come home with me to the old wigwam & burial mounds of the tribe. He has identified himself with the forms at least of the old church of the New England Puritans: his nature was eminently loyal, not in the least adventurous or democratical, and his whole being leaned backward on the departed, so that he seemed one of the rear guard of this great camp & army which have filled the world with fame, and with him passes out of sight almost the last banner & guide's flag of a mighty epoch; for these men, however in our last days they have declined into ritualists, solemnized the heyday of their strength by the planting and the liberating of America. Great, grim, earnest men! I belong by natural affinity to other thoughts & schools than yours but my affection hovers respectfully about your retiring footprints, your unpainted churches, strict platforms & sad offices, the iron gray deacon and the wearisome prayer rich with the diction of ages. Well the new is only the seed of the old. What is this abolition and Nonresistance & Temperance but the continuation of Puritanism, though it operate inevitably the destruction of the Church in which it grew, as the new is always making the old superfluous.

. . . I am your affectionate Waldo E.

September–October, 1841. . . . I told H.T. [Henry Thoreau] that his freedom is in the form, but he does not disclose new matter. I am very familiar with all his thoughts, —they are my own quite originally drest. But if the question be, What new ideas has he thrown into circulation, he has not yet told what that is which he was created to say. . . .

October 12, 1841. I would that I could, I know afar off that I can not give the lights & shades, the hopes & outlooks that come to me in these strange, cold-warm attractive-repelling conversations with Margaret, whom I always admire, most revere when I nearest see, and sometimes love, yet whom I freeze, & who freezes me to silence, when we seem to promise to come nearest. Yet perhaps my old motto holds true here also—

"And the more falls I get, move faster on."

October 16, 1841. In town I also heard some admirable music. It seemed, as I groped for the meaning, as if I were hearing a history of the adventures of fairy knights,—some Wace, or Monstrelet, or Froissart, was telling, in a language which I very imperfectly understood, the most minute & laughable particulars of the tournaments & loves & quarrels & religion & tears & fate of airy adventurers, small as moths, fine as light, swifter than shadows,—and these anecdotes were illustrated with all sorts of mimicry & scene painting, all fun & humor & grief, and, now & then, the very persons described broke in & answered, & danced, & fought, & sung for themselves.

October, 1841. In the republic must always happen what happened here that the steamboats & stages & hotels vote one way & the nation votes the other: and it seems to every meeting of readers & writers as if it were intolerable that Broad Street paddies & barroom politicians, the sots & loafers & all manner of ragged & unclean & foul-mouthed persons without a dollar in their pocket should control the property of the country & make the lawgiver & the law. But is that any more than their share whilst you hold property selfishly? They are opposed to you: yes, but first you are opposed to them: they to be sure, malevolently, menacingly, with songs & rowdies & mobs: you cunningly, plausibly, & well bred; you cheat & they strike: you sleep & eat at their expense;

they vote & threaten & sometimes throw stones, at yours.

"What are you doing Zek?" said Judge Webster to his eldest boy.
"Nothing."
"What are you doing, Daniel?"
"Helping Zek."
A tolerably correct account of most of our activity today.

October 23, 1841. A glance at my own MSS. might teach me that all my poems are unfinished, heaps of sketches but no masterpiece, yet when I open a printed volume of poems, I look imperatively for art.

November–December, 1841. All writing is by the grace of God. People do not deserve to have good writing, they are so pleased with bad. In these sentences that you show me I can find no beauty, for I see death in every clause & every word. There is a fossil or a mummy character which pervades this book. The best sepulchres, the vastest catacombs, Thebes & Cairo pyramids are sepulchres to me. I like gardens and nurseries. Give me initiative, spermatic, prophesying, man-making words.

. . . . .

It is never worth while to worry people with your contritions. We shed our follies & absurdities as fast as the rose-bugs drop off in July & leave the apple tree which they so threatened. Nothing dies so fast as a fault & the memory of a fault. I am awkward, sour, saturnine, lumpish, pedantic, & thoroughly disagreeable & oppressive to the people around me. Yet if I am born to write a few good sentences or verses, these shall endure & my disgraces utterly perish out of memory.

. . . . .

Woman should not be expected to write or fight or build or compose scores, she does all by inspiring man to do all. The poet finds her eyes anticipating all his ode, the sculptor his god, the architect his house. She looks it. She is the requiring genius.

January 28, 1842. Yesterday night at 15 minutes after eight my little Waldo ended his life.

January 30, 1842. What he looked upon is better, what he

looked not upon is insignificant. The morning of Friday I woke at 3 o'clock, & every cock in every barnyard was shrilling with the most unnecessary noise. The sun went up the morning sky with all his light, but the landscape was dishonored by this loss. For this boy in whose remembrance I have both slept & awaked so oft, decorated for me the morning star, & the evening cloud, how much more all the particulars of daily economy; for he had touched with his lively curiosity every trivial fact & circumstance in the household, the hard coal & the soft coal which I put into my stove, the wood of which he brought his little quota for Grandmother's fire, the hammer, the pincers, & file, he was so eager to use; the microscope, the magnet, the little globe, & every trinket & instrument in the study; the loads of gravel on the meadow, the nests in the henhouse and many & many a little visit to the doghouse and to the barn.—For every thing he had his own name & way of thinking, his own pronunciation & manner. And every word came mended from that tongue.

A boy of early wisdom, of a grave & even majestic deportment, of a perfect gentleness.

Every tramper that ever tramped is abroad but the little feet are still.

He gave up his little innocent breath like a bird.

. . . . .

Sorrow makes us all children again, destroys all differences of intellect. The wisest knows nothing.

It seems as if I ought to call upon the winds to describe my boy, my fast receding boy. A child of so large & generous a nature that I cannot paint him by specialties, as I might another.

. . . . .

If I go down to the bottom of the garden it seems as if some one had fallen into the brook.

Every place is handsome or tolerable where he has been. Once he sat in the pew.

His house he proposed to build in summer of burs & in winter of snow.

January 30(?), 1842. I see that a man ought to renounce writing for his townsmen or his countrymen & express his spiritual history & motions in such images as have a private significance to him.

February 21, 1842. Home again from Providence to the deserted house. Dear friends find I, but the wonderful Boy is gone. What a looking for miracles have I! As his walking into the room where we are, would not surprise Ellen, so it would seem to me the most natural of all things.

March 20(?), 1842. The least differences in intellect are immeasureable. This beloved and now departed Boy, this Image in every part beautiful, how he expands in his dimensions in this fond Memory to the dimensions of Nature!

. . . . .

The chrysalis which he brought in with care & tenderness & gave to his Mother to keep is still alive and he most beautiful of the children of men is not here.

I comprehend nothing of this fact but its bitterness. Explanation I have none, consolation none that rises out of the fact itself; only diversion; only oblivion of this & pursuit of new objects.

March–April, 1842. Hell is better than Heaven, if the man in Hell honors his place, & the man in heaven does not. It is in vain you pretend that you are not responsible for the evil law because you are not a magistrate, or a party to a civil process, or do not vote. You eat the law in a crust of bread, you wear it in your hat & shoes.

. . . . .

What for the visions of the Night? Our life is so safe & regular that we hardly know the emotion of terror. Neither public nor private violence; neither natural catastrophes, as earthquake, volcano, or deluge; nor the expectation of supernatural agents in the form of ghosts or of purgatory & devils & hellfire, disturb the sleepy circulations of our blood in these calm well-spoken days. And yet dreams acquaint us with what the day omits. Eat a hearty supper, tuck up your bed tightly, put an additional bedspread over your three blankets, & lie on your back, & you may, in the course of an hour or two, have this neglected part of your education in some measure supplied. Let me consider: I found myself in a garret disturbed by the noise of some one sawing wood. On walking towards the sound, I saw lying in a crib an insane person whom I very well knew, and the noise instantly stopped: there was no saw, a mere stirring among several trumpery matters, fur-muffs & empty baskets that lay on the floor. As I tried to approach, the muffs swelled themselves a little as with wind, & whirled off into a corner of the garret, as if alive, and a kind of animation appeared in all the objects in that corner. Seeing this, and instantly aware that here was Witchcraft, that here was a devilish Will which signified itself plainly enough in the stir & the sound of the wind, I was unable to move; my limbs were frozen with fear; I was bold & would go forward, but my limbs I could not move; I mowed the defiance I could not articulate & woke with the ugly sound I made. After I woke and recalled the impressions, my brain tingled with repeated vibrations of terror,—and yet was the sensation pleasing, as it was a sort of rehearsal of a Tragedy.

April 6(?), 1842. I am *Defeated* all the time; yet to Victory I am born.

April 22, 1842. This P.M. I found Edmund Hosmer in his field after traversing his orchard where two of his boys were grafting trees; Mr H. was ploughing and Andrew driving the oxen. I could not help feeling the highest respect as I approached this brave labourer. Here is the Napoleon, the Alexander of the soil, conquering & to conquer, after how many & many a hard fought summer's day & winter's day, not like Napoleon of Sixty battles only but of 6000, & out of every one he has come victor, & here he stands with Atlantic strength & cheer, invincible still. I am ashamed of these slight & useless limbs of mine before this strong soldier. What good this man has or has had he has earned. No rich father left him any inheritance of land or money; he borrowed the money with which he bought his farm & has supported his large family of ten children, given them a good education and improved his land in every way year by year, & is a man, every inch of him.

April, 1842. We look wishfully to emergences, to eventful revolutionary times from the desart of our ennui. And think how easy to have taken our part when the drum was rolling & the house was burning over our heads. But is not Peace greater than War and has it not greater wars & victories? Is there no progress? To wish for war is atheism.

• • • • •

Queenie [1] says, "Save me from magnificent souls. I like a small common sized one."

May, 1842. . . . The surfaces threaten to carry it in nature. The fox & musquash, the hawk & snipe & bittern, when nearly seen are found to have no more root than man, to be just such superficial tenants in the globe. Then this new molecular philosophy goes to show that there are astronomical interspaces betwixt atom & atom; that the world is all outside; it has no inside.

June 26, 1842. Nelly [2] waked & fretted at night & put all sleep of her seniors to rout. Seniors grew very cross, but Nell conquered soon by the pathos & eloquence of childhood & its words of fate. Thus after wishing it would be morning, she broke out into sublimity; "Mother, it must be morning." Presently, after, in her sleep, she rolled out of bed; I heard the little feet running round on the floor, and then, "O dear! Where's my bed?" She slept again, and then woke; "Mother I am afraid; I wish I could sleep in the bed beside of you. I am afraid I shall tumble into the waters— It is all water." What else could papa do? He jumped out of bed & laid himself down by the little mischief, & soothed her the best he might.

June–July, 1842. In town I also talked with Sampson Reed, of Swedenborg & the rest. "It is not so in your experience, but is so in the other world."—Other world? I reply, there is no other world; here or nowhere is the whole fact; all the Universe over, there is but one thing,—this old double, Creator-creature, mind-matter, right-wrong. He would have devils, objective devils. I replied, That pure malignity exists, is an absurd proposition. Goodness & Being are one. Your proposition is not to be entertained by a rational agent: it is atheism; it is the last profanation. In regard to Swedenborg, I commended him as a grand Poet: Reed wished that if I admired the poetry, I should feel it as a fact. I told him, All my concern is with the subjective truth of Jesus's or Swedenborg's or Homer's remark, not at all with the object. . . .

[1] Emerson's wife.
[2] Emerson's daughter Ellen.

October 15(?), 1842. Rabelais is not to be skipped in literary history as he is source of so much proverb, story & joke which are derived from him into all modern books in all languages. He is the Joe Miller of modern literature.

Thou shalt read Homer, Æschylus, Sophocles, Euripides, Aristophanes, Plato, Proclus, Plotinus, Iamblichus, Porphyry, Aristotle, Virgil, Plutarch, Apuleius, Chaucer, Dante, Rabelais, Montaigne, Cervantes, Shakspear, Jonson, Ford, Chapman, Beaumont & Fletcher, Bacon, Herbert, Marvell, More, Milton, Molière, Swedenborg, Goethe.

October 26(?), 1842. Read Cornelius Agrippa this morning on the Vanity of Arts & Sciences. . . . Another specimen of that scribaciousness which distinguishes the immense readers of his time. Robert Burton is the head of the class. They had read infinitely & now must disburthen themselves. So they take any loose general topic like Melancholy or Praise of science or Praise of Folly, & write & quote without method or end. One must have a great deal of time who can read them. They do not pay you. Now & then out of that affluence of their learning comes a fine sentence from Theophrastus or Boethius and perhaps six or seven in the entire volume, but no high method, no high inspiring state. One cannot afford to read for a few sentences. He will learn more by praying. They are good to read as a dictionary is, for suggestion, and I use them much for that. Plato or Shakspeare are not suggestive; their method is so high & fine, that they take too much possession of us.

November 26(?), 1842. No man can be criticized but by a greater than he. Do not then read the reviews. Wordsworth dismisses a whole regiment of poets from their vocation.

• • • • •

The world is waking to the idea of Union and already we have Communities, Phalanxes and Aesthetic Families, & Pestalozzian institutions. It is & will be magic. Men will live & communicate & ride & plough & reap & govern as by lightning and galvanic & etherial power; as now by respiration & expiration exactly together they lift a heavy man from the ground by the little finger only, & without a sense of weight. But this Union is to be reached by a reverse of the methods they use. It is Spiritual and must not be actualized. The

Union is only perfect when all the Uniters are absolutely isolated. Each man being the Universe, if he attempt to join himself to others, he instantly is jostled, crowded, cramped, halved, quartered, or on all sides diminished of his proportion. . . .

. . . . .

This old Bible if you pitch it out of the window with a fork, comes bounce back again.

November, 1842. Transcendentalism is the Saturnalia of faith. It is faith run mad. Nature is transcendental, primarily, necessarily exists & works & proceeds yet takes no thought for the morrow. Man feels the dignity of the life that exults around him in chemistry & tree & animal & in his own body, heaves the heart & the lungs, & forms the limbs, & makes himself a spectacle to him yet is baulked when he tries to fling himself into this enchanted circle where all is done without degradation.

December, 1842–January, 1843. The harvest will be better preserved & go farther laid up in private bins, in each farmer's cornbarn, & each woman's basket, than if it were kept in national granaries. In like manner, an amount of money will go farther if expended by each man & woman for their own wants, & in the feeling that this is their all, than if expended by a great Steward, or National Commissioners of the Treasury. Take away from me the feeling that I must depend on myself, give me the least hint that I have good friends & backers there in reserve who will gladly help me, & instantly I relax my diligence, I obey the first impulse of generosity that is to cost me nothing, and a certain slackness will creep over all my conduct of my affairs. Here is a bank note found of 100 dollars. Let it fall into the hands of an easy man who never earned the estate he spends, & see how little difference it will make in his affairs. At the end of the year he is just as much behindhand as ever, & could not have done at all without that hundred. Let it fall into the hands of a poor & prudent woman, and every shilling & every cent of it tells, goes to reduce debt or to add to instant & constant comfort, mends a window, buys a blanket or a pelisse, gets a stove instead of the old cavernous fire place all chimney. . . .

January 7, 1843. Baltimore . . . Here today from Philadelphia. The railroad which was but a toy coach the other day is now a dowdy lumbering country wagon. Yet it is not prosaic, as people say, but highly poetic, this strong shuttle which shoots across the forest, swamp, rivers, & arms of the sea, binding city to city. The Americans take to the little contrivance as if it were the cradle in which they were born.

January 16(?), 1843. I understand poverty much better than riches; and it is odd that one of my friends who is rich seems to me always accidentally so, & in character made to be poor.

February 7, 1843. I am greatly pleased with the merchants. In railcar & hotel it is common to meet only the successful class, & so we have favorable specimens: but these discover more manly power of all kinds than scholars; behave a great deal better, converse better, and have independent & sufficient manners.

Dreamlike travelling on the railroad. The towns through which I pass between Philadelphia & New York, make no distinct impression. They are like pictures on a wall. The more, that you can read all the way in the car a French novel.

February–March, 1843. There is no line that does not return; I suppose the mathematicians will tell us that what are called straight lines are lines with long curves, and that there is no straight line in nature.

. . . . .

Cheap literature makes new markets. We have thought only of a box audience, or at most of box & pit; but now it appears there is also slip audience, & galleries one, two, three; & backstairs, & street listeners, besides. Greeley tells me that Graham's Magazine has 70000 subscribers. And I may write a lecture, if I will, to 70000 readers.

. . . . .

Since I have been here in N.Y. I have grown less diffident of my political opinions. I supposed once the Democracy might be right. I see that they are aimless. Whigs have the best men, Democrats the best cause. But the last are destructive, not constructive. What hope, what end have they?

March 12, 1843. . . . If Government in our present clumsy fashion must go on,—could it not assume the charge of providing each citizen, on his coming of age, with a pair of acres, to enable him to get his bread honestly? Perhaps one day it will be done, by the state's assuming to distribute the estates of the dead. In the U.S. almost every State owns so much public land, that it would be practicable to give what they have, & devise a system by which the state should continue to possess a fund of this sort.

March, 1843. At the Five Points, I heard a woman swearing very liberally, as she talked with her companions; but when I looked at her face, I saw that she was no worse than other women; that she used the dialect of her class, as all others do, & are neither better, nor worse for it; but under this bad costume was the same repose, the same probity as in Broadway. Nor was she misinterpreted by her mates. There is a virtue of vice as well as of virtue.

. . . . .

March(?), 1843. In Nature the doubt recurs whether the Man is the cause or the effect. Are beasts & plants degradations of man? or are these the prophecies & preparations of nature practising for her masterpiece in Man? Culminate we do not; but that point of imperfection which we occupy— is it on the way *up,* or *down?*

March–April, 1843. Much poor talk concerning Woman which at least had the effect of revealing the true sex of several of the party who usually go disguised in the form of the other sex. Thus Mrs B is a man. The finest people marry the two sexes in their own person. Hermaphrodite is then the symbol of the finished soul. It was agreed that in every act should appear the married pair: the two elements should mix in every act.

To me it sounded hoarsely the attempt to prescribe didactically to woman her duties. Man can never tell woman what her duties are: he will certainly end in describing a man in female attire, as Harriet Martineau, a masculine woman, solved her problem of Woman. No. Woman only can tell the heights of feminine nature, & the only way in which man can help her, is by observing woman reverentially & whenever she speaks from herself & catches him in inspired moments up to a heaven of honor & religion, to hold her to that point by reverential recognition of the divinity that speaks through her.

April 10(?), 1843. Nature is the strictest economist, & works up all that is wasted today into tomorrow's creation. . . . She flung us out in her plenty, but we cannot shed a hair or the paring of a nail, but instantly she snatches at the shred & appropriates it to the general stock. Our condition is like that of the poor wolves, if one of the flock wound himself, or so much as limp, the rest eat him up incontinently.

May 20(?), 1843. Man sheds grief as his skin sheds rain. A preoccupied mind an immense protection. There is a great concession on all hands to the ideal decorum in grief, as well as joy, but few hearts are broken.

. . . . .

I enjoy all the hours of life. Few persons have such susceptibility to pleasure; as a countryman will say "I was at sea a month & never missed a meal" so I eat my dinner & sow my turnips yet do I never, I think, fear death. It seems to me so often a relief, a rendering up of responsibility, a quittance of so many vexatious trifles.

May–June, 1843. It is greatest to believe & to hope well of the world, because he who does so, quits the world of experience, & makes the world he lives in.

August–September, 1843. The charge which a lady in much trust made to me against her companions was that people on whom beforehand all persons would put the utmost reliance were not responsible. They saw the necessity that the work must be done, & did it not; and it of course fell to be done by herself and the few principals. I replied, that, in my experience good people were as bad as rogues, that the conscience of the conscientious ran in veins, & the most punctilious in some particulars, were latitudinarian in others. And, in Mr Tuttle's opinion, "Mankind is a damned rascal."

. . . . .

H.D.T. [Henry David Thoreau] sends me a paper with the old fault of unlimited contradiction. The trick of his rhetoric is soon learned: it consists in substituting for the obvious word & thought its diametrical antagonist. He praises wild mountains & winter forests for their domestic air; snow & ice for their warmth; villagers & wood choppers for their urbanity and the wilderness for resembling Rome & Paris. With the constant inclination to dispraise cities & civilization, he yet can find no way to honour woods & woodmen except by paralleling them with towns & townsmen. W E C [William Ellery Channing] declares the piece is excellent: but it makes me nervous & wretched to read it, with all its merits.

. . . . .

... "To work from dark to dark for fifty cents the day" as the poor woman in the shanty told us, is but pitiful wages for a married man.

September 3(?), 1843. . . . The capital defect of my nature for society (as it is of so many others) is the want of animal spirits. They seem to me a thing incredible, as if God should raise the dead. I hear of what others perform by their aid, with fear. . . .

September 13(?), 1843. Fear haunts the building railroad but it will be American power & beauty, when it is done. And these peaceful shovels are better, dull as they are, than pikes in the hands of these Kernes; and this stern day's work of 15 or 16 hours though deplored by all the humanity of the neighborhood & though all Concord cries shame! on the contractors, is a better police than the sheriff & his deputies to let off the peccant humours.

September–November, 1843. People came, it seems, to my lectures with expectation that I was to realize the Republic I described, & ceased to come when they found this reality no nearer. They mistook me. I am & always was a painter. I paint still with might & main, & choose the best subjects I can. Many have I seen come & go with false hopes & fears, and dubiously affected by my pictures. But I paint on. I count this distinct vocation which never leaves me in doubt what to do but in all times, places, & fortunes, gives me an open future, to be the great felicity of my lot. . . .

. . . . .

Let us not europize—neither by travel, neither by reading. Luckily for us now that steam has narrowed the Atlantic to a strait, the nervous rocky West is intruding a new & continental element into our national mind, & we shall have an American genius. . . .

December 25, 1843. At the performing of Handel's Messiah I heard some delicious strains & understood a very little of all that was told me. My ear received but a little thereof. But as the master overpowered the littleness & incapableness of the performers, & made them conductors of his electricity, so it was easy to see what efforts nature was making through so many hoarse, wooden & imperfect persons to produce beautiful voices, fluid & soul-guided men & women. The genius of nature could well be discerned. By right & might we should become participant of her invention, & not wait for morning & evening to know their peace, but prepossess it. I walked in the bright paths of sound, and liked it best when the long continuance of a chorus had made the ear insensible to the music, made it as if there was none, then I was quite solitary & at ease in the melodious uproar. Once or twice in the solos, when well sung, I could play tricks, as I like to do, with my eyes, darken the whole house & brighten & transfigure the central singer, and enjoy the enchantment.

This wonderful piece of music carries us back into the rich historical past. It is full of the Roman Church & its hierarchy & its architecture. Then further it rests on & requires so deep a faith in Christianity that it seems bereft of half & more than half its power when sung today in this unbelieving city.

December, 1843–January, 1844. We rail at trade, but the historian of the world will see that it was the principle of liberty, that it settled America, & destroyed feudalism, and made peace & keeps peace, that it will abolish slavery.

.   .   .   .   .

The two parties in life are the believers & unbelievers, variously named. The believer is poet, saint, democrat, theocrat, free-trade, no-church, no capital punishment, idealist.

January 30, 1844. . . . I am always insincere, as always knowing there are other moods.

January–March, 1844. "And fools rush in where angels fear to tread." So say I of Brook Farm. Let it live. Its merit is that it is a new life. Why should we have only two or three ways of life & not thousands & millions? This is a new one so fresh & expansive that they are all homesick when they go away. . . .

  .   .   .   .   .

The question of the annexation of Texas is one of those which look very differently to the centuries and to the years. It is very certain that the strong British race which have now overrun so much of this Continent, must also overrun that tract & Mexico & Oregon also, and it will in the course of ages be of small import by what particular occasions & methods it was done. It is a secular question. It is quite necessary & true to our New England Character that we should consider the question in its local & temporary bearings, and resist the annexation with tooth & nail.

It is a measure which goes not by right nor by wisdom but by feeling.

  .   .   .   .   .

Otherness. H.D.T. [Thoreau] said, he knew but one secret which was to do one thing at a time, and though he has his evenings for study, if he was in the day inventing machines for sawing his plumbago, he invents wheels all the evening & night also; and if this week he has some good reading & thoughts before him, his brain runs on that all day, whilst pencils pass through his hands. I find in me an opposite facility or perversity, that I never seem well to do a particular work, until another is done. I cannot write the poem though you give me a week, but if I promise to read a lecture day after tomorrow, at once the poem comes into my head & now the rhymes will flow. And let the proofs of the Dial be crowding on me from the printer, and I am full of faculty how to make the Lecture.

Somebody said of me after the lecture at Amory Hall within hearing of A.W. [Anna Ward?], "The secret of his popularity is that he has a *damn* for everybody."

March–April, 1844. I wish to have rural strength & religion for my children & I wish city facility & polish. I find with chagrin that I cannot have both.

Spring, 1844. We are impressed by a Burke or a Schiller who believes in embodying in practice ideas; because literary men, for the most part, who are cognisant of ideas, have a settled despair as to the realization of ideas in their own times.

. . . . .

In America we are such rowdies in church & state, and the very boys are so soon ripe, that I think no philosophical skepticism will make much sensation. Spinoza pronounced that there was but one substance; yea, verily; but that boy yonder told me yesterday he thought the pinelog was God, & that God was in the jakes. What can Spinoza tell the boy?

June–August, 1844. Be an opener of doors for such as come after thee and do not try to make the Universe a blind alley.

. . . . .

Novels make us skeptical by giving such prominence to wealth & social position, but I think them to be fine occasional stimulants, and, though with some shame, I am brought into an intellectual state. But great is the poverty of their inventions. The perpetual motive & means of accelerating or retarding interest is the dull device of persuading a lover that his mistress is betrothed to another. D'Israeli is well worth reading; quite a good student of his English world, and a very clever expounder of its wisdom & craft: never quite a master. Novels make us great gentlemen whilst we read them. How generous, how energetic should we be in the crisis described, but unhappy is the wife, or brother, or stranger who interrupts us, whilst we read: nothing but frowns & tart replies from the reading gentlemen for them. Our novel reading is a passion for results, we admire parks & the love of beauties, & the homage of parliaments.

. . . . .

The use of geology has been to wont the mind to a new chronology. The little dame school measures by which we had gauged everything, we have learned to disuse, & break up our European & Mosaic & Ptolemaic schemes for the grand style of nature & fact. We knew nothing rightly for want of perspective. Now we are learning the secularity of nature; & geology furnishes us with a metre or clock, a coarse kitchen clock, it is true, compared with the vaster measures which astronomy has to make us acquainted with. Now first we learn what weary patient periods must round themselves ere the rock is formed, then ere the rock is broken, & the first lichen race has disintegrated the thinnest external plate into soil, & opened the door for the remote Flora, Fauna, Pomona, & Ceres, to come in. How far off yet is the trilobite: how far the quadruped: how inconceivably remote is man. All duly arrive, & then race after race. It is a long way from granite to a woodpecker, farther yet to Plato & the preaching of the immortality of the soul. Yet all must come, as surely as the first atom has two sides. The progress of physics & of metaphysics is parallel at first, it is lowest instinctive life loathsome to the succeeding tribes like the generation of sour paste. It is animalcules, earwigs & caterpillars, writhing, wriggling, devouring & devoured. As the races advance & rise, order & rank appear, & the aurora of reason & of love. Who cares how madly the early savages fight, who sides with one or another? their rage is organic and has its animal sweetness. The world goes pregnant with Europe & with better than Europe.

Nothing interests us of these or ought to. We do not wish a world of bugs or of birds. Neither afterwards do we respect one of Scythians, or Caraibs, or Feejees. As little interests us the crimes of the recent races, the grand style of nature & her periods is what they show us, but they are not for permanence, her foot will not rest. Onward & onward that ever-going progression, that breathless haste what god can tell us whither? Who cares for the crimes of the past, for oppressing whites or oppressed blacks, any more than for bad dreams? These fangs & eaters & food are all in the harmony of nature: & there too is the germ forever protected, unfolding gigantic leaf after leaf, a newer flower, a richer fruit in every period, yet its next is not to be guessed. It will only save what is worth saving & it saves not by compassion but by power. It saves men through themselves. It appoints no police to guard the lion but his teeth & claws, no fort or city for the bird but his wings, no rescue for flies & mites but their spawning numbers, which no ravages can overcome. It deals with men after the same manner. If they are rude [or] foolish down they must go. When at last in a race a new principle appears an idea, that conserves it. Ideas only save races. If the black man is feeble & not important to the existing races, not on a par with the best race, the black man must serve & be sold & exterminated. But if the black man carries in his bosom an indispensable element of a new

& coming civilization, for the sake of that element no wrong nor strength nor circumstance can hurt him, he will survive & play his part. So now it seems to be that the arrival of such men as Toussaint if he is pure blood, or of Douglass if he is pure blood, outweighs all the English & American humanity. The Antislavery of the whole world is but dust in the balance, a poor squeamishness & nervousness. The might & the right is here. Here is the Anti-Slave. Here is Man; & if you have man, black or white is insignificance. Why at night all men are black. The intellect, that is miraculous, who has it has the talisman, his skin & bones are transparent, he is a statue of the living God, him I must love & serve & perpetually seek & desire & dream on: and who has it not is superfluous. But a compassion for that which is not & cannot be useful & lovely, is degrading & maudlin, this towing along as by ropes that which cannot go itself. Let us not be our own dupes; all the songs & newspapers & subscriptions of money & vituperation of those who do not agree with us will avail nothing against eternal fact. I say to you, you must save yourself, black or white, man or woman. Other help is none. I esteem the occasion of this jubilee to be that proud discovery that the black race can begin to contend with the white, that in the great anthem of the world which we call history, a piece of many parts & vast compass, after playing a long time a very low & subdued accompaniment they perceive the time arrived when they can strike in with force & effect & take the master's part in the music. The civilization of the world has arrived at that pitch that their moral quality is becoming indispensable, & the quality of this race is to be honoured, for itself. For this they have been preserved in sandy desarts, in rice swamps, in kitchens & shoe shops so long. Now let them emerge clothed & in their own form. I esteem this jubilee & the fifty years' movement which has preceded it to be the announcement of that fact & our Antislavery societies, boastful as we are, only the shadow & witness to that fact. The negro has saved himself, and the white man very patronisingly says, I have saved you. If the negro is a fool all the white men in the world cannot save him though they should die.

Fall, 1844(?). It is a great happiness to escape a religious education. Calvinism destroys religion of character.

. . . . . .

Intense selfishness which we all share. Planter will not hesitate to eat his negro, because he can. We eat him in milder fashion by pelting the negro's friend. We cannot lash him with a whip, because we dare not. We lash him with our tongues. I like the Southerner the best; he deals roundly, & does not cant. The northerner is surrounded with churches & Sunday Schools & is hypocritical. How gladly, how gladly, if he dared, he would seal the lips of these poor men & poor women who speak for him. I see a few persons in the church, who, I fancy, will soon look about them with some surprise to see what company they are keeping.

I do not wonder at feeble men being strong advocates for slavery. They have no feeling of worthiness which assures them of their own safety. In a new state of things they are by no means sure it would go well with them. They cannot work or facilitate work or cheer or decorate labour. No, they live by certain privileges which the actual order of the community yields them. Take those and you take all. I do not wonder that such would fain raise a mob for fear is very cruel.

Winter, 1844–1845. Putnam pleased the Boston people by railing at Goethe in his Φ B K oration because Goethe was not a New England Calvinist. If our lovers of greatness & goodness after a local type & standard could expand their scope a little they would see that a worshipper of truth and a most subtle perceiver of truth like Goethe with his impatience of all falsehood & scorn of hypocrisy was a far more useful man & incomparably more helpful ally to religion than ten thousand lukewarm church members who keep all the traditions and leave a tithe of their estates to establish them. But this clergyman should have known that the movement which in America created these Unitarian dissenters of which he is one, begun in the mind of this great man he traduces; that he is precisely the individual in whom the new ideas appeared & opened to their greatest extent & with universal application which more recently the active scholars in the different departments of Science, of State, & of the church have carried in parcels & thimblefuls to their petty occasions. Napoleon I join with him as being both representatives of the impatience & reaction of nature against the morgue of conventions, two stern realists. They want a third peer who shall stand for sentiment as they for truth & power.

RALPH WALDO EMERSON
To William Emerson

Concord, 3 Feb. 1845

Dear William,

Your letter to me & Susan's to Lidian & the precious gifts of the cousins to the cousins arrived as safely as such auspicious parcels should, which doubtless have all angels that love children to convoy them to their destination. Lidian charges me to tell you how happily chosen was Ellen's pair of books which Mr Alcott had advised papa to procure for her, but Willie has anticipated the dilatory papa. And Edie's horn of enchantments appears every morning from Grandmamma's honoured crypts, to remind her of Haven; and little Edward shakes his rattles though he has no thought or name for cousin no dream of other little hands that have held the bauble. A happy childhood have these babes of yours & mine: No cruel interferences, & what stores of happy days! We cannot look forward far, but these little felicities so natural & suitable to them should be introductory to better & not leading into any dark penumbra. We must arm them with as much good sense as we can, and throw them habitually on themselves for a moral verdict. I remember Mary Rotch of New Bedford told me, that, in her childhood, her father & mother never told her to do this or to avoid that, but only, that there was one with her who would tell her, whilst she might very easily deceive them. My little Ellen is growing up a very intelligent child, a devourer of books with an endless memory for all hymns & juvenile poems. Her vivacity procures her many a chiding from all sides in the house & I doubt not, at school; but she is reasonable & convertible. Edith never does wrong, but spends all her soft days in every body's love. I could heartily wish, as we have so often wished before, that our little nurseries were near each other,—yours & mine. As the children grow older, the wish will often repeat itself.

Mother is as well as usual this winter, and things go tolerably well with us. In the spring we shall see you: our railroad is perfect & we will no longer be denied. With kindest remembrances to Susan from me & from us all, & to the boys,

I am, as ever, yours heartily,
Waldo—

March, 1845. A despair has crept over the Whig Party in this Country. They the active, enterprizing, intelligent well-meaning & wealthy part of the people, the real bone & strength of the American People, find themselves paralyzed & defeated everywhere by the hordes of ignorant & deceivable natives & the armies of foreign voters who fill Pennsylvania, N.Y., & New Orleans, and by those unscrupulous editors & orators who have assumed to lead these masses. The creators of wealth and conscientious rational & responsible persons, those whose names are given in as fit for jurors, for referees, for offices of trust, those whose opinion is public opinion, find themselves degraded into observers, & violently turned out of all share in the action & counsels of the nation.

* * * * *

That Plato is philosophy, & philosophy Plato, is the stigma of mankind. Vain are the laurels of Rome, vain the pride of England in her Newton, Milton & Shakspeare, whilst neither Saxon nor Roman have availed to add any idea to the Categories of Plato.

March–June, 1845. We are bound hand & foot with our decorums & superstitions. England has achieved respectability at what a cost! America with a valet's eyes admires & copies in vain.

* * * * *

What argument, what eloquence can avail against the power of that one word *Niggers*? The man of the world annihilates the whole combined force of all the antislavery societies of the world by pronouncing it.

* * * * *

With our Saxon education & habit of thought we all require to be first. Each man must somehow think himself the first in his own career: if he find that he is not, he thinks himself cheated; he accuses nature & Providence. We are born with lotus in our mouths, & are very deceivable as to our merits, easily believing we are the best. But in our present system that is the basis, that I am to be the first of my kind. Meantime we have somewhere heard or dreamed of another order, to wit, purely social, where a social or loving perfection subsisted, blending the proprieties of all, & each found his beatitude in the atmosphere of his club. If an American should wake up some morning & discover that his existence was unnecessary, he would think himself excessively ill-used & would declare himself instantly against the Government of the Universe. We construct all our theories & philosophies so as to show how with many members each member may be best.

August 19(?), 1845. I am shamed in reflecting on the little new skill the years bring me, at the power trifles have over me, at the importance of my dinner, & my dress, & my house, more than at the slenderness of my acquisitions.

August 25, 1845. A practical question, you say, is, what are common people made for? You snub them, and all your plans of life & all your poetry & philosophy only contemplate the superior class. This is a verbal question, never practical. Common people, uncommon people, all sorts of people, dispose of themselves very fast, and never wait for the sentences of philosophers. The truth seems to be, there are no common people, no populace, but only juniors & seniors; the mob is made up of kings that shall be; the lords have all in their time taken place in the mob. The appearance in any assembly is of a rapid self-distribution into cliques & sets, and the best are accused of a fierce exclusiveness. Perhaps it is truer & more charitable to say, they separate as children do from old people, as oil does from water, without any love or hatred in the matter. . . .

September–October, 1845. It is easy to read Plato, difficult to read his commentators.

. . . . .

We know in one mood that which we are ignorant of in another mood, like mesmerised patients who are clairvoyant at night & in the day know nothing of that which they told.

. . . . .

The sea shore; sea seen from shore, shore seen from sea, must explain the charm of Plato. Art expresses The One, or The Same, by the Different. Thought seeks to know Unity in unity; Poetry, to show it by Variety, i.e. always by an object or symbol. Plato keeps the two vases, one of aether & one of pigment, always at his side, & invariably uses both. Things added to things, as, statistics, geography, civil history, are mere inventories or lists. Things used as language or symbols, are inexhaustibly attractive. Plato is a master of this game,

& turns incessantly the obverse & the reverse of the medal. . . .

. . . . .

The eloquent man is he who is no beautiful speaker, but who is inwardly & desperately drunk with a certain belief; it agitates & tears him, & almost bereaves him of the power of articulation. Then it rushes from him as in short abrupt screams, in torrents of meaning. The possession by the subject of his mind is so entire, that it ensures an order of expression which is the order of nature itself, and so the order of greatest force & inimitable by any art. And the main distinction between him & other well-graced actors is the conviction communicated to the hearer by every word, that his mind is contemplating a whole, and inflamed with the contemplation of the whole, & that the words & sentences uttered by him, however admirable, fall from him as unregarded parts of that terrible whole, which he sees, & means that you shall see.

. . . . .

Vedanta. The Internal Check. "He who eternally restrains this & the other world, & all beings therein, who standing in the earth is other than the earth, whom the earth knows not, whose body the earth is, who interiorly restrains the earth, the same is thy soul, and the Internal Check immortal."

. . . . .

Knowledge is the straight line;
Wisdom is the power of the straight line, or, the Square;
Virtue is the power of the Square or the solid.

Thus my friend reads in the Cultivator on the method of planting & hoeing potatoes, or he follows a farmer hoeing along the row of potato hills; that is knowledge. At last, he takes the hoe in his hands & hoes the hills; the first, with care & heed, & pulls up every root of piper grass: as the day grows hot, & the row is long, he says to himself, This is wisdom; but one hill is like another, I have mastered the art, it is mere trifling to waste my strength in doing many times the same thing: Why should I hoe more: and he desists.

But the last lesson was still unlearned: the moral power lay in the continuance, in fortitude, in working against pleasure, to the excellent end & conquering all opposition. He has knowledge, he has wisdom, but he has missed Virtue, which he only acquires who endures routine & sweat & postponement of fancy to the achievement of a worthy end.

. . . . .

Native Americans. I hate the narrowness of the native American party. It is the dog in the manger. It is precisely opposite to all the dictates of love & magnanimity: & therefore, of course, opposite to true wisdom. It is the result of science that the highest simplicity of structure is produced, not by few elements, but by the highest complexity. Man is the most composite of all creatures, the wheel insect, *volvox globator*, is at the beginning. Well, as in the old burning of the Temple at Corinth, by the melting & intermixture of silver & gold & other metals, a new compound more precious than any, called the Corinthian Brass, was formed, so in this Continent,—asylum of all nations, the energy of Irish, Germans, Swedes, Poles, & Cossacks, & all the European tribes, —of the Africans, & of the Polynesians, will construct a new race, a new religion, a new State, a new literature, which will be as vigorous as the new Europe which came out of the smelting pot of the Dark Ages, or that which earlier emerged from the Pelasgic & Etruscan barbarism.

. . . . .

. . . Rachel [the actress] possesses a certain demoniacal power which is worthy of wonder. You feel in her veiled & nowise resonant voice, in her measured & earnest acting, & in her majestic delivery, that she is incessantly brooding on this inward raging fire. But this bursts up at decisive moments.

October–November, 1845. The Indian teaching through its cloud of legends has yet a simple & grand religion like a queenly countenance seen through a rich veil. It teaches to speak the truth, love others as yourself, & to despise trifles. The East is grand,—& makes Europe appear the land of trifles.

Identity, identity! friend & foe are of one stuff, and the stuff is such & so much that the variations of surface are unimportant. All is for the soul, & the soul is Vishnu; & animals & stars are transient paintings; & light is whitewash; & durations are deceptive; and form is imprisonment and heaven itself a decoy. That which the soul seeks is resolution into Being above form, out of Tartarus & out of Heaven; liberation from existence is its name. Cheerful & noble is the genius of this cosmogony.

To William Emerson

Messrs Emerson & Prichard.
or W. E.   Concord, 16 Dec. 1845
Dear William,

Last evening I received from Wiley & Putnam
my book, "Cromwell's Letters, &c" safe & sound with an
inscription from T. Carlyle on the blank leaf.—Wiley & Putnam inclosed in the brown paper wrapper a copy of their
new two vols. & a letter. That is to say, the original envelope
has either disappeared or at all events been broken open. The
letter of W. & P. alludes to a letter already written by them
explaining the transaction, which letter I have never received.
As this new letter is addressed to Concord *N. H.*, it is likely
the other has gone thither.

It is too late then to demand of them my book, and by
the appearance of the book, which is new & uncut, they have
printed from another copy.

There remains the offence which they have committed in
retaining my parcel for three weeks, & refusing to give it up
when at last it was demanded.

On the day when it was received by them, it was worth a
thousand or fifteen hundred dollars. By keeping it for these
weeks, its value has come down to the mere price of the
volumes. It seems to me that a just judge should sentence
them to pay my friend through me this difference of value.
Is it not so?

I wish them to understand that it is not a light offence; &
that I know it to be plunder; and if you think that the laws
will not help me to remunerate Carlyle, and to keep W. & P.
hereafter from stealing from me what is confided to them, I
shall think it necessary to bethink me how I can best make
due proclamation of the men, & warn all persons in England
& America against trusting parcels or commissions to such
carriers as these.

I think it not right to let them go unchecked, and if you see
that any good may come by prosecuting them, you must do
so. It is true, I have not their letter but what can that signify?

                                    Ever yours,
                                        R. W. Emerson

April, 1846. We lie for the right. We affect a greater hope
than we feel. We idealize character. We embellish the story.

Nature loves to cross her stocks. A pure blood, Bramin on Bramin, marrying in & in, soon becomes puny & wears out. Some strong Cain son, some black blood must renew & refresh the paler veins of Seth.

. . . . .

Life is the sleep of the soul: as soon as a soul is tired, it looks out for a body as a bed; enters into a body in the season of dentition, & sleeps seventy years.

. . . . .

The "Community" in its technical sense should exist, or our vulgar community should be elevated & socialized. There ought to be in every town a permanent proprietor which should hold library, picture & sculpture gallery, museum, &c. There are so many books that are merely books of reference that no man cares to buy, yet each should have access to; so much more with the elegances, nobilities, & festivities of pictures, prints, statues, music, it is much that I should have them sometimes. How often I think could I only have music on my own terms! Could I live in a great city, & know where I could go, whenever I wished the ablution & inundation of musical waves, that were a medicine & a bath. I do not wish to own pictures & statues. I do not wish the bore of keeping & framing & exhibiting. Yet I have to buy them, because no one is here to own them for me, no duke, no noble, no municipal or collegiate gallery. It does not help that my friend buys, if not permanent here. The best use by far of these comes when they are collected in one fit stately place, & their influence can be had occasionally as a strain of music, & to be the fitting decoration of public halls.

April–May, 1846. I see not how we can live except alone. Trenchant manners, a sharp decided way will prove a lasting convenience. Society will coo & claw & caress. You must curse & swear a little: they will remember it, & it will do them good. What if they are wise & fine people? I do not want your silliness, though you be Socrates, and if you indulge them, all people are babyish. Curse them.

Understand me when I say, I love you, it is your genius & not you. I like man, but not men. The genius of humanity is very easily & accurately to be made out by the poet-mind, but it is not in Miss Nancy nor in Adoniram, with any sufficiency.

I like man, but not men.

May(?), 1846. When summer opens, I see how fast it matures, & fear it will be short; but after the heats of July & August, I am reconciled, like one who has had his swing, to the cool of autumn. So will it be with the coming of death.

. . . .

"I will get you to mow this piece of grass for me," says the prudent mechanic, "for I can earn more in the shop." And the poet replies in the same wisdom on a higher plane, to those who beg him to come in to the aid of the disturbed institutions: I can best help them by going on with the creation of my own. I am a bad bungler at laws, being afflicted with a certain inconsecutiveness of thought, impertinent association, & extreme skepticism; but I recover my eyesight & spirits, in solitude.

. . . .

The next generation will thank Dickens for showing so many mischiefs which Parliaments & Christianities had not been strong enough to remove. Punch too has done great service. . . .

Fourier, St. Simon, Bentham, Louis Blanc, Owen, Leroux, and the Chartist leader, all crazy men & so they pound on one string till the whole world knows *that*.

. . . .

Hawthorne invites his readers too much into his study, opens the process before them. As if the Confectioner should say to his customers now let us make the cake.

. . . .

If I were a member of the Massachusetts legislature, I should propose to exempt all coloured citizens from taxation because of the inability of the government to protect them by passport out of its territory. It does not give the value for which they pay the tax.

. . . .

May–June(?), 1846. . . . The poet is least a poet when he sits crowned. The transcendental & divine has the dominion of the world on the sole condition of not having it.

. . . .

The United States will conquer Mexico, but it will be as the man swallows the arsenic, which brings him down in turn. Mexico will poison us.

. . . .

The Southerner is cool & insolent. "We drive you to the wall, & will again." Yes, gentlemen, but do you know why

Massachusetts & New York are so tame? it is because we own you, and are very tender of our mortgages which cover all your property.

June–July, 1846. Do they stand immoveable. there,—the sots, & laugh at your so-called poetry? They may well laugh; it does not touch them yet. Try a deeper strain. There is no makebelieve about these fellows; they are good tests for your skill; therefore, a louder yet, & yet a louder strain. There is not one of them, but will spin fast enough when the music reaches him, but he is very deaf, try a sharper string. Angels in satinette & calico,—angels in hunting knives, & rifles,—swearing angels, roarers with liquor;—o poet, you have much to learn.

. . . America seems to have immense resources, land, men, milk, butter, cheese, timber & iron, but it is a village littleness;—village squabble & rapacity characterises its policy. It is a great strength on a basis of weakness.

July, 1846. . . . Mr Webster told them how much the war cost, that was his protest, but voted the war, & sends his son to it. They calculated rightly on Mr Webster. My friend Mr Thoreau has gone to jail rather than pay his tax. On him they could not calculate. The abolitionists denounce the war & give much time to it, but they pay the tax.

August 22, 1846. *Teachers.* The teacher should be the complement of the pupil; now for the most part they are earth's diameters wide of each other. A college professor should be elected by setting all the candidates loose on a miscellaneous gang of young men taken at large from the street. He who could get the ear of these youths after a certain number of hours, or of the greatest number of these youths should be professor. Let him see if he could interest these rowdy boys in the meaning of a list of words.

February–March, 1847. And see this terrible Atlantic stretching its stormy chaos from pole to pole, terrible by its storms, by its cold, by its ice-bergs, by its gulf stream—the desert in which no caravan loiters, but all hurry as through the valley of the Shadow of Death, as unpassable to the poor Indian through all the ages as the finer ocean that separates him from the moon; let him stand on the shore & idly entreat the birds or the wind to transport him across the roaring waste. Yet see, a man arrives at the margin with 120 dollars in his pocket, and the rude sea grows civil, and is bridged at once for the long three thousand miles to England, with a carpeted floor & painted & enamelled walls & roof, with books & gay company & feasting & music & wine.

April, 1847. I think the whole use in literature is the moral. . . .

May 24, 1847. The days come & go like muffled & veiled figures sent from a distant friendly party, but they say nothing, & if we do not use the gifts they bring, they carry them as silently away.

June, 1847. My only secret was that all men were my masters, I never saw one who was not my superior & I would so gladly have been his apprentice if his craft had been communicable.

. . . . .

The one event which never loses its romance is the alighting of superior persons at my gate.

July–August, 1847. The superstitions of our age are,
      the fear of Catholicism
      the fear of Pauperism
      the fear of immigration
      the fear of manufacturing interests
      the fear of radicalism or democracy,
      and faith in the steam engine.
Nemesis takes care of all these things, balances fear with fear, eradicates nobles by upstarts, supplants one set of nobodies by new nobodies.

. . . . .

Life consists in what a man is thinking of all day.

. . . . .

Aristocracy is the moral & independent class. Polk & Webster must have power & must truckle for it. With patrician airs they can never be gentlemen. We understand very well what they mean when they say 'Patriotism,' & unless we are very tired we do not laugh. But an aristocracy is composed of simple & sincere men for whom nature & ethics are strong enough and who say what they mean and go straight to their objects. It is a Realism. . . .

. . . . .

The artist must be sacrificed. The child had her basket full of berries, but she looked sadly tired. The scholar is pale. Schiller shuns to learn French that he may keep the purity of his German idiom. Herschel must live in the observatory & draw on his night-cap when the sun rises, & defend his eyes for nocturnal use. Michael Angelo must paint Sistine Chapels, till he can no longer read except by holding the book over his head. Nature deals with all her offspring so. See the poor moths & flies, lately so vigorous, now on the wall or the trunk of the tree, exhausted, dried up, & presently blown away. Men likewise. They must put their lives into the sting they give. What is a man good for without enthusiasm? What is enthusiasm but this daring of ruin for its object? There are thoughts beyond the reaches of our souls; we are not the less drawn to them. The moth flies into the flame of the lamp, & Swedenborg must solve the problems though he be crazed & killed.

. . . . .

H.D.T [Thoreau] when you talked of art, blotted a paper with ink, then doubled it over, & safely defied the artist to surpass his effect.

August, 1847. Laws of the world. The fish in the cave is blind. Such is the eternal relation between power & use.

August–September, 1847. Patriotism is balderdash. Our side, our state, our town is boyish enough. But it is true that every foot of soil has its proper quality, that the grape on either side of the same fence has its own flavor, and so every acre on the globe, every group of people, every point of climate has its own moral meaning whereof it is the symbol. For such a patriotism let us stand.

September–October, 1847. When people tell me they do not like poetry, and bring me Shelley or Hemans, to show that it is not likeable, I am entirely of their mind. But this only proves that they do not like slops. But I bring them Homer, and they like that, & the Cid, and that goes well; and I read them Lear & Macbeth, Robin Hood's ballads, or Lady Jane, or Fair Annie, or the Hardy Knute, or Chevy Chase, or the Cronachs cried or Bennachie, and they like that well enough. For this poetry instead of being daubs of colour, and mere mouthing, is out of the deep breast of man.

October 18(?), 1847. Religion. The Catholic religion respects masses of men & ages. If it elects, it is yet by millions, as when it divides the heathen & Christian. The Protestant, on the contrary, with its hateful "private judgment" brings parishes, families and at last individual doctrinaires & schismatics, &, verily, at last, private gentlemen into play & notice, which to the gentle musing poet is to the last degree disagreeable. This of course their respective arts & artists must build & paint. The Catholic church is ethnical & every way superior. It is in harmony with Nature, which loves the race & ruins the individual. The Protestant has his pew, which of course is only the first step to a church for every individual citizen—a church apiece.

October–December, 1847. Most of the differences between American & English, referrible to dense population here, and will certainly be lost as America fills up.

To Lidian Emerson

Manchester 1 December 1847

Dear Lidian,

What can be the reason that I have no letter by this "Caledonia" which has arrived. . . . You cannot write too often or too largely. . . .

I trust you and the children are well—that you are well,— & the children are well,—two facts & not one,—two facts highly important to an exile, you will believe. Ah perhaps you should see the tragic spectacles which these streets show, these Manchester & those Liverpool streets, by day & by night to know how much of happiest circumstance, how much of safety of dignity & of opportunity belongs to us so easily that is ravished from this population. Woman is cheap & vile in England—it is tragical to see—Childhood, too, I see oftenest in the state of absolute beggary. My dearest little Edie, to tell you the truth, costs me many a penny, day by day. I cannot go up the street but I shall see some woman in rags with a little creature just of Edie's age & size, but in coarsest ragged clothes, & barefooted, stepping beside her, and I look curiously into *her* Edies face, with some terror lest it should resemble *mine,* and the far-off Edie wins from me the halfpence for this near one. Bid Ellen & Edie thank God that they were born in New England, & bid them speak the truth and do the right forever & ever; and I hope they & theirs will not stand barefooted in the mud on a bridge in the rain all day to beg of passengers. But beggary is only the beginning & the sign of sorrow & evil here. . . .

Farewell!

Love to Mother & William.

Waldo

March 14, 1848. . . . The Englishman talks of politics & institutions, but the real thing which he values is his home, & that which belongs to it,—that general culture & high polish which in his experience no man but the Englishman possesses, & which he naturally believes have some essential connexion with his throne & laws. That is what he does not believe resides in America, & therefore his contempt of America only half-concealed.—This English tenacity in strong contrast with our facility. The facile American sheds his Puritanism when he leaves Cape Cod, runs into all English & French vices with great zest & is neither Unitarian, nor Calvinist, nor Catholic nor stands for any known thought or thing; which is very distasteful to English honour. It is a bad sign that I have met with many Americans who flattered themselves that they pass for English. Levity, levity. I do not wish to be mistaken for an Englishman, more than I wish Monadnock or Nahant or Nantucket to be mistaken for Wales or the Isle of Wight.

March(?), 1848. Dined at Lord Ashburton's, at Lady Harriet Baring's, attended Lady Palmerston's soiree; saw fine people at Lady Morgan's, & at Lady Molesworth's, Lord Lovelace's, & other houses. But a very little is enough for me, & I find that all the old deoxygenation & asphyxia that have in town or in village existed for me in that word a "party", exist unchanged in London palaces. Of course the fault is wholly mine, but I shall at least know how to save a great deal of time & temper henceforward.

I look at the immense wealth & the solid power concentrated, & am quite faint: then I look in the street at the little girls running barefoot thro' the rain with broom in hand to beg a half penny of the passenger at the crossing & at so many Lascars & pitifullest trades & think of Saadi who barefooted saw the man who had no legs, & bemoaned himself no more.

March–April, 1848. The new Religion. Yes, there will be a new church founded on moral science, at first cold & naked, a babe in a manger again, a Copernican theory, the algebra & mathematics of Ethical law, the church of men to come without shawms or psaltery or sackbut, but it will have heaven & earth for its beams & rafters, all geology & physiology, botany, chemistry, astronomy for its symbol & illustration, and it will fast enough gather beauty, music, picture, poetry.

. . . . .

If I should believe the Reviews, and I am always of their opinion, I have never written anything good. And yet, against all criticism, the books survive until this day.

. . . . .

People here expect a revolution. There will be no revolution, none that deserves to be called so. There may be a scramble for money. But as all the people we see want the things we now have, & not better things, it is very certain that they will, under whatever change of forms, keep the old system. When I see changed men, I shall look for a changed world. Whoever is skilful in heaping money now will be skilful in heaping money again. . . .

. . . . .

A curious example of the rudeness and inaccuracy of thought is the inability to distinguish between the private & the universal consciousness. I never make that blunder when I write, but the critics who read impute their confusion to me.

April, 1848. At Kew Gardens which enclose in all more than 600 acres Sir William Hooker showed us his new glass Palm house 362 ft. long, 100 wide, by 66 high; which cost £40,000. The whole Garden an admirable work of English power & taste. Good as Oxford or the British Museum. No expense spared, all climates searched. The Echinocactus Visnaga which is 1000 years old, cost many hundred pounds to transport it from the mountains in Mexico, to the sea. Here was tea growing, green & black, here was clove, cinnamon, chocolate, lotus, caoutchouc, gutta percha, kava, upas, baobab, orotava, the papaw which makes tough meat tender, the graphtophyllum pictum or caricature-plant on whose leaves were several good Punch portraits visible to me, (lately, there was one so good of Lord Brougham, appeared, that all men admired;) the ivory nut; the strelitzja Regina, named for Queen Charlotte, one of the gayest flowers in nature, it looked like a bird, and all but sung; the papyrus; the banian; a whole greenhouse or "stove" full of wonderful orchises, which are the rage of England now.

April 25, 1848. *Carlyle.* Dined with John Forster, Esq. Lincoln's Inn Fields, & found Carlyle, & Dickens, & young Pringle. Forster, who has an obstreperous cordiality, received Carlyle with loud salutation, "My prophet!" Forster called Carlyle's passion, musket-worship. There were only gentlemen present, & the conversation turned on the shameful lewdness of the London streets at night. "I hear it," [Carlyle] said, "I hear whoredom in the House of Commons. Disraeli betrays whoredom, & the whole H[ouse] of Commons universal incontinence, in every word they say." I said, that, when I came to Liverpool, I inquired whether the prostitution was always as gross in that city, as it then appeared? for, to me, it seemed to betoken a fatal rottenness in the state, & I saw not how any boy could grow up safe. But I had been told, it was not worse nor better, for years. C. & D. replied, that chastity in the male sex was as good as gone in our times; &, in England, was so rare, that they could name all the exceptions. Carlyle evidently believed that the same things were true in America.——He had heard this & that, of New York, &c. I assured them that it was not so with us; that, for the most part, young men of good standing & good education with us, go virgins to their nuptial bed, as truly as their brides. Dickens replied, "that incontinence is so much the rule in England, that if his own son were particularly chaste, he should be alarmed on his account, as if he could not be in good health." "Leigh Hunt," he said, "thought it indifferent.". . .

Carlyle is no idealist in opinions but a protectionist in political Economy, aristocrat in politics, Epicure in diet, goes for murder, money, punishment by death, slavery, & all the pretty abominations, tempering them with epigrams. His seal holds a griffin with the word, *Humilitate.* He is a covenanter-philosophe & a sans culotte-aristocrat.

. . . . .

I fancy, too, that he does not care to see anybody whom he cannot eat & reproduce tomorrow, in his pamphlet or pillory. Alcott was meat that he could not eat, & Margaret F. [Fuller] likewise, & he rejected them, at once.

He is the voice of London,—a true Londoner with no sweet country breath in him, & the instigation of these new Pamphlets is the indignation of the nightwalking in London streets. And 'tis curious, the magnificence of his genius & the poverty of his aims. He draws his weapons from the skies to fight for some wretched English property, or monopoly, or prejudice. A transcendental John Bull, delighting in the music of Bow-bells,—who cannot see across the Channel, but has skill to make divine oratorios in praise of the Strand, Kensington, & Kew.

May 6(?), 1848. TENNYSON. I saw Tennyson, first, at the house of Coventry Patmore, where we dined together. His friend Brookfield was also of the party. I was contented with him, at once. He is tall, scholastic-looking, no dandy,—but a great deal of plain strength about him, &, though cultivated, quite unaffected,—quiet sluggish sense & strength, refined, as all English are,—and good humoured. The print of his head in Horne's book is too rounded & handsome. There is in him an air of general superiority, that is very satisfactory. He lives very much with his college set, Spedding, Brookfield, Hallam, Rice, & the rest, and has the air of one who is accustomed to be petted & indulged by those he lives with, like George Bradford. Take away Hawthorne's bashfulness, & let him talk easily & fast, & you would have a pretty good Tennyson. . . .

May(?), 1848. In the Spanish Gallery in the Louvre, it is easy to see that Velasquez & Spagnoletto were painters who understood their business. I fancy them both strong swarthy men who would have made good soldiers or brigands, at a pinch. And, in running along the numberless cartoons of old masters, the eye is satisfied, that the art of expression by drawing & colour has been perfectly attained; that on that side, at least, humanity has obtained a complete transference of its thought into the symbol.

These Spaniards paint with a certain ferocity. Zurbarra who paints monks, & specially one monk with a skull in his hands, which seems the reflection of his own head, is a master so far.

. . . .

I have seen Rachel in Phedre, in Mithridate & now last night in Lucrece, (of Ponsard) in which play she took two parts, that of Lucrece & that of Tullia. The best part of her performance is the terror & energy she can throw into passages of defiance or denunciation. Her manners & carriage are throughout pleasing by their highly intellectual cast. And her expression of the character is not lost by your losing some word or look, but is continuous & is sure to be conveyed. She is extremely youthful & innocent in her appearance and when she appeared after the curtain fell to acknowledge the acclamations of the house & the heaps of flowers that were flung to her, her smile had a perfect good nature & a kind of universal intelligence.

May, 1848. So that on the whole I am thankful for Paris, as I am for the discovery of Ether & Chloroform; I like to know, that, if I should need an amputation, there is this balm; and if hard should come to hard, & I should be driven to seek some refuge of solitude & independency, why here is Paris.

May–July, 1848. In England, every man is a castle. When I get into our first class cars on the Fitchburg Road, & see sweltering men in their shirt sleeves take their seats with some well drest men & women, & see really the very little difference of level that is between them all, and then imagine the astonishment that would strike the polished inmates of English first class carriages, if such masters should enter & sit beside them, I see that it is not fit to tell Englishmen that America is like England. No, this is the Paradise of the third class; here everything is cheap; here everything is for the poor. England is the paradise of the first class; it is essentially aristocratic, and the humbler classes have made up their minds to this, & do contentedly enter into the system. In England, every man you meet is some man's son; in America, he may be some man's father. . . .

July 23, 1848. At sea. One long disgust is the sea. No personal bribe would lure one who loves the present moment. Who am I to be treated in this ignominious manner, tipped up, shoved against the side of the house, rolled over, suffocated with bilge mephitis & stewing oil?

September–October, 1848. I go twice a week over Concord with Ellery, &, as we sit on the steep park at Conantum, we still have the same regret as oft before. Is all this beauty to perish? Shall none remake this sun & wind, the skyblue river, the riverblue sky, the yellow meadow spotted with sacks & sheets of cranberry pickers, the red bushes, the iron-gray house with just the colour of the granite rock, the paths of the thicket, in which the only engineers are the cattle grazing on yonder hill; the wide straggling wild orchard in which nature has deposited every possible flavour in the apples of different trees. . . .

October–November, 1848. I see no security in laws, but only in the nature of men; & in that reactive force which develops all kinds of energy at the same time; energy of good with energy of evil; the ecstasies of devotion with the exasperations of debauchery. The sons of democrats will be whigs, and the fury of the republicanism in the father is only the immense effort of nature to engender an intolerable tyrant in the next age.

December 10, 1848. Punch notices, that in the late, hard times, Saturn has lately appeared without his rings, and that the other planets openly accuse him of having pawned them.

April 4, 1849. *Imbecility & Energy*. The key to the age is this thing, & that thing, & that other, as the young orators describe. I will tell you the key to all ages, Imbecility: imbecility in the vast majority of men at all times & in every man, even heroes, in all but certain eminent moments victims of mere gravitation, custom, fear, sense. This gives force to the strong, that the others have no habit of selfreliance or original action.

March–May, 1849. *Immortality*. I notice that as soon as writers broach this question they begin to quote. I hate quotation. Tell me what you know.

May, 1849. I meet in the street people full of life. I am, of course, at ebb tide; they at flood; they seem to have come from the south or from the west or from Europe. I see them pass with envy at this gift which includes all gifts.

May–June, 1849. *Nearness*. And really the soul is *near* things, because it is centre of the universe, so that Astronomy & history & nature & theology date from where the observer stands. There is no quality in nature's vast magazines he cannot touch; no truth in science he cannot see; no act in will he cannot verify;—there where he stands.

July 1, 1849. I cannot get enough alone to write a letter to a friend. I retreat & hide. I left the city, I hid myself in the pastures. When I bought a house, the first thing I did was to plant trees. I could not conceal myself enough. Set a hedge here, set pines there, trees & trees, set evergreens, above all, for they will keep my secret all the year round.

July 13, 1849. . . . I took my hoe & waterpail & fell upon my sleepy pear trees, broke up the soil, pulled out the weeds & grass, I manured, & mellowed, & watered, pruned, & washed, & staked, & separated the clinging boughs by shingles covered with list: I killed every slug on every leaf. The detestable pear worm, which mimics a twig, I detected & killed. The poor tree tormented by this excessive attention & industry, must do something, & began to grow.

July–August, 1849. I think if I were professor of Rhetoric—teacher of the art of writing well, to young men, I should use Dante for my text-book. Come hither, youth, & learn how the brook that flows at the bottom of your garden, or the farmer who ploughs the adjacent field,—your father & mother, your debts & credits, & your web of habits are the very best basis of poetry, & the material which you must work up. Dante knew how to throw the weight of his body into each act, and is, like Byron, Burke & Carlyle, the Rhetorician. I find him full of the *nobil volgare eloquenza*; that he knows "God damn", & can be rowdy if he please, & he does please. Yet is not Dante reason or illumination & that essence we were looking for, but only a new exhibition of the possibilities of genius. Here is an imagination that rivals in closeness & precision the senses. But we must prize him as we do a rainbow, we can appropriate nothing of him. . . .

August 1, 1849. Correcting MSS & proofs for printing,

makes apparent the value of perspective as essential to good writing. Once we said genius was health; but now we say genius is Time.

August 6(?), 1849. In Mr Levi Bartlett's farm every slope & duct was so arranged that you could not so much as spit without its being carried off to the muck-heap.

. . . . .

It is no matter how fine is your rhetoric, or how strong is your understanding, no book is good which is not written by the Instincts. A fatal frost makes cheerless & undesireable every house where animal heat is not. Cold allegory makes us yawn, whatever elegance it may have.

August 18(?), 1849. The houses in Acton seemed to be filled with fat old people who looked like old tomatoes, their faces crumpled into red collops, fatting & rotting at their ease.

August 29, 1849. Love is the bright foreigner, the foreign self.

August 29(?), 1849. Plato's vision is not illimitable, but it is not selflimited by its own obliquity, or by fogs & walls which its own vices create.

Plato is to mankind what Paris or London is to Europe. Europe concentrates itself into a capital. He has not seen Europe, who has not seen its cities. Plato codifies & catalogues & distributes. In his broad daylight things reappear as they stood in the sunlight, hardly shorn of a ray, yet now portable & reportable.

September–October, 1849. *Representative.* It is my belief that every animal in our scale of creatures leans upward on man, & man leans downward on it; that lynx, dog, tapir, lion, lizard, camel, & crocodile, all find their perfection in him; all add a support & some essential contribution to him. He is the grand lion, he the grand lynx, he the grand worm; the fish of fishes, & bird of birds, so that if one of these tribes were struck out of being he would lose some one property of his nature. And I have no doubt that to each of these creatures Man appears as of its own kind; to a lion, man appears the archlion; to a stork, the archstork.

He is the masterkey for which you must go back, to open each new door in this thousand gated Thebes.

. . . . .

Today, carpets; yesterday, the aunts; the day before, the funeral of poor S; & every day, the remembrance in the library of the rope of work which I must spin;—in this way life is dragged down & confuted. We try to listen to the hymn of gods, & must needs hear this perpetual cock-a-doodle-doo, & ke-tar-kut, right under the library windows. They, the gods, ought to respect a life, you say, whose objects are their own: but steadily they throw mud & eggs at us, roll us in the dirt, & jump on us.

December 14, 1849. *Farmers.* When I see one of our young farmers in Sunday clothes, I feel the greatest respect for & joy in them, because I know what powers & utilities are so meekly worn. What I wish to know they know, what I would so gladly do, they can do. The cold, gloomy day, the rough, rocky pasture, the swamp, are invitations & opportunities to them. And yet there is no arrogance in their bearing, but a perfect gentleness, though they know how to take care of cattle, how to raise & cure & keep their crops. Why a writer should be vain, & a farmer not, though the writer admires the farmer, & the farmer does not admire the writer, does not appear.

December, 1849–January, 1850. *Natural Aristocracy.* It is a vulgar error to suppose that a gentleman must be ready to fight. The utmost that can be demanded of the gentleman is that he be incapable of a lie. There is a man who has good sense, is well-informed, well read, obliging, cultivated, capable, and has an absolute devotion to truth. He always means what he says, & says what he means, however courteously. You may spit upon him;—nothing could induce him to spit upon you,—no praises & no possessions, no compulsion of public opinion. You may kick him; he will think it the kick of a brute: but he is not a brute, & will not kick you in return. But neither your knife & pistol, nor your gifts & courting will ever make the smallest impression on his vote or word; for he is the truth's man, & will speak & act the truth until he dies. He is the truth's Thug, & goes willingly to ruin for his Thuggee. Is not he a gentleman?

. . . . .

I easily distinguish three eras;—

1. *the Greek*; when men deified nature; Jove was in the air, Neptune in the sea, Pluto in the earth, Naiads in the fountains, dryads in the woods, oreads on the mountain; happy beautiful beatitude of nature.

2. *the Christian*; when the Soul became pronounced, and craved a heaven out of nature & above it,—looking on nature now as evil,—the world was a mere stage & school, a snare, and the powers that ruled here were devils hostile to the soul. and now lastly,

3. *the modern*; when the too idealistic tendencies of the Christian period running into the diseases of cant, monachism, and a church, demonstrating the impossibility of Christianity, have forced men to retrace their steps, & rally again on nature; but now the tendency is to marry mind to nature, to put nature under the mind, convert the world into the instrument of Right Reason. Man goes forth to the dominion of the world by Commerce, by science, & by philosophy.

. . . . .

Chladni's experiment seems to me central. He strewed sand on glass, & then struck the glass with tuneful accords, & the sand assumed symmetrical figures. With discords the sand was thrown about amorphously. It seems, then, that Orpheus is no fable; you have only to sing, and the rocks will crystallize; sing, and the plant will organize; sing, & the animal will be born.

January, 1850. *The two statements or Bipolarity.* My geometry cannot span the extreme points which I see. I affirm melioration,—which nature teaches, in pears, in the domesticated animals, and in her secular geology, & this development of complex races. I affirm also the self-equality of nature; or, that only that is true which is always true; and, that, in California, or in Greece, or in Jewry, or in Arcadia, existed the same amounts of private power, as now, & the same deductions, however differently distributed. But I cannot reconcile these two statements. I affirm the sacredness of the individual, the infinite reliance that may be put on his determination. I see also the benefits of cities, and the plausibility of phalansteries. But I cannot reconcile these oppositions. I affirm the divinity of man; but, as I know well how much is my debt to bread, & coffee, & flannel, & heated room,—I shun to be Tartuffe, & do affirm also with emphasis the value of these fomentations. But I cannot reconcile that absolute with this conditional. . . .

To William Emerson

Concord, 10 February, 1850.

Dear William

I received your Quincy-Letter, and afterwards the pacquet so carefully forwarded,—as I was departing for the Eastern country, and have had no facilities for writing a note until now. For Mr Quincy's proposition I hardly know what to say to it. This is the third application within a twelvemonth that has come to me to write a memoir of our father; the first from Dr Sprague, the second from William Ware. But I have no recollections of him that can serve me. I was eight years old when he died, & only remember a somewhat social gentleman, but severe to us children, who twice or thrice put me in mortal terror by forcing me into the salt water off some wharf or bathing house, and I still recall the fright with which, after some of this salt experience, I heard his voice one day, (as Adam that of the Lord God in the garden,) summoning us to a new bath, and I vainly endeavouring to hide myself. I have never heard any sentence or sentiment of his repeated by Mother or Aunt, and his printed or written papers, as far as I know, only show candour & taste, or I should almost say, docility, the principal merit possible to that early ignorant & transitional *Month-of-March*, in our New England culture. His literary merits really are that he fostered the Anthology & the Athenaeum. These things ripened into Buckminster, Channing & Everett. . . .

your affectionate brother Waldo.

February–April, 1850. The part that is built teaches the architect how to build the rest. The streets compress the mob into battalions. Who taught Raffaelle & Corregio how to draw? was it Signor Quadro, the perspective-master, with his rule & dividers? No, it was the weatherstains on the wall; the cloud over the house-roof yonder, with that shoulder of Hercules, & brow of Jove; it was marbled paper; it was a lucky scratch with a bit of charcoal, which taught the secret of possibility, & confounded & annihilated Signor Quadro, & themselves also.

April–May, 1850. The worst symptom I have noticed in our politics lately is the attempt to make a gibe out of Seward's appeal to a higher law than the Constitution, & Webster has taken part in it. I have seen him snubbed as *"Higher-law-*Seward." And now followed by Rufus Choate, in his phrase, "the trashy sentimentalism of our lutestring enthusiasts."

July–August, 1850. If I should be honest, I should say, my exploring of life presents little or nothing of respectable event or action, or, in myself, of a personality. Too composite to offer a positive unity, but it is a recipiency, a percipiency. And I, & far weaker persons, if it were possible, than I, who pass for nothing but imbeciles, do yet affirm by their percipiency the presence & perfection of Law, as much as all the martyrs.

December, 1850–January, 1851. *Rotation.* What an excellent principle our favourite rule of rotation in office would be if applied in industrial matters. You have been watchmaker long enough, now it is my turn to make watches, & you can bake muffins. The carpenter is to make glass this year, & the glassblower staircases. The blacksmith is to cut me a coat, & the tailor to take charge of the machine shop. Mr Benton has served an apprenticeship of thirty years to the Federal Senate, has learned the routine, has opened his views to a national scope, & must now retire to give place to Johnny Raw.

* * * * *

The odious inequality must be borne. A superintendent at the mills must have 2000 dollars, whilst the most industrious operative has only 400. Because, order & faculty are rare & costly. Why should not the wheels of the loom say, "see me, I whirl & buzz with two hundred revolutions in a minute, whilst that great lazy waterwheel down below there, only turns five times. I will not go faster than he."

* * * * *

This consideration of inflation goes into all farming value. The farmer gets 200, whilst the merchant gets 2000 dollars. But the farmer's 200 is far safer, & is more likely to remain to him. It was heavy to lift up from the soil, but it was for that reason more carefully bestowed, & will stay where it was put; so that the two sums turn out at last to be equivalent.

. . . . .

I found when I had finished my new lecture that it was a very good house, only the architect had unfortunately omitted the stairs.

January–February, 1851. To every reproach, I know now but one answer, namely, to go again to my own work. "But you neglect your relations." Yes, too true; then I will work the harder.

"But you have no genius." Yes, then I will work the harder.

"But you have no virtues." Yes, then I will work the harder.

"But you have detached yourself & acquired the aversation of all decent people. You must regain some position & relation." Yes, I will work harder.

Spring(?), 1851. Bettine is the most imaginative person in our day.

April(?), 1851. Bad times. We wake up with a painful auguring, and after exploring a little to know the cause find it is the odious news in each day's paper, the infamy that has fallen on Massachusetts, & that clouds the daylight, & takes away the comfort out of every hour. We shall never feel well again until that detestable law is nullified in Massachusetts & until the Government is assured that once for all it cannot & shall not be executed here. All I have, and all I can do shall be given & done in opposition to the execution of the law.

. . . . .

I opened a paper today in which he pounds on the old strings in a letter to the Washington Birth Day feasters at N.Y. "Liberty! liberty!" Pho! Let Mr Webster for decency's sake shut his lips once & forever on this word. The word *liberty* in the mouth of Mr Webster sounds like the word *love* in the mouth of a courtezan.

. . . . .

I may then add *the Union*. Nothing seems to me more bitterly futile than this bluster about the Union. A year ago we were all lovers & prizers of it. Before the passage of that law which Mr Webster made his own, we indulged in all the dreams which foreign nations still cherish of American destiny. But in the new attitude in which we find ourselves, the degradation & personal dishonour which now rests like miasma on every house in Massachusetts, the sentiment is entirely changed. No man can look his neighbor in the face. We sneak about with the infamy of crime in the streets, & cowardice in ourselves and frankly once for all the Union is sunk, the flag is hateful & will be hissed.

The Union! o yes, I prized that, other things being equal; but what is the Union to a man self condemned, with all sense of self-respect & chance of fair fame cut off,—with the names of conscience & religion become bitter ironies, & liberty the ghastly nothing which Mr Webster means by that word? The worst mischiefs that could follow from Secession, & new combination of the smallest fragments of the wreck were slight & medicable to the calamity your Union has brought us. Another year, and a standing army officered by Southern gentlemen, to protect the Commissioners & to hunt the fugitives will be illustrating the new sweets of Union in Boston, Worcester & Springfield. It did not appear & it was incredible that the passage of the Law would make the Union odious; but from the day it was attempted to be executed in Massachusetts, this result has appeared that the Union is no longer desireable. Whose deed is that?

. . . . .

I am surprised that lawyers can be so blind as to suffer the law to be discredited. The law rests not only in the instinct of all people, but, according to the maxims of Blackstone & the jurists, on equity, and it is the cardinal maxim that a statute contrary to natural right is illegal, is in itself null & void. The practitioners should guard this dogma well, as the palladium of the profession, as their anchor in the respect of mankind.

Against this all the arguments of Webster make no more impression than the spray of a child's squirt.

The fame of Webster ends in this nasty law.

. . . . .

It will be his distinction to have changed in one day by the most detestable law that was ever enacted by a civilized state, the fairest & most triumphant national escutcheon the sun ever shone upon, the free, the expanding, the hospitable, the irresistible America, home of the homeless & pregnant with the blessing of the world, into a jail or barracoon for the slaves of a few thousand Southern planters & all the Citizens of this hemisphere into kidnappers & drivers for the same. Is that a name will feed his hungry ambition?

· · · · ·

It is very remarkable how rare a bad law, an immoral law, is. Does Mr Everett know how few examples in Civil history there are of bad laws? I do not think it will be easy to parallel the crime of Mr Webster's law. But the crime of kidnapping is on a footing with the crimes of murder & of incest and if the Southern states should find it necessary to enact the further law in view of the too great increase of blacks that every fifth manchild should be boiled in hot water,—& obtain a majority in Congress with a speech by Mr Webster to add an article to the Fugitive Slave Bill,—that any fifth child so & so selected, having escaped into Boston should be seethed in water at 212°, will not the Mayor & Alderman boil him? Is there the smallest moral distinction between such a law, & the one now enacted? How can Mr E. [Everett] put at nought all manly qualities, all his claims to truth & sincerity, for the sake of backing up this cowardly nonsense?

· · · · ·

That is one thing; now it is not less imperative that this nation should say, this Slavery shall not be, it poisons & depraves everything it touches. There can never be peace whilst this devilish seed of war is in our soil. Root it out. Burn it up. Pay for the damage & let us have done with it. It costs a hundred millions. Twice so much were cheap for it. Boston is a little city, & yet is worth near 200 millions. Boston itself would pay a large fraction of the sum, to be clean of it. I would pay a tithe of my estate with joy; for this calamity darkens my days. It is a local accidental distemper, & the vast interests of a continent cannot be sacrificed for it.

· · · · ·

I notice, in the road, that the landscape is uninteresting enough, but a little water instantly relieves the monotony. For it is no matter what objects are near it;—a grey rock, a little grass, a crab-tree, or alder-bush, a stake,—they instantly become beautiful by being reflected. It is rhyme to the eye, & explains the charm of rhyme to the ear, & suggests the deeper rhyme or translation of every natural object into its spiritual sphere.

. . . . .

This floor holds us up by a fight with agencies that go to pull us down. The whole world is a series of balanced antagonisms.

. . . . .

The scholar goes into the attorney's office, or the carpenter's shop, &, however civilly, is treated as a trifler. Here is real business, & he is soon set aside: but Archimedes & Kant are as much realists as blacksmiths are: and they are to deal with intellections as vigorously & drastically as the joiner with his chisel & board; & set carpenter & merchant aside.

. . . . .

Lecturing. Danger of doing something. You write a discourse, & for the next weeks & months, you are carted about the country at the tail of that discourse, simply to read it over & over.

. . . . .

Webster truly represents the American people just as they are, with their vast material interests, materialized intellect, & low morals. Heretofore, their great men have led them, have been better than they, as Washington, Hamilton, & Madison. But Webster's absence of moral faculty is degrading to the country.

Of this fatal defect of course Webster himself has no perception. He does, as immoral men usually do, make very low bows to the Christian church, & goes through all the decorums of Sunday but when allusion is made to ethics & the sanctions of morality he very frankly replies as at Albany the other day—"some higher law somewhere between here & the third heaven, I do not know where."

. . . . .

America. Emigration. In the distinctions of the genius of the American race it is to be considered, that, it is not indiscriminate masses of Europe, that are shipped hitherward, but the Atlantic is a sieve through which only or chiefly the liberal, adventurous, sensitive, *America-loving* part of each city, clan, family, are brought. It is the light complexion, the blue eyes of Europe that come: the black eyes, the black drop, the Europe of Europe is left.

. . . . . .

We are glad at last to get a clear case, one on which no shadow of doubt can hang. This is not meddling with other people's affairs,—this is other people meddling with us. This is not going crusading after slaves who it is alleged are very happy & comfortable where they are: all that amiable argument falls to the ground, but defending a human being who has taken the risks of being shot or burned alive, or cast into the sea, or starved to death or suffocated in a wooden box,—taken all this risk to get away from his driver & recover the rights of man. And this man, the Statute says, you men of Massachusetts shall kidnap & send back again a thousand miles across the sea to the dog-hutch he fled from. And this filthy enactment was made in the 19th Century, by people who could read & write.

I will not obey it, by God.

May–August, 1851. I looked through the first part of Faust today, & find it a little too modern & intelligible. We can make such a fabric at several mills, though a little inferior. The miraculous, the beauty which we can manufacture at no mill, can give no account of, it wants; the cheerful, radiant, profuse beauty of which Shakspeare, of which Chaucer, had the secret.—The Faust on the contrary abounds in the disagreeable.

The vice is prurient, learned, Parisian. In the presence of Jove, Priapus may be allowed, but he should have the least to say. But here he is an equal hero. The egotism, the wit is calculated. The book is undeniably made by a great master, & stands unhappily related to the whole modern world, but it is a very disagreeable chapter of history, & accuses the author. . . .

August 11(?), 1851. Carlyle is a better painter in the Dutch style than we have had in literature before. It is terrible—his closeness & fidelity: he copies that which never was seen before. It is like seeing your figure in a glass. It is an improvement in writing, as strange as Daguerre's in picture, and rightly fell in the same age with that; and yet, there is withal an entire reserve on his own part, & the hiding of his hand. What do we know of his own life? The courage which is grand, the courage to feel that nature who made me may be trusted, & one's self painted as also a piece of nature, he has not.

August–September(?), 1851. Yes, History is a vanishing allegory, and repeats itself to tediousness, a thousand & a million times. The *Rape of the Sabines* is perpetual, and the fairest Sabine virgins are every day pounced upon by rough, victorious Romans, masquerading under mere New Hampshire & Vermont & Boston names, as Webster, Choate, Thayer, Bigelow or other obscurity.

September, 1851. Mr Eben. Francis told me, twenty years ago, that it was easy to invest a million, but by no means so easy to invest the second million. And I heard the other day that with all his care of his property, &, with all the high rates that money rents at in Boston, his property has not increased faster than six per cent for many years past.

September–October, 1851. End of Culture, Self-creation. In some sort, the end of life, is, that the man should take up the universe into himself, or, out of that quarry leave nothing unrepresented, and he is to create himself. Yonder mountain must migrate into his mind. Yonder magnificent astronomy he is at last to import, fetching away moon & planet, lunation, solstice, period, comet, & binal star, by comprehending their relation & law. Instead of the timid stripling he was, he is to be the stalwart Archimedes, Pythagoras, Columbus, Jesus, of the physic, metaphysic, & ethics of the design.

October 27, 1851. It would be hard to recall the rambles of last night's talk with H.T. [Thoreau]. But we stated over again, to sadness, almost, the eternal loneliness. I found that though the stuff of Tragedy & of Romances is in a moral union of two superior persons, and the confidence of each in the other, for long years, out of sight & in sight, and against all appearances, is at last justified by victorious proof of probity, to gods & man, causing a gush of joyful emotion, tears, glory, or whatnot,—though there be for heroes this *moral union,*—yet they too are still as far off as ever from an intellectual union, & this moral union is for comparatively low & external purposes, like the coopera-

tion of a ship's crew, or of a fire-club. But how insular &
pathetically solitary, are all the people we know! Nor dare we
tell what we think of each other, when we bow in the street.
'Tis mighty fine for us to taunt men of the world with superficial & treacherous courtesies, but are ours any better? . . .

November 1, 1851. We believe that men will not all or
always be local, spotty, trifling, but that men will come
native to all districts of nature, all related,—who will suck
the earth, the air, the sea,—be solidly related to the forest
& the mineral; amphibious, with one door down into Tartarus, & one door upward into light, belonging to both; &
when such men are possible some of the meaner kinds will
become impossible, & pass into the fossil remains.

1852. Do you think death or skulls or hospitals fit subjects
for cabinet pictures? I do not. I think the pietà or the
crucifixion must be treated with more genius than I have seen
in all the masters of Italian or Spanish art,—to be a proper
picture for houses or churches. And so with dead Romeos,
& dead princes & battles. Nature does not so. See how carefully she covers up the skeleton. The eye shall not see it, the
sun shall not shine on it, she weaves muscle & tendon &
flesh & skin, & down, & hair & beautiful colours of day
over it, forces death down under ground, & makes haste to
cover it with leaves & vines, & wipes carefully out every
trace by new creation.

Winter(?), 1852. I find one state of mind does not remember or conceive of another state. Thus I have written
within a twelvemonth verses ("Days") which I do not remember the composition or correction of, & could not write
the like today, & have only for proof of their being mine,
various external evidences as, the MS. in which I find them,
& the circumstance that I have sent copies of them to
friends, &c &c. Well, if they had been better, if it had been
a noble poem, perhaps it would have only more entirely
taken up the ladder into heaven.

· · · · ·

Eternity is very long; opportunity is a very little portion of
it, but worth the whole of it. If God gave me my choice of
the whole planet, or my little farm, I should certainly take
my farm.

March(?), 1852. Jeremiah Mason said to R.H. Dana;—"lawschool! a man must read law in the court house." And Mr A. took "Hoar's treatise on the Vine" into his garden, but could not find that kind of buds & eyes on his vines. And it is true that all the theory in the world is vain without the thumb of practice. . . .

March–April, 1852. Tin pan. I am made happy by a new thought, & like to put myself in the conditions to get it, namely, with a person who gives me thoughts in which I find my own mind; or with one who excites my own activity to that point that I think freely & newly. But how rare are these persons! Not one in all Wall street. Yet, while this thought glitters newly before me, I think Wall street nothing. I accurately record the thought, & think I have got it. After a few months, I come again to the record & it seems a mere bit of glistening tin or tinsel, and no such worldwisdom. In fact, the Universe had glowed with its eternal blaze, & I had chipped off this scale, through which its light shone, thinking this the diamond, & put it in my jewel box, & now it is nothing but a dead scale.

April, 1852. The Purist who refuses to vote, because the government does not content him in all points, should refuse to feed a starving beggar, lest he should feed his vices.

June 1, 1852. The belief of some of our friends in their duration suggests one of those musty householders who keep every broomstick & old grate, put in a box every old tooth that falls out of their heads, preserve their ancient frippery of their juvenile wardrobe, and they think God saves all the old souls which he has used up. What does he save them for?

June 7, 1852. We had a good walk, W.E.C. [Channing] & I, along the Bank of the North Branch to the swamp, & to the "Harrington Estate." C.'s young dog scampered & dived & swam at such a prodigal rate, that one could not help grudging the youth of the Universe (the animals) their Heaven. They must think us poor pedants in petticoats, as poet Cowper is painted in the Westall Editions. How much more the dog knows of nature than his master, though his master were an Indian. The dog tastes, snuffs, rubs, feels, tries, everything, everywhere, through miles of bush, brush, grass, water, mud, lilies, mountain & sky.

August 1, 1852. Nobody knows what he shall see by going to a brookside or to a ball. At the saw-mill-brook, he might see today, as I saw, a profusion of handsome flowers, among which the *Orchis fimbriata*, the stately stemmed *Eupatorium*, and the *perfoliate*, the *Noli me tangere*, the *Mimulus ringlus*, the *Thalictrum*, the *lobelia Cardinalis*, the *Lysimachia*, and some of the *mints* are conspicuous. The oldest naturalist sees something new in every walk.

August, 1852. I waked at night, & bemoaned myself, because I had not thrown myself into this deplorable question of Slavery, which seems to want nothing so much as a few assured voices. But then, in hours of sanity, I recover myself, & say, God must govern his own world, & knows his way out of this pit, without my desertion of my post which has none to guard it but me. I have quite other slaves to free than those negroes, to wit, imprisoned spirits, imprisoned thoughts, far back in the brain of man,—far retired in the heaven of invention, &, which, important to the republic of Man, have no watchman, or lover, or defender, but I.—

October, 1852. The laws find their root in the credence of the people. A two-foot stone wall guards my fine pears & melons, all summer long, from droves of hungry boys & poor men & women. If one of these people should question my right & pluck my fruit, I should set the cumbrous machinery of the law slowly in motion, & by good luck of evidence & counsel, I might get my right asserted, & that particular offender daunted. But if every passenger should make the like attempt, though the law were perfect, my house would not be worth living in, nor my fields worth planting. It is the education of these people into the ideas & laws of property, & their loyalty, that makes those stones in the low wall so virtuous.

The street, the street, is the school where language is to be learned for poet & orator.

"Pantheism," to be sure! Do you suppose the pale scholar who says, you do not know causes, or the cause of causes any better for often repeating your stupid noun,—deceives himself about his own powers? Does not he live in care, & suffer by trifles? Does not he shake with cold, & lose days by indigestion? Does not his shirt-button come off when he is dressing in haste? Does not his chimney smoke, & his wife scold? Has he not notes to pay?—and is he likely to over-estimate his powers of getting johnny cake for his breakfast, because he perceives that you use words without meaning.

A Mr Schaad who printed an orthodox pamphlet lately at Pittsburgh, Pa. says that "Mr Emerson is a pantheist by intuition, rather than by argument." So it seems our *intuitions* are mistaken. Who then can set us right?

October(?), 1852. The worst of charity, is, that the lives you are asked to preserve are not worth preserving. The calamity is the masses. I do not wish any mass at all, but honest men only, facultied men only, lovely & sweet & ac-complished women only; and no shovel-handed Irish, & no Five-Points, or Saint Gileses, or drunken crew, or mob, or stockingers, or 2 millions of paupers receiving relief or miser-able factory population, or lazzaroni, at all.

. . . . .

If Government knew how, I should like to see it check, not multiply, the population. When it reaches the true law of its action, every man that is born will be hailed as essential.

. . . . .

England has no music.
England has no art, but buys for pride.
England cannot make a pattern for a pitcher.
Hatred of transcendental ideas.

. . . . .

Fate. "The classes & the races too weak to master the new conditions of life must give way." Cor. of the Tribune Karl Ma[r]x.

December, 1852(?). What sort of respect can these preach-ers or newspapers inspire, by their weekly praises of texts & saints,—when we know, that they would say just the same things, if Belzebub had written the chapter which they read, —provided only, it stood where it does in the public opinion, which they flatter & serve.

1852(?). I find that the Americans have no passions, they have appetites.

. . . . .

Gentlemen will not go into politics. They are disgusted. Those who have gone did not well. Those who have gone—I heard it from those who knew them intimately,—were honest men—meant well—we could perfectly rely on them,—yet they voted with the basest of the populace, they ate dung, & saw not the sneer of the bully that duped them.

. . . . .

The ebb of thought drains the law, the religion, the education of the land. We send our boys to the Universities; they go thither, they look the teachers, so called teachers, in the eye;—what can they teach? The boy has doubts,—he looks at the professor with his grammar & his drill, but with frightful penetration; he says, I do not see that the professor himself is better or stronger for all he knows;—he looks into the stable at the horses, & on the whole concludes,—& I am not sure that he is not right,—that the horses can teach him most: they give him vigor & aplomb with no false pretention.

Why the presidents & professors of the University were in this very insane rabble that voted down the moral sense of mankind.

Worst to find this in the seats of Ideas,—in Courts. . . .

. . . . .

. . . This is the open secret of the world, the art of animating a private soul with inspirations from the great & public soul which we call Nature or God. When a man speaks from this, he is interesting; when he acts from it, he is strong, effective. His very silence, if conformed to it, we call character, one of the potencies of the world. . . .

The words national, public, sentiment, opinion, &c, all have real meaning in real nature though they have become disgusting cant. . . .

July 20(?), 1853. *The Sad Side of the Negro question.* The abolitionist (theoretical) wishes to abolish Slavery, but because he wishes to abolish the black man. He considers that it is violence, brute force, which, counter to intellectual rule, holds property in man; but he thinks the negro himself the very representative & exponent of that brute base force; that it is the negro in the white man which holds slaves. He attacks Legree, Macduffie, & slaveholders north & south generally, but because they are the foremost negroes of the world, & fight the negro fight. When they are extinguished,

& law, intellectual law prevails, it will then appear quickly enough that the brute instinct rallies & centres in the black man. He is created on a lower plane than the white, & eats men & kidnaps & tortures, if he can. The Negro is imitative, secondary, in short, reactionary merely in his successes, & there is no origination with him in mental & moral spheres.

July–August(?), 1853. *Abolition.* If you can get Russian tactics into your political representation, so as to ensure the fidelity of your representative to the sentiment of the constituency, by making him more afraid of his constituents than he is of his opponents, you will get your will done.

But the secret, the esoterics of abolition,—a secret, too, from the abolitionist,—is, that the negro & the negro-holder are really of one party, & that, when the apostle of freedom has gained his first point of repealing the negro laws, he will find the free negro is the type & exponent of that very animal law; standing as he does in nature below the series of thought, & in the plane of vegetable & animal existence, whose law is to prey on one another, and the strongest has it.

1853. But I thought how these antagonistic, bornés, japanning English as they build Birmingham everywhere, as they trample on nationalities to reproduce London & the Londoner in Europe, in Asia, in America, so they feel & resent the hostility of ideas, of Poetry, of religion,—ghosts which they cannot lay, and having attempted to domesticate & nationalize & dress & train the Blessed Soul itself in English broadcloth & gaiters they are tormented with an instinctive fear that herein lies a force which will sweep all their system away.

December, 1853. . . . The other day, Henry Thoreau was speaking to me about my lecture on the Anglo American, & regretting that whatever was written for a lecture, or whatever succeeded with the audience was bad, &c. I said, I am ambitious to write something which all can read, like Robinson Crusoe. And when I have written a paper or a book, I see with regret that it is not solid, with a right materialistic treatment, which delights every body. . . .

Winter, 1854. I found, in Wisconsin, that the world was laid down in large lots. The member of Congress there, said, that, up in the Pine Country, the trees were so large, & so many of them, that a man could not walk in the forest, & it was necessary to wade up the streams. Dr. Welsh at Lasalle told me that the prairie grass there was over the tops of carriages, or higher than the head of a man riding on horseback, so that really a man not accustomed to the prairie could easily get lost in the grass!

. . . . .

Metres. I amuse myself often, as I walk, with humming the rhythm of the decasyllabic quatrain, or of the octosyllabic with alternate sexsyllabic or other rhythms, & believe these metres to be organic, or derived from our human pulse, and to be therefore not proper to one nation, but to mankind. But I find a wonderful charm, heroic, & especially deeply pathetic or plaintive in the cadence, & say to myself, Ah happy! if one could fill these small measures with words approaching to the power of these beats.

. . . . .

The first men saw heavens & earths, saw noble instruments of noble souls; we see railroads, banks & mills. And we pity their poverty. There was as much creative force then as now, but it made globes instead of waterclosets. Each sees what he makes.

Realism. We shall pass for what we are. Do not fear to die, because you have not done your task. Whenever a noble soul comes, the audience awaits. And he is not judged by his performance, but by the spirit of his performance. We shall pass for what we are. The world is a masked ball & every one hides his real character, & reveals it by hiding. People have the devil's-mask stamped on their faces, & do not know it, & join the Church & talk virtue, and we are seeing the goat's foot all the time.

When you hide something we see that you hide something & usually see what you hide.

. . . . .

There are no finalities in nature. Everything is streaming. The Torricellian tube was thought to have made a vacuum; but no; over the mercury is the vapor of mercury. And the mysterious ether too enters as readily through the pores of glass as through chimney of a volcano. If I come to stoppages it is I that am wanting. To the wise navigator, beyond even the polar ice, is the Polynia, or open water,—a vast expanse.

• • • • •

Realism in literature. I have no fear but that the reality
I love will yet exist in literature. I do not go to any pope or
president for my list of books. I read what I like. I learn
what I do not already know. Only those above me can give
me this. They also do as I,—read only such as know more
than they. Thus we all depend at last on the few heads or the
one head that is nearest to the stars, nearest to the fountain
of all science & knowledge runs steadily down from class
to class, down to the lowest people, from the highest, as
water does.

February(?), 1854(?). [Negroes.] . . . 'Tis a gentle
joyous race very capable of social virtues & graces; where
manners are such an aristocratic element, why not theirs?
They are not in a hurry, they have dignity, grace, repose.
They have produced some persons of ability. But now, to be
sure, we are told, they are not men, but Chimpanzees. Mon-
tesquieu said, "It will not do to grant them to be men, lest it
appear that the whites are not". . . .

March(?), 1854. The lesson of these days is the vulgarity
of wealth. We know that wealth will vote for the same thing
which the worst & meanest of the people vote for. Wealth
will vote for rum, will vote for tyranny, will vote for slavery,
will vote against the ballot, will vote against international
copyright, will vote against schools, colleges, or any high
direction of public money.

Spring(?), 1854. The existence of evil & malignant men
does not depend on themselves or on men, it indicates the
virulence that still remains uncured in the universe, uncured
& corrupting, & hurling out these pestilent rats & tigers,
and men rat-like & wolf-like.

May–September, 1854. Heaven takes care to show us that
war is a part of our education, as much as milk or love, & is
not to be escaped. We affect to put it all back in history, as
the Trojan War, the War of the Roses, the Revolutionary
War. Not so; it is *Your* War. Has that been declared? has
that been fought out? & where did the Victory perch? The
wars of other people & of history growl at a distance, but
your war comes near, looks into your eyes, in politics, in

professional pursuit, in choices in the street, in daily habit, in all the questions of the times, in the keeping or surrendering the control of your day, & your house, & your opinion, in the terrors of the night, in the frauds & skepticism of the day.

The American independence! that is a legend. *Your Independence!* that is the question of all the present. Have you fought out that? & settled it once & again, & once for all in the minds of all persons with whom you have to do, that you & your sense of right, & fit & fair, are an invincible indestructible somewhat, which is not to be bought or cajoled or frighted away. That done, & victory inscribed on your eyes & brow & voice, the other American Freedom begins instantly to have some meaning & support.

September–October, 1854. The poor keep perpetual fast, the rich perpetual feast.

October, 1854. Intellect. I notice that I value nothing so much as the threads that spin from a thought to a fact, & from one fact to another fact, making both experiences valuable & presentable, which were insignificant before, & weaving together into rich webs all solitary observations.

. . . . .

To say, "The majority are wicked," means no malice, nor bad heart in the observer, but simply, that the majority are young, are boys, are animals, & have not yet any opinion, but borrow their opinion of the newspaper, &, of course, are not worth considering: they have not yet come to themselves, do not yet know their opinion. *That*, if they knew it, is an oracle of God, & worthy of all curiosity & respect from them & from all.

1854(?) . . . 'Tis matter of certainty that the base side will win. My rule of political prophecy, is, to ascertain which is the worst party, & the meanest action, that is the thing which will be done and I am seldom disappointed. . . .

February, 1855.

> Fortune & Hope! I've made my port,
> Farewell, ye twin deceivers;
> Ah! many a time I've been your sport;
> Go, cozen new believers.

March(?), 1855. 'Tis clear that the European is a better animal than the American. Here you can only have Webster, or Parsons, or Washington, at the first descent from a farmer or people's man. Their sons will be mediocrities but in England, in Europe, the privileged classes shall continue to furnish the best specimens. The Czars of Russia shall continue to be good stock.

. . . . .

Common Fame. I trust a good deal to common fame, as we all must. If a man has good corn, or wood, or boards, or pigs, to sell, or can make better chairs or knives or crucibles or church-organs than anybody else, you will find a broad hard beaten road to his house, though it be in the woods. And if a man knows the law, people find it out, though he live in a pine shanty, & resort to him. And if a man can pipe or sing, so as to wrap the prisoned soul in an elysium; or can paint landscape, & convey into oils & ochres all the enchantments of spring or autumn; or can liberate or intoxicate all people who hear him with delicious songs & verses; 'tis certain that the secret cannot be kept: the first witness tells it to a second, and men go by fives & tens & fifties to his door.

What a signal convenience is fame.

Well, it is still so with a thinker. If he proposes to show me any high secret, if he profess to have found the profoundly secret pass that leads from Fate to Freedom, all good heads & all mankind aspiringly & religiously wish to know it, and, though it sorely & unusually taxes their poor brain, they find out at last whether they have made the transit or no. If they have, they will know it; and his fame will surely be bruited abroad. If they come away unsatisfied, though it be easy to impute it (even in their belief) to their dulness in not being able to keep step with his snow-shoes on the icy mountain paths,—I suspect it is because the transit has not been made. 'Tis like that crooked hollow log through which the farmer's pig found access to the field; the farmer moved the log so that the pig in returning to the hole, & passing through, found himself to his astonishment still on the outside of the field: he tried it again, & was still outside; then he fled away, & would never go near it again.

Whatever transcendant abilities Fichte, Kant, Schelling, & Hegel have shown, I think they lack the confirmation of having given piggy a transit to the field. The log is very crooked, but still leaves Grumphy on the same side of the fence he was before. If they had made the transit, common fame would have found it out. So I abide by my rule of not reading the book, until I hear of it thro' the newspapers.

. . . . . .

Philip Randolph was surprised to find me speaking to the politics of Antislavery, in Philadelphia. I suppose, because he thought me a believer in General laws, and that it was a kind of distrust of my own general teachings to appear in active sympathy with these temporary heats.

He is right so far as that it is becoming in the scholar to insist on central soundness, rather than on superficial applications. I am to give a wise & just ballot, though no man else in the republic doth. I am not to compromise or mix or accommodate. I am to demand the absolute right, affirm that, & do that; but not push Boston into a false, showy & theatrical attitude, endeavoring to persuade her she is more virtuous than she is. Thereby I am robbing myself, more than I am enriching the public. After twenty, fifty, a hundred years, it will be quite easy to discriminate who stood for the right, & who for the expedient.

Out upon scholars with their pale, sickly, etiolated, indoor thoughts. Give me the out-of-door thoughts of sound men,—the thoughts, all fresh, blooming, whiskered, and with the tan on!

1855. οἱ ῥέοντες. For flowing is the secret of things & no wonder the children love masks, & to trick themselves in endless costumes, & be a horse, a soldier, a parson, or a bear; and, older, delight in theatricals; as, in nature, the egg is passing to a grub, the grub to a fly, and the vegetable eye to a bud, the bud to a leaf, a stem, a flower, a fruit; the children have only the instinct of their race, the instinct of the Universe, in which, *Becoming somewhat else* is the whole game of nature, & death the penalty of standing still. 'Tis not less in thought. I cannot conceive of any good in a thought which confines & stagnates. Liberty means the power to flow. To continue is to flow. Life is unceasing parturition.

Summer(?), 1855. A scholar is a man with this inconvenience, that, when you ask him his opinion of any matter, he must go home & look up his manuscripts to know.

1855. The first lesson of history is the good of evil. Good is a good doctor, but Bad is a better. 'Tis the oppressions of Wm Conqueror, 'tis the savage forest laws, 'tis the despotism, that made possible the inspirations of Magna Charta, under John. So Edward I. wanted money, armies, & as much as he could get. It was necessary to call the people together by shorter, swifter ways, & the House of Commons arose. With privileges, he bought subsidies. Edw. I. in his 24th year of reign, decreed, *"that no tax should be levied without consent of Lords & Commons"*: the basis of English Constitution.

Plainly, the Parliament is perpetual insurrection.

The "Thirty years' war" made Germany a nation. What calamity will make us one?

To Walt Whitman

Concord Masstts 21 July 1855

Dear Sir,

I am not blind to the worth of the wonderful gift of "Leaves of Grass." I find it the most extraordinary piece of wit & wisdom that America has yet contributed. I am very happy in reading it, as great power makes us happy. It meets the demand I am always making of what seemed the sterile & stingy Nature, as if too much handiwork or too much lymph in the temperament were making our western wits fat & mean. I give you joy of your free & brave thought. I have great joy in it. I find incomparable things said incomparably well, as they must be. I find the courage of *treatment*, which so delights us, & which large perception only can inspire.

I greet you at the beginning of a great career, which yet must have had a long foreground somewhere, for such a start. I rubbed my eyes a little to see if this sunbeam were no illusion; but the solid sense of the book is a sober certainty. It has the best merits, namely, of fortifying & encouraging.

I did not know until I, last night, saw the book advertised in a newspaper, that I could trust the name as real & available for a Post-Office. I wish to see my benefactor, & have felt much like striking my tasks, & visiting New York to pay you my respects.

R. W. Emerson.

August, 1855. 'Tis the result of Aristocracy, that its distinctions are now shared by the whole middle class. The road which grandeur levelled for its coach, toil can travel in its cart. Latin & Greek & Algebra are now cheap. 'Tis the London Times that now keeps the poet, & the chemist; & not John of Gaunt, or Lord Dorset, any longer.

August(?), 1855. Sleepy Hollow [Cemetery]. The blazing evidence of immortality is our dissatisfaction with any other solution.

December 31, 1855. I have crossed the Mississippi on foot three times.

Soft coal which comes to Rock Island from about 8 miles, sells for 16 cents a bushel: wood at 6.00 per cord. They talk "quarter sections." I will take a quarter section of that pie. . . .

January 9, 1856. Beloit. This climate & people are a new test for the wares of a man of letters. All his thin watery matter freezes; 'tis only the smallest portion of alcohol that remains good. At the lyceum, the stout Illinoian, after a short trial, walks out of the hall. The Committee tell you that the people want a hearty laugh, & Stark, & Saxe, & Park Benjamin, who give them that, are heard with joy. Well I think with Gov. Reynolds, the people are always right (in a sense) & that the man of letters is to say, these are the new conditions to which I must conform. The architect who is asked to build a house to go upon the sea, must not build a parthenon or a square house, but a ship. And Shakspeare or Franklin or Aesop coming to Illinois, would say, I must give my wisdom a comic form, instead of tragics or elegiacs, & well I know to do it, and he is no master who cannot vary his forms, & carry his own end triumphantly through the most difficult.

Winter(?), 1856. The railroads have pretended low fares, and, instead of 75 cents, I pay for a passage to Boston from Concord, 60 cents; & the trip costs one hour instead of 2½ hours. Well, I have really paid, in the depreciation of my railroad stock, six or seven hundred dollars a year, for the last few years, or, say a hundred a year, since the roads were built. And I shall be glad to know that I am at the end of my losses on this head.

March(?), 1856. Now & then leaps a word or a fact to light which is no man's invention, but the common instinct. Thus, "all men are born free and equal"—though denied by all politics, is the key-word of our modern civilization.

1856. Wise man was Napoleon. "The kindness of Kings consists in strength & strict justice." He sees the same law running through all things. "Whatever they may tell you, believe that one fights with cannon as with fists;—" "When once the fire is begun, the least want of ammunition renders what you have done already, useless."

I find it easy to translate all his technics into all of mine, & his official advices are to me more literary & philosophical than the Memoires of the Academy. . . .

1856(?). *Qu'est-ce qu'un classique?* The classic art was the art of necessity: modern romantic art bears the stamp of caprice & chance. This is the most general distinction we can give between classic & romantic art.

. . . . .

Eugene Sue, Dumas, &c., when they begin a story, do not know how it will end; but Walter Scott when he began the Bride of Lammermoor had no choice, nor Shakspeare in Macbeth. But Mme George Sand, though she writes fast & miscellaneously, is yet fundamentally classic & necessitated: and I, who tack things strangely enough together, & consult my ease rather than my strength, & often write *on the other side*, am yet an adorer of the *One*. To be classic, then, *de rigueur*, is the prerogative of a vigorous mind who is able to execute what he conceives.

. . . . .

Thy voice is sweet, Musketaquid,
⟨ & ⟩ repeats the music of the rain
but sweeter ⟨ is the ⟩ ↑ ⟨ flows ⟩ ↓ ↑ rivers ↓ silent ⟨ stream ⟩ ↑ flit ↓
⟨ which flows ever ⟩ through thee
as thou through ⟨ the land ⟩ ↑ Concord plain ↓.
Thou art shut in thy banks;
but the stream I love, flows
in thy water, & flows through rocks & through the
air & through rays of light as well, & through
darkness, & through men & women. I hear & see the
inundation & eternal spending of the stream in
winter & in summer in men & animals, in passion &
thought. Happy are they who can hear it.

. . . . .

I know a song which is more hurtful than strychnine or

the kiss of the asp. It blasts those who hear it, changes their color & shape, & dissipates their substance. It is called Time

> Yet they who hear it shed their age
> And take their youth again.

Whipple said of the author of "Leaves of Grass," that he had every leaf but the figleaf.

* * * * *

Education. Don't let them eat their seed-corn; don't let them anticipate, or antedate, & be young men, before they have finished their boyhood. Let them have the fields & woods, & learn their secret & the base- & foot-ball & wrestling, & brickbats, & suck all the strength & courage that lies for them in these games; let them ride bareback, & catch their horse in his pasture, let them hook & spear their fish, & shin a post and a tall tree, & shoot their partridge & trap the woodchuck, before they begin to dress like collegians & sing in serenades, & make polite calls.

March(?), 1857. The democratic party is the party of the Poor marshalled against the Rich. They are sure they are excluded from rich houses & society, & they vote with the poor against you. That is the sting that exasperates them, & makes a strong party. But they are always officered by a few self-seeking deserters from the Rich or Whig Party. They know the incapacity of their own rank & file, and would reject one of their own nobodies as a leader. A few rich men or Whigs are therefore always ready to accept the place of Captain & Major & Colonel & President, & wear their colors for the rewards which are only to be given to the officers, & never to rank & file. But these leaders are Whigs, & associate with Whigs, that is, they are the dining, drinking & dancing & investing class, & by no means the digging & hoeing class.

March–May, 1857. *Art.* You cannot make a cheap palace.

* * * * *

Because our education is defective, because we are superficial & ill-read, we were forced to make the most of that position, of ignorance; to idealize ignorance. Hence America is a vast Know-Nothing party, & we disparage books, & cry up intuition. With a few clever men we have made a reputable thing of that, & denouncing libraries & severe culture, & magnifying the motherwit swagger of bright boys from the country colleges, we have even come so far as to deceive every body, except ourselves, into an admiration of un-learning and inspiration forsooth.

July 8, 1857, Wednesday. This morning I had the remains of my mother & of my son Waldo removed from the tomb of Mrs Ripley to my lot in "Sleepy Hollow." The sun shone brightly on the coffins, of which Waldo's was well preserved —now fifteen years. I ventured to look into the coffin. I gave a few white-oak leaves to each coffin, after they were put in the new vault, & the vault was then covered with two slabs of granite.

1857(?). I took such pains not to keep my money in the house, but to put it out of the reach of burglars by buying stock, & had no guess that I was putting it into the hands of these very burglars now grown wiser & standing dressed as Railway Directors.

. . . . .

If men should take off their clothes, I think the aristocracy would not be less, but more pronounced than now.

June(?), 1858. Your fate is what you do, because first it is what you are.

Spring(?), 1859. Love. All the renovation of Spring connects itself with love; the marriage of the plants, the wedding of the birds, the pairing of all animals. Even the frog & his mate have a new & gayer coat for this benign occasion.

. . . . .

I have now for more than a year, I believe, ceased to write in my Journal, in which I formerly wrote almost daily. I see few intellectual persons, & even those to no purpose, & sometimes believe that I have no new thoughts, and that my life is quite at an end. But the magnet that lies in my drawer for years, may believe it has no magnetism, and, on touching it with steel, it shows the old virtue; and, this morning, came by a man with knowledge & interests like mine, in his head, and suddenly I had thoughts again.

. . . . .

I have been writing & speaking what were once called

novelties, for twenty five or thirty years, & have not now one disciple. Why? not that what I said was not true; not that it has not found intelligent receivers; but because it did not go from any wish in me to bring men to me, but to themselves. I delight in driving them from me. What could I do, if they came to me? they would interrupt & encumber me. This is my boast that I have no school & no followers. I should account it a measure of the impurity of insight, if it did not create independence.

August, 1859. *Beatitudes of Intellect.* Am I not, one of these days, to write consecutively of the beatitude of intellect? It is too great for feeble souls, and they are over-excited. The wineglass shakes, & the wine is spilled. What then? The joy which will not let me sit in my chair, which brings me bolt upright to my feet, & sends me striding around my room, like a tiger in his cage, and I cannot have composure & concentration enough even to set down in English words the thought which thrills me—is not that joy a certificate of the elevation? What if I never write a book or a line? For a moment, the eyes of my eyes were opened, the affirmative experience remains, & consoles through all suffering.

Fall(?), 1859. It may be that we have no right here as individuals; that the existence of an embodied man marks fall & sin. To be pure, we must live in God radiant & flowing, constituting the health & conservation of the universe. We have stopped, we have stagnated, we have appropriated or become selfish, before we could arrest our immortality into this callus or wen of an individual, & have been punished by the wars, infirmities & fate, of human life. The wise east Indian seeks Nirwana or reabsorption, as felicity. It is for this reason that we are dualists, & know the law of our members as opposed to the good. And hence the inexplicable jangle of Fate & freedom, matter & spirit. Hence the indignation of the poet, the scorn of the idealist, to whom geology & zoology are often an impertinence.

May(?), 1860. Advantages of old age. I reached the other day the end of my fifty seventh year, and am easier in my mind than hitherto. I could never give much reality to evil & pain. But now when my wife says, perhaps this tumor on your shoulder is a cancer, I say, what if it is? It would not make the gentleman on his way in a cart to the gallows very unhappy, to tell him that the pain in his knee threatened a white swelling.

November 15, 1860. . . . Yesterday eve I attended at the Lyceum in the Town Hall the Exhibition of Stereoscopic views magnified on the wall, which seems to me the last & most important application of this wonderful art: for here was London, Paris, Switzerland, Spain, &, at last, Egypt, brought visibly & accurately to Concord, for authentic examination by women & children, who had never left their state. Cornelius Agrippa was fairly outdone. And the lovely manner in which one picture was changed for another beat the faculty of dreaming. . . .

January–February, 1861. Gurowski asked "Where is this bog? I wish to earn some money: I wish to dig peat."—"O no, indeed, sir, you cannot do this kind of degrading work." —"I cannot be degraded. I am Gurowski."

. . . . .

Do the duty of the day. Just now, the supreme public duty of all thinking men is to assert freedom. Go where it is threatened, & say, 'I am for it, & do not wish to live in the world a moment longer than it exists.' Phillips has the supreme merit in this time, that he & he alone stands in the gap & breach against the assailants. Hold up his hands. He did me the honor to ask me to come to the meeting at Tremont Temple, &, esteeming such invitation a command, though sorely against my inclination & habit, I went, and, though I had nothing to say, showed myself. If I were dumb, yet I would have gone & mowed & muttered or made signs. The mob roared whenever I attempted to speak, and after several beginnings, I withdrew.

February 27, 1861. . . . In the South, slavery & hunting & horsemanship & the climate, & politics, give the men self-reliance; & the South is well officered, &, with some right, they despise the peaceful north people, leaning on the law, & on each other. In proportion to the number of self-reliant persons, will the power & attitude of the state be.

February–March, 1861. I like dry light, & hard clouds, hard expressions, & hard manners.

. . . . .

At Mrs Hooper's, 23 February, we had a conversation or Genius, in which I enumerated the traits of Genius.

1. Love of truth, distinguished from *talent*, which Mackintosh defined *"habitual facility of execution."*

2. Surprises; incalculable.

3. Always the term Genius, when used with emphasis, implies imagination, use of symbols, figurative speech.

4. Creative, advancing, leading by new ways to the ever-new or infinite.

Coleridge said, "its accompaniment is the carrying the feelings & freshness of youth into the powers of manhood."

Most men in their life & ways make us feel the arrested development; in Genius, the unfolding goes on,—perfect metamorphosis, & again, new metamorphosis. And every soul is potentially genius, if not arrested.

5. Moral. Genius is always moral.

And finally, my definition is, Genius is a sensibility to the laws of the world. Things make a natural impression on him, —belong to us as well.

January, 1862. Fluxional Quantities. Fluxions, I believe, treat of flowing numbers, as, for example, the path through space of a point on the rim of a cart-wheel. Flowing or varying. Most of my values are very variable. My estimate of America which sometimes runs very low, sometimes to ideal prophetic proportions. My estimate of my own mental means & resources is all or nothing, in happy hours, life looking infinitely rich; & sterile at others. My value of my club is as elastic as steam or gunpowder, so great now, so little anon. Literature looks now all-sufficient, but in high & happy conversation, it shrinks away to poor experimenting.

Our only safe rule in politics heretofore, was, always to believe that the worst would be done. Then we were not deceived.

May–June, 1862. Resources or feats. I like people who can do things. When Edward & I struggled in vain to drag our big calf into the barn, the Irish girl put her finger into the calf's mouth, & led her in directly. When you find your boat full of water at the shore of the pond & strive to drag it ashore to empty it, Tom puts a round stick underneath, & 'tis on wheels directly.

June, 1862. Art. Two things in picture;

1. representation of nature, which a photograph gives better than any pencil, and a *camera obscura* better than a photograph, and which is a miracle of delight to every eye.

2. an ideal representation, which, by selection & much omission, & by adding something not in nature, but profoundly related to the subject, & so suggesting the heart of the thing, gives a higher delight, & shows an artist, a creator.

June–July, 1862. I defend myself against failure in my main design by making every inch of the road to it pleasant.

November, 1862. It is said Mr Lincoln has a policy & adheres to it. He thinks emancipation almost morally wrong, & resorts to it only as a desperate measure, & means never to put radicals into power. When he puts one into office, as Fremont, or Phelps, or Lane, he takes care to neutralize him by a democrat or a Kentuckian who will thwart him. And prudent people say, "quite right, for these hot heads have no administrative talent." Perhaps not; but they can not have less than the ruling party, which has shown none whatever. Perhaps, also, they have a great deal. They respect principles, which it may still be believed, have a certain force, if not in the Whig Club, yet in the Universe of men.

Besides, those defeats are incidents & not crises to a well principled man, not affecting the general result (which he contemplates as a forgone conclusion), any more than headwinds or calms to a good sailor, who uses them also to make his port.

Moral tendency is the regnant west wind, resulting from the astronomic motion of the planet.

. . . . .

There never was a nation great except through trial. A religious revolution cuts sharpest, & tests the faith & endurance. A civil war sweeps away all the false issues on which it began, & arrives presently at real & lasting questions.

. . . . .

. . . The question stands thus: reconstruction is no longer matter of doubt. All our action now is new & unconstitutional, & necessarily so. To bargain or treat at all with the rebels, to make arrangements with them about exchange of prisoners or hospitals or truces to bury the dead, all unconstitutional & enough to drive a strict constructionist out of his wits. Much more in our future action touching peace any & every arrangement short of forcible subjugation o: the rebel country, will be flat disloyalty, on our part.

Then how to reconstruct? I say, this time, go to work right. Go down to the pan, see that your works turn on a jewel.

Do not make an impossible mixture. Do not lay your corner stone on a shaking morass that will let down the superstructure into a bottomless pit again.

Leave slavery out. Since (unfortunately as some may think) God is God, & nothing satisfies all men but justice, let us have that, & let us stifle our prejudices against common sense & humanity, & agree that every man shall have what he honestly earns, and, if he is a sane & innocent man, have an equal vote in the state, and a fair chance in society.

February–March, 1863. I am a bard least of bards.

I cannot, like them, make lofty arguments in stately, continuous verse, constraining the rocks, trees, animals, & the periodic stars to say my thoughts,—for that is the gift of great poets; but I am a bard because I stand near them, & apprehend all they utter, & with pure joy hear that which I also would say, &, moreover, I speak interruptedly words & half stanzas which have the like scope & aim.

Spring(?), 1863. It is never quite so dismal weather out of doors as it appears from the house window. Neither is the hardship of campaigning so dreary as it seems to us who see not the reaction. Neither is the battlefield so horrible, nor wounds, nor death, as we imagine.

June, 1863. All decomposition is recomposition. What we call consumption is energetic growth of the fungus or whatever new order. War disorganizes, but it also organizes. It forces individuals & states to combine & act with larger views, & under the best heads, & keeps the population together, producing the effect of cities; for camps are wandering cities.

1863. It is impossible to extricate oneself from the questions in which our age is involved. You can no more keep out of politics than out of the frost.

Nature says to the American, I understand mensuration &

numbers. I have measured out to you by weight & tally the
powers you need. I give you the land & sea, the forest &
the mine; the elemental forces; nervous energy, & a good
brain. See to it that you hold & administer the continent for
Mankind.

March(?), 1864. Barriers of man impassable. They who
should be friends cannot pass into each other. Friends are
fictions founded on some single momentary experience.

Thoughts let us into realities. Nothing of religious tradition, not the immortality of the soul is incredible, after we
have experienced an insight, a thought. But what we want is
consecutiveness. 'Tis with us a flash of light, & then a long
darkness, & then a flash again. This separation of our days
by a sleep almost destroys identity. Ah! could we turn these
fugitive sparkles into an astronomy of Copernican worlds!
Scarcely a link of memory holds yesterday & today together,
with most men; I mean, in their minds. Their house &
trade & families serve them as ropes to give a coarse continuity. But they have forgotten the thoughts of yesterday,
and they say today what occurs to them, & something else
tomorrow.

April–May, 1864. How to say it, I know not, but I know
that the point of praise of Shakspeare, is, the pure poetic
power: he is the chosen closet companion, who can, at any
moment, by incessant surprises, work the miracle of
mythologising every fact of the common life; as snow, or
moonlight, or the level rays of sunrise,—lend a momentary
glory to every pump & woodpile.

June–September, 1864. The test of civilization is the
power of drawing the most benefit out of cities.

September 24–October, 1864. The American Nationality
is now within the Republican Party. Hence its security. In
like manner, in view of all the nationalities of the world,
the battle of humanity is now in the American Union, &
hence the weakness of English & European opposition.

. . . . .

Napoleon's word, that, in 25 years, the United States would
dictate the polity of the world, was a little early; but the
sense was just, with a Jewish interpretation of the "forty
days" & "seventy weeks." It is true, that, if we escape bravely

from the present war, America will be the controlling power.

October 9, 1864. . . . These Tennessee slaveholders in the land of Midian are far in advance of our New-England politicians. They see & front the real questions. The two points would seem to be absolute Emancipation,—establishing the fact that the United States henceforward knows no color, no race, in its law, but legislates for all alike,—one law for all men,—that first; and, secondly, make the confiscation of rebel property final, as you did with the tories in the Revolution.
Thereby you at once open the whole south to the enterprise & genius of new men of all nations, & extend New England from Canada to the Gulf, & to the Pacific. You redeem your wicked Indian policy, & leave no murderous complications to sow the sure seed of future wars. . . .

May, 1865. All the victories of religion belong to the moral sentiment. The poor soul sees the Law blazing through such impediments as he has, & they are many & he yields himself to humility & joy. The parson calls it Justification by Faith. All the victories, all the convictions, all the anxieties of Revivals are the old Eternal fact of remorse for wrong, & joy in the Right.
It is becoming to the Americans to dare in religion to be simple, as they have been in government, in trade, in social life.
They are to break down prisons, capital punishment, slavery, tariff, disfranchisement, caste; and they have rightly pronounced Toleration,—that no religious test shall be put. They are to abolish laws against atheism.
They are not to allow immorality, they are to be strict in laws of marriage; they are to be just to women, in property, in votes, in personal rights,
And they are to establish the pure religion, Justice, Asceticism, self devotion, Bounty;
They will lead their language round the globe, & they will lead religion & freedom with them.

1865(?). *Benefits of the War.* . . . We see the dawn of a new era, worth to mankind all the treasure & all the lives it has cost, yes, worth to the world the lives of all this generation of American men, if they had been demanded.
. . . The present war, on a prodigiously enlarged scale, has

cost us how many valuable lives; but it has made many lives valuable that were not so before, through the start & expansion it has given. It has fired selfish old men to an incredible liberality, & young men to the last devotion. The journals say, it has demoralized many rebel regiments, but also it has *moralized* many of our regiments, & not only so, but *moralized* cities & states. It added to every house & heart a vast enlargement. In every house & shop, an American map has been unrolled, & daily studied,—& now that peace has come, every citizen finds himself a skilled student of the condition, means, & future, of this continent.

.   .   .   .   .

The War has made the Divine Providence credible to a good many people. They did not believe that Heaven was quite honest. I think it a singular & marked result, that it has established a conviction in so many minds that the right will get done; has established a chronic hope for a chronic despair.

August, 1865. Then in the Revue des D.M. [Deux Mondes] found a paper on the Future Life, which suggested the thought, that one abstains,—I abstain, for example,—from printing a chapter on the Immortality of the Soul, because, when I have come to the end of my statement, the hungry eyes that run through it will close disappointed; *That is not here which we desire*: & I shall be as much wronged by their hasty conclusion, as they feel themselves by my short-comings. I mean, that I am a better believer, & all serious souls are better believers in the Immortality, than we give grounds for. The real evidence is too subtle, or is higher, than we can write down in propositions, & therefore Wordsworth's Ode is the best modern Essay on the subject.

August–November, 1865. The conduct of intellect must respect nothing so much as preserving the sensibility. That mind is best which is most impressionable. There are times when the cawing of crows, a flowering weed, a snowflake, a boy's willow whistle or a porter's wheelbarrow is more suggestive to the mind than the *YoSemite Gorge* or *the Vatican* would be in another hour. In like mood, an old verse, or particular words gleam with rare significance. How to keep, how, how, to recover at will this sensibility?

November 5, 1865. We hoped that in the Peace, after such a war, a great expansion would follow in the mind of the country: grand views in every direction,—true freedom in politics, in religion, in social science, in thought. But the energy of the nation seems to have expended itself in the war, and every interest is found as sectional & timorous as before. The Episcopal Church is baser than ever,—perfect Yahoo; the Southerner just the same Gambia negro chief; addicted to crowing, garotting, & stealing, as ever: the Democrat as false & truckling; the Union party as timid & compromising, the scholars pale & expectant, never affirmative; only Phillips & Frank Bird, only Wilson & Sumner unreconciled, aggressive, & patriotic still.

July, 1866. I see with joy the Irish emigrants landing at Boston, at New York, & say to myself, There they go—to school.

. . . . .

There is this to be said in favor of drinking, that it takes the drunkard first out of society, then out of the world.

August, 1866. In the history of intellect no more important fact than the Hindoo theology, teaching that the beatitude or supreme good is to be attained through science; namely, by the perception of the real & unreal, setting aside matter, & qualities, & affections or emotions and persons, & actions, as Maias or illusions, & thus arriving at the contemplation of the one eternal Life & Cause, & a perpetual approach & assimilation to Him, thus escaping new births or transmigration.

1866(?). I am so purely a spectator that I have absolute confidence that all pure spectators will agree with me, whenever I make a careful report. I told Alcott that every one of my expressions concerning "God," or the "Soul," &c. is entitled to attention as testimony, because it is independent, not calculated, not part of any system, but spontaneous, & the nearest word I could find to the thing.

. . . . .

We Americans have got suppled into the state of melioration. We have lived fast in ten years, in four years, last past. We have seen our rocks covered with gold, our states floored with coal, the rifts are now gushing oil. We have seen railroad & telegraph subdue our enormous geography. We have seen the snowy desarts on the northwest, the seals & Esquimaux become lands of promise: we have seen slavery disappear like a painted scene in a theatre. We have seen the old oligarchs tumbled out of their powerful chairs into poverty, exile & shame. Those who were their victims occupy their places & dictate their fate. Sumner in the Foreign Affairs. We have seen total revolution in the politics of the nation. We have seen China opened to European & American ministers & commerce, Japan likewise. Our arts & our productions begin to penetrate both. Negroes too are a new nation of customers. Now we are working the new Siberian Telegraph, & mean to perforate & deal with the old ball of the Earth as a carpenter does with wood.

The plasticity of the tough old planet is wonderful. As the walls of a modern house are pierced with waterpipes, soundpipes, gas-pipes & heatpipes, so the geography & geology are beginning to yield to man's power & convenience. Everything has grown ductile. The very Constitution is amended & is construed in a new spirit. Things once not possible are probable now. Women dispose of their own property. Women will vote. Women lecture, preach, are physicians, artists.

Nationality is babyish. But stand where you are & make the best of it. I cannot find any bar in the way of social life here. The travellers for whom London & Paris spoil their homes, can be spared here to return to those cities. I not only see a career at home for more genius than we have, but for more than there is now in the world. I see, too, happy homes, & true gentlemen to live & die for, & friends to die with.

Spring(?), 1867. The good writer seems to be writing about himself, but has his eye always on that thread of the Universe which runs through himself, & all things.

• • • • •

The word *miracle*, as it is used, only indicates the savage ignorance of the devotee, staring with wonder to see water turned into wine, & heedless of the stupendous fact of himself being there present. If the water became wine, became fire, became a chorus of angels, it would not compare with the familiar fact of his own perception. Here he stands, a lonely thought, harmoniously organized into correspondence with the Universe of mind & matter.

April–May, 1867. You complain that the negroes are a base class. Who makes & keeps the jew or the negro base, who but you, who exclude them from the rights which others enjoy?

. . . . .

If I were rich, I should get the education I have always wished by persuading Agassiz to let me carry him to Canada; & Dr. Gray to go to examine the trans-Mississippi Flora; & Wyman should find me necessary to his excavations; and Alvan Clark should make a telescope for me too, & I can easily see how to find the gift for each master that would domesticate me with him for a time. . . .

October–December, 1867. In this old matter of Originality & Quotation, a few points to be made distinctly.

The apparently immense amount of debt to the old. By necessity & by proclivity, & by delight, we all quote. We quote books, & arts, & science, & religion, & customs, & laws, yes, & houses, tables & chairs. At first view, 'tis all quotation,—all we have. But presently we make distinction. 1. By wise quotation. Vast difference in the mode of quotation. One quotes so well, that the person quoted is the gainer. The quoter's selection honors & celebrates the author. The quoter gives more fame than he receives aid. Thus Coleridge. Quoting is often merely of a suggestion which the quoter drew but of which the author is quite innocent.

For good quoting, then, there must be originality in the quoter,—bent, bias, delight in the truth, & only valuing the Author in the measure of his agreement with the truth which we see, & which he had the luck to see first.

And originality, what is that? It is being; being somebody, being yourself, & reporting accurately what you see & are. If another's words describe your fact, use them as freely as you use the language & the alphabet, whose use does not impair your originality. Neither will another's sentiment or distinction impugn your sufficiency. Yet in proportion to your reality of life & perception, will be your difficulty of finding yourself expressed in others' words or deeds. . . .

Winter(?), 1868. I have no knowledge of trade & there is not the sciolist who cannot shut my mouth & my understanding by strings of facts that seem to prove the wisdom of tariffs. But my faith in freedom of trade, as the rule, returns always. If the Creator has made oranges, coffee, & pineapples in Cuba, & refused them to Massachusetts, I cannot see why we should put a fine on the Cubans for bringing these to us, —a fine so heavy as to enable Massachusetts men to build costly palm-houses & glass conservatories, under which to coax these poor plants to ripen under our hard skies, & thus discourage the poor planter from sending them to gladden the very cottages here. We punish the planter there & punish the consumer here for adding these benefits to life. Tax opium, tax poisons, tax brandy, gin, wine, hasheesh, tobacco, & whatever articles of pure luxury, but not healthy & delicious food.

. . . . .

I wish the American Poet should let old times go & write on Tariff; universal suffrage; woman's suffrage; Science shall not be abused to make guns. The poet shall bring out the blazing truth, that he who kills his brother commits suicide. . . .

April–May, 1868. . . . Coleridge, Goethe, the New Naturalists in astronomy, geology, zoology, the correlations, the Social Science, the new readings of history through Niebuhr, Mommsen, Max Muller, Champollion, Lepsius astonish the mind, & detach it effectually from a hopeless routine. 'Come out of that,' they say, 'you lie sick & doting, only shifting from bed to bed.' And they dip the patient in this Russian bath, & he is at least well awake, & capable of sane activity. The perceptions which metaphysical & natural science cast upon the religious traditions, are every day forcing people in conversation to take new & advanced position. We have been building on the ice, & lo! the ice has floated. And the man is reconciled to his losses, when he sees the grandeur of his gains.

1868(?). 1869(?). When I find in people narrow religion, I find also narrow reading.

July–September, 1869. I am interested not only in my advantages, but in my disadvantages, that is, in my fortunes proper; that is, in watching my fate, to notice, after each act of mine, what result? is it prosperous? is it adverse? & thus I find a pure entertainment of the intellect, alike in what is called good or bad.

October 21, 1869. I read a good deal of experimental

poetry in the new books. The author has said to himself, 'Who knows but this may please, & become famous? Did not Goethe experiment? Does not this read like the ancients?' But good poetry was not written thus, but it delighted the poet first; he said & wrote it for joy, & it pleases the reader for the same reason.

March 15, 1870. My New book [*Society and Solitude*] sells faster, it appears, than either of its foregoers. This is not for its merit, but only shows that old age is a good advertisement. Your name has been seen so often that your book must be worth buying.

July 21, 1870. I am filling my house with books which I am bound to read, & wondering whether the new heavens which await the soul (after the fatal hour), will allow the consultation of these?

December, 1870–February, 1871. California is teaching in its history & its poetry the good of evil, & confirming my thought one day in Five Points in New York, twenty years ago, that the ruffians & Amazons in that district were only superficially such, but carried underneath this bronze about the same morals as their civil & well-dressed neighbors.

May–October, 1871. The splendors of this age outshine all other recorded ages. In my lifetime, have been wrought five miracles, namely, 1. the steamboat; 2. the railroad; 3. the Electric telegraph; 4. the application of the spectroscope to astronomy; 5. the photograph; five miracles which have altered the relations of nations to each other. Add Cheap Postage; and the Sewing machine; &, in agriculture, the Mowing machine & the horse-rake. A corresponding power has been given to manufactures by the machine for pegging shoes, & the power-loom; & the power-press of the printers. And in dentistry & in surgery Dr Jackson's discovery of anaesthesis. It only needs to add the power which up to this hour eludes all human ingenuity, namely, a rudder to the balloon, to give us the dominion of the air, as well as of the sea & the land. But the account is not complete until we add the discovery of Oersted, of the identity of Electricity & Magnetism, & the generalization of that conversion by its application to light, heat, & gravitation. The geologist has found the correspondence of the age of stratified remains to the ascending scale of structure in animal life. Add now, the daily predictions of the weather for the next 24 hours for North America, by the Observatory at Washington.

1872(?). When a boy I used to go to the wharves, & pick up shells out of the sand which vessels had brought as ballast, & also plenty of stones, gypsum, which, I discovered would be luminous when I rubbed two bits together in a dark closet, to my great wonder,—& I do not know why luminous to this day. That, & the magnetising my penknife, till it would hold a needle; & the fact that blue & gamboge would make green in my pictures of mountains; & the charm of drawing vases by scrawling with ink heavy random lines, & then doubling the paper, so as to make another side symmetrical,—what was chaos, becoming symmetrical; then hallooing to an echo at the pond, & getting wonderful replies.

Still earlier, what silent wonder is waked in the boy by blowing bubbles from soap & water with a pipe.

August 31, 1872, Naushon. I thought today, in these rare seaside woods, that if absolute leisure were offered me, I should run to the College or the Scientific School which offered best lectures on Geology, Chemistry, Minerals, Botany, & seek to make the alphabets of those sciences clear to me. How could leisure or labor be better employed? 'Tis never late to learn them, and every secret opened goes to authorize our aesthetics. Cato learned Greek at eighty years, but these are older bibles & oracles than Greek.

1858(?)–1870(?). . . . Nat. Sciences have made a great stride by means of Hegel's dogma which put Nature and thought, matter and spirit, in right relation, one the expression or externisation of the other. Observation was the right method, & metaphysics was nature & subject to observation also.

But philosophy (Hegel and all his followers) shunned to apply the new arm to what most of all belonged to it, to anthropology, morals, politics, &c.

For this at once touched conservatism, church, jurisprudence, &c.

Therefore the Nat. Sciences made great progress & philosophy none. But Nat. Science, without philosophy, without ethics, was unsouled.

Presently Nat. Science which the governments have befriended will disclose the liberalizing as well as the dynamic strength, then Nat. Science will be persecuted as e.g., geology, astronomy, ethnology, as contradicting the Bible.

Difference of the two: Natural Sciences, a circle, Morals and Metaphysics a line of advance;

one, the basis;

the other, the completion.

· · · · ·

Writing should be the settlement of dew on the leaf, of stalactites on the cavern wall, the deposit of flesh from the blood, of woody fibre from the sap.

· · · · ·

The poem is made up of lines each of which filled the sky of the poet in its turn; so that mere synthesis produces a work quite superhuman. . . . For that reason, a true poem by no means yields all its virtue at the first reading, but is best when we have slowly and by repeated attention felt the truth of all the details.

· · · · ·

Detachment. The distinction of a man is that he think. Let that be so. For a man cannot otherwise compare with a steam engine or the self-acting spinning-mule which is never tired, & makes no fault. But a man thinks & adapts. A man is not a man, then, until he have his own thoughts: that first; then, that he can detach them. But what thought of his own is in Abner or Guy? They are clean, well-built men enough to look at, have money, & houses & books, but they are not yet arrived at humanity, but remain idiots & minors.

· · · · ·

Scholar's Creed. I believe that all men are born free and equal *quoad* the laws;

that all men have a right to their life, *quoad* the laws.

I believe in freedom of opinion religious and political.

I believe in the justice of universal suffrage,[1] in public schools, in free trade.

I believe the soul makes the body.

I believe that causality is perfect.

[1] With the exception that known crime should withdraw the right of suffrage. [Emerson's note.]

II. ESSAYS AND ADDRESSES

NATURE.

A subtle chain of countless rings
The next unto the farthest brings;
The eye reads omens where it goes,
And speaks all languages the rose;
And, striving to be man, the worm
Mounts through all the spires of form.

INTRODUCTION

Our age is retrospective. It builds the sepulchres of the fathers. It writes biographies, histories, and criticism. The foregoing generations beheld God and nature face to face; we, through their eyes. Why should not we also enjoy an original relation to the universe? Why should not we have a poetry and philosophy of insight and not of tradition, and a religion by revelation to us, and not the history of theirs? Embosomed for a season in nature, whose floods of life stream around and through us, and invite us by the powers they supply, to action proportioned to nature, why should we grope among the dry bones of the past, or put the living generation into masquerade out of its faded wardrobe? The sun shines to-day also. There is more wool and flax in the fields. There are new lands, new men, new thoughts. Let us demand our own works and laws and worship.

Undoubtedly we have no questions to ask which are unanswerable. We must trust the perfection of the creation so far, as to believe that whatever curiosity the order of things has awakened in our minds, the order of things can satisfy. Every man's condition is a solution in hieroglyphic to those inquiries he would put. He acts it as life, before he apprehends it as truth. In like manner, nature is already, in its forms and tendencies, describing its own design. Let us interrogate the great apparition, that shines so peacefully around us. Let us inquire, to what end is nature?

All science has one aim, namely, to find a theory of nature. We have theories of races and of functions, but scarcely yet a remote approach to an idea of creation. We are now so far from the road to truth, that religious teachers dispute and hate each other, and speculative men are esteemed unsound and frivolous. But to a sound judgment, the most abstract truth is the most practical. Whenever a true theory appears, it will be its own evidence. Its test is, that it will explain all phenomena. Now many are thought not only unexplained but inexplicable; as language, sleep, madness, dreams, beasts, sex.

Philosophically considered, the universe is composed of Nature and the Soul. Strictly speaking, therefore, all that is separate from us, all which Philosophy distinguishes as the NOT ME, that is, both nature and art, all other men and my own body, must be ranked under this name, NATURE. In enumerating the values of nature and casting up their sum, I shall use the word in both senses,—in its common and in its philosophical import. In inquiries so general as our present one, the inaccuracy is not material; no confusion of thought will occur. *Nature*, in the common sense, refers to essences unchanged by man; space, the air, the river, the leaf. *Art* is applied to the mixture of his will with the same things, as in a house, a canal, a statue, a picture. But his operations taken together are so insignificant, a little chipping, baking, patching, and washing, that in an impression so grand as that of the world on the human mind, they do not vary the result.

CHAPTER I.

To go into solitude, a man needs to retire as much from his chamber as from society. I am not solitary whilst I read and write, though nobody is with me. But if a man would be alone, let him look at the stars. The rays that come from those heavenly worlds will separate between him and what he touches. One might think the atmosphere was made transparent with this design, to give man, in the heavenly bodies, the perpetual presence of the sublime. Seen in the streets of cities, how great they are! If the stars should appear one night in a thousand years, how would men believe and adore; and preserve for many generations the remembrance of the city of God which had been shown! But every night come out these envoys of beauty, and light the universe with their admonishing smile.

The stars awaken a certain reverence, because though always present, they are inaccessible; but all natural objects make a kindred impression, when the mind is open to their influence. Nature never wears a mean appearance. Neither does the wisest man extort her secret, and lose his curiosity by finding out all her perfection. Nature never became a toy to a wise spirit. The flowers, the animals, the mountains, reflected the wisdom of his best hour, as much as they had delighted the simplicity of his childhood.

When we speak of nature in this manner, we have a distinct but most poetical sense in the mind. We mean the integrity of impression made by manifold natural objects. It is this which distinguishes the stick of timber of the woodcutter, from the tree of the poet. The charming landscape which I saw this morning is indubitably made up of some twenty or thirty farms. Miller owns this field, Locke that, and Manning the woodland beyond. But none of them owns the landscape. There is a property in the horizon which no man has but he whose eye can integrate all the parts, that is, the poet. This is the best part of these men's farms, yet to this their warranty-deeds give no title.

To speak truly, few adult persons can see nature. Most persons do not see the sun. At least they have a very superficial seeing. The sun illuminates only the eye of the man, but shines into the eye and the heart of the child. The lover of nature is he whose inward and outward senses are still truly adjusted to each other; who has retained the spirit of infancy even into the era of manhood. His intercourse with heaven and earth, becomes part of his daily food. In the presence of nature, a wild delight runs through the man, in spite of real sorrows. Nature says,—he is my creature, and maugre all his impertinent griefs, he shall be glad with me. Not the sun or the summer alone, but every hour and season yields its tribute of delight; for every hour and change corresponds to and authorizes a different state of the mind, from breathless noon to grimmest midnight. Nature is a setting that fits equally well a comic or a mourning piece. In good health, the air is a cordial of incredible virtue. Crossing a bare common, in snow puddles, at twilight, under a clouded sky, without having in my thoughts any occurrence of special good fortune, I have enjoyed a perfect exhilaration. I am glad to the brink of fear. In the woods too, a man casts off his years, as the snake his slough, and at what period soever of life, is always a child. In the woods, is perpetual youth. Within these plantations of God, a decorum and sanctity reign, a perennial festival is dressed, and the guest sees not how he should tire of them in a thousand years. In the woods, we return to reason and faith. There I feel that nothing can befall me in life,—no disgrace, no calamity (leaving me my eyes), which nature cannot repair. Standing on the bare ground,—my head bathed by the blithe air, and uplifted into infinite space,—all mean egotism vanishes. I become a transparent eyeball; I am nothing; I see all; the currents of the Universal Being circulate through me; I am part or particle of God. The name of the nearest friend sounds then foreign and accidental: to be brothers, to be acquaintances,—master or servant, is then a trifle and a disturbance. I am the lover of uncontained and immortal beauty. In the wilderness, I find something more dear and connate than in streets or villages. In the tranquil landscape, and especially in the distant line of the horizon, man beholds somewhat as beautiful as his own nature.

The greatest delight which the fields and woods minister, is the suggestion of an occult relation between man and the vegetable. I am not alone and unacknowledged. They nod to me, and I to them. The waving of the boughs in the storm, is new to me and old. It takes me by surprise, and yet is not unknown. Its effect is like that of a higher thought or a better emotion coming over me, when I deemed I was thinking justly or doing right.

Yet it is certain that the power to produce this delight does not reside in nature, but in man, or in a harmony of both. It is necessary to use these pleasures with great temperance. For, nature is not always tricked in holiday attire, but the same scene which yesterday breathed perfume and glittered as for the frolic of the nymphs, is overspread with melancholy today. Nature always wears the colors of the spirit. To a man laboring under calamity, the heat of his own fire hath sadness in it. Then, there is a kind of contempt of the landscape felt by him who has just lost by death a dear friend. The sky is less grand as it shuts down over less worth in the population.

CHAPTER II.

COMMODITY.

Whoever considers the final cause of the world, will discern a multitude of uses that enter as parts into that result. They all admit of being thrown into one of the following classes: Commodity; Beauty; Language; and Discipline.

Under the general name of Commodity, I rank all those advantages which our senses owe to nature. This, of course, is a benefit which is temporary and mediate, not ultimate, like its service to the soul. Yet although low, it is perfect in its kind, and is the only use of nature which all men apprehend. The misery of man appears like childish petulance, when we explore the steady and prodigal provision that has been made for his support and delight on this green ball which floats him through the heavens. What angels invented these splendid ornaments, these rich conveniencies, this ocean of air above, this ocean of water beneath, this firmament of earth between? this zodiac of lights, this tent of dropping clouds, this striped coat of climates, this fourfold year? Beasts, fire, water, stones, and corn serve him. The field is at once his floor, his workyard, his play-ground, his garden, and his bed.

"More servants wait on man
Than he'll take notice of."

Nature, in its ministry to man, is not only the material, but is also the process and the result. All the parts incessantly work into each other's hands for the profit of man. The wind sows the seed; the sun evaporates the sea; the wind blows the vapor to the field; the ice, on the other side of the planet, condenses rain on this; the rain feeds the plant; the plant feeds the animal; and thus the endless circulations of the divine charity nourish man.

The useful arts are reproductions or new combinations by the wit of man, of the same natural benefactors. He no longer waits for favoring gales, but by means of steam, he realizes the fable of Æolus's bag, and carries the two-and-thirty winds in the boiler of his boat. To diminish friction, he paves the road with iron bars, and, mounting a coach with a ship-load of men, animals, and merchandise behind him, he darts through the country from town to town, like an eagle or a swallow through the air. By the aggregate of these aids, how is the face of the world changed, from the era of Noah to that of Napoleon! The private poor man hath cities, ships, canals, bridges, built for him. He goes to the post-office, and the human race run on his errands; to the book-shop, and the human race read and write of all that happens, for him; to the court-house, and nations repair his wrongs. He sets his house upon the road, and the human race go forth every morning, and shovel out the snow, and cut a path for him.

But there is no need of specifying particulars in this class of uses. The catalogue is endless, and the examples so obvious, that I shall leave them to the reader's reflection, with the general remark, that this mercenary benefit is one which has respect to a further good. A man is fed, not that he may be fed, but that he may work.

CHAPTER III.

BEAUTY.

A nobler want of man is served by nature, namely, the love of beauty.

The ancient Greeks called the world κόσμος beauty. Such

is the constitution of all things, or such the plastic power of the human eye, that the primary forms, as the sky, the mountain, the tree, the animal, give us a delight *in and for themselves;* a pleasure arising from outline, color, motion, and grouping, This seems partly owing to the eye itself. The eye is the best of artists. By the mutual action of its structure and of the laws of light, perspective is produced, which integrates every mass of objects, of what character soever, into a well-colored and shaded globe, so that where the particular objects are mean and unaffecting, the landscape which they compose is round and symmetrical. And as the eye is the best composer, so light is the first of painters. There is no object so foul that intense light will not make beautiful. And the stimulus it affords to the sense, and a sort of infinitude which it hath, like space and time, make all matter gay. Even the corpse has its own beauty. But besides this general grace diffused over nature, almost all the individual forms are agreeable to the eye, as is proved by our endless imitations of some of them, as the acorn, the grape, the pine-cone, the wheat-ear, the egg, the wings and forms of most birds, the lion's claw, the serpent, the butterfly, sea-shells, flames, clouds, buds, leaves, and the forms of many trees, as the palm.

For better consideration, we may distribute the aspects of Beauty in a threefold manner.

1. First, the simple perception of natural forms is a delight. The influence of the forms and actions in nature is so needful to man, that, in its lowest functions, it seems to lie on the confines of commodity and beauty. To the body and mind which have been cramped by noxious work or company, nature is medicinal and restores their tone. The tradesman, the attorney comes out of the din and craft of the street, and sees the sky and the woods, and is a man again. In their eternal calm, he finds himself. The health of the eye seems to demand a horizon. We are never tired, so long as we can see far enough.

But in other hours, Nature satisfies by its loveliness, and without any mixture of corporeal benefit. I see the spectacle of morning from the hill-top over against my house, from day-break to sunrise, with emotions which an angel might share. The long slender bars of cloud float like fishes in the sea of crimson light. From the earth, as a shore, I look out into that silent sea. I seem to partake its rapid transformations: the active enchantment reaches my dust, and I dilate and conspire wih the morning wind. How does Nature deify us with a few and cheap elements! Give me health and a day, and I will make the pomp of emperors ridiculous. The dawn is my Assyria; the sunset and moonrise my Paphos, and unimaginable realms of faerie; broad noon shall be my England of the senses and the understanding; the night shall be my Germany of mystic philosophy and dreams.

Not less excellent, except for our less susceptibility in the afternoon, was the charm, last evening, of a January sunset. The western clouds divided and subdivided themselves into pink flakes modulated with tints of unspeakable softness; and the air had so much life and sweetness, that it was a pain to come within doors. What was it that nature would say? Was there no meaning in the live repose of the valley behind the mill, and which Homer or Shakespeare could not re-form for me in words? The leafless trees become spires of flame in the sunset, with the blue east for their background, and the stars of the dead calices of flowers, and every withered stem and stubble rimed with frost, contribute something to the mute music.

The inhabitants of cities suppose that the country landscape is pleasant only half the year. I please myself with the graces of the winter scenery, and believe that we are as much touched by it as by the genial influences of summer. To the attentive eye, each moment of the year has its own beauty, and in the same field, it beholds, every hour, a picture which was never seen before, and which shall never be seen again. The heavens change every moment, and reflect their glory or gloom on the plains beneath. The state of the crop in the surrounding farms alters the expression of the earth from week to week. The succession of native plants in the pastures and roadsides, which makes the silent clock by which time tells the summer hours, will make even the divisions of the day sensible to a keen observer. The tribes of birds and insects, like the plants punctual to their time, follow each other, and the year has room for all. By water-courses, the variety is greater. In July, the blue pontederia or pickerel-weed blooms in large beds in the shallow parts of our pleasant river, and swarms with yellow butterflies in continual motion. Art cannot rival this pomp of purple and gold. Indeed the river is a perpetual gala, and boasts each month a new ornament.

But this beauty of Nature which is seen and felt as beauty,

is the least part. The shows of day, the dewy morning, the rainbow, mountains, orchards in blossom, stars, moonlight, shadows in still water, and the like, if too eagerly hunted, become shows merely, and mock us with their unreality. Go out of the house to see the moon, and 't is mere tinsel; it will not please as when its light shines upon your necessary journey. The beauty that shimmers in the yellow afternoons of October, who ever could clutch it? Go forth to find it, and it is gone: 't is only a mirage as you look from the windows of diligence.

2. The presence of a higher, namely, of the spiritual element is essential to its perfection. The high and divine beauty which can be loved without effeminacy, is that which is found in combination with the human will. Beauty is the mark God sets upon virtue. Every natural action is graceful. Every heroic act is also decent, and causes the place and the by-standers to shine. We are taught by great actions that the universe is the property of every individual in it. Every rational creature has all nature for his dowry and estate. It is his, if he will. He may divest himself of it; he may creep into a corner, and abdicate his kingdom, as most men do, but he is entitled to the world by his constitution. In proportion to the energy of his thought and will, he takes up the world into himself. "All those things for which men plough, build, or sail, obey virtue," said Sallust. "The winds and waves," said Gibbon, "are always on the side of the ablest navigators." So are the sun and moon and all the stars of heaven. When a noble act is done,—perchance in a scene of great natural beauty; when Leonidas and his three hundred martyrs consume one day in dying, and the sun and moon come each and look at them once in the steep defile of Thermopylæ; when Arnold Winkelried, in the high Alps, under the shadow of the avalanche, gathers in his side a sheaf of Austrian spears to break the line for his comrades; are not these heroes entitled to add the beauty of the scene to the beauty of the deed? When the bark of Columbus nears the shore of America;—before it, the beach lined with savages, fleeing out of all their huts of cane; the sea behind; and the purple mountains of the Indian Archipelago around, can we separate the man from the living picture? Does not the New World clothe his form with her palm-groves and savannahs as fit drapery? Ever does natural beauty steal in like air, and envelope great actions. When Sir Harry Vane was dragged

up the Tower-hill, sitting on a sled to suffer death, as the champion of the English laws, one of the multitude cried out to him, "You never sat on so glorious a seat." Charles II., to intimidate the citizens of London, caused the patriot Lord Russell to be drawn in an open coach, through the principal streets of the city, on his way to the scaffold. "But," his biographer says, "the multitude imagined they saw liberty and virtue sitting by his side." In private places, among sordid objects, an act of truth or heroism seems at once to draw to itself the sky as its temple, the sun as its candle. Nature stretcheth out her arms to embrace man, only let his thoughts be of equal greatness. Willingly does she follow his steps with the rose and the violet, and bend her lines of grandeur and grace to the decoration of her darling child. Only let his thoughts be of equal scope, and the frame will suit the picture. A virtuous man is in unison with her works, and makes the central figure of the visible sphere. Homer, Pindar, Socrates, Phocion, associate themselves fitly in our memory with the geography and climate of Greece. The visible heavens and earth sympathize with Jesus. And in common life, whosoever has seen a person of powerful character and happy genius will have remarked how easily he took all things along with him,—the persons, the opinions, and the day, and nature became ancillary to a man.

3. There is still another aspect under which the beauty of the world may be viewed, namely, as it becomes an object of the intellect. Beside the relation of things to virtue, they have a relation to thought. The intellect searches out the absolute order of things as they stand in the mind of God, and without the colors of affection. The intellectual and the active powers seem to succeed each other, and the exclusive activity of the one generates the exclusive activity of the other. There is something unfriendly in each to the other, but they are like the alternate periods of feeding and working in animals; each prepares and will be followed by the other. Therefore does beauty, which, in relation to actions, as we have seen, comes unsought, and comes because it is unsought, remain for the apprehension and pursuit of the intellect; and then again, in its turn, of the active power. Nothing divine dies. All good is eternally reproductive. The beauty of nature re-forms itself in the mind, and not for barren contemplation, but for new creation.

All men are in some degree impressed by the face of the

world; some men even to delight. This love of beauty is Taste. Others have the same love in such excess, that, not content with admiring, they seek to embody it in new forms. The creation of beauty is Art.

The production of a work of art throws a light upon the mystery of humanity. A work of art is an abstract or epitome of the world. It is the result or expression of nature, in miniature. For, although the works of nature are innumerable and all different, the result or the expression of them all is similar and single. Nature is a sea of forms radically alike and even unique. A leaf, a sunbeam, a landscape, the ocean, make an analogous impression on the mind. What is common to them all,—that perfectness and harmony, is beauty. The standard of beauty is the entire circuit of natural forms,—the totality of nature; which the Italians expressed by defining beauty "il più nell' uno." Nothing is quite beautiful alone; nothing but is beautiful in the whole. A single object is only so far beautiful as it suggests this universal grace. The poet, the painter, the sculptor, the musician, the architect, seek each to concentrate this radiance of the world on one point, and each in his several work to satisfy the love of beauty which stimulates him to produce. Thus is Art, a nature passed through the alembic of man. Thus in art, does nature work through the will of a man filled with the beauty of her first works.

The world thus exists to the soul to satisfy the desire of beauty. This element I call an ultimate end. No reason can be asked or given why the soul seeks beauty. Beauty, in its largest and profoundest sense, is one expression for the universe. God is the all-fair. Truth and goodness and beauty are but different faces of the same All. But beauty in nature is not ultimate. It is the herald of inward and internal beauty, and is not alone a solid and satisfactory good. It must stand as a part, and not as yet the last or highest expression of the final cause of Nature.

CHAPTER IV.

LANGUAGE.

Language is a third use which Nature subserves to man. Nature is the vehicle of thought, and in a simple, double, and threefold degree.

1. Words are signs of natural facts.

2. Particular natural facts are symbols of particular spiritual facts.

3. Nature is the symbol of spirit.

1. Words are signs of natural facts. The use of natural history is to give us aid in supernatural history: the use of the outer creation, to give us language for the beings and changes of the inward creation. Every word which is used to express a moral or intellectual fact, if traced to its root, is found to be borrowed from some material appearance. *Right* means *straight; wrong* means *twisted. Spirit* primarily means *wind; transgression,* the crossing of a *line; supercilious,* the *raising of the eyebrow.* We say the *heart* to express emotion, the *head* to denote thought; and *thought* and *emotion* are words borrowed from sensible things, and now appropriated to spiritual nature. Most of the process by which this transformation is made is hidden from us in the remote time when language was framed; but the same tendency may be daily observed in children. Children and savages use only nouns or names of things, which they convert into verbs, and apply to analogous mental acts.

2. But this origin of all words that convey a spiritual import—so conspicuous a fact in the history of language—is our least debt to nature. It is not words only that are emblematic; it is things which are emblematic. Every natural fact is a symbol of some spiritual fact. Every appearance in nature corresponds to some state of the mind, and that state of the mind can only be described by presenting that natural appearance as its picture. An enraged man is a lion, a cunning man is a fox, a firm man is a rock, a learned man is a torch. A lamb is innocence; a snake is subtle spite; flowers express to us the delicate affections. Light and darkness are our familiar expression for knowledge and ignorance; and heat

for love. Visible distance behind and before us is respectively our image of memory and hope.

Who looks upon a river in a meditative hour, and is not reminded of the flux of all things? Throw a stone into the stream, and the circles that propagate themselves are the beautiful type of all influence. Man is conscious of a universal soul within or behind his individual life, wherein, as in a firmament, the natures of Justice, Truth, Love, Freedom, arise and shine. This universal soul, he calls Reason: it is not mine or thine, or his, but we are its; we are its property and men. And the blue sky in which the private earth is buried, the sky with its eternal calm, and full of everlasting orbs, is the type of Reason. That which, intellectually considered, we call Reason, considered in relation to nature, we call Spirit. Spirit is the Creator. Spirit hath life in itself. And man in all ages and countries embodies it in his language, as the FATHER.

It is easily seen that there is nothing lucky or capricious in these analogies, but that they are constant, and pervade nature. These are not the dreams of a few poets, here and there, but man is an analogist, and studies relations in all objects. He is placed in the centre of beings, and a ray of relation passes from every other being to him. And neither can man be understood without these objects, nor these objects without man. All the facts in natural history taken by themselves have no value, but are barren like a single sex. But marry it to human history, and it is full of life. Whole Floras, all Linnæus's and Buffon's volumes, are dry catalogues of facts; but the most trivial of these facts, the habit of a plant, the organs, or work, or noise of an insect, applied to the illustration of a fact in intellectual philosophy, or, in any way, associated to human nature, affects us in the most lively and agreeable manner. The seed of a plant,—to what affecting analogies in the nature of man is that little fruit made use of, in all discourse, up to the voice of Paul, who calls the human corpse a seed,—"It is sown a natural body; it is raised a spiritual body." The motion of the earth round its axis, and round the sun, makes the day, and the year. These are certain amounts of brute light and heat. But is there no intent of an analogy between man's life and the seasons? And do the seasons gain no grandeur or pathos from that analogy? The instincts of the ant are very unimportant, considered as the ant's; but the moment a ray of relation is seen to extend from it to man, and the little drudge is seen to be a monitor, a little body with a mighty heart, then all its habits, even that said to be recently observed, that it never sleeps, become sublime.

Because of this radical correspondence between visible things and human thoughts, savages, who have only what is necessary, converse in figures. As we go back in history, language becomes more picturesque, until its infancy, when it is all poetry; or all spiritual facts are represented by natural symbols. The same symbols are found to make the original elements of all languages. It has moreover been observed, that the idioms of all languages approach each other in passages of the greatest eloquence and power. And as this is the first language, so is it the last. This immediate dependence of language upon nature, this conversion of an outward phenomenon into a type of somewhat in human life, never loses its power to affect us. It is this which gives that piquancy to the conversation of a strong-natured farmer or backwoodsman, which all men relish.

A man's power to connect his thought with its proper symbol, and so to utter it, depends on the simplicity of his character, that is, upon his love of truth, and his desire to communicate it without loss. The corruption of man is followed by the corruption of language. When simplicity of character and the sovereignty of ideas is broken up by the prevalence of secondary desires, the desire of riches, of pleasure, of power, and of praise,—and duplicity and falsehood take place of simplicity and truth, the power over nature as an interpreter of the will is in a degree lost; new imagery ceases to be created, and old words are perverted to stand for things which are not; a paper currency is employed, when there is no bullion in the vaults. In due time, the fraud is manifest, and words lose all power to stimulate the understanding or the affections. Hundreds of writers may be found in every long-civilized nation, who for a short time believe, and make others believe, that they see and utter truths, who do not of themselves clothe one thought in its natural garment, but who feed unconsciously on the language created by the primary writers of the country, those, namely, who hold primarily on nature.

But wise men pierce this rotten diction and fasten words again to visible things; so that picturesque language is at once a commanding certificate that he who employs it is a man in alliance with truth and God. The moment our discourse rises above the ground line of familiar facts, and is inflamed with passion or exalted by thought, it clothes itself in images. A man conversing in earnest, if he watch his intellectual processes, will find that a material image, more or less luminous, arises in his mind, cotemporaneous with every thought, which furnishes the vestment of the thought. Hence, good writing and brilliant discourse are perpetual allegories. This imagery is spontaneous. It is the blending of experience with the present action of the mind. It is proper creation. It is the working of the Original Cause through the instruments he has already made.

These facts may suggest the advantage which the country life possesses for a powerful mind, over the artificial and curtailed life of cities. We know more from nature than we can at will communicate. Its light flows into the mind evermore, and we forget its presence. The poet, the orator, bred in the woods, whose senses have been nourished by their fair and appeasing changes, year after year, without design and without heed,—shall not lose their lesson altogether, in the roar of cities or the broil of politics. Long hereafter, amidst agitation and terror in national councils,—in the hour of revolution,—these solid images shall reappear in their morning lustre, as fit symbols and words of the thoughts which the passing events shall awaken. At the call of a noble sentiment, again the woods wave, the pines murmur, the river rolls and shines, and the cattle low upon the mountains, as he saw and heard them in his infancy. And with these forms, the spells of persuasion, the keys of power are put into his hands.

3. We are thus assisted by natural objects in the expression of particular meanings. But how great a language to convey such pepper-corn informations! Did it need such noble races of creatures, this profusion of forms, this host of orbs in heaven, to furnish man with the dictionary and grammar of his municipal speech? Whilst we use this grand cipher to expedite the affairs of our pot and kettle, we feel that we have not yet put it to its use, neither are able. We are like travellers using the cinders of a volcano to roast their eggs. Whilst we see that it always stands ready to clothe what we would say, we cannot avoid the question, whether the characters are not significant of themselves. Have mountains, and waves, and skies, no significance but what we consciously give them, when we employ them as emblems of our thoughts? The

word is emblematic. Parts of speech are metaphors, because the whole of nature is a metaphor of the human mind. The laws of moral nature answer to those of matter as face to face in a glass. "The visible world and the relation of its parts, is the dial-plate of the invisible." The axioms of physics translate the laws of ethics. Thus, "the whole is greater than its part"; "reaction is equal to action"; "the smallest weight may be made to lift the greatest, the difference of weight being compensated by time"; and many the like propositions, which have an ethical as well as physical sense. These propositions have a much more extensive and universal sense when applied to human life, than when confined to technical use.

In like manner, the memorable words of history, and the proverbs of nations, consist usually of a natural fact, selected as a picture or parable of a moral truth. Thus; A rolling stone gathers no moss; A bird in the hand is worth two in the bush; A cripple in the right way will beat a racer in the wrong; Make hay while the sun shines; 'T is hard to carry a full cup even; Vinegar is the son of wine; The last ounce broke the camel's back; Long-lived trees make roots first; and the like. In their primary sense these are trivial facts, but we repeat them for the value of their analogical import. What is true of proverbs is true of all fables, parables, and allegories.

This relation between the mind and matter is not fancied by some poet, but stands in the will of God, and so is free to be known by all men. It appears to men, or it does not appear. When in fortunate hours we ponder this miracle, the wise man doubts, if, at all other times, he is not blind and deaf;

> "Can these things be,
> And overcome us like a summer's cloud,
> Without our special wonder?"

for the universe becomes transparent, and the light of higher laws than its own shines through it. It is the standing problem which has exercised the wonder and the study of every fine genius since the world began; from the era of the Egyptians and the Brahmins, to that of Pythagoras, of Plato, of Bacon, of Leibnitz, of Swedenborg. There sits the Sphinx at the roadside, and from age to age, as each prophet comes by, he tries his fortune at reading her riddle. There seems to be a necessity in spirit to manifest itself in material forms; and day and night, river and storm, beast and bird, acid and alkali, pre-exist in necessary Ideas in the mind of God, and are what they are by virtue of preceding affections, in the world of spirit. A Fact is the end or last issue of spirit. The visible creation is the terminus or the circumference of the invisible world. "Material objects," said a French philosopher, "are necessarily kinds of *scoriæ* of the substantial thoughts of the Creator, which must always preserve an exact relation to their first origin; in other words, visible nature must have a spiritual and moral side."

This doctrine is abstruse, and though the images of "garment," "scoriæ," "mirror," &c., may stimulate the fancy, we must summon the aid of subtler and more vital expositors to make it plain. "Every scripture is to be interpreted by the same spirit which gave it forth," is the fundamental law of criticism. A life in harmony with nature, the love of truth and of virtue, will purge the eyes to understand her text. By degrees we may come to know the primitive sense of the permanent objects of nature, so that the world shall be to us an open book, and every form significant of its hidden life and final cause.

A new interest surprises us, whilst, under the view now suggested, we contemplate the fearful extent and multitude of objects; since "every object rightly seen unlocks a new faculty of the soul." That which was unconscious truth becomes, when interpreted and defined in an object, a part of the domain of knowledge,—a new weapon in the magazine of power.

CHAPTER V.

DISCIPLINE.

In view of the significance of nature, we arrive at once at a new fact, that nature is a discipline. This use of the world includes the preceding uses, as parts of itself.

Space, time, society, labor, climate, food, locomotion, the animals, the mechanical forces, give us sincerest lessons, day by day, whose meaning is unlimited. They educate both the Understanding and the Reason. Every property of matter is a school for the understanding,—its solidity or resistance, its inertia, its extension, its figure, its divisibility. The under-standing adds, divides, combines, measures, and finds nutri-ment and room for its activity in this worthy scene. Mean-time, Reason transfers all these lessons into its own world of thought, by perceiving the analogy that marries Matter and Mind.

1. Nature is a discipline of the understanding in intellectual truths. Our dealing with sensible objects is a constant exer-cise in the necessary lessons of difference, of likeness, of order, of being and seeming, of progressive arrangement; of ascent from particular to general; of combination to one end of manifold forces. Proportioned to the importance of the organ to be formed, is the extreme care with which its tuition is provided,—a care pretermitted in no single case. What tedious training, day after day, year after year, never ending, to form the common sense; what continual reproduction of annoyances, inconveniences, dilemmas; what rejoicing over us of little men; what disputing of prices, what reckonings of interest,—and all to form the Hand of the mind;—to instruct us that "good thoughts are no better than good dreams, unless they be executed!"

The same good office is performed by Property and its filial systems of debt and credit. Debt, grinding debt, whose iron face the widow, the orphan, and the sons of genius fear and hate;—debt, which consumes so much time, which so cripples and disheartens a great spirit with cares that seem so base, is a preceptor whose lessons cannot be foregone, and is needed most by those who suffer from it most. Moreover, property, which has been well compared to snow,—"if it fall level to-day, it will be blown into drifts to-morrow,"—is the surface action of internal machinery, like the index on the face of a clock. Whilst now it is the gymnastics of the under-standing, it is hiving in the foresight of the spirit, experience in profounder laws.

The whole character and fortune of the individual are af-fected by the least inequalities in the culture of the under-standing; for example, in the perception of differences. There-fore is Space, and therefore Time, that man may know that things are not huddled and lumped, but sundered and in-dividual. A bell and a plough have each their use, and neither can do the office of the other. Water is good to drink, coal to burn, wool to wear; but wool cannot be drunk, nor water spun, nor coal eaten. The wise man shows his

wisdom in separation, in gradation, and his scale of creatures and of merits is as wide as nature. The foolish have no
range in their scale, but suppose every man is as every other
man. What is not good they call the worst, and what is not
hateful, they call the best.

In like manner, what good heed, Nature forms in us! She
pardons no mistakes. Her yea is yea, and her nay, nay.

The first steps in Agriculture, Astronomy, Zoölogy (those
first steps which the farmer, the hunter, and the sailor take),
teach that Nature's dice are always loaded; that in her heaps
and rubbish are concealed sure and useful results.

How calmly and genially the mind apprehends one after
another the laws of physics! What noble emotions dilate the
mortal as he enters into the counsels of the creation, and
feels by knowledge the privilege to BE! His insight refines
him. The beauty of nature shines in his own breast. Man is
greater that he can see this, and the universe less, because
Time and Space relations vanish as laws are known.

Here again we are impressed and even daunted by the immense Universe to be explored. "What we know, is a point
to what we do not know." Open any recent journal of science,
and weigh the problems suggested concerning Light, Heat,
Electricity, Magnetism, Physiology, Geology, and judge
whether the interest of natural science is likely to be soon
exhausted.

Passing by many particulars of the discipline of nature, we
must not omit to specify two.

The exercise of the Will or the lesson of power is taught in
every event. From the child's successive possession of his
several senses up to the hour when he saith, "Thy will be
done!" he is learning the secret, that he can reduce under
his will, not only particular events, but great classes, nay the
whole series of events, and so conform all facts to his character. Nature is thoroughly mediate. It is made to serve. It
receives the dominion of man as meekly as the ass on which
the Saviour rode. It offers all its kingdoms to man as the
raw material which he may mould into what is useful. He is
never weary of working it up. He forges the subtile and
delicate air into wise and melodious words, and gives them
wing as angels of persuasion and command. One after another, his victorious thought comes up with and reduces all
things, until the world becomes, at last, only a realized will,
—the double of the man.

2. Sensible objects conform to the premonitions of Reason and reflect the conscience. All things are moral; and in their boundless changes have an unceasing reference to spiritual nature. Therefore is nature glorious with form, color, and motion, that every globe in the remotest heaven; every chemical change from the rudest crystal up to the laws of life; every change of vegetation from the first principle of growth in the eye of a leaf, to the tropical forest and ante-diluvian coal-mine; every animal function from the sponge up to Hercules, shall hint or thunder to man the laws of right and wrong, and echo the Ten Commandments. Therefore is nature ever the ally of Religion: lends all her pomp and riches to the religious sentiment. Prophet and priest, David, Isaiah, Jesus, have drawn deeply from this source. This ethical character so penetrates the bone and marrow of nature, as to seem the end for which it was made. Whatever private purpose is answered by any member or part, this is its public and universal function, and is never omitted. Nothing in nature is exhausted in its first use. When a thing has served an end to the uttermost, it is wholly new for an ulterior service. In God, every end is converted into a new means. Thus the use of commodity, regarded by itself, is mean and squalid. But it is to the mind an education in the doctrine of Use, namely, that a thing is good only so far as it serves; that a conspiring of parts and efforts to the production of an end, is essential to any being. The first and gross manifestation of this truth is our inevitable and hated training in values and wants, in corn and meat.

It has already been illustrated, that every natural process is a version of a moral sentence. The moral law lies at the centre of nature and radiates to the circumference. It is the pith and marrow of every substance, every relation, and every process. All things with which we deal preach to us. What is a farm but a mute gospel? The chaff and the wheat, weeds and plants, blight, rain, insects, sun,—it is a sacred emblem from the first furrow of spring to the last stack which the snow of winter overtakes in the fields. But the sailor, the shepherd, the miner, the merchant, in their several resorts, have each an experience precisely parallel, and leading to the same conclusion: because all organizations are radically alike. Nor can it be doubted that this moral sentiment which thus scents the air, grows in the grain, and impregnates the waters of the world, is caught by man and sinks into his soul. The moral influence of nature upon every individual is that amount of truth which it illustrates to him. Who can estimate this? Who can guess how much firmness the sea-beaten rock has taught the fisherman? how much tranquillity has been reflected to man from the azure sky, over whose unspotted deeps the winds forevermore drive flocks of stormy clouds, and leave no wrinkle or stain? how much industry and providence and affection we have caught from the pantomime of brutes? What a searching preacher of self-command is the varying phenomenon of Health!

Herein is especially apprehended the unity of Nature,—the unity in variety,—which meets us everywhere. All the endless variety of things make an identical impression. Xenophanes complained in his old age, that, look where he would, all things hastened back to unity: he was weary of seeing the same entity in the tedious variety of forms. The fable of Proteus has a cordial truth. A leaf, a drop, a crystal, a moment of time is related to the whole, and partakes of the perfection of the whole. Each particle is a microcosm, and faithfully renders the likeness of the world.

Not only resemblances exist in things whose analogy is obvious, as when we detect the type of the human hand in the flipper of the fossil saurus, but also in objects wherein there is great superficial unlikeness. Thus architecture is called "frozen music," by De Stael and Goethe. Vitruvius thought an architect should be a musician. "A Gothic church," said Coleridge, "is a petrified religion." Michael Angelo maintained, that, to an architect, a knowledge of anatomy is essential. In Haydn's oratorios, the notes present to the imagination not only motions, as, of the snake, the stag, and the elephant, but colors also; as the green grass. The law of harmonic sounds reappears in the harmonic colors. The granite is differenced in its laws only by the more or less of heat, from the river that wears it away. The river, as it flows, resembles the air that flows over it; the air resembles the light which traverses it with more subtile currents; the light resembles the heat which rides with it through Space. Each creature is only a modification of the other; the likeness in them is more than the difference, and their radical law is one and the same. A rule of one art, or a law of one organization, holds true throughout nature. So intimate is this Unity, that, it is easily seen, it lies under the undermost garment of nature, and betrays its source in Universal Spirit.

For it pervades Thought also. Every universal truth which
we express in words implies or supposes every other truth.
Omne verum vero consonat. It is like a great circle on a
sphere, comprising all possible circles; which, however, may
be drawn, and comprise it, in like manner. Every such truth
is the absolute Ens seen from one side. But it has innumerable
sides.

The central Unity is still more conspicuous in actions.
Words are finite organs of the infinite mind. They cannot
cover the dimensions of what is in truth. They break, chop,
and impoverish it. An action is the perfection and publication
of thought. A right action seems to fill the eye, and to be
related to all nature. "The wise man, in doing one thing,
does all; or, in the one thing he does rightly, he sees the likeness of all which is done rightly."

Words and actions are not the attributes of brute nature.
They introduce us to the human form, of which all other organizations appear to be degradations. When this appears
among so many that surround it, the spirit prefers it to all
others. It says: "From such as this have I drawn joy and
knowledge; in such as this have I found and beheld myself;
I will speak to it; it can speak again; it can yield me thought
already formed and alive." In fact, the eye—the mind—is
always accompanied by these forms, male and female; and
these are incomparably the richest informations of the power
and order that lie at the heart of things. Unfortunately, every
one of them bears the marks as of some injury; is marred
and superficially defective. Nevertheless, far different from
the deaf and dumb nature around them, these all rest like
fountain-pipes on the unfathomed sea of thought and virtue
whereto they alone, of all organizations, are the entrances.

It were a pleasant inquiry to follow into detail their ministry to our education, but where would it stop? We are associated in adolescent and adult life with some friends, who,
like skies and waters, are coextensive with our idea; who, answering each to a certain affection of the soul, satisfy our desire on that side; whom we lack power to put at such focal
distance from us, that we can mend or even analyze them.
We cannot choose but love them. When much intercourse
with a friend has supplied us with a standard of excellence,
and has increased our respect for the resources of God who
thus sends a real person to outgo our ideal; when he has,
moreover, become an object of thought, and, whilst his char-

acter retains all its unconscious effect, is converted in the mind into solid and sweet wisdom,—it is a sign to us that his office is closing, and he is commonly withdrawn from our sight in a short time.

CHAPTER VI.

IDEALISM.

Thus is the unspeakable but intelligible and practicable meaning of the world conveyed to man, the immortal pupil, in every object of sense. To this one end of Discipline, all parts of nature conspire.

A noble doubt perpetually suggests itself, whether this end be not the Final Cause of the Universe; and whether nature outwardly exists. It is a sufficient account of that Appearance we call the World, that God will teach a human mind, and so makes it the receiver of a certain number of congruent sensations, which we call sun and moon, man and woman, house and trade. In my utter impotence to test the authenticity of the report of my senses, to know whether the impressions they make on me correspond with outlying objects, what difference does it make, whether Orion is up there in heaven, or some god paints the image in the firmament of the soul? The relations of parts and the end of the whole remaining the same, what is the difference, whether land and sea interact, and worlds revolve and intermingle without number or end,—deep yawning under deep, and galaxy balancing galaxy, throughout absolute space,—or, whether, without relations of time and space, the same appearances are inscribed in the constant faith of man? Whether nature enjoy a substantial existence without, or is only in the apocalypse of the mind, it is alike useful and alike venerable to me. Be it what it may, it is ideal to me, so long as I cannot try the accuracy of my senses.

The frivolous make themselves merry with the Ideal theory, as if its consequences were burlesque; as if it affected the stability of nature. It surely does not. God never jests with us, and will not compromise the end of nature, by permitting any inconsequence in its procession. Any distrust of the permanence of laws would paralyze the faculties of man. Their permanence is sacredly respected, and his faith therein is perfect. The wheels and springs of man are all set to the hypothesis of the permanence of nature. We are not built like a ship to be tossed, but like a house to stand. It is a natural consequence of this structure, that, so long as the active powers predominate over the reflective, we resist with indignation any hint that nature is more short-lived or mutable than spirit. The broker, the wheelwright, the carpenter, the tollman, are much displeased at the intimation.

But whilst we acquiesce entirely in the permanence of natural laws, the question of the absolute existence of nature still remains open. It is the uniform effect of culture on the human mind, not to shake our faith in the stability of particular phenomena, as of heat, water, azote; but to lead us to regard nature as a phenomenon, not a substance; to attribute necessary existence to spirit; to esteem nature as an accident and an effect.

To the senses and the unrenewed understanding belongs a sort of instinctive belief in the absolute existence of nature. In their view, man and nature are indissolubly joined. Things are ultimates, and they never look beyond their sphere. The presence of Reason mars this faith. The first effort of thought tends to relax this despotism of the senses, which binds us to nature as if we were a part of it, and shows us nature aloof, and, as it were, afloat. Until this higher agency intervened, the animal eye sees, with wonderful accuracy, sharp outlines and colored surfaces. When the eye of Reason opens, to outline and surface are at once added grace and expression. These proceed from imagination and affection, and abate somewhat of the angular distinctness of objects. If the Reason be stimulated to more earnest vision, outlines and surfaces become transparent, and are no longer seen; causes and spirits are seen through them. The best moments of life are these delicious awakenings of the higher powers, and the reverential withdrawing of nature before its God.

Let us proceed to indicate the effects of culture.

1. Our first institution in the Ideal philosophy is a hint from Nature herself.

Nature is made to conspire with spirit to emancipate us. Certain mechanical changes, a small alteration in our local position apprises us of a dualism. We are strangely affected by seeing the shore from a moving ship, from a balloon, or through the tints of an unusual sky. The least change in our point of view gives the whole world a pictorial air. A man who seldom rides needs only to get into a coach and traverse his own town, to turn the street into a puppet-show. The men, the women,—talking, running, bartering, fighting,—the earnest mechanic, the lounger, the beggar, the boys, the dogs, are unrealized at once, or at least wholly detached from all relation to the observer, and seen as apparent, not substantial beings. What new thoughts are suggested by seeing a face of country quite familiar, in the rapid movement of the railroad car! Nay, the most wonted objects (make a very slight change in the point of vision) please us most. In a camera obscura, the butcher's cart and the figure of one of our own family amuse us. So a portrait of a well-known face gratifies us. Turn the eyes upside down, by looking at the landscape through your legs, and how agreeable is the picture, though you have seen it any time these twenty years!

In these cases, by mechanical means, is suggested the difference between the observer and the spectacle, between man and nature. Hence arises a pleasure mixed with awe; I may say, a low degree of the sublime is felt from the fact, probably, that man is hereby apprised, that, whilst the world is a spectacle, something in himself is stable.

2. In a higher manner, the poet communicates the same pleasure. By a few strokes he delineates, as on air, the sun, the mountain, the camp, the city, the hero, the maiden, not different from what we know them, but only lifted from the ground and afloat before the eye. He unfixes the land and the sea, makes them revolve around the axis of his primary thought, and disposes them anew. Possessed himself by a heroic passion, he uses matter as symbols of it. The sensual man conforms thoughts to things; the poet conforms things to his thoughts. The one esteems nature as rooted and fast; the other, as fluid, and impresses his being thereon. To him, the refractory world is ductile and flexible; he invests dust and stones with humanity, and makes them the words of the Reason. The Imagination may be defined to be, the use which the Reason makes of the material world. Shakespeare possesses the power of subordinating nature for the purposes of expression, beyond all poets. His imperial muse tosses the creation like a bauble from hand to hand, and uses it to embody any caprice of thought that is uppermost in his mind. The remotest spaces of nature are visited, and the farthest

sundered things are brought together, by a subtle spiritual connection. We are made aware that magnitude of material things is relative, and all objects shrink and expand to serve the passion of the poet. Thus, in his sonnets, the lays of birds, the scents and dyes of flowers, he finds to be the *shadow* of his beloved; time, which keeps her from him, is his *chest;* the suspicion she has awakened is her *ornament;*

> The ornament of beauty is Suspect,
> A crow which flies in heaven's sweetest air.

His passion is not the fruit of chance; it swells, as he speaks, to a city, or a state.

> No, it was builded far from accident;
> It suffers not in smiling pomp, nor falls
> Under the brow of thralling discontent;
> It fears not policy, that heretic,
> That works on leases of short numbered hours,
> But all alone stands hugely politic.

In the strength of his constancy, the Pyramids seem to him recent and transitory. The freshness of youth and love dazzles him with its resemblance to morning.

> Take those lips away
> Which so sweetly were forsworn;
> And those eyes,—the break of day,
> Lights that do mislead the morn.

The wild beauty of this hyperbole, I may say, in passing, it would not be easy to match in literature.

This transfiguration which all material objects undergo through the passion of the poet,—this power which he exerts to dwarf the great, to magnify the small,—might be illustrated by a thousand examples from his Plays. I have before me the Tempest, and will cite only these few lines.

> ARIEL.   The strong based promontory
> Have I made shake, and by the spurs plucked up
> The pine and cedar.

Prospero calls for music to soothe the frantic Alonzo, and his companions;

> A solemn air, and the best comforter
> To an unsettled fancy, cure thy brains
> Now useless, boiled within thy skull.

Again;

> The charm dissolves apace,
> And, as the morning steals upon the night,
> Melting the darkness, so their rising senses
> Begin to chase the ignorant fumes that mantle
> Their clearer reason.
>   Their understanding
> Begins to swell: and the approaching tide
> Will shortly fill the reasonable shores
> That now lie foul and muddy.

The perception of real affinities between events (that is to say, of *ideal* affinities, for those only are real) enables the poet thus to make free with the most imposing forms and phenomena of the world, and to assert the predominance of the soul.

3. Whilst thus the poet animates nature with his own thoughts, he differs from the philosopher only herein, that the one proposes Beauty as his main end; the other Truth. But the philosopher, not less than the poet, postpones the apparent order and relations of things to the empire of thought. "The problem of philosophy," according to Plato, "is, for all that exists conditionally, to find a ground unconditioned and absolute." It proceeds on the faith that a law determines all phenomena, which being known, the phenomena can be predicted. That law, when in the mind, is an idea. Its beauty is infinite. The true philosopher and the true poet are one, and a beauty, which is truth, and a truth, which is beauty, is the aim of both. Is not the charm of one of Plato's or Aristotle's definitions, strictly like that of the Antigone of Sophocles? It is, in both cases, that a spiritual life has been imparted to nature; that the solid seeming block of matter has been pervaded and dissolved by a thought; that this feeble human being has penetrated the vast masses of nature with an informing soul, and recognized itself in their harmony, that is, seized their law. In physics, when this is attained, the memory disburdens itself of its cumbrous catalogues of particulars, and carries centuries of observation in a single formula.

Thus even in physics, the material is degraded before the spiritual. The astronomer, the geometer, rely on their irrefragable analysis, and disdain the results of observation. The sublime remark of Euler on his law of arches, "This will be found contrary to all experience, yet is true," had already transferred nature into the mind, and left matter like an outcast corpse.

4. Intellectual science has been observed to beget invariably a doubt of the existence of matter. Turgot said, "He that has never doubted the existence of matter may be assured he has no aptitude for metaphysical inquiries." It fastens the attention upon immortal necessary uncreated natures, that is, upon Ideas; and in their presence, we feel that the outward circumstance is a dream and a shade. Whilst we wait in this Olympus of gods, we think of nature as an appendix to the soul. We ascend into their region, and know that these are the thoughts of the Supreme Being. "These are they who were set up from everlasting, from the beginning, or ever the earth was. When he prepared the heavens, they were there; when he established the clouds above, when he strengthened the fountains of the deep. Then they were by him, as one brought up with him. Of them took he counsel."

Their influence is proportionate. As objects of science, they are accessible to few men. Yet all men are capable of being raised by piety or by passion into their region. And no man touches these divine natures, without becoming, in some degree, himself divine. Like a new soul, they renew the body. We become physically nimble and lightsome; we tread on air; life is no longer irksome, and we think it will never be so. No man fears age or misfortune or death, in their serene company, for he is transported out of the district of change. Whilst we behold unveiled the nature of Justice and Truth, we learn the difference between the absolute and the conditional or relative. We apprehend the absolute. As it were, for the first time, *we exist*. We become immortal, for we learn that time and space are relations of matter; that, with a perception of truth, or a virtuous will, they have no affinity.

5. Finally, religion and ethics, which may be fitly called, —the practice of ideas, or the introduction of ideas into life,—have an analogous effect with all lower culture, in degrading nature and suggesting its dependence on spirit. Ethics and religion differ herein; that the one is the system of human duties commencing from man; the other, from God. Religion includes the personality of God; Ethics does not. They are one to our present design. They both put nature under foot. The first and last lesson of religion is, "The things that are seen, are temporal; the things that are unseen, are eternal." It puts an affront upon nature. It does that for the unschooled, which philosophy does for Berkeley and

Viasa. The uniform language that may be heard in the churches of the most ignorant sects, is, "Contemn the unsubstantial shows of the world; they are vanities, dreams, shadows, unrealities; seek the realities of religion." The devotee flouts nature. Some theosophists have arrived at a certain hostility and indignation towards matter, as the Manichean and Plotinus. They distrusted in themselves any looking back to these flesh-pots of Egypt. Plotinus was ashamed of his body. In short, they might all say of matter, what Michael Angelo said of external beauty, "It is the frail and weary weed, in which God dresses the soul, which he has called into time."

It appears that motion, poetry, physical and intellectual science, and religion, all tend to affect our convictions of the reality of the external world. But I own there is something ungrateful in expanding too curiously the particulars of the general proposition, that all culture tends to imbue us with idealism. I have no hostility to nature, but a child's love to it. I expand and live in the warm day like corn and melons. Let us speak her fair. I do not wish to fling stones at my beautiful mother, nor soil my gentle nest. I only wish to indicate the true position of nature in regard to man, wherein to establish man, all right education tends; as the ground which to attain is the object of human life, that is, of man's connection with nature. Culture inverts the vulgar views of nature, and brings the mind to call that apparent, which it uses to call real, and that real, which it uses to call visionary. Children, it is true, believe in the external world. The belief that it appears only, is an afterthought, but with culture, this faith will as surely arise on the mind as did the first.

The advantage of the ideal theory over the popular faith is this, that it presents the world in precisely that view which is most desirable to the mind. It is, in fact, the view which Reason, both speculative and practical, that is, philosophy and virtue, take. For, seen in the light of thought, the world always is phenomenal; and virtue subordinates it to the mind. Idealism sees the world in God. It beholds the whole circle of persons and things, of actions and events, of country and religion, not as painfully accumulated, atom after atom, act after act, in an aged creeping Past, but as one vast picture, which God paints on the instant eternity, for the contemplation of the soul. Therefore the soul holds itself off from a too trivial and microscopic study of the universal tablet. It respects the end too much, to immerse itself in the means. It sees something more important in Christianity than the scandals of ecclesiastical history, or the niceties of criticism; and, very incurious concerning persons or miracles, and not at all disturbed by chasms of historical evidence, it accepts from God the phenomenon, as it finds it, as the pure and awful form of religion in the world. It is not hot and passionate at the appearance of what it calls its own good or bad fortune, at the union or opposition of other persons. No man is its enemy. It accepts whatsoever befalls, as part of its lesson. It is a watcher more than a doer, and it is as a doer, only that it may the better watch.

CHAPTER VII.

SPIRIT.

It is essential to a true theory of nature and of man, that it should contain somewhat progressive. Uses that are exhausted or that may be, and facts that end in the statement, cannot be all that is true of this brave lodging wherein man is harbored, and wherein all his faculties find appropriate and endless exercise. And all the uses of nature admit of being summed in one, which yields the activity of man an infinite scope. Through all its kingdoms, to the suburbs and outskirts of things, it is faithful to the cause whence it had its origin. It always speaks of Spirit. It suggests the absolute. It is a perpetual effect. It is a great shadow pointing always to the sun behind us.

The aspect of nature is devout. Like the figure of Jesus, she stands with bended head, and hands folded upon the breast. The happiest man is he who learns from nature the lesson of worship.

Of that ineffable essence which we call Spirit, he that thinks most, will say least. We can foresee God in the coarse, as it were, distant phenomena of matter; but when we try to define and describe himself, both language and thought desert us, and we are as helpless as fools and savages. That essence refuses to be recorded in propositions, but when man has worshipped him intellectually, the noblest ministry of nature is to stand as the apparition of God. It is the organ through which the universal spirit speaks to the individual, and strives to lead back the individual to it.

When we consider Spirit, we see that the views already presented do not include the whole circumference of man. We must add some related thoughts.

Three problems are put by nature to the mind; What is matter? Whence is it? and Whereto? The first of these questions only, the ideal theory answers. Idealism saith: matter is a phenomenon, not a substance. Idealism acquaints us with the total disparity between the evidence of our own being, and the evidence of the world's being. The one is perfect; the other, incapable of any assurance; the mind is a part of the nature of things; the world is a divine dream, from which we may presently awake to the glories and certainties of day. Idealism is a hypothesis to account for nature by other principles than those of carpentry and chemistry. Yet, if it only deny the existence of matter, it does not satisfy the demands of the spirit. It leaves God out of me. It leaves me in the splendid labyrinth of my perceptions, to wander without end. Then the heart resists it, because it balks the affections in denying substantive being to men and women. Nature is so pervaded with human life, that there is something of humanity in all, and in every particular. But this theory makes nature foreign to me, and does not account for that consanguinity which we acknowledge to it.

Let it stand, then, in the present state of our knowledge, merely as a useful introductory hypothesis, serving to apprise us of the eternal distinction between the soul and the world.

But when, following the invisible steps of thought, we come to inquire, Whence is matter? and Whereto? many truths arise to us out of the recesses of consciousness. We learn that the highest is present to the soul of man, that the dread universal essence, which is not wisdom, or love, or beauty, or power, but all in one, and each entirely, is that for which all things exist, and that by which they are; that spirit creates; that behind nature, throughout nature, spirit is present; one and not compound, it does not act upon us from without, that is, in space and time, but spiritually, or through ourselves: therefore, that spirit, that is, the Supreme Being, does not build up nature around us, but puts it forth through us, as the life of the tree puts forth new branches and leaves through the pores of the old. As a plant upon the earth, so a man rests upon the bosom of God; he is nourished by unfailing fountains, and draws, at his need, inexhaustible power. Who can set bounds to the possibilities of man? Once inhale the upper air, being admitted to behold the absolute natures of justice and truth, and we learn that man has access to the entire mind of the Creator, is himself the creator in the finite. This view, which admonishes me where the sources of wisdom and power lie, and points to virtue as to

> "The golden key
> Which opes the palace of eternity,"

carries upon its face the highest certificate of truth, because it animates me to create my own world through the purification of my soul.

The world proceeds from the same spirit as the body of man. It is a remoter and inferior incarnation of God, a projection of God in the unconscious. But it differs from the body in one important respect. It is not, like that, now subjected to the human will. Its serene order is inviolable by us. It is, therefore, to us, the present expositor of the divine mind. It is a fixed point whereby we may measure our departure. As we degenerate, the contrast between us and our house is more evident. We are as much strangers in nature, as we are aliens from God. We do not understand the notes of birds. The fox and the deer run away from us; the bear and tiger rend us. We do not know the uses of more than a few plants, as corn and the apple, the potato and the vine. Is not the landscape, every glimpse of which hath a grandeur, a face of him? Yet this may show us what discord is between man and nature, for you cannot freely admire a noble landscape, if laborers are digging in the field hard by. The poet finds something ridiculous in his delight, until he is out of the sight of men.

CHAPTER VIII.

PROSPECTS.

In inquiries respecting the laws of the world and the frame of things, the highest reason is always the truest. That which seems faintly possible—it is so refined, is often faint and dim because it is deepest seated in the mind among the eternal verities. Empirical science is apt to cloud the sight, and, by the very knowledge of functions and processes, to bereave the student of the manly contemplation of the whole. The savant becomes unpoetic. But the best read naturalist who lends an entire and devout attention to truth, will see that there remains much to learn of his relation to the world, and that it is not to be learned by any addition or subtraction or other comparison of known quantities, but is arrived at by untaught sallies of the spirit, by a continual self-recovery, and by entire humility. He will perceive that there are far more excellent qualities in the student than preciseness and infallibility; that a guess is often more fruitful than an indisputable affirmation, and that a dream may let us deeper into the secret of nature than a hundred concerted experiments.

For, the problems to be solved are precisely those which the physiologist and the naturalist omit to state. It is not so pertinent to man to know all the individuals of the animal kingdom, as it is to know whence and whereto is this tyrannizing unity in his constitution, which evermore separates and classifies things, endeavoring to reduce the most diverse to one form. When I behold a rich landscape, it is less to my purpose to recite correctly the order and superposition of the strata, than to know why all thought of multitude is lost in a tranquil sense of unity. I cannot greatly honor minuteness in details, so long as there is no hint to explain the relation between things and thoughts; no ray upon the *metaphysics* of conchology, of botany, of the arts, to show the relation of the forms of flowers, shells, animals, architecture, to the mind, and build science upon ideas. In a cabinet of natural history, we become sensible of a certain occult recognition and sympathy in regard to the most unwieldy and eccentric forms of beast, fish, and insect. The American who has been confined, in his own country, to the sight of buildings designed after foreign models, is surprised on entering York Minster or St. Peter's at Rome, by the feeling that these structures are imitations also,—faint copies of an invisible archetype. Nor has science sufficient humanity, so long as the naturalist overlooks that wonderful congruity which subsists between man and the world; of which he is lord, not because he is the most subtile inhabitant, but because he is its head and heart, and finds something of him-

self in every great and small thing, in every mountain
stratum, in every new law of color, fact of astronomy, or
atmospheric influence which observation or analysis lay open.
A perception of this mystery inspires the muse of George
Herbert, the beautiful psalmist of the seventeenth century.
The following lines are part of his little poem on Man.

> "Man is all symmetry,
> Full of proportions, one limb to another,
> And to all the world besides.
> Each part may call the farthest, brother;
> For head with foot hath private amity,
> And both with moons and tides.
>
> "Nothing hath got so far
> But man hath caught and kept it as his prey;
> His eyes dismount the highest star;
> He is in little all the sphere.
> Herbs gladly cure our flesh, because that they
> Find their acquaintance there.
>
> "For us, the winds do blow,
> The earth doth rest, heaven move, and fountains flow;
> Nothing we see, but means our good,
> As our delight, or as our treasure;
> The whole is either our cupboard of food,
> Or cabinet of pleasure.
>
> "The stars have us to bed:
> Night draws the curtain; which the sun withdraws.
> Music and light attend our head.
> All things unto our flesh are kind,
> In their descent and being; to our mind,
> In their ascent and cause.
>
> "More servants wait on man
> Than he'll take notice of. In every path,
> He treads down that which doth befriend him
> When sickness makes him pale and wan.
> O mighty love! Man is one world, and hath
> Another to attend him."

The perception of this class of truths makes the attraction
which draws men to science, but the end is lost sight of in
attention to the means. In view of this half-sight of science,
we accept the sentence of Plato, that "poetry comes nearer
to vital truth than history." Every surmise and vaticination
of the mind is entitled to a certain respect, and we learn to
prefer imperfect theories, and sentences, which contain
glimpses of truth, to digested systems which have no one

valuable suggestion. A wise writer will feel that the ends of study and composition are best answered by announcing undiscovered regions of thought, and so communicating, through hope, new activity to the torpid spirit.

I shall therefore conclude this essay with some traditions of man and nature, which a certain poet sang to me; and which, as they have always been in the world, and perhaps reappear to every bard, may be both history and prophecy.

'The foundations of man are not in matter, but in spirit. But the element of spirit is eternity. To it, therefore, the longest series of events, the oldest chronologies are young and recent. In the cycle of the universal man, from whom the known individuals proceed, centuries are points, and all history is but the epoch of one degradation.

'We distrust and deny inwardly our sympathy with nature. We own and disown our relation to it, by turns. We are, like Nebuchadnezzar, dethroned, bereft of reason, and eating grass like an ox. But who can set limits to the remedial force of spirit?

'A man is a god in ruins. When men are innocent, life shall be longer, and shall pass into the immortal, as gently as we awake from dreams. Now, the world would be insane and rabid, if these disorganizations should last for hundreds of years. It is kept in check by death and infancy. Infancy is the perpetual Messiah, which comes into the arms of fallen men, and pleads with them to return to paradise.

'Man is the dwarf of himself. Once he was permeated and dissolved by spirit. He filled nature with his overflowing currents. Out from him sprang the sun and moon; from man, the sun; from woman, the moon. The laws of his mind, the periods of his actions externized themselves into day and night, into the year and the seasons. But, having made for himself this huge shell, his waters retired; he no longer fills the veins and veinlets; he is shrunk to a drop. He sees, that the structure still fits him, but fits him colossally. Say, rather, once it fitted him, now it corresponds to him from far and on high. He adores timidly his own work. Now is man the follower of the sun, and woman the follower of the moon. Yet sometimes he starts in his slumber, and wonders at himself and his house, and muses strangely at the resemblance betwixt him and it. He perceives that if his law is still paramount, if still he have elemental power, if his word is sterling yet in nature, it is not conscious power, it is not inferior but superior to his will. It is Instinct.' Thus my Orphic poet sang.

At present, man applies to nature but half his force. He works on the world with his understanding alone. He lives in it, and masters it by a penny-wisdom; and he that works most in it, is but a half-man, and whilst his arms are strong and his digestion good, his mind is imbruted, and he is a selfish savage. His relation to nature, his power over it, is through the understanding; as by manure; the economic use of fire, wind, water, and the mariner's needle; steam, coal, chemical agriculture; the repairs of the human body by the dentist and the surgeon. This is such a resumption of power, as if a banished king should buy his territories inch by inch, instead of vaulting at once into his throne. Meantime, in the thick darkness, there are not wanting gleams of a better light, —occasional examples of the action of man upon nature with his entire force,—with reason as well as understanding. Such examples are; the traditions of miracles in the earliest antiquity of all nations; the history of Jesus Christ; the achievements of a principle, as in religious and political revolutions, and in the abolition of the Slave-trade; the miracles of enthusiasm, as those reported of Swedenborg, Hohenlohe, and the Shakers; many obscure and yet contested facts, now arranged under the name of Animal Magnetism; prayer; eloquence; self-healing; and the wisdom of children. These are examples of Reason's momentary grasp of the sceptre; the exertions of a power which exists not in time or space, but an instantaneous in-streaming causing power. The difference between the actual and the ideal force of man is happily figured by the schoolmen, in saying, that the knowledge of man is an evening knowledge, *vespertina cognitio*, but that of God is a morning knowledge, *matutina cognitio*.

The problem of restoring to the world original and eternal beauty, is solved by the redemption of the soul. The ruin or the blank, that we see when we look at nature, is in our own eye. The axis of vision is not coincident with the axis of things, and so they appear not transparent but opaque. The reason why the world lacks unity, and lies broken and in heaps, is, because man is disunited with himself. He cannot be a naturalist, until he satisfies all the demands of the spirit. Love is as much its demand, as perception. Indeed, neither can be perfect without the other. In the uttermost meaning of the words, thought is devout, and devotion is thought. Deep calls unto deep. But in actual life, the marriage is not celebrated. There are innocent men who worship God after the tradition of their fathers, but their sense of duty has not yet extended to the use of all their faculties. And there are patient naturalists, but they freeze their subject under the wintry light of the understanding. Is not prayer also a study of truth,—a sally of the soul into the unfound infinite? No man ever prayed heartily, without learning something. But when a faithful thinker, resolute to detach every object from personal relations, and see it in the light of thought, shall, at the same time, kindle science with the fire of the holiest affections, then will God go forth anew into the creation.

It will not need, when the mind is prepared for study, to search for objects. The invariable mark of wisdom is to see the miraculous in the common. What is a day? What is a year? What is summer? What is woman? What is a child? What is sleep? To our blindness, these things seem unaffecting. We make fables to hide the baldness of the fact and conform it, as we say, to the higher law of the mind. But when the fact is seen under the light of an idea, the gaudy fable fades and shrivels. We behold the real higher law. To the wise, therefore, a fact is true poetry, and the most beautiful of fables. These wonders are brought to our own door. You also are a man. Man and woman, and their social life, poverty, labor, sleep, fear, fortune, are known to you. Learn that none of these things is superficial, but that each phenomenon has its roots in the faculties and affections of the mind. Whilst the abstract question occupies your intellect, nature brings it in the concrete to be solved by your hands. It were a wise inquiry for the closet, to compare, point by point, especially at remarkable crises in life, our daily history, with the rise and progress of ideas in the mind.

So shall we come to look at the world with new eyes. It shall answer the endless inquiry of the intellect,—What is truth? and of the affections,—What is good? by yielding itself passive to the educated Will. Then shall come to pass what my poet said: 'Nature is not fixed but fluid. Spirit alters, moulds, makes it. The immobility or bruteness of nature, is the absence of spirit; to pure spirit, it is fluid, it is volatile, it is obedient. Every spirit builds itself a house; and beyond its house a world; and beyond its world, a heaven. Know then, that the world exists for you. For you is the phenomenon perfect. What we are, that only can we see. All that Adam had, all that Cæsar could, you have and can do.

Adam called his house, heaven and earth; Cæsar called his house, Rome; you perhaps call yours, a cobbler's trade; a hundred acres of ploughed land; or a scholar's garret. Yet line for line and point for point, your dominion is as great as theirs, though without fine names. Build, therefore, your own world. As fast as you conform your life to the pure idea in your mind, that will unfold its great proportions. A correspondent revolution in things will attend the influx of the spirit. So fast will disagreeable appearances, swine, spiders, snakes, pests, mad-houses, prisons, enemies, vanish; they are temporary and shall be no more seen. The sordor and filths of nature, the sun shall dry up, and the wind exhale. As when the summer comes from the south; the snow-banks melt, and the face of the earth becomes green before it, so shall the advancing spirit create its ornaments along its path, and carry with it the beauty it visits, and the song which enchants it; it shall draw beautiful faces, warm hearts, wise discourse, and heroic acts, around its way, until evil is no more seen. The kingdom of man over nature, which cometh not with observation,—a dominion such as now is beyond his dream of God,—he shall enter without more wonder than the blind man feels who is gradually restored to perfect sight.'

1836

THE AMERICAN SCHOLAR.

Mr. President and Gentlemen:—

I greet you on the re-commencement of our literary year. Our anniversary is one of hope, and, perhaps, not enough of labor. We do not meet for games of strength or skill, for the recitation of histories, tragedies, and odes, like the ancient Greeks; for parliaments of love and poesy, like the Troubadours; nor for the advancement of science, like our contemporaries in the British and European capitals. Thus far, our holiday has been simply a friendly sign of the survival of the love of letters amongst a people too busy to give to letters any more. As such, it is precious as the sign of an indestructible instinct. Perhaps the time is already come, when it ought to be, and will be, something else; when the sluggard intellect of this continent will look from under its iron lids, and fill the postponed expectation of the world with something better than the exertions of mechanical skill. Our day of dependence, our long apprenticeship to the learning of other lands, draws to a close. The millions, that around us are rushing into life, cannot always be fed on the sere remains of foreign harvests. Events, actions arise, that must be sung, that will sing themselves. Who can doubt, that poetry will revive and lead in a new age, as the star in the constellation Harp, which now flames in our zenith, astronomers announce, shall one day be the pole-star for a thousand years?

In this hope, I accept the topic which not only usage, but the nature of our association, seem to prescribe to this day,— the AMERICAN SCHOLAR. Year by year, we come up hither to read one more chapter of his biography. Let us inquire what light new days and events have thrown on his character, and his hopes.

It is one of those fables, which, out of an unknown antiquity, convey an unlooked-for wisdom, that the gods, in the beginning, divided Man into men, that he might be more helpful to himself; just as the hand was divided into fingers, the better to answer its end.

The old fable covers a doctrine ever new and sublime; that there is One Man,—present to all particular men only partially, or through one faculty; and that you must take the whole society to find the whole man. Man is not a farmer, or a professor, or an engineer, but he is all. Man is priest, and scholar, and statesman, and producer, and soldier. In the *divided* or social state, these functions are parcelled out to individuals, each of whom aims to do his stint of the joint work, whilst each other performs his. The fable implies, that the individual, to possess himself, must sometimes return from his own labor to embrace all the other laborers. But unfortunately, this original unit, this fountain of power, has been so distributed to multitudes, has been so minutely subdivided and peddled out, that it is spilled into drops, and cannot be gathered. The state of society is one in which the members have suffered amputation from the trunk, and strut about so many walking monsters,—a good finger, a neck, a stomach, an elbow, but never a man.

Man is thus metamorphosed into a thing, into many things. The planter, who is Man sent out into the field to gather food, is seldom cheered by any idea of the true dignity of his ministry. He sees his bushel and his cart, and nothing beyond, and sinks into the farmer, instead of Man on the farm.

The tradesman scarcely ever gives an ideal worth to his work, but is ridden by the routine of his craft, and the soul is subject to dollars. The priest becomes a form; the attorney, a statute-book; the mechanic, a machine; the sailor, a rope of a ship.

In this distribution of functions, the scholar is the delegated intellect. In the right state, he is, *Man Thinking*. In the degenerate state, when the victim of society, he tends to become a mere thinker, or, still worse, the parrot of other men's thinking.

In this view of him, as Man Thinking, the theory of his office is contained. Him Nature solicits with all her placid, all her monitory pictures; him the past instructs; him the future invites. Is not, indeed, every man a student, and do not all things exist for the student's behoof? And, finally, is not the true scholar the only true master? But the old oracle said: 'All things have two handles: beware of the wrong one.' In life, too often, the scholar errs with mankind and forfeits his privilege. Let us see him in his school, and consider him in reference to the main influences he receives.

I. The first in time and the first in importance of the influences upon the mind is that of nature. Every day, the sun; and, after sunset, night and her stars. Ever the winds blow; ever the grass grows. Every day, men and women, conversing, beholding and beholden. The scholar is he of all men whom this spectacle most engages. He must settle its value in his mind. What is nature to him? There is never a beginning, there is never an end, to the inexplicable continuity of this web of God, but always circular power returning into itself. Therein it resembles his own spirit, whose beginning, whose ending, he never can find,—so entire, so boundless. Far, too, as her splendors shine, system on system shooting like rays, upward, downward, without centre, without circumference, —in the mass and in the particle, nature hastens to render account of herself to the mind. Classification begins. To the young mind, everything is individual, stands by itself. By and by, it finds how to join two things, and see in them one nature; then three, then three thousand; and so tyrannized over by its own unifying instinct, it goes on tying things together, diminishing anomalies, discovering roots running under ground, whereby contrary and remote things cohere, and flower out from one stem. It presently learns, that, since the dawn of history, there has been a constant accumulation and classifying of facts. But what is classification but the perceiving that these objects are not chaotic, and are not foreign, but have a law which is also a law of the human mind? The astronomer discovers that geometry, a pure abstraction of the human mind, is the measure of planetary motion. The chemist finds proportions and intelligible method throughout matter; and science is nothing but the finding of analogy, identity in the most remote parts. The ambitious soul sits down before each refractory fact; one after another, reduces all strange constitutions, all new powers, to their class and their law, and goes on forever to animate the last fibre of organization, the outskirts of nature, by insight.

Thus to him, to this school-boy under the bending dome of day, is suggested, that he and it proceed from one root; one is leaf and one is flower; relation, sympathy, stirring in every vein. And what is that Root? Is not that the soul of his soul?—A thought too bold,—a dream too wild. Yet when this spiritual light shall have revealed the law of more earthly natures,—when he has learned to worship the soul, and to see that the natural philosophy that now is, is only the first gropings of its gigantic hand, he shall look forward to an ever-expanding knowledge as to a becoming creator. He shall see that nature is the opposite of the soul, answering to it part for part. One is seal, and one is print. Its beauty is the beauty of his own mind. Its laws are the laws of his own mind. Nature then becomes to him the measure of his attainments. So much of nature as he is ignorant of, so much of his own mind does he not yet possess. And, in fine, the ancient precept, "Know thyself," and the modern precept, "Study nature," become at last one maxim.

II. The next great influence into the spirit of the scholar is, the mind of the Past,—in whatever form, whether of literature, of art, of institutions, that mind is inscribed. Books are the best type of the influence of the past, and perhaps we shall get at the truth,—learn the amount of this influence more conveniently,—by considering their value alone.

The theory of books is noble. The scholar of the first age received into him the world around; brooded thereon; gave it the new arrangement of his own mind, and uttered it again. It came into him, life; it went out from him, truth. It came to him, short-lived actions; it went out from him, immortal thoughts. It came to him, business; it went from him, poetry. It was dead fact; now, it is quick thought. It can stand, and it can go. It now endures, it now flies, it now inspires. Precisely in proportion to the depth of mind from which it issued, so high does it soar, so long does it sing.

Or, I might say, it depends on how far the process had gone, of transmuting life into truth. In proportion to the completeness of the distillation, so will the purity and imperishableness of the product be. But none is quite perfect. As no air-pump can by any means make a perfect vacuum, so neither can any artist entirely exclude the conventional, the local, the perishable from his book, or write a book of pure thought, that shall be as efficient, in all respects, to a remote posterity, as to cotemporaries, or rather to the second age. Each age, it is found, must write its own books; or rather, each generation for the next succeeding. The books of an older period will not fit this.

Yet hence arises a grave mischief. The sacredness which attaches to the act of creation,—the act of thought,—is transferred to the record. The poet chanting, was felt to be a divine man: henceforth the chant is divine also. The writer was a just and wise spirit: henceforward it is settled, the book is perfect; as love of the hero corrupts into worship of his statue. Instantly, the book becomes noxious: the guide is a tyrant. The sluggish and perverted mind of the multitude, slow to open to the incursions of Reason, having once so opened, having once received this book, stands upon it, and makes an outcry, if it is disparaged. Colleges are built on it. Books are written on it by thinkers, not by Man Thinking; by men of talent, that is, who start wrong, who set out from accepted dogmas, not from their own sight of principles. Meek young men grow up in libraries, believing it their duty to accept the views, which Cicero, which Locke, which Bacon, have given, forgetful that Cicero, Locke, and Bacon were only young men in libraries, when they wrote these books.

Hence, instead of Man Thinking, we have the bookworm. Hence, the book-learned class, who value books, as such; not as related to nature and the human constitution, but as making a sort of Third Estate with the world and the soul. Hence, the restorers of readings, the emendators, the bibliomaniacs of all degrees.

Books are the best of things, well used; abused, among the worst. What is the right use? What is the one end, which

all means go to effect? They are for nothing but to inspire.
I had better never see a book, than to be warped by its attraction clean out of my own orbit, and made a satellite instead of a system. The one thing in the world, of value, is
the active soul. This every man is entitled to; this every man
contains within him, although, in almost all men, obstructed,
and as yet unborn. The soul active sees absolute truth; and
utters truth, or creates. In this action it is genius; not the
privilege of here and there a favorite, but the sound estate of
every man. In its essence, it is progressive. The book, the
college, the school of art, the institution of any kind, stop
with some past utterance of genius. This is good, say they,
—let us hold by this. They pin me down. They look backward and not forward. But genius looks forward; the eyes of
man are set in his forehead, not in his hindhead; man hopes;
genius creates. Whatever talents may be, if the man create
not, the pure efflux of the Deity is not his; cinders and smoke
there may be, but not yet flame. There are creative manners,
there are creative actions and creative words; manners, actions, words, that is, indicative of no custom or authority,
but springing spontaneous from the mind's own sense of
good and fair.

On the other part, instead of being its own seer, let it receive from another mind its truth, though it were in torrents
of light, without periods of solitude, inquest, and self-recovery, and a fatal disservice is done. Genius is always sufficiently the enemy of genius by over-influence. The literature
of every nation bear me witness. The English dramatic poets
have Shakespearized now for two hundred years.

Undoubtedly there is a right way of reading, so it be stern-
ly subordinated. Man Thinking must not be subdued by his
instruments. Books are for the scholar's idle times. When he
can read God directly, the hour is too precious to be wasted
in other men's transcripts of their readings. But when the intervals of darkness come, as come they must,—when the sun
is hid, and the stars withdraw their shining,—we repair to
the lamps which were kindled by their ray, to guide our
steps to the East again, where the dawn is. We hear, that we
may speak. The Arabian proverb says, "A fig-tree, looking on
a fig-tree, becometh fruitful."

It is remarkable, the character of the pleasure we derive
from the best books. They impress us with the conviction,
that one nature wrote and the same reads. We read the

verses of one of the great English poets, of Chaucer, of Marvell, of Dryden, with the most modern joy,—with a pleasure, I mean, which is in great part caused by the abstraction of all *time* from their verses. There is some awe mixed with the joy of our surprise, when this poet, who lived in some past world, two or three hundred years ago, says that which lies close to my own soul, that which I also had wellnigh thought and said. But for the evidence thence afforded to the philosophical doctrine of the identity of all minds, we should suppose some pre-established harmony, some foresight of souls that were to be, and some preparation of stores for their future wants, like the fact observed in insects, who lay up food before death for the young grub they shall never see.

I would not be hurried by any love of system, by any exaggeration of instincts, to underrate the Book. We all know, that, as the human body can be nourished on any food, though it were boiled grass and the broth of shoes, so the human mind can be fed by any knowledge. And great and heroic men have existed, who had almost no other information than by the printed page. I only would say, that it needs a strong head to bear that diet. One must be an inventor to read well. As the proverb says, "He that would bring home the wealth of the Indies, must carry out the wealth of the Indies." There is then creative reading as well as creative writing. When the mind is braced by labor and invention, the page of whatever book we read becomes luminous with manifold allusion. Every sentence is doubly significant, and the sense of our author is as broad as the world. We then see, what is always true, that, as the seer's hour of vision is short and rare among heavy days and months, so is its record, perchance, the least part of his volume. The discerning will read, in his Plato or Shakespeare, only that least part,— only the authentic utterances of the oracle; all the rest he rejects, were it never so many times Plato's and Shakespeare's.

Of course, there is a portion of reading quite indispensable to a wise man. History and exact science he must learn by laborious reading. Colleges, in like manner, have their indispensable office,—to teach elements. But they can only highly serve us, when they aim not to drill, but to create; when they gather from far every ray of various genius to their hospitable halls, and, by the concentrated fires, set the hearts of their youth on flame. Thought and knowledge are natures in which apparatus and pretension avail nothing. Gowns, and pecuniary foundations, though of towns of gold, can never countervail the least sentence or syllable of wit. Forget this, and our American colleges will recede in their public importance, whilst they grow richer every year.

III. There goes in the world a notion, that the scholar should be a recluse, a valetudinarian,—as unfit for any handiwork or public labor, as a penknife for an axe. The so-called 'practical men' sneer at speculative men, as if, because they speculate or *see*, they could do nothing. I have heard it said that the clergy—who are always, more universally than any other class, the scholars of their day—are addressed as women; that the rough, spontaneous conversation of men they do not hear, but only a mincing and diluted speech. They are often virtually disfranchised; and, indeed, there are advocates for their celibacy. As far as this is true of the studious classes, it is not just and wise. Action is with the scholar subordinate, but it is essential. Without it, he is not yet man. Without it, thought can never ripen into truth. Whilst the world hangs before the eye as a cloud of beauty, we cannot even see its beauty. Inaction is cowardice, but there can be no scholar without the heroic mind. The preamble of thought, the transition through which it passes from the unconscious to the conscious, is action. Only so much do I know, as I have lived. Instantly we know whose words are loaded with life, and whose not.

The world—this shadow of the soul, or *other me*—lies wide around. Its attractions are the keys which unlock my thoughts and make me acquainted with myself. I run eagerly into this resounding tumult. I grasp the hands of those next me, and take my place in the ring to suffer and to work, taught by an instinct, that so shall the dumb abyss be vocal with speech. I pierce its order; I dissipate its fear; I dispose of it within the circuit of my expanding life. So much only of life as I know by experience, so much of the wilderness have I vanquished and planted, or so far have I extended my being, my dominion. I do not see how any man can afford, for the sake of his nerves and his nap, to spare any action in which he can partake. It is pearls and rubies to his discourse. Drudgery, calamity, exasperation, want, are instructors in eloquence and wisdom. The true scholar grudges every opportunity of action past by, as a loss of power. It is the raw material out of which the intellect moulds her splendid products. A strange process too, this, by which experience is converted into thought, as a mulberry leaf is converted into satin. The manufacture goes forward at all hours.

The actions and events of our childhood and youth are now matters of calmest observation. They lie like fair pictures in the air. Not so with our recent actions,—with the business which we now have in hand. On this we are quite unable to speculate. Our affections as yet circulate through it. We no more feel or know it, than we feel the feet, or the hand, or the brain of our body. The new deed is yet a part of life,—remains for a time immersed in our unconscious life. In some contemplative hour, it detaches itself from the life like a ripe fruit, to become a thought of the mind. Instantly, it is raised, transfigured; the corruptible has put on incorruption. Henceforth it is an object of beauty, however base its origin and neighborhood. Observe, too, the impossibility of antedating this act. In its grub state, it cannot fly, it cannot shine, it is a dull grub. But suddenly, without observation, the selfsame thing unfurls beautiful wings, and is an angel of wisdom. So is there no fact, no event, in our private history, which shall not, sooner or later, lose its adhesive, inert form, and astonish us by soaring from our body into the empyrean. Cradle and infancy, school and playground, the fear of boys, and dogs, and ferules, the love of little maids and berries, and many another fact that once filled the whole sky, are gone already; friend and relative, profession and party, town and country, nation and world, must also soar and sing.

Of course, he who has put forth his total strength in fit actions has the richest return of wisdom. I will not shut myself out of this globe of action, and transplant an oak into a flower-pot, there to hunger and pine; nor trust the revenue of some single faculty, and exhaust one vein of thought, much like those Savoyards, who, getting their livelihood by carving shepherds, shepherdesses, and smoking Dutchmen, for all Europe, went out one day to the mountain to find stock, and discovered that they had whittled up the last of their pine-trees. Authors we have, in numbers, who have written out their vein, and who, moved by a commendable prudence, sail for Greece or Palestine, follow the trapper into the prairie, or ramble round Algiers, to replenish their merchantable stock.

If it were only for a vocabulary, the scholar would be

covetous of action. Life is our dictionary. Years are well spent in country labors; in town,—in the insight into trades and manufactures; in frank intercourse with many men and women; in science; in art; to the one end of mastering in all their facts a language by which to illustrate and embody our perceptions. I learn immediately from any speaker how much he has already lived, through the poverty or the splendor of his speech. Life lies behind us as the quarry from whence we get tiles and cope-stones for the masonry of to-day. This is the way to learn grammar. Colleges and books only copy the language which the field and the work-yard made.

But the final value of action, like that of books, and better than books, is, that it is a resource. That great principle of Undulation in nature, that shows itself in the inspiring and expiring of the breath; in desire and satiety; in the ebb and flow of the sea; in day and night; in heat and cold; and as yet more deeply ingrained in every atom and every fluid, is known to us under the name of Polarity,—these "fits of easy transmission and reflection," as Newton called them, are the law of nature because they are the law of spirit.

The mind now thinks; now acts; and each fit reproduces the other. When the artist has exhausted his materials, when the fancy no longer paints, when thoughts are no longer apprehended, and books are a weariness,—he has always the resource *to live*. Character is higher than intellect. Thinking is the function. Living is the functionary. The stream retreats to its source. A great soul will be strong to live, as well as strong to think. Does he lack organ or medium to impart his truths? He can still fall back on this elemental force of living them. This is a total act. Thinking is a partial act. Let the grandeur of justice shine in his affairs. Let the beauty of affection cheer his lowly roof. Those 'far from fame,' who dwell and act with him, will feel the force of his constitution in the doings and passages of the day better than it can be measured by any public and designed display. Time shall teach him that the scholar loses no hour which the man lives. Herein he unfolds the sacred germ of his instinct, screened from influence. What is lost in seemliness is gained in strength. Not out of those, on whom systems of education have exhausted their culture, comes the helpful giant to destroy the old or to build the new, but out of unhandselled savage nature, out of terrible Druids and Berserkirs, come at last Alfred and Shakespeare.

I hear therefore with joy whatever is beginning to be said of the dignity and necessity of labor to every citizen. There is virtue yet in the hoe and the spade, for learned as well as for unlearned hands. And labor is everywhere welcome; always we are invited to work; only be this limitation observed, that a man shall not for the sake of wider activity sacrifice any opinion to the popular judgments and modes of action.

I have now spoken of the education of the scholar by nature, by books, and by action. It remains to say somewhat of his duties.

They are such as become Man Thinking. They may all be comprised in self-trust. The office of the scholar is to cheer, to raise, and to guide men by showing them facts amidst appearances. He plies the slow, unhonored, and unpaid task of observation. Flamsteed and Herschel, in their glazed observatories, may catalogue the stars with the praise of all men, and, the results being splendid and useful, honor is sure. But he, in his private observatory, cataloguing obscure and nebulous stars of the human mind, which as yet no man has thought of as such,—watching days and months, sometimes, for a few facts; correcting still his old records,— must relinquish display and immediate fame. In the long period of his preparation, he must betray often an ignorance and shiftlessness in popular arts, incurring the disdain of the able who shoulder him aside. Long he must stammer in his speech; often forego the living for the dead. Worse yet, he must accept—how often!—poverty and solitude. For the ease and pleasure of treading the old road, accepting the fashions, the education, the religion of society, he takes the cross of making his own, and, of course, the self-accusation, the faint heart, the frequent uncertainty and loss of time, which are the nettles and tangling vines in the way of the self-relying and self-directed; and the state of virtual hostility in which he seems to stand to society, and especially to educated society. For all this loss and scorn, what offset? He is to find consolation in exercising the highest functions of human nature. He is one, who raises himself from private considerations, and breathes and lives on public and illustrious thoughts. He is the world's eye. He is the world's heart. He is to resist the vulgar prosperity that retrogrades ever to barbarism, by preserving and communicating heroic sentiments, noble biographies, melodious verse, and the conclusions of history. Whatsoever oracles the human heart, in all emergencies, in all solemn hours, has uttered as its commentary on the world of actions,—these he shall receive and impart. And whatsoever new verdict Reason from her inviolable seat pronounces on the passing men and events of today,—this he shall hear and promulgate.

These being his functions, it becomes him to feel all confidence in himself, and to defer never to the popular cry. He and he only knows the world. The world of any moment is the merest appearance. Some great decorum, some fetish of a government, some ephemeral trade, or war, or man, is cried up by half mankind and cried down by the other half, as if all depended on this particular up or down. The odds are that the whole question is not worth the poorest thought which the scholar has lost in listening to the controversy. Let him not quit his belief that a popgun is a popgun, though the ancient and honorable of the earth affirm it to be the crack of doom. In silence, in steadiness, in severe abstraction, let him hold by himself; add observation to observation, patient of neglect, patient of reproach; and bide his own time,— happy enough, if he can satisfy himself alone, that this day he has seen something truly. Success treads on every right step. For the instinct is sure, that prompts him to tell his brother what he thinks. He then learns, that in going down into the secrets of his own mind, he has descended into the secrets of all minds. He learns that he who has mastered any law in his private thoughts is master to that extent of all men whose language he speaks, and of all into whose language his own can be translated. The poet, in utter solitude remembering his spontaneous thoughts and recording them, is found to have recorded that, which men in crowded cities find true for them also. The orator distrusts at first the fitness of his frank confessions,—his want of knowledge of the persons he addresses,—until he finds that he is the complement of his hearers; that they drink his words because he fulfils for them their own nature; the deeper he dives into his privatest, secretest presentiment, to his wonder he finds, this is the most acceptable, most public, and universally true. The people delight in it; the better part of every man feels, This is my music; this is myself.

In self-trust all the virtues are comprehended. Free should the scholar be,—free and brave. Free even to the definition of freedom, "without any hindrance that does not arise out of his own constitution." Brave; for fear is a thing which a scholar by his very function puts behind him. Fear always springs from ignorance. It is a shame to him if his tranquillity, amid dangerous times, arise from the presumption, that, like children and women, his is a protected class; or if he seek a temporary peace by the diversion of his thoughts from politics or vexed questions, hiding his head like an ostrich in the flowering bushes, peeping into microscopes, and turning rhymes, as a boy whistles to keep his courage up. So is the danger a danger still; so is the fear worse. Manlike let him turn and face it. Let him look into its eye and search its nature, inspect its origin,—see the whelping of this lion,— which lies no great way back; he will then find in himself a perfect comprehension of its nature and extent; he will have made his hands meet on the other side, and can henceforth defy it, and pass on superior. The world is his, who can see through its pretension. What deafness, what stoneblind custom, what overgrown error you behold, is there only by sufferance,—by your sufferance. See it to be a lie, and you have already dealt it its mortal blow.

Yes, we are the cowed,—we the trustless. It is a mischievous notion that we are come late into nature; that the world was finished a long time ago. As the world was plastic and fluid in the hands of God, so it is ever to so much of his attributes as we bring to it. To ignorance and sin, it is flint. They adapt themselves to it as they may; but in proportion as a man has anything in him divine, the firmament flows before him and takes his signet and form. Not he is great who can alter matter, but he who can alter my state of mind. They are the kings of the world who give the color of their present thought to all nature and all art, and persuade men by the cheerful serenity of their carrying the matter, that this thing which they do, is the apple which the ages have desired to pluck, now at last ripe, and inviting nations to the harvest. The great man makes the great thing. Wherever Macdonald sits, there is the head of the table. Linnæus makes botany the most alluring of studies, and wins it from the farmer and the herb-woman; Davy, chemistry; and Cuvier, fossils. The day is always his, who works in it with serenity and great aims. The unstable estimates of men crowd to him whose mind is filled with a truth, as the heaped waves of the Atlantic follow the moon.

For this self-trust, the reason is deeper than can be fath-
omed,—darker than can be enlightened. I might not carry
with me the feeling of my audience in stating my own belief. But I have already shown the ground of my hope, in
adverting to the doctrine that man is one. I believe man has
been wronged; he has wronged himself. He has almost lost
the light, that can lead him back to his prerogatives. Men
are become of no account. Men in history, men in the world
of to-day are bugs, are spawn, and are called 'the mass' and
'the herd.' In a century, in a millennium, one or two men;
that is to say,—one or two approximations to the right state
of every man. All the rest behold in the hero or the poet
their own green and crude being,—ripened; yes, and are
content to be less, so *that* may attain to its full stature.
What a testimony,—full of grandeur, full of pity, is borne
to the demands of his own nature, by the poor clansman, the
poor partisan, who rejoices in the glory of his chief. The
poor and the low find some amends to their immense moral
capacity, for their acquiescence in a political and social inferiority. They are content to be brushed like flies from the
path of a great person, so that justice shall be done by him
to that common nature which it is the dearest desire of all to
see enlarged and glorified. They sun themselves in the great
man's light, and feel it to be their own element. They cast
the dignity of man from their down-trod selves upon the
shoulders of a hero, and will perish to add one drop of blood
to make that great heart beat, those giant sinews combat
and conquer. He lives for us, and we live in him.

Men such as they are, very naturally seek money or power;
and power because it is as good as money,—the "spoils,"
so called, "of office." And why not? for they aspire to the
highest, and this, in their sleep-walking, they dream is highest. Wake them, and they shall quit the false good, and leap
to the true, and leave governments to clerks and desks. This
revolution is to be wrought by the gradual domestication of
the idea of Culture. The main enterprise of the world for
splendor, for extent, is the upbuilding of a man. Here are
the materials strown along the ground. The private life of
one man shall be a more illustrious monarchy,—more formidable to its enemy, more sweet and serene in its influence to
its friend, than any kingdom in history. For a man, rightly
viewed, comprehendeth the particular natures of all men.
Each philosopher, each bard, each actor, has only done for

me, as by a delegate, what one day I can do for myself. The books which once we valued more than the apple of the eye, we have quite exhausted. What is that but saying, that we have come up with the point of view which the universal mind took through the eyes of one scribe; we have been that man, and have passed on. First, one; then, another; we drain all cisterns, and, waxing greater by all these supplies, we crave a better and more abundant food. The man has never lived that can feed us ever. The human mind cannot be enshrined in a person, who shall set a barrier on any one side to this unbounded, unboundable empire. It is one central fire, which, flaming now out of the lips of Etna, lightens the capes of Sicily; and, now out of the throat of Vesuvius, illuminates the towers and vineyards of Naples. It is one light which beams out of a thousand stars. It is one soul which animates all men.

But I have dwelt perhaps tediously upon this abstraction of the Scholar. I ought not to delay longer to add what I have to say, of nearer reference to the time and to this country.

Historically, there is thought to be a difference in the ideas which predominate over successive epochs, and there are data for marking the genius of the Classic, of the Romantic, and now of the Reflective or Philosophical age. With the views I have intimated of the oneness or the identity of the mind through all individuals, I do not much dwell on these differences. In fact, I believe each individual passes through all three. The boy is a Greek; the youth, romantic; the adult, reflective. I deny not, however, that a revolution in the leading idea may be distinctly enough traced.

Our age is bewailed as the age of Introversion. Must that needs be evil? We, it seems, are critical; we are embarrassed with second thoughts; we cannot enjoy anything for hankering to know whereof the pleasure consists; we are lined with eyes; we see with our feet; the time is infected with Hamlet's unhappiness,—

"Sicklied o'er with the pale cast of thought."

Is it so bad then? Sight is the last thing to be pitied. Would we be blind? Do we fear lest we should outsee nature and God, and drink truth dry? I look upon the discontent of the literary class, as a mere announcement of the fact, that they find themselves not in the state of mind of their fathers, and regret the coming state as untried; as a boy dreads the water before he has learned that he can swim. If there is any period one would desire to be born in,—is it not the age of Revolution; when the old and the new stand side by side, and admit of being compared; when the energies of all men are searched by fear and by hope; when the historic glories of the old can be compensated by the rich possibilities of the new era? This time, like all times, is a very good one, if we but know what to do with it.

I read with joy some of the auspicious signs of the coming days, as they glimmer already through poetry and art, through philosophy and science, through church and state.

One of these signs is the fact, that the same movement which effected the elevation of what was called the lowest class in the state assumed in literature a very marked and as benign an aspect. Instead of the sublime and beautiful; the near, the low, the common, was explored and poetized. That, which had been negligently trodden under foot by those who were harnessing and provisioning themselves for long journeys into far countries, is suddenly found to be richer than all foreign parts. The literature of the poor, the feelings of the child, the philosophy of the street, the meaning of household life, are the topics of the time. It is a great stride. It is a sign—is it not?—of new vigor, when the extremities are made active, when currents of warm life run into the hands and the feet. I ask not for the great, the remote, the romantic; what is doing in Italy or Arabia; what is Greek art, or Provençal minstrelsy; I embrace the common, I explore and sit at the feet of the familiar, the low. Give me insight into to-day, and you may have the antique and future worlds. What would we really know the meaning of? The meal in the firkin; the milk in the pan; the ballad in the street; the news of the boat; the glance of the eye; the form and the gait of the body;—show me the ultimate reason of these matters; show me the sublime presence of the highest spiritual cause lurking, as always it does lurk, in these suburbs and extremities of nature; let me see every trifle bristling with the polarity that ranges it instantly on an eternal law; and the shop, the plough, and the ledger, referred to the like cause by which light undulates and poets sing; and the world lies no longer a dull miscellany and lumber-room, but has form and order; there is no trifle; there is no puzzle; but one design unites and animates the farthest pinnacle and the lowest trench.

This idea has inspired the genius of Goldsmith, Burns, Cowper, and, in a newer time, of Goethe, Wordsworth, and Carlyle. This idea they have differently followed and with various success. In contrast with their writing, the style of Pope, of Johnson, of Gibbon, looks cold and pedantic. This writing is blood-warm. Man is surprised to find that things near are not less beautiful and wondrous than things remote. The near explains the far. The drop is a small ocean. A man is related to all nature. This perception of the worth of the vulgar is fruitful in discoveries. Goethe, in this very thing the most modern of the moderns, has shown us, as none ever did, the genius of the ancients.

There is one man of genius, who has done much for this philosophy of life, whose literary value has never yet been rightly estimated;—I mean Emanuel Swedenborg. The most imaginative of men, yet writing with the precision of a mathematician, he endeavored to engraft a purely philosophical Ethics on the popular Christianity of his time. Such an attempt, of course, must have difficulty, which no genius could surmount. But he saw and showed the connection between nature and the affections of the soul. He pierced the emblematic or spiritual character of the visible, audible, tangible world. Especially did his shade-loving muse hover over and interpret the lower parts of nature; he showed the mysterious bond that allies moral evil to the foul material forms, and has given in epical parables a theory of insanity, of beasts, of unclean and fearful things.

Another sign of our times, also marked by an analogous political movement, is, the new importance given to the single person. Everything that tends to insulate the individual— to surround him with barriers of natural respect, so that each man shall feel the world as his, and man shall treat with man as a sovereign state with a sovereign state—tends to true union as well as greatness. "I learned," said the melancholy Pestalozzi, "that no man in God's wide earth is either willing or able to help any other man." Help must come from the bosom alone. The scholar is that man who must take up into himself all the ability of the time, all the contributions of the past, all the hopes of the future. He must be an university of knowledges. If there be one lesson more than another, which should pierce his ear, it is: The world is nothing, the man is all; in yourself is the law of all nature, and you know not yet how a globule of sap ascends; in yourself slumbers the whole of Reason; it is for you to know all, it is for you to dare all. Mr. President and Gentlemen, this confidence in the unsearched might of man belongs, by all motives, by all prophecy, by all preparation, to the American Scholar. We have listened too long to the courtly muses of Europe. The spirit of the American freeman is already suspected to be timid, imitative, tame. Public and private avarice make the air we breathe thick and fat. The scholar is decent, indolent, complaisant. See already the tragic consequence. The mind of this country, taught to aim at low objects, eats upon itself. There is no work for any but the decorous and the complaisant. Young men of the fairest promise, who begin life upon our shores, inflated by the mountain winds, shined upon by all the stars of God, find the earth below not in unison with these,—but are hindered from action by the disgust which the principles on which business is managed inspire, and turn drudges, or die of disgust,— some of them suicides. What is the remedy? They did not yet see, and thousands of young men as hopeful now crowding to the barriers for the career, do not yet see, that if the single man plant himself indomitably on his instincts, and there abide, the huge world will come round to him. Patience, —patience;—with the shades of all the good and great for company; and for solace, the perspective of your own infinite life; and for work, the study and the communication of principles, the making those instincts prevalent, the conversion of the world. Is it not the chief disgrace in the world, not to be an unit;—not to be reckoned one character; —not to yield that peculiar fruit which each man was created to bear, but to be reckoned in the gross, in the hundred, or the thousand, of the party, the section, to which we belong; and our opinion predicted geographically, as the north, or the south? Not so, brothers and friends,—please God, ours shall not be so. We will walk on our own feet; we will work with our own hands; we will speak our own minds. The study of letters shall be no longer a name for pity, for doubt, and for sensual indulgence. The dread of man and the love of man shall be a wall of defence and a wreath of joy around all. A nation of men will for the first time exist, because each believes himself inspired by the Divine Soul which also inspires all men.

1837

DIVINITY SCHOOL ADDRESS.

In this refulgent summer it has been a luxury to draw the breath of life. The grass grows, the buds burst, the meadow is spotted with fire and gold in the tint of flowers. The air is full of birds, and sweet with the breath of the pine, the balm-of-Gilead, and the new hay. Night brings no gloom to the heart with its welcome shade. Through the transparent darkness the stars pour their almost spiritual rays. Man under them seems a young child, and his huge globe a toy. The cool night bathes the world as with a river, and prepares his eyes again for the crimson dawn. The mystery of nature was never displayed more happily. The corn and the wine have been freely dealt to all creatures, and the never-broken silence with which the old bounty goes forward has not yielded yet one word of explanation. One is constrained to respect the perfection of this world, in which our senses converse. How wide; how rich; what invitation from every property it gives to every faculty of man! In its fruitful soils; in its navigable sea; in its mountains of metal and stone; in its forests of all woods; in its animals; in its chemical ingredients; in the powers and path of light, heat, attraction, and life, it is well worth the pith and heart of great men to subdue and enjoy it. The planters, the mechanics, the inventors, the astronomers, the builders of cities, and the captains, history delights to honor.

But when the mind opens, and reveals the laws which traverse the universe, and make things what they are, then shrinks the great world at once into a mere illustration and fable of this mind. What am I? and What is? asks the human spirit with a curiosity new-kindled, but never to be quenched. Behold these out-running laws, which our imperfect apprehension can see tend this way and that, but not come full circle. Behold these infinite relations, so like, so unlike; many, yet one. I would study, I would know, I would admire forever. These works of thought have been the entertainments of the human spirit in all ages.

A more secret, sweet, and overpowering beauty appears to man when his heart and mind open to the sentiment of virtue. Then he is instructed in what is above him. He learns that his being is without bound; that, to the good, to the perfect, he is born, low as he now lies in evil and weakness. That which he venerates is still his own, though he has not realized it yet. *He ought.* He knows the sense of that grand word, though his analysis fails entirely to render account of it. When in innocency, or when by intellectual perception, he attains to say,—'I love the Right; Truth is beautiful within and without, forevermore. Virtue, I am thine: save me: use me: thee will I serve, day and night, in great, in small, that I may be not virtuous, but virtue';—then is the end of the creation answered, and God is well pleased.

The sentiment of virtue is a reverence and delight in the presence of certain divine laws. It perceives that this homely game of life we play covers, under what seem foolish details, principles that astonish. The child amidst his baubles is learning the action of light, motion, gravity, muscular force; and in the game of human life, love, fear, justice, appetite, man, and God, interact. These laws refuse to be adequately stated. They will not be written out on paper, or spoken by the tongue. They elude our persevering thought; yet we read them hourly in each other's faces, in each other's actions, in our own remorse. The moral traits which are all globed into every virtuous act and thought,—in speech, we must sever, and describe or suggest by painful enumeration of many particulars. Yet, as this sentiment is the essence of all religion, let me guide your eye to the precise objects of the sentiment, by an enumeration of some of those classes of facts in which this element is conspicuous.

The intuition of the moral sentiment is an insight of the perfection of the laws of the soul. These laws execute themselves. They are out of time, out of space, and not subject to circumstance. Thus; in the soul of man there is a justice whose retributions are instant and entire. He who does a good deed, is instantly ennobled. He who does a mean deed, is by the action itself contracted. He who puts off impurity, thereby puts on purity. If a man is at heart just, then in so far is he God; the safety of God, the immortality of God, the majesty of God, do enter into that man with justice. If a man dissemble, deceive, he deceives himself, and goes out of acquaintance with his own being. A man in the view of absolute goodness, adores, with total humility. Every step so downward, is a step upward. The man who renounces himself, comes to himself.

See how this rapid intrinsic energy worketh everywhere, righting wrongs, correcting appearances, and bringing up facts to a harmony with thoughts. Its operation in life, though slow to the senses, is, at last, as sure as in the soul. By it, a man is made the Providence to himself, dispensing good to his goodness, and evil to his sin. Character is always known. Thefts never enrich; alms never impoverish; murder will speak out of stone walls. The least admixture of a lie—for example, the taint of vanity, the least attempt to make a good impression, a favorable appearance—will instantly vitiate the effect. But speak the truth, and all nature and all spirits help you with unexpected furtherance. Speak the truth, and all things alive or brute are vouchers, and the very roots of the grass underground there, do seem to stir and move to bear you witness. See again the perfection of the Law as it applies itself to the affections, and becomes the law of society. As we are, so we associate. The good, by affinity, seek the good; the vile, by affinity, the vile. Thus of their own volition, souls proceed into heaven, into hell.

These facts have always suggested to man the sublime creed, that the world is not the product of manifold power, but of one will, of one mind; and that one mind is everywhere active, in each ray of the star, in each wavelet of the pool; and whatever opposes that will is everywhere balked and baffled, because things are made so, and not otherwise. Good is positive. Evil is merely privative, not absolute: it is like cold which is the privation of heat. All evil is so much death or nonentity. Benevolence is absolute and real. So much benevolence as a man hath, so much life hath he. For all things proceed out of this same spirit, which is differently named love, justice, temperance, in its different applications, just as the ocean receives different names on the several shores which it washes. All things proceed out of the same spirit, and all things conspire with it. Whilst a man seeks good ends, he is strong by the whole strength of nature. In so far as he roves from these ends, he bereaves himself of power, of auxiliaries; his being shrinks out of all remote channels, he becomes less and less, a mote, a point, until absolute badness is absolute death.

The perception of this law of laws awakens in the mind a sentiment which we call the religious sentiment, and which makes our highest happiness. Wonderful is its power to charm and to command. It is a mountain air. It is the embalmer of the world. It is myrrh and storax, and chlorine and rosemary. It makes the sky and the hills sublime, and the silent song of the stars is it. By it, is the universe made safe and habitable, not by science or power. Thought may work cold and intransitive in things, and find no end or unity; but the dawn of the sentiment of virtue on the heart gives and is the assurance that Law is sovereign over all natures; and the worlds, time, space, eternity, do seem to break out into joy.

This sentiment is divine and deifying. It is the beatitude of man. It makes him illimitable. Through it, the soul first knows itself. It corrects the capital mistake of the infant man, who seeks to be great by following the great, and hopes to derive advantages *from another*,—by showing the fountain of all good to be in himself, and that he, equally with every man, is an inlet into the deeps of Reason. When he says, "I ought"; when love warms him; when he chooses, warned from on high, the good and great deed; then, deep melodies wander through his soul from Supreme Wisdom. Then he can worship, and be enlarged by his worship; for he can never go behind this sentiment. In the sublimest flights of the soul, rectitude is never surmounted, love is never outgrown.

This sentiment lies at the foundation of society, and successively creates all forms of worship. The principle of veneration never dies out. Man fallen into superstition, into sensuality, is never quite without the visions of the moral sentiment. In like manner, all the expressions of this sentiment are sacred and permanent in proportion to their purity. The expressions of this sentiment affect us more than all other compositions. The sentences of the oldest time, which ejaculate this piety, are still fresh and fragrant. This thought dwelled always deepest in the minds of men in the devout and contemplative East; not alone in Palestine, where it reached its purest expression, but in Egypt, in Persia, in India, in China. Europe has always owed to Oriental genius its divine impulses. What these holy bards said, all sane men found agreeable and true. And the unique impression of Jesus upon mankind, whose name is not so much written as ploughed into the history of this world, is proof of the subtle virtue of this infusion.

Meantime, whilst the doors of the temple stand open, night and day, before every man, and the oracles of this truth cease never, it is guarded by one stern condition: this, namely; it is an intuition. It cannot be received at second hand. Truly speaking, it is not instruction, but provocation, that I can receive from another soul. What he announces, I must find true in me, or wholly reject; and on his word, or as his second, be he who he may, I can accept nothing. On the contrary, the absence of this primary faith is the presence of degradation. As is the flood so is the ebb. Let this faith depart, and the very words it spake, and the things it made, become false and hurtful. Then falls the church, the state, art, letters, life. The doctrine of the divine nature being forgotten, a sickness infects and dwarfs the constitution. Once man was all; now he is an appendage, a nuisance. And because the indwelling Supreme Spirit cannot wholly be got rid of, the doctrine of it suffers this perversion, that the divine nature is attributed to one or two persons, and denied to all the rest, and denied with fury. The doctrine of inspiration is lost; the base doctrine of the majority of voices usurps the place of the doctrine of the soul. Miracles, prophecy, poetry; the ideal life, the holy life, exist as ancient history merely; they are not in the belief, nor in the aspiration of society; but, when suggested, seem ridiculous. Life is comic or pitiful, as soon as the high ends of being fade out of sight, and man becomes near-sighted, and can only attend to what addresses the senses.

These general views, which, whilst they are general, none will contest, find abundant illustration in the history of religion, and especially in the history of the Christian Church. In that, all of us have had our birth and nurture. The truth contained in that, you, my young friends, are now setting forth to teach. As the Cultus, or established worship of the civilized world, it has great historical interest for us. Of its blessed words, which have been the consolation of humanity, you need not that I should speak. I shall endeavor to discharge my duty to you, on this occasion, by pointing out two errors in its administration, which daily appear more gross from the point of view we have just now taken.

Jesus Christ belonged to the true race of prophets. He saw with open eye the mystery of the soul. Drawn by its severe harmony, ravished with its beauty, he lived in it, and had his being there. Alone in all history, he estimated the greatness of man. One man was true to what is in you and me. He saw that God incarnates himself in man, and evermore goes forth anew to take possession of his world. He said, in this jubilee of sublime emotion, 'I am divine. Through me, God acts; through me, speaks. Would you see

God, see me; or, see thee, when thou also thinkest as I now think.' But what a distortion did his doctrine and memory suffer in the same, in the next, and the following ages! There is no doctrine of the Reason which will bear to be taught by the Understanding. The understanding caught this high chant from the poet's lips, and said, in the next age, 'This was Jehovah come down out of heaven. I will kill you, if you say he was a man.' The idioms of his language, and the figures of his rhetoric, have usurped the place of his truth; and churches are not built on his principles, but on his tropes. Christianity became a Mythus, as the poetic teaching of Greece and of Egypt, before. He spoke of miracles; for he felt that man's life was a miracle, and all that man doth, and he knew that his daily miracle shines, as the character ascends. But the word Miracle, as pronounced by Christian churches, gives a false impression; it is Monster. It is not one with the blowing clover and the falling rain.

He felt respect for Moses and the prophets; but no unfit tenderness at postponing their initial revelations, to the hour and the man that now is; to the eternal revelation in the heart. Thus was he a true man. Having seen that the law in us is commanding, he would not suffer it to be commanded. Boldly, with hand, and heart, and life, he declared it was God. Thus is he, as I think, the only soul in history who has appreciated the worth of a man.

1. In this point of view we become very sensible of the first defect of historical Christianity. Historical Christianity has fallen into the error that corrupts all attempts to communicate religion. As it appears to us, and as it has appeared for ages, it is not the doctrine of the soul, but an exaggeration of the personal, the positive, the ritual. It has dwelt, it dwells, with noxious exaggeration about the *person* of Jesus. The soul knows no persons. It invites every man to expand to the full circle of the universe, and will have no preferences but those of spontaneous love. But by this eastern monarchy of a Christianity, which indolence and fear have built, the friend of man is made the injurer of man. The manner in which his name is surrounded with expressions, which were once sallies of admiration and love, but are now petrified into official titles, kills all generous sympathy and liking. All who hear me, feel, that the language that describes Christ to Europe and America, is not the style of friendship and enthusiasm to a good and noble heart, but is appropriated and for-

mal,—paints a demi-god as the Orientals or the Greeks would describe Osiris or Apollo. Accept the injurious impositions of our early catechetical instruction, and even honesty and self-denial were but splendid sins, if they did not wear the Christian name. One would rather be

> 'A pagan, suckled in a creed outworn,'

than to be defrauded of his manly right in coming into nature, and finding not names and places, not land and professions, but even virtue and truth foreclosed and monopolized. You shall not be a man even. You shall not own the world; you shall not dare, and live after the infinite Law that is in you, and in company with the infinite Beauty which heaven and earth reflect to you in all lovely forms; but you must subordinate your nature to Christ's nature; you must accept our interpretations; and take his portrait as the vulgar draw it.

That is always best which gives me to myself. The sublime is excited in me by the great stoical doctrine, Obey thyself. That which shows God in me, fortifies me. That which shows God out of me, makes me a wart and a wen. There is no longer a necessary reason for my being. Already the long shadows of untimely oblivion creep over me, and I shall decease forever.

The divine bards are the friends of my virtue, of my intellect, of my strength. They admonish me, that the gleams which flash across my mind, are not mine, but God's; that they had the like, and were not disobedient to the heavenly vision. So I love them. Noble provocations go out from them, inviting me to resist evil; to subdue the world; and to Be. And thus by his holy thoughts, Jesus serves us, and thus only. To aim to convert a man by miracles, is a profanation of the soul. A true conversion, a true Christ, is now, as always, to be made, by the reception of beautiful sentiments. It is true that a great and rich soul, like his, falling among the simple, does so preponderate, that, as his did, it names the world. The world seems to them to exist for him, and they have not yet drunk so deeply of his sense, as to see that only by coming again to themselves, or to God in themselves, can they grow forevermore. It is a low benefit to give me something; it is a high benefit to enable me to do somewhat of myself. The time is coming when all men will see, that the gift of God to the soul is not a vaunting, overpowering, excluding sanctity, but a sweet, natural goodness, a goodness like thine and mine, and that so invites thine and mine to be and to grow.

The injustice of the vulgar tone of preaching is not less flagrant to Jesus, than to the souls which it profanes. The preachers do not see that they make his gospel not glad, and shear him of the locks of beauty and the attributes of heaven. When I see a majestic Epaminondas, or Washington; when I see among my contemporaries, a true orator, an upright judge, a dear friend; when I vibrate to the melody and fancy of a poem; I see beauty that is to be desired. And so lovely, and with yet more entire consent of my human being, sounds in my ear the severe music of the bards that have sung of the true God in all ages. Now do not degrade the life and dialogues of Christ out of the circle of this charm, by insulation and peculiarity. Let them lie as they befell, alive and warm, part of human life, and of the landscape, and of the cheerful day.

2. The second defect of the traditional and limited way of using the mind of Christ is a consequence of the first; this, namely; that the Moral Nature, that Law of laws, whose revelations introduce greatness,—yea, God himself, into the open soul, is not explored as the fountain of the established teaching in society. Men have come to speak of the revelation as somewhat long ago given and done, as if God were dead. The injury to faith throttles the preacher; and the goodliest of institutions becomes an uncertain and inarticulate voice.

It is very certain that it is the effect of conversation with the beauty of the soul, to beget a desire and need to impart to others the same knowledge and love. If utterance is denied, the thought lies like a burden on the man. Always the seer is a sayer. Somehow his dream is told: somehow he publishes it with solemn joy: sometimes with pencil on canvas; sometimes with chisel on stone; sometimes in towers and aisles of granite, his soul's worship is builded; sometimes in anthems or indefinite music; but clearest and most permanent, in words.

The man enamored of this excellency, becomes its priest or poet. The office is coeval with the world. But observe the condition, the spiritual limitation of the office. The spirit only can teach. Not any profane man, not any sensual, not any liar, not any slave can teach, but only he can give, who has; he only can create, who is. The man on whom the soul descends, through whom the soul speaks, alone can teach. Courage, piety, love, wisdom, can teach; and every man can open his door to these angels, and they shall bring him the gift of tongues. But the man who aims to speak as books enable, as synods use, as the fashion guides, and as interest commands, babbles. Let him hush.

To this holy office you propose to devote yourselves. I wish you may feel your call in throbs of desire and hope. The office is the first in the world. It is of that reality that it cannot suffer the deduction of any falsehood. And it is my duty to say to you, that the need was never greater of new revelation than now. From the views I have already expressed, you will infer the sad conviction, which I share, I believe, with numbers, of the universal decay and now almost death of faith in society. The soul is not preached. The Church seems to totter to its fall, almost all life extinct. On this occasion, any complaisance would be criminal, which told you, whose hope and commission it is to preach the faith of Christ, that the faith of Christ is preached.

It is time that this ill-suppressed murmur of all thoughtful men against the famine of our churches; this moaning of the heart because it is bereaved of the consolation, the hope, the grandeur, that come alone out of the culture of the moral nature; should be heard through the sleep of indolence, and over the din of routine. This great and perpetual office of the preacher is not discharged. Preaching is the expression of the moral sentiment in application to the duties of life. In how many churches, by how many prophets, tell me, is man made sensible that he is an infinite Soul; that the earth and heavens are passing into his mind; that he is drinking forever the soul of God? Where now sounds the persuasion, that by its very melody imparadises my heart, and so affirms its own origin in heaven? Where shall I hear words such as in elder ages drew men to leave all and follow,—father and mother, house and land, wife and child? Where shall I hear these august laws of moral being so pronounced, as to fill my ear, and I feel ennobled by the offer of my uttermost action and passion? The test of the true faith, certainly, should be its power to charm and command the soul, as the laws of nature control the activity of the hands,—so commanding that we find pleasure and honor in obeying. The faith should blend with the light of rising and of setting suns, with the flying cloud, the singing bird, and the breath of flowers. But now

the priest's Sabbath has lost the splendor of nature; it is un-
lovely; we are glad when it is done; we can make, we do
make, even sitting in our pews, a far better, holier, sweeter,
for ourselves.

Whenever the pulpit is usurped by a formalist, then is the
worshipper defrauded and disconsolate. We shrink as soon
as the prayers begin, which do not uplift, but smite and offend
us. We are fain to wrap our cloaks about us, and secure, as
best we can, a solitude that hears not. I once heard a preacher
who sorely tempted me to say I would go to church no more.
Men go, thought I, where they are wont to go, else had no
soul entered the temple in the afternoon. A snow-storm was
falling around us. The snow-storm was real; the preacher
merely spectral; and the eye felt the sad contrast in looking
at him, and then out of the window behind him, into the
beautiful meteor of the snow. He had lived in vain. He had
no one word intimating that he had laughed or wept, was
married or in love, had been commended, or cheated, or cha-
grined. If he had ever lived and acted, we were none the
wiser for it. The capital secret of his profession, namely, to
convert life into truth, he had not learned. Not one fact in
all his experience had he yet imported into his doctrine.
This man had ploughed, and planted, and talked, and bought,
and sold; he had read books; he had eaten and drunken; his
head aches; his heart throbs; he smiles and suffers; yet was
there not a surmise, a hint, in all the discourse, that he had
ever lived at all. Not a line did he draw out of real history.
The true preacher can be known by this, that he deals out to
the people his life,—life passed through the fire of thought.
But of the bad preacher, it could not be told from his sermon,
what age of the world he fell in; whether he had a father or
a child; whether he was a freeholder or a pauper; whether
he was a citizen or a countryman; or any other fact of his
biography. It seemed strange that the people should come to
church. It seemed as if their houses were very unentertain-
ing, that they should prefer this thoughtless clamor. It shows
that there is a commanding attraction in the moral sentiment,
that can lend a faint tint of light to dulness and ignorance,
coming in its name and place. The good hearer is sure he
has been touched sometimes; is sure there is somewhat to be
reached, and some word that can reach it. When he listens to
these vain words, he comforts himself by their relation to

his remembrance of better hours, and so they clatter and echo unchallenged.

I am not ignorant that when we preach unworthily, it is not always quite in vain. There is a good ear, in some men, that draws supplies to virtue out of very indifferent nutriment. There is poetic truth concealed in all the commonplaces of prayer and of sermons, and though foolishly spoken, they may be wisely heard; for, each is some select expression that broke out in a moment of piety from some stricken or jubilant soul, and its excellency made it remembered. The prayers and even the dogmas of our church are like the zodiac of Denderah, and the astronomical monuments of the Hindoos, wholly insulated from anything now extant in the life and business of the people. They mark the height to which the waters once rose. But this docility is a check upon the mischief from the good and devout. In a large portion of the community, the religious service gives rise to quite other thoughts and emotions. We need not chide the negligent servant. We are struck with pity, rather, at the swift retribution of his sloth. Alas for the unhappy man that is called to stand in the pulpit, and *not* give bread of life. Everything that befalls, accuses him. Would he ask contributions for the missions, foreign or domestic? Instantly his face is suffused with shame, to propose to his parish, that they should send money a hundred or a thousand miles, to furnish such poor fare as they have at home, and would do well to go the hundred or the thousand miles to escape. Would he urge people to a godly way of living; and can he ask a fellow-creature to come to Sabbath meetings, when he and they all know what is the poor uttermost they can hope for therein? Will he invite them privately to the Lord's Supper? He dares not. If no heart warm this rite, the hollow, dry, creaking formality is too plain, than that he can face a man of wit and energy, and put the invitation without terror. In the street, what has he to say to the bold village blasphemer? The village blasphemer sees fear in the face, form, and gait of the minister.

Let me not taint the sincerity of this plea by any oversight of the claims of good men. I know and honor the purity and strict conscience of numbers of the clergy. What life the public worship retains, it owes to the scattered company of pious men, who minister here and there in the churches, and who, sometimes accepting with too great tenderness the tenet of the elders, have not accepted from others, but from their own heart, the genuine impulses of virtue, and so still command our love and awe, to the sanctity of character. Moreover, the exceptions are not so much to be found in a few eminent preachers, as in the better hours, the truer inspirations of all,—nay, in the sincere moments of every man. But with whatever exception, it is still true, that tradition characterizes the preaching of this country; that it comes out of the memory, and not out of the soul; that it aims at what is usual, and not at what is necessary and eternal; that thus historical Christianity destroys the power of preaching, by withdrawing it from the exploration of the moral nature of man, where the sublime is, where are the resources of astonishment and power. What a cruel injustice it is to that Law, the joy of the whole earth, which alone can make thought dear and rich; that Law whose fatal sureness the astronomical orbits poorly emulate, that it is travestied and depreciated, that it is behooted and behowled, and not a trait, not a word of it articulated. The pulpit in losing sight of this Law, loses its reason, and gropes after it knows not what. And for want of this culture, the soul of the community is sick and faithless. It wants nothing so much as a stern, high, stoical, Christian discipline, to make it know itself and the divinity that speaks through it. Now man is ashamed of himself; he skulks and sneaks through the world, to be tolerated, to be pitied, and scarcely in a thousand years does any man dare to be wise and good, and so draw after him the tears and blessings of his kind.

Certainly there have been periods when, from the inactivity of the intellect on certain truths, a greater faith was possible in names and persons. The Puritans in England and America, found in the Christ of the Catholic Church, and in the dogmas inherited from Rome, scope for their austere piety, and their longings for civil freedom. But their creed is passing away, and none arises in its room. I think no man can go with his thoughts about him, into one of our churches, without feeling, that what hold the public worship had on men is gone, or going. It has lost its grasp on the affection of the good, and the fear of the bad. In the country, neighborhoods, half parishes are *signing off*,—to use the local term. It is already beginning to indicate character and religion to withdraw from the religious meetings. I have heard a devout person, who prized the Sabbath, say in bitterness of heart, "On Sundays, it seems wicked to go to church." And the motive that holds the best there, is now only a hope and a waiting. What was once a mere circumstance, that the best and the worst men in the parish, the poor and the rich, the learned and the ignorant, young and old, should meet one day as fellows in one house, in sign of an equal right in the soul,—has come to be a paramount motive for going thither.

My friends, in these two errors, I think, I find the causes of a decaying church and a wasting unbelief. And what greater calamity can fall upon a nation than the loss of worship? Then all things go to decay. Genius leaves the temple, to haunt the senate, or the market. Literature becomes frivolous. Science is cold. The eye of youth is not lighted by the hope of other worlds, and age is without honor. Society lives to trifles, and when men die, we do not mention them.

And now, my brothers, you will ask, What in these desponding days can be done by us? The remedy is already declared in the ground of our complaint of the Church. We have contrasted the Church with the Soul. In the soul, then, let the redemption be sought. Wherever a man comes, there comes revolution. The old is for slaves. When a man comes, all books are legible, all things transparent, all religions are forms. He is religious. Man is the wonder-worker. He is seen amid miracles. All men bless and curse. He saith yea and nay, only. The stationariness of religion; the assumption that the age of inspiration is past, that the Bible is closed; the fear of degrading the character of Jesus by representing him as a man; indicate with sufficient clearness the falsehood of our theology. It is the office of a true teacher to show us that God is, not was; that he speaketh, not spake. The true Christianity—a faith like Christ's in the infinitude of man— is lost. None believeth in the soul of man, but only in some man or person old and departed. Ah me! no man goeth alone. All men go in flocks to this saint or that poet, avoiding the God who seeth in secret; they cannot see in secret; they love to be blind in public. They think society wiser than their soul, and know not that one soul, and their soul, is wiser than the whole world. See how nations and races flit by on the sea of time, and leave no ripple to tell where they floated or sunk, and one good soul shall make the name of Moses, or of Zeno, or of Zoroaster, reverend forever. None assayeth the stern ambition to be the Self of the nation, and of nature, but each would be an easy secondary to some Christian scheme, or sectarian connection, or some eminent man. Once leave your own knowledge of God, your own sentiment, and take secondary knowledge, as St. Paul's, or George Fox's, or Swedenborg's, and you get wide from God with every year this secondary form lasts, and if, as now, for centuries,— the chasm yawns to that breadth, that men can scarcely be convinced there is in them anything divine.

Let me admonish you, first of all, to go alone; to refuse the good models, even those which are sacred in the imagination of men, and dare to love God without mediator or veil. Friends enough you shall find who will hold up to your emulation Wesleys and Oberlins, Saints and Prophets. Thank God for these good men, but say, 'I also am a man.' Imitation cannot go above its model. The imitator dooms himself to hopeless mediocrity. The inventor did it, because it was natural to him, and so in him it has a charm. In the imitator, something else is natural, and he bereaves himself of his own beauty, to come short of another man's.

Yourself a new-born bard of the Holy Ghost,—cast behind you all conformity, and acquaint men at first hand with Deity. Look to it first and only, that fashion, custom, authority, pleasure, and money are nothing to you,—are not bandages over your eyes, that you cannot see,—but live with the privilege of the immeasurable mind. Not too anxious to visit periodically all families and each family in your parish connection,—when you meet one of these men or women, be to them a divine man; be to them thought and virtue; let their timid aspirations find in you a friend; let their trampled instincts be genially tempted out in your atmosphere; let their doubts know that you have doubted, and their wonder feel that you have wondered. By trusting your own heart, you shall gain more confidence in other men. For all our penny-wisdom, for all our soul-destroying slavery to habit, it is not to be doubted, that all men have sublime thoughts; that all men value the few real hours of life; they love to be heard; they love to be caught up into the vision of principles. We mark with light in the memory the few interviews we have had, in the dreary years of routine and of sin, with souls that made our souls wiser; that spoke what we thought; that told us what we knew; that gave us leave to be what we inly were. Discharge to men the priestly office, and, present or absent, you shall be followed with their love as by an angel.

And, to this end, let us not aim at common degrees of merit. Can we not leave, to such as love it, the virtue that glitters for the commendation of society, and ourselves pierce the deep solitudes of absolute ability and worth? We easily come up to the standard of goodness in society. Society's praise can be cheaply secured, and almost all men are content with those easy merits; but the instant effect of conversing with God, will be to put them away. There are persons who are not actors, not speakers, but influences; persons too great for fame, for display; who disdain eloquence; to whom all we call art and artist, seems too nearly allied to show and by-ends, to the exaggeration of the finite and selfish, and loss of the universal. The orators, the poets, the commanders encroach on us only as fair women do, by our allowance and homage. Slight them by preoccupation of mind, slight them, as you can well afford to do, by high and universal aims, and they instantly feel that you have right, and that it is in lower places that they must shine. They also feel your right; for they with you are open to the influx of the all-knowing Spirit, which annihilates before its broad noon the little shades and gradations of intelligence in the compositions we call wiser and wisest.

In such high communion, let us study the grand strokes of rectitude; a bold benevolence, an independence of friends, so that not the unjust wishes of those who love us, shall impair our freedom, but we shall resist for truth's sake the freest flow of kindness, and appeal to sympathies far in advance; and—what is the highest form in which we know this beautiful element—a certain solidity of merit, that has nothing to do with opinion, and which is so essentially and manifestly virtue, that it is taken for granted, that the right, the brave, the generous step will be taken by it, and nobody thinks of commending it. You would compliment a coxcomb doing a good act, but you would not praise an angel. The silence that accepts merit as the most natural thing in the world, is the highest applause. Such souls, when they appear, are the Imperial Guard of Virtue, the perpetual reserve, the dictators of fortune. One needs not praise their courage,— they are the heart and soul of nature. O my friends, there are resources in us on which we have not drawn. There are men who rise refreshed on hearing a threat; men to whom a crisis which intimidates and paralyzes the majority,—demanding not the faculties of prudence and thrift, but comprehension,

immovableness, the readiness of sacrifice,—comes graceful
and beloved as a bride. Napoleon said of Massena, that he
was not himself until the battle began to go against him;
then, when the dead began to fall in ranks around him,
awoke his powers of combination, and he put on terror and
victory as a robe. So it is in rugged crises, in unwearable
endurance, and in aims which put sympathy out of question,
that the angel is shown. But these are heights that we can
scarce remember and look up to, without contrition and
shame. Let us thank God that such things exist.

And now let us do what we can to rekindle the smoulder-
ing, nigh quenched fire on the altar. The evils of the church
that now is are manifest. The question returns, What shall
we do? I confess, all attempts to project and establish a
Cultus with new rites and forms, seem to me vain. Faith
makes us, and not we it, and faith makes its own forms. All
attempts to contrive a system are as cold as the new worship introduced by the French to the goddess of Reason,—to-
day, pasteboard and filigree, and ending to-morrow in madness and murder. Rather let the breath of new life be breathed
by you through the forms already existing. For, if once you
are alive, you shall find they shall become plastic and new.
The remedy to their deformity is, first, soul, and second,
soul, and evermore, soul. A whole popedom of forms, one
pulsation of virtue can uplift and vivify. Two inestimable advantages Christianity has given us: first, the Sabbath, the
jubilee of the whole world; whose light dawns welcome alike
into the closet of the philosopher, into the garret of toil, and
into prison cells, and everywhere suggests, even to the vile,
the dignity of spiritual being. Let it stand forevermore, a
temple, which new love, new faith, new sight shall restore to
more than its first splendor to mankind. And secondly, the
institution of preaching,—the speech of man to men,—essentially the most flexible of all organs, of all forms. What
hinders that now, everywhere, in pulpits, in lecture-rooms,
in houses, in fields, wherever the invitation of men or your
own occasions lead you, you speak the very truth, as your
life and conscience teach it, and cheer the waiting, fainting
hearts of men with new hope and new revelation?

I look for the hour when that supreme Beauty, which ravished the souls of those Eastern men, and chiefly of those
Hebrews, and through their lips spoke oracles to all time,
shall speak in the West also. The Hebrew and Greek Scrip-

tures contain immortal sentences, that have been bread of life to millions. But they have no epical integrity; are fragmentary; are not shown in their order to the intellect. I look for the new Teacher, that shall follow so far those shining laws, that he shall see them come full circle; shall see their rounding complete grace; shall see the world to be the mirror of the soul; shall see the identity of the law of gravitation with purity of heart; and shall show that the Ought, that Duty, is one thing with Science, with Beauty, and with Joy.

1838

SELF-RELIANCE.*

"Ne te quæsiveris extra."

"Man is his own star; and the soul that can
  Render an honest and a perfect man,
  Commands all light, all influence, all fate;
  Nothing to him falls early or too late.
  Our acts our angels are, or good or ill,
  Our fatal shadows that walk by us still."
  Epilogue to Beaumont and Fletcher's Honest Man's Fortune.

Cast the bantling on the rocks,
  Suckle him with the she-wolf's teat;
Wintered with the hawk and fox,
Power and speed be hands and feet.

I read the other day some verses written by an eminent painter which were original and not conventional. The soul always hears an admonition in such lines, let the subject be what it may. The sentiment they instil is of more value than any thought they may contain. To believe your own thought, to believe that what is true for you in your private heart is true for all men,—that is genius. Speak your latent conviction, and it shall be the universal sense; for the inmost in due time becomes the outmost,—and our first thought is rendered back to us by the trumpets of the Last Judgment.

* From *Essays, First Series.*

Familiar as the voice of the mind is to each, the highest
merit we ascribe to Moses, Plato, and Milton is, that they set
at naught books and traditions, and spoke not what men
but what they thought. A man should learn to detect and
watch that gleam of light which flashes across his mind
from within, more than the lustre of the firmament of bards
and sages. Yet he dismisses without notice his thought, because it is his. In every work of genius we recognize our own
rejected thoughts: they come back to us with a certain alienated majesty. Great works of art have no more affecting lesson for us than this. They teach us to abide by our spontaneous impression with good-humored inflexibility then most
when the whole cry of voices is on the other side. Else, to-
morrow a stranger will say with masterly good sense precisely
what we have thought and felt all the time, and we shall be
forced to take with shame our own opinion from another.

There is a time in every man's education when he arrives
at the conviction that envy is ignorance; that imitation is suicide; that he must take himself for better, for worse, as his
portion; that though the wide universe is full of good, no
kernel of nourishing corn can come to him but through his
toil bestowed on that plot of ground which is given to him
to till. The power which resides in him is new in nature,
and none but he knows what that is which he can do nor
does he know until he has tried. Not for nothing one face,
one character, one fact, makes much impression on him, and
another none. This sculpture in the memory is not without
pre-established harmony. The eye was placed where one ray
should fall, that it might testify of that particular ray. We
but half express ourselves, and are ashamed of that divine
idea which each of us represents. It may be safely trusted as
proportionate and of good issues, so it be faithfully imparted,
but God will not have his work made manifest by cowards. A
man is relieved and gay when he has put his heart into his
work and done his best; but what he has said or done otherwise, shall give him no peace. It is a deliverance which does
not deliver. In the attempt his genius deserts him; no muse
befriends; no invention, no hope.

Trust thyself: every heart vibrates to that iron string. Accept the place the divine providence has found for you, the
society of your contemporaries, the connection of events.
Great men have always done so, and confided themselves
childlike to the genius of their age, betraying their perception

that the absolutely trustworthy was seated at their heart, working through their hands, predominating in all their being. And we are now men, and must accept in the highest mind the same transcendent destiny; and not minors and invalids in a protected corner, not cowards fleeing before a revolution, but guides, redeemers, and benefactors, obeying the Almighty effort, and advancing on Chaos and the Dark.

What pretty oracles nature yields us on this text, in the face and behavior of children, babes, and even brutes! That divided and rebel mind, that distrust of a sentiment because our arithmetic has computed the strength and means opposed to our purpose, these have not. Their mind being whole, their eye is as yet unconquered, and when we look in their faces we are disconcerted. Infancy conforms to nobody: all conform to it, so that one babe commonly makes four or five out of the adults who prattle and play to it. So God has armed youth and puberty and manhood no less with its own piquancy and charm, and made it enviable and gracious and its claims not to be put by, if it will stand by itself. Do not think the youth has no force, because he cannot speak to you and me. Hark! in the next room his voice is sufficiently clear and emphatic. It seems he knows how to speak to his contemporaries. Bashful or bold, then, he will know how to make us seniors very unnecessary.

The nonchalance of boys who are sure of a dinner, and would disdain as much as a lord to do or say aught to conciliate one, is the healthy attitude of human nature. A boy is in the parlor what the pit is in the playhouse; independent, irresponsible, looking out from his corner on such people and facts as pass by, he tries and sentences them on their merits, in the swift, summary way of boys, as good, bad, interesting, silly, eloquent, troublesome. He cumbers himself never about consequences, about interests: he gives an independent, genuine verdict. You must court him: he does not court you. But the man is, as it were, clapped into jail by his consciousness. As soon as he has once acted or spoken with eclat, he is a committed person, watched by the sympathy or the hatred of hundreds, whose affections must now enter into his account. There is no Lethe for this. Ah, that he could pass again into his neutrality! Who can thus avoid all pledges, and having observed, observe again from the same unaffected, unbiassed, unbribable, unaffrighted innocence, must always be formidable. He would utter opinions on all passing affairs, which being seen to be not private, but necessary, would sink like darts into the ear of men, and put them in fear.

These are the voices which we hear in solitude, but they grow faint and inaudible as we enter into the world. Society everywhere is in conspiracy against the manhood of every one of its members. Society is a joint-stock company, in which the members agree, for the better securing of his bread to each shareholder, to surrender the liberty and culture of the eater. The virtue in most request is conformity. Self-reliance is its aversion. It loves not realities and creators, but names and customs.

Whoso would be a man must be a nonconformist. He who would gather immortal palms must not be hindered by the name of goodness, but must explore if it be goodness. Nothing is at last sacred but the integrity of your own mind. Absolve you to yourself, and you shall have the suffrage of the world. I remember an answer which when quite young I was prompted to make a valued adviser, who was wont to importune me with the dear old doctrines of the church. On my saying, What have I to do with the sacredness of traditions, if I live wholly from within? my friend suggested: "But these impulses may be from below, not from above." I replied: "They do not seem to me to be such; but if I am the Devil's child, I will live then from the Devil." No law can be sacred to me but that of my nature. Good and bad are but names very readily transferable to that or this; the only right is what is after my constitution, the only wrong what is against it. A man is to carry himself in the presence of all opposition, as if everything were titular and ephemeral but he. I am ashamed to think how easily we capitulate to badges and names, to large societies and dead institutions. Every decent and well-spoken individual affects and sways me more than is right. I ought to go upright and vital, and speak the rude truth in all ways. If malice and vanity wear the coat of philanthropy, shall that pass? If an angry bigot assumes this bountiful cause of Abolition, and comes to me with his last news from Barbadoes, why should I not say to him: 'Go love thy infant; love thy woodchopper: be good-natured and modest: have that grace; and never varnish your hard, uncharitable ambition with this incredible tenderness for black folk a thousand miles off. Thy love afar is spite at home.' Rough and graceless would be such greeting, but truth is handsomer than the affectation of love. Your goodness must have some edge to it,—else it is none. The doctrine of hatred must be preached as the counteraction of the doctrine of love when that pules and whines. I shun father and mother and wife and brother, when my genius calls me. I would write on the lintels of the door-post, *Whim*. I hope it is somewhat better than whim at last, but we cannot spend the day in explanation. Expect me not to show cause why I seek or why I exclude company. Then, again, do not tell me, as a good man did to-day, of my obligation to put all poor men in good situations. Are they *my* poor? I tell thee, thou foolish philanthropist, that I grudge the dollar, the dime, the cent, I give to such men as do not belong to me and to whom I do not belong. There is a class of persons to whom by all spiritual affinity I am bought and sold; for them I will go to prison, if need be; but your miscellaneous popular charities; the education at college of fools; the building of meeting-houses to the vain end to which many now stand; alms to sots; and the thousand-fold Relief Societies;—though I confess with shame I sometimes succumb and give the dollar, it is a wicked dollar which by and by I shall have the manhood to withhold.

Virtues are, in the popular estimate, rather the exception than the rule. There is the man *and* his virtues. Men do what is called a good action, as some piece of courage or charity, much as they would pay a fine in expiation of daily non-appearance on parade. Their works are done as an apology or extenuation of their living in the world,—as invalids and the insane pay a high board. Their virtues are penances. I do not wish to expiate, but to live. My life is for itself and not for a spectacle. I much prefer that it should be of a lower strain, so it be genuine and equal, than that it should be glittering and unsteady. I wish it to be sound and sweet, and not to need diet and bleeding. I ask primary evidence that you are a man, and refuse this appeal from the man to his actions. I know that for myself it makes no difference whether I do or forbear those actions which are reckoned excellent. I cannot consent to pay for a privilege where I have intrinsic right. Few and mean as my gifts may be, I actually am, and do not need for my own assurance or the assurance of my fellows any secondary testimony.

What I must do is all that concerns me, not what the people think. This rule, equally arduous in actual and in intellectual life, may serve for the whole distinction between greatness and meanness. It is the harder, because you will always find those who think they know what is your duty better than you know it. It is easy in the world to live after the world's opinion; it is easy in solitude to live after our own; but the great man is he who in the midst of the crowd keeps with perfect sweetness the independence of solitude.

The objection to conforming to usages that have become dead to you is, that it scatters your force. It loses your time and blurs the impression of your character. If you maintain a dead church, contribute to a dead Bible society, vote with a great party either for the government or against it, spread your table like base housekeepers,—under all these screens I have difficulty to detect the precise man you are. And, of course, so much force is withdrawn from your proper life. But do your work, and I shall know you. Do your work, and you shall reinforce yourself. A man must consider what a blind-man's-buff is this game of conformity. If I know your sect, I anticipate your argument. I hear a preacher announce for his text and topic the expediency of one of the institutions of his church. Do I not know beforehand that not possibly can he say a new and spontaneous word? Do I not know that, with all this ostentation of examining the grounds of the institution, he will do no such thing? Do I not know that he is pledged to himself not to look but at one side,—the permitted side, not as a man, but as a parish minister? He is a retained attorney, and these airs of the bench are the emptiest affectation. Well, most men have bound their eyes with one or another handkerchief, and attached themselves to some one of these communities of opinion. This conformity makes them not false in a few particulars, authors of a few lies, but false in all particulars. Their every truth is not quite true. Their two is not the real two, their four not the real four; so that every word they say chagrins us, and we know not where to begin to set them right. Meantime nature is not slow to equip us in the prison-uniform of the party to which we adhere. We come to wear one cut of face and figure, and acquire by degrees the gentlest asinine expression. There is a mortifying experience in particular, which does not fail to wreak itself also in the general history; I mean "the foolish face of praise," the forced smile which we put on in company where we do not feel at ease in answer to conversation which does not interest us. The muscles, not spontaneously moved, but moved by a low usurping wilfulness, grow tight about the outline of the face with the most disagreeable sensation.

For non-conformity the world whips you with its displeasure. And therefore a man must know how to estimate a sour face. The bystanders look askance on him in the public street or in the friend's parlor. If this aversation had its origin in contempt and resistance like his own, he might well go home with a sad countenance; but the sour faces of the multitude, like their sweet faces, have no deep cause, but are put on and off as the wind blows and a newspaper directs. Yet is the discontent of the multitude more formidable than that of the senate and the college. It is easy enough for a firm man who knows the world to brook the rage of the cultivated classes. Their rage is decorous and prudent, for they are timid as being very vulnerable themselves. But when to their feminine rage the indignation of the people is added, when the ignorant and the poor are aroused, when the unintelligent brute force that lies at the bottom of society is made to growl and mow, it needs the habit of magnanimity and religion to treat it godlike as a trifle of no concernment.

The other terror that scares us from self-trust is our consistency; a reverence for our past act or word, because the eyes of others have no other data for computing our orbit than our past acts, and we are loath to disappoint them.

But why should you keep your head over your shoulder? Why drag about this corpse of your memory, lest you contradict somewhat you have stated in this or that public place? Suppose you should contradict yourself; what then? It seems to be a rule of wisdom never to rely on your memory alone, scarcely even in acts of pure memory, but to bring the past for judgment into the thousand-eyed present, and live ever in a new day. In your metaphysics you have denied personality to the Deity: yet when the devout motions of the soul come, yield to them heart and life, though they should clothe God with shape and color. Leave your theory, as Joseph his coat in the hand of the harlot, and flee.

A foolish consistency is the hobgoblin of little minds, adored by little statesmen and philosophers and divines. With consistency a great soul has simply nothing to do. He may as well concern himself with his shadow on the wall. Speak what you think now in hard words and to-morrow speak what to-morrow thinks in hard words again, though it contradict everything you said to-day.—'Ah, so you shall be sure to be misunderstood?'—Is it so bad, then, to be misunderstood? Pythagoras was misunderstood, and Socrates, and Jesus, and Luther, and Copernicus, and Galileo, and Newton, and every pure and wise spirit that ever took flesh. To be great is to be misunderstood.

I suppose no man can violate his nature. All the sallies of his will are rounded in by the law of his being, as the inequalities of Andes and Himmaleh are insignificant in the curve of the sphere. Nor does it matter how you gauge and try him. A character is like an acrostic or Alexandrian stanza;—read it forward, backward, or across, it still spells the same thing. In this pleasing, contrite wood-life which God allows me, let me record day by day my honest thought without prospect or retrospect, and, I cannot doubt, it will be found symmetrical, though I mean it not and see it not. My book should smell of pines and resound with the hum of insects. The swallow over my window should interweave that thread or straw he carries in his bill into my web also. We pass for what we are. Character teaches above our wills. Men imagine that they communicate their virtue or vice only by overt actions, and do not see that virtue or vice emit a breath every moment.

There will be an agreement in whatever variety of actions, so they be each honest and natural in their hour. For of one will, the actions will be harmonious, however unlike they seem. These varieties are lost sight of at a little distance, at a little height of thought. One tendency unites them all. The voyage of the best ship is a zigzag line of a hundred tacks. See the line from a sufficient distance, and it straightens itself to the average tendency. Your genuine action will explain itself, and will explain your other genuine actions. Your conformity explains nothing. Act singly, and what you have already done singly will justify you now. Greatness appeals to the future. If I can be firm enough to-day to do right, and scorn eyes, I must have done so much right before as to defend me now. Be it how it will, do right now. Always scorn appearances, and you always may. The force of character is cumulative. All the foregone days of virtue work their health into this. What makes the majesty of the heroes of the senate and the field, which so fills the imagination? The consciousness of a train of great days and victories behind. They shed an united light on the advancing actor. He is attended as by a visible escort of angels. That is it which throws thunder into Chatham's voice, and dignity into Washington's port, and America into Adams's eye. Honor is venerable to us because it is no ephemeris. It is always ancient virtue. We worship it to-day because it is not of to-day. We love it and pay it homage, because it is not a trap for our love and homage, but is self-dependent, self-derived, and therefore of an old immaculate pedigree, even if shown in a young person.

I hope in these days we have heard the last of conformity and consistency. Let the words be gazetted and ridiculous henceforward. Instead of the gong for dinner, let us hear a whistle from the Spartan fife. Let us never bow and apologize more. A great man is coming to eat at my house. I do not wish to please him; I wish that he should wish to please me. I will stand here for humanity, and though I would make it kind, I would make it true. Let us affront and reprimand the smooth mediocrity and squalid contentment of the times, and hurl in the face of custom, and trade, and office, the fact which is the upshot of all history, that there is a great responsible Thinker and Actor working wherever a man works; that a true man belongs to no other time or place, but is the centre of things. Where he is, there is nature. He measures you, and all men, and all events. Ordinarily, everybody in society reminds us of somewhat else, or of some other person. Character, reality, reminds you of nothing else; it takes place of the whole creation. The man must be so much, that he must make all circumstances indifferent. Every true man is a cause, a country, and an age; requires infinite spaces and numbers and time fully to accomplish his design;—and posterity seems to follow his steps as a train of clients. A man Cæsar is born, and for ages after we have a Roman Empire. Christ is born, and millions of minds so grow and cleave to his genius, that he is confounded with virtue and the possible of man. An institution is the lengthened shadow of one man; as Monachism, of the Hermit Antony; the Reformation, of Luther; Quakerism, of Fox; Methodism, of Wesley; Abolition, of Clarkson. Scipio, Milton called "the height of Rome"; and all history resolves itself very easily into the biography of a few stout and earnest persons.

Let a man then know his worth, and keep things under his feet. Let him not peep or steal, or skulk up and down with the air of a charity-boy, a bastard, or an interloper, in the world which exists for him. But the man in the street, finding no worth in himself which corresponds to the force which built a tower or sculptured a marble god, feels poor when he looks on these. To him a palace, a statue, or a costly book have an alien and forbidding air, much like a gay equipage, and seems to say like that, 'Who are you, sir?' Yet they all are his suitors for his notice, petitioners to his faculties that they will come out and take possession. The picture waits for my verdict: it is not to command me, but I am to settle its claims to praise. That popular fable of the sot who was picked up dead drunk in the street, carried to the duke's house, washed and dressed and laid in the duke's bed, and, on his waking, treated with all obsequious ceremony like the duke, and assured that he had been insane, owes its popularity to the fact, that it symbolizes so well the state of man, who is in the world a sort of sot, but now and then wakes up, exercises his reason and finds himself a true prince.

Our reading is mendicant and sycophantic. In history, our imagination plays us false. Kingdom and lordship, power and estate, are a gaudier vocabulary than private John and Edward in a small house and common day's work; but the things of life are the same to both; the sum total of both are the same. Why all this deference to Alfred, and Scanderbeg, and Gustavus? Suppose they were virtuous; did they wear out virtue? As great a stake depends on your private act to-day, as followed their public and renowned steps. When private men shall act with original views, the lustre will be transferred from the actions of kings to those of gentlemen.

The world has been instructed by its kings, who have so magnetized the eyes of nations. It has been taught by this colossal symbol the mutual reverence that is due from man to man. The joyful loyalty with which men have everywhere suffered the king, the noble, or the great proprietor to walk among them by a law of his own, make his own scale of men and things and reverse theirs, pay for benefits not with money but with honor, and represent the law in his person, was the hieroglyphic by which they obscurely signified their consciousness of their own right and comeliness, the right of every man.

The magnetism which all original action exerts is explained when we inquire the reason of self-trust. Who is the Trustee? What is the aboriginal Self, on which a universal reliance may be grounded? What is the nature and power of that science-baffling star, without parallax, without calculable elements, which shoots a ray of beauty even into trivial and impure actions, if the least mark of independence appear? The inquiry leads us to that source, at once the essence of genius, of virtue, and of life, which we call Spontaneity or Instinct. We denote this primary wisdom as Intuition, whilst all later teachings are tuitions. In that deep force, the last fact behind which analysis cannot go, all things find their common origin. For, the sense of being which in calm hours rises, we know not how, in the soul, is not diverse from things, from space, from light, from time, from man, but one with them, and proceeds obviously from the same source whence their life and being also proceed. We first share the life by which things exist, and afterwards see them as appearances in nature, and forget that we have shared their cause. Here is the fountain of action and of thought. Here are the lungs of that inspiration which giveth man wisdom, and which cannot be denied without impiety and atheism. We lie in the lap of immense intelligence, which makes us receivers of its truth and organs of its activity. When we discern justice, when we discern truth, we do nothing of ourselves, but allow a passage to its beams. If we ask whence this comes, if we seek to pry into the soul that causes, all philosophy is at fault. Its presence or its absence is all we can affirm. Every man discriminates between the voluntary acts of his mind, and his involuntary perceptions, and knows that to his involuntary perceptions a perfect faith is due. He may err in the expression of them, but he knows that these things are so, like day and night, not to be disputed. My wilful actions and acquisitions are but roving; —the idlest revery, the faintest native emotion, command my curiosity and respect. Thoughtless people contradict as readily the statement of perceptions as of opinions, or rather much more readily; for, they do not distinguish between perception and notion. They fancy that I choose to see this or that thing. But perception is not whimsical, but fatal. If I see a trait, my children will see it after me, and in course of time, all mankind,—although it may chance that no one has seen it before me. For my perception of it is as much a fact as the sun.

The relations of the soul to the divine spirit are so pure, that it is profane to seek to interpose helps. It must be that when God speaketh he should communicate, not one thing, but all things; should fill the world with his voice; should scatter forth light, nature, time, souls, from the centre of the present thought; and new date and new create the whole. Whenever a mind is simple, and receives a divine wisdom, old things pass away,—means, teachers, texts, temples fall; it lives now, and absorbs past and future into the present hour. All things are made sacred by relation to it,—one as much as another. All things are dissolved to their centre by their cause, and, in the universal miracle, petty and particular miracles disappear. If, therefore, a man claims to know and speak of God, and carries you backward to the phraseology of some old mouldered nation in another country, in another world, believe him not. Is the acorn better than the oak which is its fulness and completion? Is the parent better than the child into whom he has cast his ripened being? Whence, then, this worship of the past? The centuries are conspirators against the sanity and authority of the soul. Time and space are but physiological colors which the eye makes, but the soul is light; where it is, is day; where it was, is night; and history is an impertinence and an injury, if it be anything more than a cheerful apologue or parable of my being and becoming.

Man is timid and apologetic; he is no longer upright; he dares not say 'I think,' 'I am,' but quotes some saint or sage. He is ashamed before the blade of grass or the blowing rose. These roses under my window make no reference to former roses or to better ones; they are for what they are; they exist with God to-day. There is no time to them. There is simply the rose; it is perfect in every moment of its existence. Before a leaf-bud has burst, its whole life acts; in the full-blown flower there is no more; in the leafless root there is no less. Its nature is satisfied, and it satisfies nature, in all moments alike. But man postpones or remembers; he does not live in the present, but with reverted eye laments the past, or, heedless of the riches that surround him, stands on tiptoe to foresee the future. He cannot be happy and strong until he too lives with nature in the present, above time.

This should be plain enough. Yet see what strong intellects dare not yet hear God himself, unless he speak the phraseology of I know not what David, or Jeremiah, or

Paul. We shall not always set so great a price on a few texts, on a few lives. We are like children who repeat by rote the sentences of grandames and tutors, and, as they grow older, of the men of talents and character they chance to see,—painfully recollecting the exact words they spoke; afterwards, when they come into the point of view which those had who uttered these sayings, they understand them, and are willing to let the words go; for, at any time, they can use words as good when occasion comes. If we live truly, we shall see truly. It is as easy for the strong man to be strong, as it is for the weak to be weak. When we have new perception, we shall gladly disburden the memory of its hoarded treasures as old rubbish. When a man lives with God, his voice shall be as sweet as the murmur of the brook and the rustle of the corn.

And now at last the highest truth on this subject remains unsaid; probably cannot be said; for all that we say is the far-off remembering of the intuition. That thought, by what I can now nearest approach to say it, is this. When good is near you, when you have life in yourself, it is not by any known or accustomed way; you shall not discern the footprints of any other; you shall not see the face of man; you shall not hear any name; the way, the thought, the good, shall be wholly strange and new. It shall exclude example and experience. You take the way from man, not to man. All persons that ever existed are its forgotten ministers. Fear and hope are alike beneath it. There is somewhat low even in hope. In the hour of vision, there is nothing that can be called gratitude, nor properly joy. The soul raised over passion beholds identity and eternal causation, perceives the self-existence of Truth and Right, and calms itself with knowing that all things go well. Vast spaces of nature, the Atlantic Ocean, the South Sea,—long intervals of time, years, centuries,—are of no account. This which I think and feel underlay every former state of life and circumstances, as it does underlie my present, and what is called life, and what is called death.

Life only avails, not the having lived. Power ceases in the instant of repose; it resides in the moment of transition from a past to a new state, in the shooting of the gulf, in the darting to an aim. This one fact the world hates, that the soul *becomes;* for that forever degrades the past, turns all riches to poverty, all reputation to a shame, confounds the saint with the rogue, shoves Jesus and Judas equally aside. Why, then, do we prate of self-reliance? Inasmuch as the soul is present, there will be power not confident but agent. To talk of reliance is a poor external way of speaking. Speak rather of that which relies, because it works and is. Who has more obedience than I masters me, though he should not raise his finger. Round him I must revolve by the gravitation of spirits. We fancy it rhetoric, when we speak of eminent virtue. We do not yet see that virtue is Height, and that a man or a company of men, plastic and permeable to principles, by the law of nature must overpower and ride all cities, nations, kings, rich men, poets, who are not.

This is the ultimate fact which we so quickly reach on this, as on every topic, the resolution of all into the ever-blessed ONE. Self-existence is the attribute of the Supreme Cause, and it constitutes the measure of good by the degree in which it enters into all lower forms. All things real are so by so much virtue as they contain. Commerce, husbandry, hunting, whaling, war, eloquence, personal weight, are somewhat, and engage my respect as examples of its presence and impure action. I see the same law working in nature for conservation and growth. Power is in nature the essential measure of right. Nature suffers nothing to remain in her kingdoms which cannot help itself. The genesis and maturation of a planet, its poise and orbit, the bended tree recovering itself from the strong wind, the vital resources of every animal and vegetable, are demonstrations of the self-sufficing, and therefore self-relying soul.

Thus all concentrates: let us not rove; let us sit at home with the cause. Let us stun and astonish the intruding rabble of men and books and institutions, by a simple declaration of the divine fact. Bid the invaders take the shoes from off their feet, for God is here within. Let our simplicity judge them, and our docility to our own law demonstrate the poverty of nature and fortune beside our native riches.

But now we are a mob. Man does not stand in awe of man, nor is his genius admonished to stay at home, to put itself in communication with the internal ocean, but it goes abroad to beg a cup of water of the urns of other men. We must go alone. I like the silent church before the service begins, better than any preaching. How far off, how cool, how chaste the persons look, begirt each one with a precinct or sanctuary! So let us always sit. Why should we assume the faults of our friend, or wife, or father, or child, because they sit around our hearth, or are said to have the same blood? All men have my blood, and I have all men's. Not for that will I adopt their petulance or folly, even to the extent of being ashamed of it. But your isolation must not be mechanical, but spiritual, that is, must be elevation. At times the whole world seems to be in conspiracy to importune you with emphatic trifles. Friend, client, child, sickness, fear, want, charity, all knock at once at thy closet door, and say, 'Come out unto us.' But keep thy state; come not into their confusion. The power men possess to annoy me, I give them by a weak curiosity. No man can come near me but through my act. "What we love that we have, but by desire we bereave ourselves of the love."

If we cannot at once rise to the sanctities of obedience and faith, let us at least resist our temptations; let us enter into the state of war, and wake Thor and Woden, courage and constancy in our Saxon breasts. This is to be done in our smooth times by speaking the truth. Check this lying hospitality and lying affection. Live no longer to the expectation of these deceived and deceiving people with whom we converse. Say to them, 'O father, O mother, O wife, O brother, O friend, I have lived with you after appearances hitherto. Henceforward I am the truth's. Be it known unto you that henceforward I obey no law less than the eternal law. I will have no convenants but proximities. I shall endeavor to nourish my parents, to support my family, to be the chaste husband of one wife,—but these relations I must fill after a new and unprecedented way. I appeal from your customs. I must be myself. I cannot break myself any longer for you, or you. If you can love me for what I am, we shall be the happier. If you cannot, I will still seek to deserve that you should. I will not hide my tastes or aversions. I will so trust that what is deep is holy, that I will do strongly before the sun and moon whatever inly rejoices me, and the heart appoints. If you are noble, I will love you; if you are not, I will not hurt you and myself by hypocritical attentions. If you are true, but not in the same truth with me, cleave to your companions; I will seek my own. I do this not selfishly, but humbly and truly. It is alike your interest, and mine, and all men's, however long we have dwelt in lies, to live in truth. Does this sound harsh to-day? You will soon love what is dictated by your nature as well as mine, and, if we follow the truth, it will bring us out safe at last.' But so you may give these friends pain. Yes, but I cannot sell my liberty and my power, to save their sensibility. Besides, all persons have their moments of reason, when they look out into the region of absolute truth; then will they justify me, and do the same thing.

The populace think that your rejection of popular standards is a rejection of all standard, and mere antinomianism; and the bold sensualist will use the name of philosophy to gild his crimes. But the law of consciousness abides. There are two confessionals, in one or the other of which we must be shriven. You may fulfil your round of duties by clearing yourself in the *direct*, or in the *reflex* way. Consider whether you have satisfied your relations to father, mother, cousin, neighbor, town, cat, and dog; whether any of these can upbraid you. But I may also neglect this reflex standard, and absolve me to myself. I have my own stern claims and perfect circle. It denies the name of duty to many offices that are called duties. But if I can discharge its debts, it enables me to dispense with the popular code. If any one imagines that this law is lax, let him keep its commandment one day.

And truly it demands something godlike in him who has cast off the common motives of humanity, and has ventured to trust himself for a taskmaster. High be his heart, faithful his will, clear his sight, that he may in good earnest be doctrine, society, law, to himself, that a simple purpose may be to him as strong as iron necessity is to others!

If any man consider the present aspects of what is called by distinction *society*, he will see the need of these ethics. The sinew and heart of man seem to be drawn out, and we are become timorous, desponding whimperers. We are afraid of truth, afraid of fortune, afraid of death, and afraid of each other. Our age yields no great and perfect persons. We want men and women who shall renovate life and our social state, but we see that most natures are insolvent, cannot satisfy their own wants, have an ambition out of all proportion to their practical force, and do lean and beg day and night continually. Our housekeeping is mendicant, our arts, our occupations, our marriages, our religions, we have not chosen, but society has chosen for us. We are parlor soldiers. We shun the rugged battle of fate, where strength is born.

If our young men miscarry in their first enterprises, they lose all heart. If the young merchant fails, men say he is *ruined*. If the finest genius studies at one of our colleges, and is not installed in an office within one year afterwards in the cities or suburbs of Boston or New York, it seems to his friends and to himself that he is right in being disheartened, and in complaining the rest of his life. A sturdy lad from New Hampshire or Vermont, who in turn tries all the professions, who *teams it, farms it, peddles*, keeps a school, preaches, edits a newspaper, goes to Congress, buys a township, and so forth, in successive years, and always, like a cat, falls on his feet, is worth a hundred of these city dolls. He walks abreast with his days, and feels no shame in not 'studying a profession,' for he does not postpone his life, but lives already. He has not one chance, but a hundred chances. Let a Stoic open the resources of man, and tell men they are not leaning willows, but can and must detach themselves; that with the exercise of self-trust, new powers shall appear; that a man is the word made flesh, born to shed healing to the nations, that he should be ashamed of our compassion, and that the moment he acts from himself, tossing the laws, the books, idolatries, and customs out of the window, we pity him no more, but thank and revere him,—and that teacher shall restore the life of man to splendor, and make his name dear to all history.

It is easy to see that a greater self-reliance must work a revolution in all the offices and relations of men; in their religion; in their education; in their pursuits; their modes of living; their association; in their property; in their speculative views.

1. In what prayers do men allow themselves! That which they call a holy office is not so much as brave and manly. Prayer looks abroad and asks for some foreign addition to come through some foreign virtue, and loses itself in endless mazes of natural and supernatural, and mediatorial and miraculous. Prayer that craves a particular commodity,—anything less than all good,—is vicious. Prayer is the contemplation of the facts of life from the highest point of view. It is the soliloquy of a beholding and jubilant soul. It is the spirit of God pronouncing his works good. But prayer as a means to effect a private end is meanness and theft. It supposes dualism and not unity in nature and consciousness. As soon as the man is at one with God, he will not beg.

He will then see prayer in all action. The prayer of the farmer kneeling in his field to weed it, the prayer of the rower kneeling with the stroke of his oar, are true prayers heard throughout nature though for cheap ends. Caratach, in Fletcher's Bonduca, when admonished to inquire the mind of the god Audate, replies,—

> "His hidden meaning lies in our endeavors;
> Our valors are our best gods."

Another sort of false prayers are our regrets. Discontent is the want of self-reliance: it is infirmity of will. Regret calamities, if you can thereby help the sufferer; if not, attend your own work, and already the evil begins to be repaired. Our sympathy is just as base. We come to them who weep foolishly, and sit down and cry for company, instead of imparting to them truth and health in rough electric shocks, putting them once more in communication with their own reason. The secret of fortune is joy in our hands. Welcome evermore to gods and men is the self-helping man. For him all doors are flung wide: him all tongues greet, all honors crown, all eyes follow with desire. Our love goes out to him and embraces him, because he did not need it. We solicitously and apologetically caress and celebrate him, because he held on his way and scorned our disapprobation. The gods love him because men hated him. "To the persevering mortal," said Zoroaster, "the blessed Immortals are swift."

As men's prayers are a disease of the will, so are their creeds a disease of the intellect. They say with those foolish Israelites, 'Let not God speak to us, lest we die. Speak thou, speak any man with us, and we will obey.' Everywhere I am hindered of meeting God in my brother, because he has shut his own temple doors, and recites fables merely of his brother's, or his brother's brother's God. Every new mind is a new classification. If it prove a mind of uncommon activity and power, a Locke, a Lavoisier, a Hutton, a Bentham, a Fourier, it imposes its classification on other men, and lo! a new system. In proportion to the depth of the thought, and so to the number of the objects it touches and brings within reach of the pupil, is his complacency. But chiefly is this apparent in creeds and churches, which are also classifications of some powerful mind acting on the elemental thought of duty, and man's relation to the Highest. Such is Calvinism, Quakerism, Swedenborgism. The pupil takes the same delight in subordinating everything to the new terminology, as a girl who has just learned botany in seeing a new earth and new seasons thereby. It will happen for a time, that the pupil will find his intellectual power has grown by the study of his master's mind. But in all unbalanced minds, the classification is idolized, passes for the end, and not for a speedily exhaustible means, so that the walls of the system blend to their eye in the remote horizon with the walls of the universe; the luminaries of heaven seem to them hung on the arch their master built. They cannot imagine how you aliens have any right to see,—how you can see; 'It must be somehow that you stole the light from us.' They do not yet perceive, that light, unsystematic, indomitable, will break into any cabin, even into theirs. Let them chirp awhile and call it their own. If they are honest and do well, presently their neat new pinfold will be too strait and low, will crack, will lean, will rot and vanish, and the immortal light, all young and joyful, million-orbed, million-colored, will beam over the universe as on the first morning.

2. It is for want of self-culture that the superstition of Travelling, whose idols are Italy, England, Egypt, retains its fascination for all educated Americans. They who made England, Italy, or Greece venerable in the imagination did so by sticking fast where they were, like an axis of the earth. In manly hours, we feel that duty is our place. The soul is no traveller; the wise man stays at home, and when his necessities, his duties, on any occasion call him from his house, or into foreign lands, he is at home still, and shall make men sensible by the expression of his countenance, that he goes the missionary of wisdom and virtue, and visits cities and men like a sovereign, and not like an interloper or a valet.

I have no churlish objection to the circumnavigation of the globe, for the purposes of art, of study, and benevolence, so that the man is first domesticated, or does not go abroad with the hope of finding somewhat greater than he knows. He who travels to be amused, or to get somewhat which he does not carry, travels away from himself, and grows old even in youth among old things. In Thebes, in Palmyra, his will and mind have become old and dilapidated as they. He carries ruins to ruins.

Travelling is a fool's paradise. Our first journeys discover to us the indifference of places. At home I dream that at Naples, at Rome, I can be intoxicated with beauty, and lose my sadness. I pack my trunk, embrace my friends, embark on the sea, and at last wake up in Naples, and there beside me is the stern fact, the sad self, unrelenting, identical, that I fled from. I seek the Vatican, and the palaces. I affect to be intoxicated with sights and suggestions, but I am not intoxicated. My giant goes with me wherever I go.

3. But the rage of travelling is a symptom of a deeper unsoundness affecting the whole intellectual action. The intellect is vagabond, and our system of education fosters restlessness. Our minds travel when our bodies are forced to stay at home. We imitate; and what is imitation but the travelling of the mind? Our houses are built with foreign taste; our shelves are garnished with foreign ornaments; our opinions, our tastes, our faculties, lean, and follow the Past and the Distant. The soul created the arts wherever they have flourished. It was in his own mind that the artist sought his model. It was an application of his own thought to the thing to be done and the conditions to be observed. And why need we copy the Doric or the Gothic model? Beauty, convenience, grandeur of thought, and quaint expression are as near to us as to any, and if the American artist will study with hope and love the precise thing to be done by him, considering the climate, the soil, the length of the day, the wants of the people, the habit and form of the government, he will create a house in which all these will find themselves fitted, and taste and sentiment will be satisfied also.

Insist on yourself; never imitate. Your own gift you can present every moment with the cumulative force of a whole life's cultivation; but of the adopted talent of another, you have only an extemporaneous, half possession. That which each can do best, none but his Maker can teach him. No man yet knows what it is, nor can, till that person has exhibited it. Where is the master who could have taught Shakespeare? Where is the master who could have instructed Franklin, or Washington, or Bacon, or Newton? Every great man is a unique. The Scipionism of Scipio is precisely that part he could not borrow. Shakespeare will never be made by the study of Shakespeare. Do that which is assigned you, and you cannot hope too much or dare too much. There is at this moment for you an utterance brave and grand as that of the colossal chisel of Phidias, or trowel of the Egyptians, or the pen of Moses, or Dante, but different from all these. Not possibly will the soul all rich, all eloquent, with thousand-cloven tongue, design to repeat itself; but if you can hear what these patriarchs say, surely you can reply to them in the same pitch of voice; for the ear and the tongue are two organs of one nature. Abide in the simple and noble regions of thy life, obey thy heart, and thou shalt reproduce the Foreworld again.

4. As our Religion, our Education, our Art look abroad, so does our spirit of society. All men plume themselves on the improvement of society, and no man improves.

Society never advances. It recedes as fast on one side as it gains on the other. It undergoes continual changes; it is barbarous, it is civilized, it is Christianized, it is rich, it is scientific; but this change is not amelioration. For everything that is given, something is taken. Society acquires new arts, and loses old instincts. What a contrast between the well-clad, reading, writing, thinking American, with a watch, a pencil, and a bill of exchange in his pocket, and the naked New-Zealander, whose property is a club, a spear, a mat, and an undivided twentieth of a shed to sleep under! But compare the health of the two men, and you shall see that the white man has lost his aboriginal strength. If the traveller tell us truly, strike the savage with a broad axe, and in a day or two the flesh shall unite and heal as if you struck the blow into soft pitch, and the same blow shall send the white man to his grave.

The civilized man has built a coach, but has lost the use of his feet. He is supported on crutches, but lacks so much support of muscle. He has a fine Geneva watch, but he fails of the skill to tell the hour by the sun. A Greenwich nautical almanac he has, and so being sure of the information when he wants it, the man in the street does not know a star in the sky. The solstice he does not observe; the equinox he knows as little; and the whole bright calendar of the year is without a dial in his mind. His note-books impair his memory; his libraries overload his wit; the insurance office increases the number of accidents; and it may be a question whether machinery does not encumber; whether we have not lost by refinement some energy, by a Christianity intrenched in establishments and forms, some vigor of wild virtue. For every Stoic was a Stoic; but in Christendom where is the Christian?

There is no more deviation in the moral standard than in the standard of height or bulk. No greater men are now than ever were. A singular equality may be observed between the great men of the first and of the last ages; nor can all the science, art, religion, and philosophy of the nineteenth century avail to educate greater men than Plutarch's heroes, three or four and twenty centuries ago. Not in time is the race progressive. Phocion, Socrates, Anaxagoras, Diogenes, are great men, but they leave no class. He who is really of their class will not be called by their name, but will be his own man, and, in his turn, the founder of a sect. The arts and inventions of each period are only its costume, and do not invigorate men. The harm of the improved machinery may compensate its good. Hudson and Behring accomplished so much in their fishing-boats, as to astonish Parry and Franklin, whose equipment exhausted the resources of science and art. Galileo, with an opera-glass, discovered a more splendid series of celestial phenomena than any one since. Columbus found the New World in an undecked boat. It is curious to see the periodical disuse and perishing of means and machinery, which were introduced with loud laudation a few years or centuries before. The great genius returns to essential man. We reckoned the improvements of the art of war among the triumphs of science, and yet Napoleon conquered Europe by the bivouac, which consisted of falling back on naked valor, and disencumbering it of all aids. The Emperor held it impossible to make a perfect army, says Las Casas, "without abolishing our arms, magazines, commissaries, and carriages, until, in imitation of the Roman custom, the soldier should receive his supply of corn, grind it in his hand-mill, and bake his bread himself."

Society is a wave. The wave moves onward, but the water of which it is composed does not. The same particle does not rise from the valley to the ridge. Its unity is only phenomenal. The persons who make up a nation to-day, next year die, and their experience with them.

And so the reliance on Property, including the reliance on governments which protect it, is the want of self-reliance. Men have looked away from themselves and at things so long, that they have come to esteem the religious, learned, and civil institutions as guards of property, and they deprecate assaults on these, because they feel them to be assaults on property. They measure their esteem of each other by what each has, and not by what each is. But a cultivated man becomes ashamed of his property, out of new respect for his nature. Especially he hates what he has, if he see that it is accidental,—came to him by inheritance, or gift, or crime; then he feels that it is not having; it does not belong to him, has no root in him, and merely lies there, because no revolution or no robber takes it away. But that which a man is does always by necessity acquire, and what the man acquires is living property, which does not wait the beck of rulers, or mobs, or revolutions, or fire, or storm, or bankruptcies, but perpetually renews itself wherever the man breathes. "Thy lot or portion of life," said the Caliph Ali, "is seeking after thee; therefore be at rest from seeking after it." Our dependence on these foreign goods leads us to our slavish respect for numbers. The political parties meet in numerous conventions; the greater the concourse, and with each new uproar of announcement, The delegation from Essex! The Democrats from New Hampshire! The Whigs of Maine! the young patriot feels himself stronger than before by a new thousand of eyes and arms. In like manner the reformers summon conventions, and vote and resolve in multitude. Not so, O friends, will the God deign to enter and inhabit you, but by a method precisely the reverse. It is only as a man puts off all foreign support, and stands alone, that I see him to be strong and to prevail. He is weaker by every recruit to his banner. Is not a man better than a town? Ask nothing of men, and in the endless mutation, thou only firm column must presently appear the upholder of all that surrounds thee. He who knows that power is inborn, that he is weak because he has looked for good out of him and elsewhere, and so perceiving, throws himself unhesitatingly on his thought, instantly rights himself, stands in the erect position, commands his limbs, works miracles; just as a man who stands on his feet is stronger than a man who stands on his head.

So use all that is called Fortune. Most men gamble with her, and gain all, and lose all, as her wheel rolls. But do thou leave as unlawful these winnings, and deal with Cause and Effect, the chancellors of God. In the Will work and acquire, and thou hast chained the wheel of Chance, and shalt sit hereafter out of fear from her rotations. A political victory, a rise of rents, the recovery of your sick, or the return of your absent friend, or some other favorable event, raises

280 RALPH WALDO EMERSON

your spirits, and you think good days are preparing for you.
Do not believe it. Nothing can bring you peace but yourself.
Nothing can bring you peace but the triumph of principles.

1841

THE OVER-SOUL.*

"But souls that of his own good life partake,
He loves as his own self; dear as his eye
They are to Him: He'll never them forsake:
When they shall die, then God himself shall die:
They live, they live in blest eternity."

HENRY MORE.

Space is ample, east and west,
But two cannot go abreast,
Cannot travel in it two:
Yonder masterful cuckoo
Crowds every egg out of the nest,
Quick or dead, except its own;
A spell is laid on sod and stone,
Night and Day were tampered with,
Every quality and pith
Surcharged and sultry with a power
That works its will on age and hour.

There is a difference between one and another hour of life,
in their authority and subsequent effect. Our faith comes in
moments; our vice is habitual. Yet there is a depth in those
brief moments which constrains us to ascribe more reality to
them than to all other experiences. For this reason, the argument which is always forthcoming to silence those who conceive extraordinary hopes of man, namely, the appeal to experience, is forever invalid and vain. We give up the past to
the objector, and yet we hope. He must explain this hope.
We grant that human life is mean; but how did we find out
that it was mean? What is the ground of this uneasiness of
ours; of this old discontent? What is the universal sense of
want and ignorance, but the fine innuendo by which the soul
makes its enormous claim? Why do men feel that the natural
history of man has never been written, but he is always leav-

* From *Essays, First Series*.

ing behind what you have said of him, and it becomes old, and books of metaphysics worthless? The philosophy of six thousand years has not searched the chambers and magazines of the soul. In its experiments there has always remained, in the last analysis, a residuum it could not resolve. Man is a stream whose source is hidden. Our being is descending into us from we know not whence. The most exact calculator has no prescience that somewhat incalculable may not balk the very next moment. I am constrained every moment to acknowledge a higher origin for events than the will I call mine.

As with events, so is it with thoughts. When I watch that flowing river, which, out of regions I see not, pours for a season its streams into me, I see that I am a pensioner; not a cause, but a surprised spectator of this ethereal water; that I desire and look up, and put myself in the attitude of reception, but from some alien energy the visions come.

The Supreme Critic on the errors of the past and the present, and the only prophet of that which must be, is that great nature in which we rest, as the earth lies in the soft arms of the atmosphere; that Unity, that Over-soul, within which every man's particular being is contained and made one with all other; that common heart, of which all sincere conversation is the worship, to which all right action is submission; that overpowering reality which confutes our tricks and talents, and constrains every one to pass for what he is, and to speak from his character, and not from his tongue, and which evermore tends to pass into our thought and hand, and become wisdom, and virtue, and power, and beauty. We live in succession, in division, in parts, in particles. Meantime within man is the soul of the whole; the wise silence; the universal beauty, to which every part and particle is equally related; the eternal ONE. And this deep power in which we exist, and whose beatitude is all accessible to us, is not only self-sufficing and perfect in every hour, but the act of seeing and the thing seen, the seer and the spectacle, the subject and the object, are one. We see the world piece by piece, as the sun, the moon, the animal, the tree; but the whole, of which these are the shining parts, is the soul. Only by the vision of that Wisdom can the horoscope of the ages be read, and by falling back on our better thoughts, by yielding to the spirit of prophecy which is innate in every man, we can know what it saith. Every man's words, who speaks from that life,

must sound vain to those who do not dwell in the same
thought on their own part. I dare not speak for it. My words
do not carry its august sense; they fall short and cold. Only
itself can inspire whom it will, and behold! their speech shall
be lyrical, and sweet, and universal as the rising of the wind.
Yet I desire, even by profane words, if I may not use sacred,
to indicate the heaven of this deity, and to report what hints
I have collected of the transcendent simplicity and energy of
the Highest Law.

If we consider what happens in conversation, in reveries, in
remorse, in times of passion, in surprises, in the instructions
of dreams, wherein often we see ourselves in masquerade,—
the droll disguises only magnifying and enhancing a real element, and forcing it on our distinct notice,—we shall catch
many hints that will broaden and lighten into knowledge of
the secret of nature. All goes to show that the soul in man
is not an organ, but animates and exercises all the organs; is
not a function like the power of memory, of calculation, of
comparison, but uses these as hands and feet; is not a
faculty, but a light; is not the intellect or the will, but the
master of the intellect and the will; is the background of our
being, in which they lie,—an immensity not possessed and
that cannot be possessed. From within or from behind, a
light shines through us upon things, and makes us aware that
we are nothing, but the light is all. A man is the façade of a
temple wherein all wisdom and all good abide. What we commonly call man, the eating, drinking, planting, counting man,
does not, as we know him, represent himself, but misrepre-
sents himself. Him we do not respect, but the soul, whose
organ he is, would he let it appear through his action, would
make our knees bend. When it breathes through his intellect,
it is genius; when it breathes through his will, it is virtue;
when it flows through his affection, it is love. And the blindness of the intellect begins, when it would be something of itself. The weakness of the will begins, when the individual
would be something of himself. All reform aims, in some
one particular, to let the soul have its way through us; in
other words, to engage us to obey.

Of this pure nature every man is at some time sensible.
Language cannot paint it with his colors. It is too subtile. It
is undefinable, unmeasurable, but we know that it pervades
and contains us. We know that all spiritual being is in man.
A wise old proverb says, "God comes to see us without bell";

that is, as there is no screen or ceiling between our heads and the infinite heavens, so is there no bar or wall in the soul where man, the effect, ceases, and God, the cause, begins. The walls are taken away. We lie open on one side to the deeps of spiritual nature, to the attributes of God. Justice we see and know, Love, Freedom, Power. These natures no man ever got above, but they tower over us, and most in the moment when our interests tempt us to wound them.

The sovereignty of this nature whereof we speak is made known by its independency of those limitations which circumscribe us on every hand. The soul circumscribes all things. As I have said, it contradicts all experience. In like manner it abolishes time and space. The influence of the senses has, in most men, overpowered the mind to that degree, that the walls of time and space have come to look real and insurmountable; and to speak with levity of these limits is, in the world, the sign of insanity. Yet time and space are but inverse measures of the force of the soul. The spirit sports with time,—

> "Can crowd eternity into an hour,
> Or stretch an hour to eternity."

We are often made to feel that there is another youth and age than that which is measured from the year of our natural birth. Some thoughts always find us young and keep us so. Such a thought is the love of the universal and eternal beauty. Every man parts from that contemplation with the feeling that it rather belongs to ages than to mortal life. The least activity of the intellectual powers redeems us in a degree from the conditions of time. In sickness, in languor, give us a strain of poetry, or a profound sentence, and we are refreshed; or produce a volume of Plato, or Shakespeare, or remind us of their names, and instantly we come into a feeling of longevity. See how the deep, divine thought reduces centuries, and millenniums, and makes itself present through all ages. Is the teaching of Christ less effective now than it was when first his mouth was opened? The emphasis of facts and person in my thought has nothing to do with time. And so, always, the soul's scale is one; the scale of the senses and the understanding is another. Before the revelations of the soul, Time, Space, and Nature shrink away. In common speech, we refer all things to time, as we habitually refer the immensely sundered stars to one concave sphere. And so we say that the Judgment is distant or near, that the Millennium approaches, that a day of certain political, moral, social reforms is at hand, and the like, when we mean, that, in the nature of things, one of the facts we contemplate is external and fugitive, and the other is permanent and connate with the soul. The things we now esteem fixed shall, one by one, detach themselves, like ripe fruit, from our experience and fall. The wind shall blow them none knows whither. The landscape, the figures, Boston, London, are facts as fugitive as any institution past, or any whiff of mist or smoke, and so is society, and so is the world. The soul looketh steadily forwards, creating a world before her, leaving worlds behind her. She has no dates, nor rites, nor persons, nor specialties, nor men. The soul knows only the soul; the web of events is the flowing robe in which she is clothed.

After its own law and not by arithmetic is the rate of its progress to be computed. The soul's advances are not made by gradation, such as can be represented by motion in a straight line; but rather by ascension of state, such as can be represented by metamorphosis,—from the egg to the worm, from the worm to the fly. The growths of genius are of a certain *total* character, that does not advance the elect individual first over John, then Adam, then Richard, and give to each the pain of discovered inferiority, but by every throe of growth the man expands there where he works, passing, at each pulsation, classes, populations, of men. With each divine impulse the mind rends the thin rinds of the visible and finite, and comes out into eternity, and inspires and expires its air. It converses with truths that have always been spoken in the world, and becomes conscious of a closer sympathy with Zeno and Arrian, than with persons in the house.

This is the law of moral and of mental gain. The simple rise as by specific levity, not into a particular virtue, but into the region of all the virtues. They are in the spirit which contains them all. The soul requires purity, but purity is not it; requires justice, but justice is not that; requires beneficence, but is somewhat better; so that there is a kind of descent and accommodation felt when we leave speaking of moral nature, to urge a virtue which it enjoins. To the well-born child, all the virtues are natural, and not painfully acquired. Speak to his heart, and the man becomes suddenly virtuous.

Within the same sentiment is the germ of intellectual

growth, which obeys the same law. Those who are capable of
humility, of justice, of love, of aspiration, stand already on a
platform that commands the sciences and arts, speech and
poetry, action and grace. For whoso dwells in this moral
beatitude already anticipates those special powers which men
prize so highly. The lover has no talent, no skill, which
passes for quite nothing with his enamored maiden, however
little she may possess of related faculty; and the heart which
abandons itself to the Supreme Mind finds itself related to all
its works, and will travel a royal road to particular knowledges and powers. In ascending to this primary and aboriginal
sentiment, we have come from our remote station on the circumference instantaneously to the centre of the world,
where, as in the closet of God, we see causes, and anticipate
the universe, which is but a slow effect.

One mode of the divine teaching is the incarnation of the
spirit in a form,—in forms, like my own. I live in society;
with persons who answer to thoughts in my own mind, or
express a certain obedience to the great instincts to which I
live. I see its presence to them. I am certified of a common
nature; and these other souls, these separated selves, draw me
as nothing else can. They stir in me the new emotions we
call passion; of love, hatred, fear, admiration, pity; thence
comes conversation, competition, persuasion, cities, and war.
Persons are supplementary to the primary teaching of the
soul. In youth we are mad for persons. Childhood and youth
see all the world in them. But the larger experience of man
discovers the identical nature appearing through them all.
Persons themselves acquaint us with the impersonal. In all
conversation between two persons, tacit reference is made,
as to a third party, to a common nature. That third party or
common nature is not social; it is impersonal; is God. And
so in groups where debate is earnest, and especially on high
questions, the company become aware that the thought rises
to an equal level in all bosoms, that all have a spiritual property in what was said, as well as the sayer. They all become
wiser than they were. It arches over them like a temple, this
unity of thought, in which every heart beats with nobler sense
of power and duty, and thinks and acts with unusual solemni-
ty. All are conscious of attaining to a higher self-possession.
There is a certain wisdom of humanity which is common to
the greatest men with the lowest, and which our ordinary
education often labors to silence and obstruct. The mind is

one, and the best minds, who love truth for its own sake, think much less of property in truth. They accept it thankfully everywhere, and do not label or stamp it with any man's name, for it is theirs long beforehand, and from eternity. The learned and the studious of thought have no monopoly of wisdom. Their violence of direction in some degree disqualifies them to think truly. We owe many valuable observations to people who are not very acute or profound, and who say the thing without effort, which we want and have long been hunting in vain. The action of the soul is oftener in that which is felt and left unsaid, than in that which is said in any conversation. It broods over every society, and they unconsciously seek for it in each other. We know better than we do. We do not yet possess ourselves, and we know at the same time that we are much more. I feel the same truth how often in my trivial conversation with my neighbors, that somewhat higher in each of us overlooks this by-play, and Jove nods to Jove from behind each of us.

Men descend to meet. In their habitual and mean service to the world, for which they forsake their native nobleness, they resemble those Arabian sheiks, who dwell in mean houses, and affect an external poverty, to escape the rapacity of the Pacha, and reserve all their display of wealth for their interior and guarded retirements.

As it is present in all persons, so it is in every period of life. It is adult already in the infant man. In my dealing with my child, my Latin and Greek, my accomplishments and my money, stead me nothing; but as much soul as I have avails. If I am wilful, he sets his will against mine, one for one, and leaves me, if I please, the degradation of beating him by my superiority of strength. But if I renounce my will, and act for the soul, setting that up as umpire between us two, out of his young eyes looks the same soul; he reveres and loves with me.

The soul is the perceiver and revealer of truth. We know truth when we see it, let sceptic and scoffer say what they choose. Foolish people ask you, when you have spoken what they do not wish to hear, 'How do you know it is truth, and not an error of your own?' We know truth when we see it, from opinion, as we know when we are awake that we are awake. It was a grand sentence of Emanuel Swedenborg, which would alone indicate the greatness of that man's perception,—"It is no proof of a man's understanding to be able to confirm whatever he pleases; but to be able to discern that what is true is true, and that what is false is false, this is the mark and character of intelligence." In the book I read, the good thought returns to me, as every truth will, the image of the whole soul. To the bad thought which I find in it, the same soul becomes a discerning, separating sword, and lops it away. We are wiser than we know. If we will not interfere with our thought, but will act entirely, or see how the thing stands in God, we know the particular thing, and everything, and every man. For the Maker of all things and all persons stands behind us, and casts his dread omniscience through us over things.

But beyond this recognition of its own in particular passages of the individual's experience, it also reveals truth. And here we should seek to reinforce ourselves by its very presence, and to speak with a worthier, loftier strain of that advent. For the soul's communication of truth is the highest event in nature, since it then does not give somewhat from itself, but it gives itself, or passes into and becomes that man whom it enlightens; or, in proportion to that truth he receives, it takes him to itself.

We distinguish the announcements of the soul, its manifestations of its own nature, by the term *Revelation*. These are always attended by the emotion of the sublime. For this communication is an influx of the Divine mind into our mind. It is an ebb of the individual rivulet before the flowing surges of the sea of life. Every distinct apprehension of this central commandment agitates men with awe and delight. A thrill passes through all men at the reception of new truth, or at the performance of a great action, which comes out of the heart of nature. In these communications, the power to see is not separated from the will to do, but the insight proceeds from obedience, and the obedience proceeds from a joyful perception. Every moment when the individual feels himself invaded by it is memorable. By the necessity of our constitution, a certain enthusiasm attends the individual's consciousness of that Divine presence. The character and duration of this enthusiasm varies with the state of the individual, from an ecstasy and trance and prophetic inspiration,—which is its rarer appearance,—to the faintest glow of virtuous emotion, in which form it warms, like our household fires, all the families and associations of men, and makes society possible. A certain tendency to insanity has always attended the opening of the religious sense in men, as if they had been "blasted with excess of light." The trances of Socrates, the "union" of Plotinus, the vision of Porphyry, the conversion of Paul, the aurora of Behmen, the convulsions of George Fox and his Quakers, the illumination of Swedenborg, are of this kind. What was in the case of these remarkable persons a ravishment has, in innumerable instances in common life, been exhibited in less striking manner. Everywhere the history of religion betrays a tendency to enthusiasm. The rapture of the Moravian and Quietist; the opening of the internal sense of the Word, in the language of the New Jerusalem Church; the *revival* of the Calvinistic churches; the *experiences* of the Methodists, are varying forms of that shudder of awe and delight with which the individual soul always mingles with the universal soul.

The nature of these revelations is the same; they are perceptions of the absolute law. They are solutions of the soul's own questions. They do not answer the questions which the understanding asks. The soul answers never by words, but by the thing itself that is inquired after.

Revelation is the disclosure of the soul. The popular notion of a revelation is, that it is a telling of fortunes. In past oracles of the soul, the understanding seeks to find answers to sensual questions, and undertakes to tell from God how long men shall exist, what their hands shall do, and who shall be their company, adding names, and dates, and places. But we must pick no locks. We must check this low curiosity. An answer in words is delusive; it is really no answer to the questions you ask. Do not require a description of the countries towards which you sail. The description does not describe them to you, and to-morrow you arrive there, and know them by inhabiting them. Men ask concerning the immortality of the soul, the employments of heaven, the state of the sinner, and so forth. They even dream that Jesus has left replies to precisely these interrogatories. Never a moment did that sublime spirit speak in their *patois*. To truth, justice, love, the attributes of the soul, the idea of immutableness is essentially associated. Jesus, living in these moral sentiments, heedless of sensual fortunes, heeding only the manifestations of these, never made the separation of the idea a duration from the essence of these attributes, nor uttered a syllable concerning the duration of the soul. It was left to his disciples to sever duration from the moral elements, and to teach the immortality of the soul as a doctrine, and maintain it by evidence. The moment the doctrine of the immortality is separately taught, man is already fallen. In the flowing of love, in the adoration of humility, there is no question of continuance. No inspired man ever asks this question, or condescends to these evidences. For the soul is true to itself, and the man in whom it is shed abroad cannot wander from the present, which is infinite, to a future which would be finite.

These questions which we lust to ask about the future are a confession of sin. God has no answer for them. No answer in words can reply to a question of things. It is not in an arbitrary "decree of God," but in the nature of man, that a veil shuts down on the facts of to-morrow; for the soul will not have us read any other cipher than that of cause and effect. By this veil, which curtains events, it instructs the children of men to live in to-day. The only mode of obtaining an answer to these questions of the senses is to forego all low curiosity, and, accepting the tide of being which floats us into the secret of nature, work and live, work and live, and all unawares the advancing soul has built and forged for itself a new condition, and the question and the answer are one.

By the same fire, vital, consecrating, celestial, which burns until it shall dissolve all things into the waves and surges of an ocean of light, we see and know each other, and what spirit each is of. Who can tell the grounds of his knowledge of the character of the several individuals in his circle of friends? No man. Yet their acts and words do not disappoint him. In that man, though he knew no ill of him, he put no trust. In that other, though they had seldom met, authentic signs had yet passed, to signify that he might be trusted as one who had an interest in his own character. We know each other very well,—which of us has been just to himself, and whether that which we teach or behold is only an aspiration, or is our honest effort also.

We are all discerners of spirits. That diagnosis lies aloft in our life or unconscious power. The intercourse of society,— its trade, its religion, its friendships, its quarrels,—is one wide, judicial investigation of character. In full court, or in small committee, or confronted face to face, accuser and accused, men offer themselves to be judged. Against their will they exhibit those decisive trifles by which character is read. But who judges? and what? Not our understanding. We do not read them by learning or craft. No; the wisdom of the wise man consists herein, that he does not judge them; he lets them judge themselves, and merely reads and records their own verdict.

By virtue of this inevitable nature, private will is overpowered, and, maugre our efforts or our imperfections, your genius will speak from you, and mine from me. That which we are, we shall teach, not voluntarily, but involuntarily. Thoughts come into our minds by avenues which we never left open, and thoughts go out of our minds through avenues which we never voluntarily opened. Character teaches over our head. The infallible index of true progress is found in the tone the man takes. Neither his age, nor his breeding, nor company, nor books, nor actions, nor talents, nor all together, can hinder him from being deferential to a higher spirit than his own. If he have not found his home in God, his manners, his forms of speech, the turn of his sentences, the build, shall I say, of all his opinions, will involuntarily confess it, let him brave it out how he will. If he have found his centre, the Deity will shine through him, through all the disguises of ignorance, of ungenial temperament, of unfavorable circumstance. The tone of seeking is one, and the tone of having is another.

The great distinction between teachers sacred or literary, —between poets like Herbert, and poets like Pope,—between philosophers like Spinoza, Kant, and Coleridge, and philosophers like Locke, Paley, Mackintosh, and Stewart,—between men of the world, who are reckoned accomplished talkers, and here and there a fervent mystic, prophesying, half insane under the infinitude of his thought,—is, that one class speak *from within*, or from experience, as parties and possessors of the fact; and the other class, *from without*, as spectators merely, or perhaps as acquainted with the fact on the evidence of third persons. It is of no use to preach to me from without. I can do that too easily myself. Jesus speaks always from within, and in a degree that transcends all others. In that is the miracle. I believe beforehand that it ought so to be. All men stand continually in the expectation of the appearance of such a teacher. But if a man do not speak from within the veil, where the word is one with that it tells of, let him lowly confess it.

The same Omniscience flows into the intellect, and makes what we call genius. Much of the wisdom of the world is not wisdom, and the most illuminated class of men are no doubt superior to literary fame, and are not writers. Among the multitude of scholars and authors, we feel no hallowing presence; we are sensible of a knack and skill rather than of inspiration; they have a light, and know not whence it comes, and call it their own; their talent is some exaggerated faculty, some overgrown member, so that their strength is a disease. In these instances the intellectual gifts do not make the impression of virtue, but almost of vice; and we feel that a man's talents stand in the way of his advancement in truth. But genius is religious. It is a larger imbibing of the common heart. It is not anomalous, but more like, and not less like other men. There is, in all great poets, a wisdom of humanity which is superior to any talents they exercise. The author, the wit, the partisan, the fine gentleman, does not take place of the man. Humanity shines in Homer, in Chaucer, in Spenser, in Shakespeare, in Milton. They are content with truth. They use the positive degree. They seem frigid and phlegmatic to those who have been spiced with the frantic passion and violent coloring of inferior, but popular writers. For they are poets by the free course which they allow to the informing soul, which through their eyes beholds again, and blesses the things which it hath made. The soul is superior to its knowledge; wiser than any of its works. The great poet makes us feel our own wealth, and then we think less of his compositions. His best communication to our mind is to teach us to despise all he has done. Shakespeare carries us to such a lofty strain of intelligent activity, as to suggest a wealth which beggars his own; and we then feel that the splendid works which he has created, and which in other hours we extol as a sort of self-existent poetry, take no stronger hold of real nature than the shadow of a passing traveller on the rock. The inspiration which uttered itself in Hamlet and Lear could utter things as good from day to day, forever. Why, then, should I make account of Hamlet and Lear, as if we had not the soul from which they fell as syllables from the tongue?

This energy does not descend into individual life on any other condition than entire possession. It comes to the lowly and simple; it comes to whomsoever will put off what is foreign and proud; it comes as insight! it comes as serenity and grandeur. When we see those whom it inhabits, we are apprised of new degrees of greatness. From that inspiration the man comes back with a changed tone. He does not talk with men with an eye to their opinion. He tries them. It requires of us to be plain and true. The vain traveller attempts to embellish his life by quoting my lord, and the prince, and the countess, who thus said or did to *him*. The ambitious vulgar show you their spoons, and brooches, and rings, and preserve their cards and compliments. The more cultivated, in their account of their own experience, cull out the pleasing, poetic circumstance,—the visit to Rome, the man of genius they saw, the brilliant friend they know; still further on, perhaps, the gorgeous landscape, the mountain lights, the mountain thoughts, they enjoyed yesterday,—and so seek to throw a romantic color over their life. But the soul that ascends to worship the great God is plain and true; has no rose-color, no fine friends, no chivalry, no adventures; does not want admiration; dwells in the hour that now is, in the earnest experience of the common day,—by reason of the present moment and the mere trifle having become porous to thought, and bibulous of the sea of light.

Converse with a mind that is grandly simple, and literature looks like word-catching. The simplest utterances are worthiest to be written, yet are they so cheap, and so things of course, that, in the infinite riches of the soul, it is like gathering a few pebbles off the ground, or bottling a little air in a phial, when the whole earth and the whole atmosphere are ours. Nothing can pass there, or make you one of the circle, but the casting aside your trappings, and dealing man to man in naked truth, plain confession, and omniscient affirmation.

Souls such as these treat you as gods would; walk as gods in the earth, accepting without any admiration your wit, your bounty, your virtue even,—say rather your act of duty, for your virtue they own as their proper blood, royal as themselves, and over-royal, and the father of the gods. But what rebuke their plain fraternal bearing casts on the mutual flattery with which authors solace each other and wound themselves! These flatter not. I do not wonder that these men go to see Cromwell, and Christina, and Charles the Second, and James the First, and the Grand Turk. For they are, in their own elevation, the fellows of kings, and must feel the servile tone of conversation in the world. They must always be a godsend to princes, for they confront them, a king to a king, without ducking or concession, and give a high nature the refreshment and satisfaction of resistance, of plain humanity, of even companionship, and of new ideas. They leave them wiser and superior men. Souls like these make us feel that sincerity is more excellent than flattery. Deal so plainly with man and woman, as to constrain the utmost sincerity, and destroy all hope of trifling with you. It is the highest compliment you can pay. Their "highest praising," said Milton, "is not flattery, and their plainest advice is a kind of praising."

Ineffable is the union of man and God in every act of the soul. The simplest person, who in his integrity worships God, becomes God: yet for ever and ever the influx of this better and universal self is new and unsearchable. It inspires awe and astonishment. How dear, how soothing to man, arises the idea of God, peopling the lonely place, effacing the scars of our mistakes and disappointments! When we have broken our god of tradition, and ceased from our God of rhetoric, then may God fire the heart with his presence. It is the doubling of the heart itself, nay, the infinite enlargement of the heart with a power of growth to a new infinity on every side. It inspires in man an infallible trust. He has not the conviction, but the sight, that the best is the true, and may in that thought easily dismiss all particular uncertainties and fears, and adjourn to the sure revelation of time, the solution of his private riddles. He is sure that his welfare is dear to the heart of being. In the presence of law to his mind, he is overflowed with a reliance so universal, that it sweeps away all cherished hopes and the most stable projects of mortal condition in its flood. He believes that he cannot escape from his good. The things that are really for thee gravitate to thee. You are running to seek your friend. Let your feet run, but your mind need not. If you do not find him, will you not acquiesce that it is best you should not find him? for there is a power, which, as it is in you, is in him also, and could therefore very well bring you together, if it were for the best. You are preparing with eagerness to go and render a service to which your talent and your taste invite you, the love of men and the hope of fame. Has it not occurred to you, that you have no right to go, unless you are equally willing to be prevented from going? O, believe, as thou livest, that every sound that is spoken over the round world, which thou oughtest to hear, will vibrate on thine ear! Every proverb, every book, every byword that belongs to thee for aid or comfort, shall surely come home through open or winding passages. Every friend whom not thy fantastic will, but the great and tender heart in thee craveth, shall lock thee in his embrace. And this, because the heart in thee is the heart of all; not a valve, not a wall, not an intersection is there anywhere in nature, but one blood rolls uninterruptedly an endless circulation through all men, as the water of the globe is all one sea, and, truly seen, its tide is one.

Let man, then, learn the revelation of all nature and all thought to his heart; this, namely; that the Highest dwells with him; that the sources of nature are in his own mind, if the sentiment of duty is there. But if he would know what the great God speaketh, he must 'go into his closet and shut the door,' as Jesus said. God will not make himself manifest to cowards. He must greatly listen to himself, withdrawing himself from all the accents of other men's devotion. Even their prayers are hurtful to him, until he have made his own. Our religion vulgarly stands on numbers of believers. Whenever the appeal is made—no matter how indirectly—to numbers, proclamation is then and there made, that religion is not. He that finds God a sweet, enveloping thought to him never counts his company. When I sit in that presence, who shall dare to come in? When I rest in perfect humility, when I burn with pure love, what can Calvin or Swedenborg say?

It makes no difference whether the appeal is to numbers or to one. The faith that stands on authority is not faith. The reliance on authority measures the decline of religion, the withdrawal of the soul. The position men have given to Jesus, now for many centuries of history, is a position of authority. It characterizes themselves. It cannot alter the eternal facts. Great is the soul, and plain. It is no flatterer, it is no follower; it never appeals from itself. It believes in itself. Before the immense possibilities of man, all mere experience, all past biography, however spotless and sainted, shrinks away. Before that heaven which our presentiments foreshow us, we cannot easily praise any form of life we have seen or read of. We not only affirm that we have few great men, but, absolutely speaking, that we have none; that we have no history, no record of any character or mode of living, that entirely contents us. The saints and demigods whom history worships we are constrained to accept with a grain of allowance. Though in our lonely hours we draw a new strength out of their memory, yet, pressed on our attention, as they are by the thoughtless and customary, they fatigue and invade. The soul gives itself, alone, original, and pure, to the Lonely, Original, and Pure, who on that condition, gladly inhabits, leads, and speaks through it. Then is it glad, young, and nimble. It is not wise, but it sees through all things. It is not called religious, but it is innocent. It calls the light its own, and feels that the grass grows and the stone falls by a law inferior to, and dependent on, its nature. Behold, it saith, I am born into the great, the universal mind. I, the imperfect, adore my own Perfect. I am somehow receptive of the great soul, and thereby I do overlook the sun and the stars, and feel them to be the fair accidents and effects which change and pass. More and more the surges of everlasting nature enter into me, and I become public and human in my regards and actions. So come I to live in thoughts, and act with energies, which are immortal. Thus revering the soul, and learning, as the ancient said, that "its beauty is immense," man will come to see that the world is the perennial miracle which the soul worketh, and be less astonished at particular wonders; he will learn that there is no profane history; that all history is sacred; that the universe is represented in an atom, in a moment of time. He will weave no longer a spotted life of shreds and patches, but he will live with a divine unity. He will cease from what is base and frivolous in his life, and be content with all places and with any service he can render. He will calmly front the morrow in the negligency of that trust which carries God with it, and so hath already the whole future in the bottom of the heart.

1841

CIRCLES.*

Nature centres into balls,
And her proud ephemerals,
Fast to surface and outside,
Scan the profile of the sphere;
Knew they what that signified.
A new genesis were here.

* From *Essays, First Series*.

The eye is the first circle; the horizon which it forms is the second; and throughout nature this primary figure is repeated without end. It is the highest emblem in the cipher of the world. St. Augustine described the nature of God as a circle whose centre was everywhere, and its circumference nowhere. We are all our lifetime reading the copious sense of this first of forms. One moral we have already deduced, in considering the circular or compensatory character of every human action. Another analogy we shall now trace; that every action admits of being outdone. Our life is an apprenticeship to the truth, that around every circle another can be drawn; that there is no end in nature, but every end is a beginning; that there is always another dawn risen on mid-noon, and under every deep a lower deep opens.

This fact, as far as it symbolizes the moral fact of the Unattainable, the flying Perfect, around which the hands of man can never meet, at once the inspirer and the condemner of every success, may conveniently serve us to connect many illustrations of human power in every department.

There are no fixtures in nature. The universe is fluid and volatile. Permanence is but a word of degrees. Our globe seen by God is a transparent law, not a mass of facts. The law dissolves the fact and holds it fluid. Our culture is the predominance of an idea which draws after it this train of cities and institutions. Let us rise into another idea: they will disappear. The Greek sculpture is all melted away, as if it had been statues of ice; here and there a solitary figure or fragment remaining, as we see flecks and scraps of snow left in cold dells and mountain clefts, in June and July. For the genius that created it creates now somewhat else. The Greek letters last a little longer, but are already passing under the same sentence, and tumbling into the inevitable pit which the creation of new thought opens for all that is old. The new continents are built out of the ruins of an old planet; the new races fed out of the decomposition of the foregoing. New arts destroy the old. See the investment of capital in aqueducts made useless by hydraulics; fortifications, by gunpowder; roads and canals, by railways; sails, by steam; steam by electricity.

You admire this tower of granite, weathering the hurts of so many ages. Yet a little waving hand built this huge wall, and that which builds is better than that which is built. The hand that built can topple it down much faster. Better than the hand, and nimbler, was the invisible thought which wrought through it; and thus ever, behind the coarse effect, is a fine cause, which, being narrowly seen, is itself the effect of a finer cause. Everything looks permanent until its secret is known. A rich estate appears to woman a firm and lasting fact; to a merchant, one easily created out of any materials, and easily lost. An orchard, good tillage, good grounds, seem a fixture, like a gold-mine, or a river, to a citizen; but to a large farmer, not much more fixed than the state of the crop. Nature looks provokingly stable and secular, but it has a cause like all the rest; and when once I comprehend that, will these fields stretch so immovably wide, these leaves hang so individually considerable? Permanence is a word of degrees. Everything is medial. Moons are no more bounds to spiritual power than bat-balls.

The key to every man is his thought. Sturdy and defying though he look, he has a helm which he obeys, which is the idea after which all his facts are classified. He can only be reformed by showing him a new idea which commands his own. The life of man is a self-evolving circle, which, from a ring imperceptibly small, rushes on all sides outwards to new and larger circles, and that without end. The extent to which this generation of circles, wheel without wheel, will go, depends on the force or truth of the individual soul. For it is the inert effort of each thought, having formed itself into a circular wave of circumstance,—as, for instance, an empire, rules of an art, a local usage, a religious rite,—to heap itself on that ridge, and to solidify and hem in the life. But if the soul is quick and strong, it bursts over that boundary on all sides, and expands another orbit on the great deep, which also runs up into a high wave, with attempt again to stop and to bind. But the heart refuses to be imprisoned; in its first and narrowest pulses, it already tends outward with a vast force, and to immense and innumerable expansions.

Every ultimate fact is only the first of a new series. Every general law only a particular fact of some more general law presently to disclose itself. There is no outside, no enclosing wall, no circumference to us. The man finishes his story,— how good! how final! how it puts a new face on all things! He fills the sky. Lo! on the other side rises also a man, and draws a circle around the circle we had just pronounced the outline of the sphere. Then already is our first speaker not

man, but only a first speaker. His only redress is forthwith
to draw a circle outside of his antagonist. And so men do by
themselves. The result of to-day, which haunts the mind and
cannot be escaped, will presently be abridged into a word,
and the principle that seemed to explain nature will itself be
included as one example of a bolder generalization. In the
thought of to-morrow there is a power to upheave all thy
creed, all the creeds, all the literatures, of the nations, and
marshal thee to a Heaven which no epic dream has yet de-
picted. Every man is not so much a workman in the world,
as he is a suggestion of that he should be. Men walk as
prophecies of the next age.

Step by step we scale this mysterious ladder: the steps are
actions; the new prospect is power. Every several result is
threatened and judged by that which follows. Every one
seems to be contradicted by the new; it is only limited by
the new. The new statement is always hated by the old, and,
to those dwelling in the old, comes like an abyss of scepticism. But the eye soon gets wonted to it, for the eye and it are
effects of one cause; then its innocency and benefit appear,
and presently, all its energy spent, it pales and dwindles
before the revelation of the new hour.

Fear not the new generalization. Does the fact look crass
and material, threatening to degrade thy theory of spirit?
Resist it not; it goes to refine and raise thy theory of matter
just as much.

There are no fixtures to men, if we appeal to consciousness. Every man supposes himself not to be fully understood;
and if there is any truth in him, if he rests at last on the
divine soul, I see not how it can be otherwise. The last
chamber, the last closet, he must feel, was never opened;
there is always a residuum unknown, unanalyzable. That is,
every man believes that he has a greater possibility.

Our moods do not believe in each other. To-day I am full
of thoughts, and can write what I please. I see no reason
why I should not have the same thought, the same power
of expression, to-morrow. What I write, whilst I write it,
seems the most natural thing in the world; but yesterday I
saw a dreary vacuity in this direction in which now I see so
much; and a month hence, I doubt not, I shall wonder who he
was that wrote so many continuous pages. Alas for this
infirm faith, this will not strenuous, this vast ebb of a vast
flow! I am God in nature; I am a weed by the wall.

The continual effort to raise himself above himself, to work a pitch above his last height, betrays itself in a man's relations. We thirst for approbation, yet cannot forgive the approver. The sweet of nature is love; yet, if I have a friend, I am tormented by my imperfections. The love of me accuses the other party. If he were high enough to slight me, then could I love him, and rise by my affection to new heights. A man's growth is seen in the successive choirs of his friends. For every friend whom he loses for truth, he gains a better. I thought as I walked in the woods and mused on my friends, why should I play with them this game of idolatry? I know and see too well, when not voluntarily blind, the speedy limits of persons called high and worthy. Rich, noble, and great they are by the liberality of our speech, but truth is sad. O blessed Spirit, whom I forsake for these, they are not thou! Every personal consideration that we allow costs us heavenly state. We sell the thrones of angels for a short and turbulent pleasure.

How often must we learn this lesson? Men cease to interest us when we find their limitations. The only sin is limitation. As soon as you once come up with a man's limitations, it is all over with him. Has he talents? has he enterprise? has he knowledge? it boots not. Infinitely alluring and attractive was he to you yesterday, a great hope, a sea to swim in; now, you have found his shores, found it a pond, and you care not if you never see it again.

Each new step we take in thought reconciles twenty seemingly discordant facts, as expressions of one law. Aristotle and Plato are reckoned the respective heads of two schools. A wise man will see that Aristotle Platonizes. By going one step farther back in thought, discordant opinions are reconciled, by being seen to be two extremes of one principle, and we can never go so far back as to preclude a still higher vision.

Beware when the great God lets loose a thinker on this planet. Then all things are at risk. It is as when a conflagration has broken out in a great city, and no man knows what is safe, or where it will end. There is not a piece of science, but its flank may be turned to-morrow; there is not any literary reputation, not the so-called eternal names of fame, that may not be revised and condemned. The very hopes of man, the thoughts of his heart, the religion of nations, the manners and morals of mankind, are all at the mercy of a new generalization. Generalization is always a new influx of the divinity into the mind. Hence the thrill that attends it.

Valor consists in the power of self-recovery, so that a man cannot have his flank turned, cannot be out-generalled, but put him where you will, he stands. This can only be by his preferring truth to his past apprehension of truth; and his alert acceptance of it, from whatever quarter; the intrepid conviction that his laws, his relations to society, his Christianity, his world, may at any time be superseded and decease.

There are degrees in idealism. We learn first to play with it academically, as the magnet was once a toy. Then we see in the heyday of youth and poetry that it may be true, that it is true in gleams and fragments. Then, its countenance waxes stern and grand, and we see that it must be true. It now shows itself ethical and practical. We learn that God IS; that he is in me; and that all things are shadows of him. The idealism of Berkeley is only a crude statement of the idealism of Jesus, and that again is a crude statement of the fact, that all nature is the rapid efflux of goodness executing and organizing itself. Much more obviously is history and the state of the world at any one time directly dependent on the intellectual classification then existing in the minds of men. The things which are dear to men at this hour are so on account of the ideas which have emerged on their mental horizon, and which cause the present order of things as a tree bears its apples. A new degree of culture would instantly revolutionize the entire system of human pursuits.

Conversation is a game of circles. In conversation we pluck up the *termini* which bound the common of silence on every side. The parties are not to be judged by the spirit they partake and even express under this Pentecost. To-morrow they will have receded from this high-water-mark. To-morrow you shall find them stooping under the old pack-saddles. Yet let us enjoy the cloven flame whilst it glows on our walls. When each new speaker strikes a new light, emancipates us from the oppression of the last speaker, to oppress us with the greatness and exclusiveness of his own thought, then yields us to another redeemer, we seem to recover our rights, to become men. O, what truths profound and executable only in ages and orbs are supposed in the announcement of every truth? In common hours, society sits cold and statuesque. We all stand waiting, empty,—knowing, possibly, that we can be full, surrounded by mighty symbols which are not symbols to us, but prose and trivial toys. Then cometh the god, and converts the statues into fiery men, and by a flash of his eye burns up the veil which shrouded all things, and the meaning of the very furniture, of cup and saucer, of chair and clock and tester, is manifest. The facts which loomed so large in the fogs of yesterday,—property, climate, breeding, personal beauty, and the like, have strangely changed their proportions. All that we reckoned settled shakes and rattles; and literatures, cities, climates, religions, leave their foundations, and dance before our eyes. And yet here again see the swift circumspection! Good as is discourse, silence is better, and shames it. The length of the discourse indicates the distance of thought betwixt the speaker and the hearer. If they were at a perfect understanding in any part, no words would be necessary thereon. If at one in all parts, no words would be suffered.

Literature is a point outside of our hodiernal circle, through which a new one may be described. The use of literature is to afford us a platform whence we may command a view of our present life, a purchase by which we may move it. We fill ourselves with ancient learning, install ourselves the best we can in Greek, in Punic, in Roman houses, only that we may wiselier see French, English, and American houses and modes of living. In like manner, we see literature best from the midst of wild nature, or from the din of affairs, or from a high religion. The field cannot be well seen from within the field. The astronomer must have his diameter of the earth's orbit as a base to find the parallax of any star.

Therefore we value the poet. All the argument and all the wisdom is not in the encyclopædia, or the treatise on metaphysics, or the Body of Divinity, but in the sonnet or the play. In my daily work I incline to repeat my old steps, and do not believe in remedial force, in the power of change and reform. But some Petrarch or Ariosto, filled with the new wine of his imagination, writes me an ode or a brisk romance, full of daring thought and action. He smites and arouses me with his shrill tones, breaks up my whole chain of habits, and I open my eye on my own possibilities. He claps wings to the sides of all the solid old lumber of the world, and I am capable once more of choosing a straight path in theory and practice.

We have the same need to command a view of the religion

of the world. We can never see Christianity from the catechism:—from the pastures, from a boat in the pond, from
amidst the songs of wood-birds, we possibly may. Cleansed by
the elemental light and wind, steeped in the sea of beautiful
forms which the field offers us, we may chance to cast a
right glance back upon biography. Christianity is rightly
dear to the best of mankind; yet was there never a young
philosopher whose breeding had fallen into the Christian
church, by whom that brave text of Paul's was not specially
prized: "Then shall also the Son be subject unto Him who put
all things under him, that God may be all in all." Let the
claims and virtues of persons be never so great and welcome,
the instinct of man presses eagerly onward to the impersonal
and illimitable, and gladly arms itself against the dogmatism
of bigots with this generous word out of the book itself.

The natural world may be conceived of as a system of con-
centric circles, and we now and then detect in nature slight
dislocations, which apprise us that this surface on which we
now stand is not fixed, but sliding. These manifold tenacious
qualities, this chemistry and vegetation, these metals and animals, which seem to stand there for their own sake, are means
and methods only,—are words of God, and as fugitive as
other words. Has the naturalist or chemist learned his craft,
who has explored the gravity of atoms and the elective affinities, who has not yet discerned the deeper law whereof
this is only a partial or approximate statement, namely, that
like draws to like; and that the goods which belong to you
gravitate to you, and need not be pursued with pains and
cost? Yet is that statement approximate also, and not final.
Omnipresence is a higher fact. Not through subtle, subterranean channels need friend and fact be drawn to their coun-
terpart, but, rightly considered, these things proceed from
the eternal generation of the soul. Cause and effect are two
sides of one fact.

The same law of eternal procession ranges all that we call
the virtues, and extinguishes each in the light of a better.
The great man will not be prudent in the popular sense; all
his prudence will be so much deduction from his grandeur.
But it behooves each to see, when he sacrifices prudence, to
what god he devotes it; if to ease and pleasure, he had
better be prudent still; if to a great trust, he can well spare his
mule and panniers who has a winged chariot instead. Geof-
frey draws on his boots to go through the woods, that his feet

may be safer from the bite of snakes; Aaron never thinks of such a peril. In many years neither is harmed by such an accident. Yet it seems to me, that, with every precaution you take against such an evil, you put yourself into the power of the evil. I suppose that the highest prudence is the lowest prudence. Is this too sudden a rushing from the centre to the verge of our orbit? Think how many times we shall fall back into pitiful calculations before we take up our rest in the great sentiment, or make the verge of to-day the new centre. Besides, your bravest sentiment is familiar to the humblest men. The poor and the low have their way of expressing the last facts of philosophy as well as you. "Blessed be nothing," and "the worse things are, the better they are," are proverbs which express the transcendentalism of common life.

One man's justice is another's injustice; one man's beauty, another's ugliness; one man's wisdom, another's folly; as one beholds the same objects from a higher point. One man thinks justice consists in paying debts, and has no measure in his abhorrence of another who is very remiss in this duty, and makes the creditor wait tediously. But that second man has his own way of looking at things; asks himself, Which debt must I pay first,—the debt to the rich, or the debt to the poor? the debt of money, or the debt of thought to mankind, of genius to nature? For you, O broker! there is no other principle but arithmetic. For me, commerce is of trivial import; love, faith, truth of character, the aspiration of man, these are sacred; nor can I detach one duty, like you, from all other duties, and concentrate my forces mechanically on the payment of moneys. Let me live onward; you shall find that, though slower, the progress of my character will liquidate all these debts without injustice to higher claims. If a man should dedicate himself to the payment of notes, would not this be injustice? Does he owe no debt but money? And are all claims on him to be postponed to a landlord's or a banker's?

There is no virtue which is final; all are initial. The virtues of society are vices of the saint. The terror of reform is the discovery that we must cast away our virtues, or what we have always esteemed such, into the same pit that has consumed our grosser vices.

"Forgive his crimes, forgive his virtues too,
    Those smaller faults, half converts to the right."

It is the highest power of divine moments that they abolish our contritions also. I accuse myself of sloth and unprofitableness day by day; but when these waves of God flow into me, I no longer reckon lost time. I no longer poorly compute my possible achievement by what remains to me of the month or the year; for these moments confer a sort of omnipresence and omnipotence which asks nothing of duration, but sees that the energy of the mind is commensurate with the work to be done, without time.

And thus, O circular philosopher, I hear some reader exclaim, you have arrived at a fine Pyrrhonism, at an equivalence and indifferency of all actions, and would fain teach us that, *if we are true*, forsooth, our crimes may be lively stones out of which we shall construct the temple of the true God!

I am not careful to justify myself. I own I am gladdened by seeing the predominance of the saccharine principle throughout vegetable nature, and not less by beholding in morals that unrestrained inundation of the principle of good into every chink and hole that selfishness has left open, yea, into selfishness and sin itself; so that no evil is pure, nor hell itself without its extreme satisfactions. But lest I should mislead any when I have my own head and obey my whims, let me remind the reader that I am only an experimenter. Do not set the least value on what I do, or the least discredit on what I do not, as if I pretended to settle anything as true or false. I unsettle all things. No facts are to me sacred; none are profane; I simply experiment, an endless seeker, with no Past at my back.

Yet this incessant movement and progression which all things partake could never become sensible to us but by contrast to some principle of fixture or stability in the soul. Whilst the eternal generation of circles proceeds, the eternal generator abides. That central life is somewhat superior to creation, superior to knowledge and thought, and contains all its circles. Forever it labors to create a life and thought as large and excellent as itself; but in vain; for that which is made instructs how to make a better.

Thus there is no sleep, no pause, no preservation, but all things renew, germinate, and spring. Why should we import rags and relics into the new hour? Nature abhors the old, and old age seems the only disease; all others run into this one. We call it by many names,—fever, intemperance, insanity, stupidity, and crime; they are all forms of old age; they are rest, conservatism, appropriation, inertia, not newness, not the way onward. We grizzle every day. I see no need of it. Whilst we converse with what is above us, we do not grow old, but grow young. Infancy, youth, receptive, aspiring, with religious eye looking upward, counts itself nothing, and abandons itself to the instruction flowing from all sides. But the man and woman of seventy assume to know all, they have outlived their hope, they renounce aspiration, accept the actual for the necessary, and talk down to the young. Let them, then, become organs of the Holy Ghost; let them be lovers; let them behold truth; and their eyes are uplifted, their wrinkles smoothed, they are perfumed again with hope and power. This old age ought not to creep on a human mind. In nature every moment is new; the past is always swallowed and forgotten; the coming only is sacred. Nothing is secure but life, transition, the energizing spirit. No love can be bound by oath or covenant to secure it against a higher love. No truth so sublime but it may be trivial tomorrow in the light of new thoughts. People wish to be settled; only as far as they are unsettled is there any hope for them.

Life is a series of surprises. We do not guess to-day the mood, the pleasure, the power of to-morrow, when we are building up our being. Of lower states,—of acts of routine and sense,—we can tell somewhat; but the masterpieces of God, the total growths and universal movements of the soul, he hideth; they are incalculable. I can know that truth is divine and helpful; but how it shall help me I can have no guess, for *so to be* is the sole inlet of *so to know*. The new position of the advancing man has all the powers of the old, yet has them all new. It carries in its bosom all the energies of the past, yet is itself an exhalation of the morning. I cast away in this new moment all my once hoarded knowledge, as vacant and vain. Now, for the first time, seem I to know anything rightly. The simplest words,—we do not know what they mean, except when we love and aspire.

The difference between talents and character is adroitness to keep the old and trodden round, and power and courage to make a new road to new and better goals. Character makes an overpowering present; a cheerful, determined hour, which fortifies all the company, by making them see that much is possible and excellent that was not thought of. Character dulls the impression of particular events. When we see the conqueror, we do not think much of any one battle or success. We see that we had exaggerated the difficulty. It was easy to him. The great man is not convulsible or tormentable; events pass over him without much impression. People say sometimes, "See what I have overcome; see how cheerful I am; see how completely I have triumphed over these black events." Not if they still remind me of the black event. True conquest is the causing the calamity to fade and disappear, as an early cloud of insignificant result in a history so large and advancing.

The one thing which we seek with insatiable desire is to forget ourselves, to be surprised out of our propriety, to lose our sempiternal memory, and to do something without knowing how or why; in short, to draw a new circle. Nothing great was ever achieved without enthusiasm. The way of life is wonderful; it is by abandonment. The great moments of history are the facilities of performance through the strength of ideas, as the works of genius and religion. "A man," said Oliver Cromwell, "never rises so high as when he knows not whither he is going." Dreams and drunkenness, the use of opium and alcohol are the semblance and counterfeit of this oracular genius, and hence their dangerous attraction for men. For the like reason, they ask the aid of wild passions, as in gaming and war, to ape in some manner these flames and generosities of the heart.

1841

THE POET.*

A moody child and wildly wise
Pursued the game with joyful eyes,
Which chose, like meteors, their way,
And rived the dark with private ray:
They overleapt the horizon's edge,
Searched with Apollo's privilege;
Through man, and woman, and sea, and star,
Saw the dance of nature forward far;
Through worlds, and races, and terms, and times,
Saw musical order, and pairing rhymes.

* From *Essays, Second Series.*

> Olympian bards who sung
>   Divine ideas below,
> Which always find us young,
>   And always keep us so.

Those who are esteemed umpires of taste are often persons who have acquired some knowledge of admired pictures or sculptures, and have an inclination for whatever is elegant; but if you inquire whether they are beautiful souls, and whether their own acts are like fair pictures, you learn that they are selfish and sensual. Their cultivation is local, as if you should rub a log of dry wood in one spot to produce fire, all the rest remaining cold. Their knowledge of the fine arts is some study of rules and particulars, or some limited judgment of color or form, which is exercised for amusement or for show. It is a proof of the shallowness of the doctrine of beauty, as it lies in the minds of our amateurs, that men seem to have lost the perception of the instant dependence of form upon soul. There is no doctrine of forms in our philosophy. We were put into our bodies, as fire is put into a pan, to be carried about; but there is no accurate adjustment between the spirit and the organ, much less is the latter the germination of the former. So in regard to other forms, the intellectual men do not believe in any essential dependence of the material world on thought and volition. Theologians think it a pretty air-castle to talk of the spiritual meaning of a ship or a cloud, of a city or a contract, but they prefer to come again to the solid ground of historical evidence; and even the poets are contented with a civil and conformed manner of living, and to write poems from the fancy, at a safe distance from their own experience. But the highest minds of the world have never ceased to explore the double meaning, or, shall I say, the quadruple, or the centuple, or much more manifold meaning, of every sensuous fact: Orpheus, Empedocles, Heraclitus, Plato, Plutarch, Dante, Swedenborg, and the masters of sculpture, picture, and poetry. For we are not pans and barrows, nor even porters of the fire and torch-bearers, but children of the fire, made of it, and only the same divinity transmuted, and at two or three removes, when we know least about it. And this hidden truth, that the fountains whence all this river of Time, and its creatures, floweth, are intrinsically ideal and beautiful, draws us to the consideration of the nature and functions of the Poet, or the man of Beauty, to the means and materials he uses, and to the general aspect of the art in the present time.

The breadth of the problem is great, for the poet is representative. He stands among partial men for the complete man, and apprises us not of his wealth, but of the commonwealth. The young man reveres men of genius, because, to speak truly, they are more himself than he is. They receive of the soul as he also receives, but they more. Nature enhances her beauty to the eye of loving men, from their belief that the poet is beholding her shows at the same time. He is isolated among his contemporaries, by truth and by his art, but with this consolation in his pursuits, that they will draw all men sooner or later. For all men live by truth, and stand in need of expression. In love, in art, in avarice, in politics, in labor, in games, we study to utter our painful secret. The man is only half himself, the other half is his expression.

Notwithstanding this necessity to be published, adequate expression is rare. I know not how it is that we need an interpreter; but the great majority of men seem to be minors, who have not yet come into possession of their own, or mutes, who cannot report the conversation they have had with nature. There is no man who does not anticipate a supersensual utility in the sun, and stars, earth and water. These stand and wait to render him a peculiar service. But there is some obstruction, or some excess of phlegm in our constitution, which does not suffer them to yield the due effect. Too feeble fall the impressions of nature on us to make us artists. Every touch should thrill. Every man should be so much an artist, that he could report in conversation what had befallen him. Yet, in our experience, the rays or appulses have sufficient force to arrive at the senses, but not enough to reach the quick, and compel the reproduction of themselves in speech. The poet is the person in whom these powers are in balance, the man without impediment, who sees and handles that which others dream of, traverses the whole scale of experience, and is representative of man, in virtue of being the largest power to receive and to impart.

For the Universe has three children, born at one time, which reappear, under different names, in every system of thought, whether they be called cause, operation, and effect; or, more poetically, Jove, Pluto, Neptune; or theologically, the Father, the Spirit, and the Son; but which we will call here, the Knower, the Doer, and the Sayer. These stand respectively for the love of truth, for the love of good, and for the love of beauty. These three are equal. Each is that which he is essentially, so that he cannot be surmounted or analyzed, and each of these three has the power of the others latent in him, and his own patent.

The poet is the sayer, the namer, and represents beauty. He is a sovereign, and stands on the centre. For the world is not painted, or adorned, but is from the beginning beautiful; and God has not made some beautiful things, but Beauty is the creator of the universe. Therefore the poet is not any permissive potentate, but is emperor in his own right. Criticism is infested with a cant of materialism, which assumes that manual skill and activity is the first merit of all men, and disparages such as say and do not, overlooking the fact, that some men, namely, poets, are natural sayers, sent into the world to the end of expression, and confounds them with those whose province is action, but who quit it to imitate the sayers. But Homer's words are as costly and admirable to Homer, as Agamemnon's victories are to Agamemnon. The poet does not wait for the hero or the sage, but, as they act and think primarily, so he writes primarily what will and must be spoken, reckoning the others, though primaries also, yet, in respect to him, secondaries and servants; as sitters or models in the studio of a painter, or as assistants who bring building materials to an architect.

For poetry was all written before time was, and whenever we are so finely organized that we can penetrate into that region where the air is music, we hear those primal warblings, and attempt to write them down, but we lose ever and anon a word, or a verse, and substitute something of our own, and thus miswrite the poem. The men of more delicate ear write down these cadences more faithfully, and these transcripts, though imperfect, become the songs of the nations. For nature is as truly beautiful as it is good, or as it is reasonable, and must as much appear, as it must be done, or be known. Words and deeds are quite indifferent modes of the divine energy. Words are also actions, and actions are a kind of words.

The sign and credentials of the poet are, that he announces that which no man foretold. He is the true and only doctor; he knows and tells; he is the only teller of news, for he was present and privy to the appearance which he describes. He is a beholder of ideas, and an utterer of the necessary and casual. For we do not speak now of men of poetical talents, or of industry and skill in metre, but of the true poet. I took part in a conversation, the other day, concerning a recent writer of lyrics, a man of subtle mind, whose head appeared to be a music-box of delicate tunes and rhythms, and whose skill and command of language we could not sufficiently praise. But when the question arose, whether he was not only a lyrist, but a poet, we were obliged to confess that he is plainly a contemporary, not an eternal man. He does not stand out of our low limitations, like a Chimborazo under the line, running up from a torrid base through all the climates of the globe, with belts of the herbage of every latitude on its high and mottled sides; but this genius is the landscape-garden of a modern house, adorned with fountains and statues, with well-bred men and women standing and sitting in the walks and terraces. We hear, through all the varied music, the ground-tone of conventional life. Our poets are men of talents who sing, and not the children of music. The argument is secondary, the finish of the verses is primary.

For it is not metres, but a metre-making argument, that makes a poem,—a thought so passionate and alive, that, like the spirit of a plant or an animal, it has an architecture of its own, and adorns nature with a new thing. The thought and the form are equal in the order of time, but in the order of genesis the thought is prior to the form. The poet has a new thought: he has a whole new experience to unfold; he will tell us how it was with him, and all men will be the richer in his fortune. For the experience of each new age requires a new confession, and the world seems always waiting for its poet. I remember, when I was young, how much I was moved one morning by tidings that genius had appeared in a youth who sat near me at table. He had left his work, and gone rambling none knew whither, and had written hundreds of lines, but could not tell whether that which was in him was therein told: he could tell nothing but that all was changed,—man, beast, heaven, earth, and sea. How gladly we listened! how credulous! Society seemed to be compromised. We sat in the aurora of a sunrise which was to put out all the stars. Boston seemed to be at twice the distance it had the night before, or was much farther than that. Rome, —what was Rome? Plutarch and Shakespeare were in the yellow leaf, and Homer no more should be heard of. It is much to know that poetry has been written this very day, under this very roof, by your side. What! that wonderful spirit has not expired! These stony moments are still sparkling and animated! I had fancied that the oracles were all silent, and nature had spent her fires, and behold! all night, from every pore, these fine auroras have been streaming. Every one has some interest in the advent of the poet, and no one knows how much it may concern him. We know that the secret of the world is profound, but who or what shall be our interpreter, we know not. A mountain ramble, a new style of face, a new person, may put the key into our hands. Of course, the value of genius to us is in the veracity of its report. Talent may frolic and juggle; genius realizes and adds. Mankind, in good earnest, have arrived so far in understanding themselves and their work, that the foremost watchman on the peak announces his news. It is the truest word ever spoken, and the phrase will be the fittest, most musical, and the unerring voice of the world for that time.

All that we call sacred history attests that the birth of a poet is the principal event in chronology. Man, never so often deceived, still watches for the arrival of a brother who can hold him steady to a truth, until he has made it his own. With what joy I begin to read a poem, which I confide in as an inspiration! And now my chains are to be broken; I shall mount above these clouds and opaque airs in which I live,— opaque, though they seem transparent,—and from the heaven of truth I shall see and comprehend my relations. That will reconcile me to life, and renovate nature, to see trifles animated by a tendency, and to know what I am doing. Life will no more be a noise; now I shall see men and women, and know the signs by which they may be discerned from fools and satans. This day shall be better than my birthday: then I became an animal: now I am invited into the science of the real. Such is the hope, but the fruition is postponed. Oftener it falls that this winged man, who will carry me into the heaven, whirls me into mists, then leaps and frisks about with me as it were from cloud to cloud, still affirming that he is bound heavenward; and I, being myself a novice, am slow in perceiving that he does not know the way into the heavens, and is merely bent that I should admire his skill to rise, like a fowl or a flying-fish, a little way from the ground or the water; but the all-piercing, all-feeding, and ocular air of heaven, that man shall never inhabit. I tumble down again soon into my old nooks, and lead the life of exaggerations as before, and have lost my faith in the possibility of any guide who can lead me thither where I would be.

But, leaving these victims of vanity, let us, with new hope, observe how nature, by worthier impulses, has insured the poet's fidelity to his office of announcement and affirming, namely, by the beauty of things, which becomes a new and higher beauty, when expressed. Nature offers all her creatures to him as a picture-language. Being used as a type, a second wonderful value appears in the object, far better than its old value, as the carpenter's stretched cord, if you hold your ear close enough, is musical in the breeze. "Things more excellent than every image," says Jamblichus, "are expressed through images." Things admit of being used as symbols, because nature is a symbol, in the whole, and in every part. Every line we can draw in the sand has expression; and there is nobody without its spirit or genius. All form is an effect of character; all condition, of the quality of the life; all harmony, of health; (and, for this reason, a perception of beauty should be sympathetic, or proper only to the good.) The beautiful rests on the foundations of the necessary. The soul makes the body, as the wise Spenser teaches:—

> "So every spirit, as it is more pure,
> And hath in it the more of heavenly light,
> So it the fairer body doth procure
> To habit in, and it more fairly dight,
> With cheerful grace and amiable sight.
> For, of the soul, the body form doth take,
> For soul is form, and doth the body make."

Here we find ourselves, suddenly, not in a critical speculation, but in a holy place, and should go very warily and reverently. We stand before the secret of the world, there where Being passes into Appearance, and Unity into Variety.

The Universe is the externization of the soul. Wherever the life is, that bursts into appearance around it. Our science is sensual, and therefore superficial. The earth and the heavenly bodies, physics, and chemistry, we sensually treat, as if they were self-existent; but these are the retinue of that Being we have. "The mighty heaven," said Proclus, "exhibits, in its transfigurations, clear images of the splendor of intellectual perceptions; being moved in conjunction with the un-apparent periods of intellectual natures." Therefore, science always goes abreast with the just elevation of the man, keeping step with religion and metaphysics; or, the state of science is an index of our self-knowledge. Since everything in nature answers to a moral power, if any phenomenon remains brute and dark, it is because the corresponding faculty in the observer is not yet active.

No wonder, then, if these waters be so deep, that we hover over them with a religious regard. The beauty of the fable proves the importance of the sense; to the poet, and to all others; or, if you please, every man is so far a poet as to be susceptible of these enchantments of nature; for all men have the thoughts whereof the universe is the celebration. I find that the fascination resides in the symbol. Who loves nature? Who does not? Is it only poets, and men of leisure and cultivation, who live with her? No; but also hunters, farmers, grooms, and butchers, though they express their affection in their choice of life, and not in their choice of words. The writer wonders what the coachman or the hunter values in riding, in horses, and dogs. It is not superficial qualities. When you talk with him, he holds these at as slight a rate as you. His worship is sympathetic; he has no definitions, but he is commanded in nature, by the living power which he feels to be there present. No imitation, or playing of these things, would content him; he loves the earnest of the north wind, of rain, of stone, and wood, and iron. A beauty not explicable is dearer than a beauty which we can see to the end of. It is nature the symbol, nature certifying the supernatural, body overflowed by life, which he worships, with coarse but sincere rites.

The inwardness and mystery of this attachment drive men of every class to the use of emblems. The schools of poets, and philosophers, are not more intoxicated with their symbols, than the populace with theirs. In our political parties, compute the power of badges and emblems. See the huge wooden ball lately rolled from Baltimore to Bunker Hill! In the political processions, Lowell goes in a loom, and Lynn in a shoe, and Salem in a ship. Witness the cider-barrel, the log-cabin, the hickory-stick, the palmetto, and all the cognizances of party. See the power of national emblems. Some stars, lilies, leopards, a crescent, a lion, an eagle, or other figure, which came into credit God knows how, on an old rag of bunting, blowing in the wind, on a fort, at the ends of the earth, shall make the blood tingle under the rudest or the most conventional exterior. The people fancy they hate poetry, and they are all poets and mystics!

Beyond this universality of the symbolic language, we are apprised of the divineness of this superior use of things, whereby the world is a temple, whose walls are covered with emblems, pictures, and commandments of the Deity, in this, that there is no fact in nature which does not carry the whole sense of nature; and the distinctions which we make in events, and in affairs, of low and high, honest and base, disappear when nature is used as a symbol. Thought makes everything fit for use. The vocabulary of an omniscient man would embrace words and images excluded from polite conversation. What would be base, or even obscene, to the obscene, becomes illustrious, spoken in a new connection of thought. The piety of the Hebrew prophets purges their grossness. The circumcision is an example of the power of poetry to raise the low and offensive. Small and mean things serve as well as great symbols. The meaner the type by which a law is expressed, the more pungent it is, and the more lasting in the memories of men: just as we choose the smallest box, or case, in which any needful utensil can be carried. Bare lists of words are found suggestive, to an imaginative and excited mind; as it is related of Lord Chatham, that he was accustomed to read in Bailey's Dictionary, when he was preparing to speak in Parliament. The poorest experience is rich enough for all the purposes of expressing thought. Why covet a knowledge of new facts? Day and night, house and garden, a few books, a few actions, serve us as well as would all trades and all spectacles. We are far from having exhausted the significance of the few symbols we use. We can come to use them yet with a terrible simplicity. It does not need that a poem should be long. Every word was once a poem. Every new relation is a new word. Also, we use defects and deformities to a sacred purpose, so expressing our sense that the evils of the world are such only to the evil eye. In the old mythology, mythologists observe, defects are ascribed to divine natures, as lameness to Vulcan, blindness to Cupid, and the like, to signify exuberances.

For, as it is dislocation and detachment from the life of God, that makes things ugly, the poet, who reattaches things to nature and the Whole,—reattaching even artificial things, and violations of nature, to nature, by a deeper insight,—disposes very easily of the most disagreeable facts. Readers of poetry see the factory village and the railway, and fancy that the poetry of the landscape is broken up by these; for these works of art are not yet consecrated in their reading; but the poet sees them fall within the great Order not less than the beehive, or the spider's geometrical web. Nature adopts them very fast into her vital circles, and the gliding train of cars she loves like her own. Besides, in a centred mind, it signifies nothing how many mechanical inventions you exhibit. Though you add millions, and never so surprising, the fact of mechanics has not gained a grain's weight. The spiritual fact remains unalterable, by many or by few particulars; as no mountain is of any appreciable height to break the curve of the sphere. A shrewd country boy goes to the city for the first time, and the complacent citizen is not satisfied with his little wonder. It is not that he does not see all the fine houses, and know that he never saw such before, but he disposes of them as easily as the poet finds place for the railway. The chief value of the new fact, is to enhance the great and constant fact of Life, which can dwarf any and every circumstance, and to which the belt of wampum, and the commerce of America, are alike.

The world being thus put under the mind for verb and noun, the poet is he who can articulate it. For, though life is great, and fascinates, and absorbs,—and though all men are intelligent of the symbols through which it is named,— yet they cannot originally use them. We are symbols, and inhabit symbols; workmen, work, and tools, words and things, birth and death, all are emblems; but we sympathize with the symbols, and, being infatuated with the economical uses of things, we do not know that they are thoughts. The poet, by an ulterior intellectual perception, gives them a power which makes their old use forgotten, and puts eyes, and a tongue, into every dumb and inanimate object. He perceives the independence of the thought on the symbol, the stability of the thought, the accidency and fugacity of the symbol. As the eyes of Lynceus were said to see through the earth, so the poet turns the world to glass, and shows us all things in their right series and procession. For, through that better perception, he stands one step nearer to things, and sees the flowing or metamorphosis; perceives that thought in multiform; that within the form of every creature is a force impelling it to ascend into a higher form; and, following with his eyes the life, uses the forms which express that life, and so his speech flows with the flowing of nature. All the facts of the animal economy,—sex, nutriment, gestation, birth, growth—are symbols of the passage of the world into the soul of man, to suffer there a change, and reappear a new and higher fact. He uses forms according to the life and not according to the form. This is true science. The poet alone knows astronomy, chemistry, vegetation, and animation, for he does not stop at these facts, but employs them as signs. He knows why the plain or meadow of space was strown with these flowers we call suns, and moons, and stars; why the great deep is adorned with animals, with men, and gods; for, in every word he speaks he rides on them as the horses of thought.

By virtue of this science the poet is the Namer, or Language-maker, naming things sometimes after their appearance, sometimes after their essence, and giving to every one its own name and not another's, thereby rejoicing the intellect, which delights in detachment or boundary. The poets made all the words, and therefore language is the archives of history, and, if we must say it, a sort of tomb of the muses. For, though the origin of most of our words is forgotten, each word was at first a stroke of genius, and obtained currency, because for the moment it symbolized the world to the first speaker and to the hearer. The etymologist finds the deadest word to have been once a brilliant picture. Language is fossil poetry. As the limestone of the continent consists of infinite masses of the shells of animalcules, so language is made up of images, or tropes, which now, in their secondary use, have long ceased to remind us of their poetic origin. But the poet names the thing because he sees it, or comes one step nearer to it than any other. This expression, or naming, is not art, but a second nature, grown out of the first, as a leaf out of a tree. What we call nature, is a certain self-regulated motion, or change; and nature does all things by her own hands, and does not leave another to baptize her, but baptizes herself; and this through the metamorphosis again. I remember that a certain poet described it to me thus:—

Genius is the activity which repairs the decays of things,

whether wholly or partly of a material and finite kind. Nature, through all her kingdoms, insures herself. Nobody cares for planting the poor fungus: so she shakes down from the gills of one agaric countless spores, any one of which, being preserved, transmits new billions of spores to-morrow or next day. The new agaric of this hour has a chance which the old one had not. This atom of seed is thrown into a new place, not subject to the accidents which destroyed its parent two rods off. She makes a man; and having brought him to ripe age, she will no longer run the risk of losing this wonder at a blow, but she detaches from him a new self, that the kind may be safe from accidents to which the individual is exposed. So when the soul of the poet has come to ripeness of thought, she detaches and sends away from it its poems or songs,—a fearless, sleepless, deathless progeny, which is not exposed to the accidents of the weary kingdom of time; a fearless, vivacious offspring, clad with wings (such was the virtue of the soul out of which they came), which carry them fast and far, and infix them irrecoverably into the hearts of men. These wings are the beauty of the poet's soul. The songs, thus flying immortal from their mortal parent, are pursued by clamorous flights of censures, which swarm in far greater numbers, and threaten to devour them; but these last are not winged. At the end of a very short leap they fall plump down, and rot, having received from the souls out of which they came no beautiful wings. But the melodies of the poet ascend, and leap, and pierce into the deeps of infinite time.

So far the bard taught me, using his freer speech. But nature has a higher end, in the production of new individuals, than security, namely, *ascension*, or, the passage of the soul into higher forms. I knew, in my younger days, the sculptor who made the statue of the youth which stands in the public garden. He was, as I remember, unable to tell directly, what made him happy, or unhappy, but by wonderful indirections he could tell. He rose one day, according to his habit, before the dawn, and saw the morning break, grand as the eternity out of which it came, and, for many days after, he strove to express this tranquillity, and, lo! his chisel had fashioned out of marble the form of a beautiful youth, Phosphorus, whose aspect is such, that, it is said, all persons who look on it become silent. The poet also resigns himself to his mood, and that thought which agitated him is expressed, but *alter idem,* in a manner totally new. The expression is organic, or, the new type which things themselves take when liberated. As, in the sun, objects paint their images on the retina of the eye, so they, sharing the aspiration of the whole universe, tend to paint a far more delicate copy of their essence in his mind. Like the metamorphosis of things into higher organic forms, is their change into melodies. Over everything stands its daemon, or soul, and, as the form of the thing is reflected by the eye, so the soul of the thing is reflected by a melody. The sea, the mountain ridge, Niagara, and every flower-bed, pre-exist, or super-exist, in pre-cantations, which sail like odors in the air, and when any man goes by with an ear sufficiently fine, he overhears them, and endeavors to write down the notes, without diluting or depraving them. And herein is the legitimation of criticism, in the mind's faith, that the poems are a corrupt version of some text in nature, with which they ought to be made to tally. A rhyme in one of our sonnets should not be less pleasing than the iterated nodes of a seashell, or the resembling difference of a group of flowers. The pairing of the birds is an idyl, not tedious as our idyls are; a tempest is a rough ode, without falsehood or rant: a summer, with its harvest sown, reaped, and stored, is an epic song, subordinating how many admirably executed parts. Why should not the symmetry and truth that modulate these glide into our spirits, and we participate the invention of nature?

This insight, which expresses itself by what is called Imagination, is a very high sort of seeing, which does not come by study, but by the intellect being where and what it sees, by sharing the path or circuit of things through forms, and so making them translucid to others. The path of things is silent. Will they suffer a speaker to go with them? A spy they will not suffer; a lover, a poet, is the transcendency of their own nature,—him they will suffer. The condition of true naming, on the poet's part, is his resigning himself to the divine *aura* which breathes through forms, and accompanying that.

It is a secret which every intellectual man quickly learns, that, beyond the energy of his possessed and conscious intellect, he is capable of a new energy (as of an intellect doubled on itself), by abandonment to the nature of things; that, beside his privacy of power as an individual man, there is a great public power, on which he can draw, by unlocking, at all risks, his human doors, and suffering the ethereal tides to roll and circulate through him: then he is caught up into the life of the Universe, his speech is thunder, his thought is law, and his words are universally intelligible as the plants and animals. The poet knows that he speaks adequately, then, only when he speaks somewhat wildly, or, "with the flower of the mind"; not with the intellect, used as an organ, but with the intellect released from all service, and suffered to take its direction from its celestial life; or, as the ancients were wont to express themselves, not with intellect alone, but with the intellect inebriated by nectar. As the traveller who has lost his way throws his reins on his horse's neck, and trusts to the instinct of the animal to find his road, so must we do with the divine animal who carries us through this world. For if in any manner we can stimulate this instinct, new passages are opened for us into nature, the mind flows into and through things hardest and highest, and the metamorphosis is possible.

This is the reason why bards love wine, mead, narcotics, coffee, tea, opium, the fumes of sandal-wood and tobacco, or whatever other procurers of animal exhilaration. All men avail themselves of such means as they can, to add this extraordinary power to their normal powers; and to this end they prize conversation, music, pictures, sculpture, dancing, theatres, travelling, war, mobs, fires, gaming, politics, or love, or science, or animal intoxication, which are several coarser or finer *quasi*-mechanical substitutes for the true nectar, which is the ravishment of the intellect by coming nearer to the fact. These are auxiliaries to the centrifugal tendency of a man, to his passage out into free space, and they help him to escape the custody of that body in which he is pent up, and of that jail-yard of individual relations in which he is enclosed. Hence a great number of such as were professionally expressors of Beauty, as painters, poets, musicians, and actors, have been more than others wont to lead a life of pleasure and indulgence: all but the few who received the true nectar; and, as it was a spurious mode of attaining freedom, as it was an emancipation not into the heavens, but into the freedom of baser places, they were punished for that advantage they won, by a dissipation and deterioration. But never can any advantage be taken of nature by a trick. The spirit of the world, the great calm presence of the Creator, comes not forth to the sorceries of opium or of wine. The sublime vision comes to the pure and simple soul in a clean and chaste body. That is not an inspiration which we owe to narcotics, but some counterfeit excitement and fury. Milton says that the lyric poet may drink wine and live generously, but the epic poet, he who shall sing of the gods, and their descent unto men, must drink water out of a wooden bowl. For poetry is not 'Devil's wine,' but God's wine. It is with this as it is with toys. We fill the hands and nurseries of our children with all manner of dolls, drums, and horses, withdrawing their eyes from the plain face and sufficing objects of nature, the sun, and moon, the animals, the water, and stones, which should be their toys. So the poet's habit of living should be set on a key so low, that the common influences should delight him. His cheerfulness should be the gift of the sunlight; the air should suffice for his inspiration, and he should be tipsy with water. That spirit which suffices quiet hearts, which seems to come forth to such from every dry knoll of sere grass, from every pine stump, and half-imbedded stone, on which the dull March sun shines, comes forth to the poor and hungry, and such as are of simple taste. If thou fill thy brain with Boston and New York, with fashion and covetousness, and wilt stimulate thy jaded senses with wine and French coffee, thou shalt find no radiance of wisdom in the lonely waste of the pine-woods.

If the imagination intoxicates the poet, it is not inactive in other men. The metamorphosis excites in the beholder an emotion of joy. The use of symbols has a certain power of emancipation and exhilaration for all men. We seem to be touched by a wand, which makes us dance and run about happily, like children. We are like persons who come out of a cave or cellar into the open air. This is the effect on us of tropes, fables, oracles, and all poetic forms. Poets are thus liberating gods. Men have really got a new sense, and found within their world another world, or nest of worlds; for, the metamorphosis once seen, we divine that it does not stop. I will not now consider how much this makes the charm of algebra and the mathematics, which also have their tropes, but it is felt in every definition; as, when Aristotle defines *space* to be an immovable vessel, in which things are contained; or, when Plato defines a *line* to be a flowing point; or, *figure* to be a bound of solid; and many the like. What a joyful sense of freedom we have, when Vitruvius announces the old opinion of artists, that no architect can build any house well, who does not know something of anatomy. When Socrates, in Charmides, tells us that the soul is cured of its maladies by certain incantations, and that these incantations are beautiful reasons, from which temperance is generated in souls; when Plato calls the world an animal; and Timæus affirms that the plants also are animals; or affirms a man to be a heavenly tree, growing with its root, which is his head, upward; and, as George Chapman, following him, writes,—

> "So in our tree of man, whose nervie root
> Springs in his top";

when Orpheus speaks of hoariness as "that white flower which marks extreme old age"; when Proclus calls the universe the statue of the intellect; when Chaucer, in his praise of 'Gentilesse,' compares good blood in mean condition to fire, which, though carried to the darkest house betwixt this and the mount of Caucasus, will yet hold its natural office, and burn as bright as if twenty thousand men did it behold; when John saw, in the Apocalypse, the ruin of the world through evil, and the stars fall from Heaven, as the fig-tree casteth her untimely fruit; when Æsop reports the whole catalogue of common daily relations through the masquerade of birds and beasts; we take the cheerful hint of the immortality of our essence, and its versatile habit and escapes, as when the gypsies say of themselves, "It is in vain to hang them, they cannot die."

The poets are thus liberating gods. The ancient British bards had for the title of their order, "Those who are free throughout the world." They are free and they make free. An imaginative book renders us much more service at first, by stimulating us through its tropes, than afterward, when we arrive at the precise sense of the author. I think nothing is of any value in books, excepting the transcendental and extraordinary. If a man is inflamed and carried away by his thought, to that degree that he forgets the authors and the public, and heeds only this one dream, which holds him like an insanity, let me read his paper, and you may have all the arguments and histories and criticism. All the value which attaches to Pythagoras, Paracelsus, Cornelius Agrippa, Cardan, Kepler, Swedenborg, Schelling, Oken, or any other who introduces questionable facts into his cosmogony, as angels, devils, magic, astrology, palmistry, mesmerism, and so on, is the certificate we have of departure from routine, and that here is a new witness. That also is the best success in conversation, the magic of liberty, which puts the world, like a ball, in our hands. How cheap even the liberty then seems; how mean to study, when an emotion communicates to the intellect the power to sap and upheave nature: how great the perspective! nations, times, systems, enter and disappear, like threads in tapestry of large figure and many colors; dream delivers us to dream, and, while the drunkenness lasts, we will sell our bed, our philosophy, our religion, in our opulence.

There is good reason why we should prize this liberation. The fate of the poor shepherd, who, blinded and lost in the snow-storm, perishes in a drift within a few feet of his cottage door, is an emblem of the state of man. On the brink of the waters of life and truth, we are miserably dying. The inaccessibleness of every thought but that we are in, is wonderful. What if you come near to it,—you are as remote, when you are nearest, as when you are farthest. Every thought is also a prison; every Heaven is also a prison. Therefore we love the poet, the inventor, who in any form, whether in an ode, or in an action, or in looks and behavior, has yielded us a new thought. He unlocks our chains, and admits us to a new scene.

This emancipation is dear to all men, and the power to impart it, as it must come from greater depth and scope of thought, is a measure of intellect. Therefore all books of the imagination endure, all which ascend to that truth, that the writer sees nature beneath him, and uses it as his exponent. Every verse or sentence, possessing this virtue, will take care of its own immortality. The religions of the world are the ejaculations of a few imaginative men.

But the quality of the imagination is to flow, and not to freeze. The poet did not stop at the color, or the form, but read their meaning, neither may he rest in this meaning, but he makes the same objects exponents of his new thought. Here is the difference betwixt the poet and the mystic, that the last nails a symbol to one sense, which was a true sense for a moment, but soon becomes old and false. For all symbols are fluxional; all language is vehicular and transitive, and is good, as ferries and horses are, for conveyance, not as farms and houses are, for homestead. Mysticism consists in the mistake of an accidental and individual symbol for an universal one. The morning redness happens to be the favorite meteor to the eyes of Jacob Behmen, and comes to stand to him for truth and faith; and he believes should stand for the same realities to every reader. But the first reader prefers as naturally the symbol of a mother and child, or a gardener and his bulb, or a jeweller polishing a gem. Either of these, or of a myriad more, are equally good to the person to whom they are significant. Only they must be held lightly, and be very willingly translated into the equivalent terms which others use. And the mystic must be steadily told, All that you say is just as true without the tedious use of that symbol as with it. Let us have a little algebra, instead of this trite rhetoric,—universal signs, instead of these village symbols,—and we shall both be gainers. The history of hierarchies seems to show, that all religious error consisted in making the symbol too stark and solid, and, at last, nothing but an excess of the organ of language.

Swedenborg, of all men in the recent ages, stands eminently for the translator of nature into thought. I do not know the man in history to whom things stood so uniformly for words. Before him the metamorphosis continually plays. Everything on which his eye rests obeys the impulses of moral nature. The figs become grapes whilst he eats them. When some of his angels affirmed a truth, the laurel twig which they held blossomed in their hands. The noise which, at a distance, appeared like gnashing and thumping, on coming nearer was found to be the voice of disputants. The men, in one of his visions, seen in heavenly light, appeared like dragons, and seemed in darkness: but, to each other, they appeared as men, and when the light from Heaven shone into their cabin, they complained of the darkness, and were compelled to shut the window that they might see.

There was this perception in him, which makes the poet or seer an object of awe and terror, namely, that the same man, or society of men, may wear one aspect to themselves and their companions, and a different aspect to higher intelligences. Certain priests, whom he describes as conversing very learnedly together, appeared to the children, who were at some distance, like dead horses; and many the like misappearances. And instantly the mind inquires whether these fishes under the bridge, yonder oxen in the pasture, those dogs in the yard, are immutably fishes, oxen, and dogs, or only so appear to me, and perchance to themselves appear upright men; and whether I appear as a man to all eyes. The Bramins and Pythagoras propounded the same question, and if any poet has witnessed the transformation, he doubtless found it in harmony with various experiences. We have all seen changes as considerable in wheat and caterpillars. He is the poet, and shall draw us with love and terror, who sees, through the flowing vest, the firm nature, and can declare it.

I look in vain for the poet whom I describe. We do not, with sufficient plainness, or sufficient profoundness, address ourselves to life, nor dare we chant our own times and social circumstance. If we filled the day with bravery, we should not shrink from celebrating it. Time and nature yield us many gifts, but not yet the timely man, the new religion, the reconciler, whom all things await. Dante's praise is, that he dared to write his autobiography in colossal cipher, or into universality. We have yet had no genius in America, with tyrannous eye, which knew the value of our incomparable materials, and saw, in the barbarism and materialism of the times, another carnival of the same gods whose picture he so much admires in Homer; then in the middle age; then in Calvinism. Banks and tariffs, the newspaper and caucus, Methodism and Unitarianism, are flat and dull to dull people, but rest on the same foundations of wonder as the town of Troy, and the temple of Delphi, and are as swiftly passing away.

Our log-rolling, our stumps and their politics, our fisheries, our Negroes, and Indians, our boasts, and our repudiations, the wrath of rogues, and the pusillanimity of honest men, the Northern trade, the Southern planting, the Western clearing, Oregon and Texas, are yet unsung. Yet America is a poem in our eyes; its ample geography dazzles the imagination, and it will not wait long for metres. If I have not found that excellent combination of gifts in my countrymen which I seek, neither could I aid myself to fix the idea of the poet by reading now and then in Chalmers's collection of five centuries of English poets. These are wits, more than poets, though there have been poets among them. But when we adhere to the ideal of the poet, we have our difficulties even with Milton and Homer. Milton is too literary, and Homer too literal and historical.

But I am not wise enough for a national criticism, and must use the old largeness a little longer, to discharge my errand from the muse to the poet concerning his art.

Art is the path of the creator to his work. The paths, or

methods, are ideal and eternal, though few men ever see them, not the artist himself for years, or for a lifetime, unless he come into the conditions. The painter, the sculptor, the composer, the epic rhapsodist, the orator, all partake one desire, namely, to express themselves symmetrically and abundantly, not dwarfishly and fragmentarily. They found or put themselves in certain conditions, as, the painter and sculptor before some impressive human figures; the orator, into the assembly of the people; and the others, in such scenes as each has found exciting to his intellect; and each presently feels the new desire. He hears a voice, he sees a beckoning. Then he is apprised, with wonder, what herds of demons hem him in. He can no more rest; he says, with the old painter, "By God, it is in me, and must come forth of me." He pursues a beauty, half seen, which flies before him. The poet pours out verses in every solitude. Most of the things he says are conventional, no doubt; but by and by he says something which is original and beautiful. That charms him. He would say nothing else but such things. In our way of talking, we say, 'That is yours, this is mine'; but the poet knows well that it is not his; that it is as strange and beautiful to him as to you; he would fain hear the like eloquence at length. Once having tasted this immortal ichor, he cannot have enough of it, and, as an admirable creative power exists in these intellections, it is of the last importance that these things get spoken. What a little of all we know is said! What drops of all the sea of our science are baled up! and by what accident it is that these are exposed, when so many secrets sleep in nature! Hence the necessity of speech and song; hence these throbs and heart-beatings in the orator, at the door of the assembly, to the end, namely, that thought may be ejaculated as Logos, or Word.

Doubt not, O poet, but persist. Say, 'It is in me, and shall out.' Stand there, balked and dumb, stuttering and stammering, hissed and hooted, stand and strive, until, at last, rage draw out of thee that *dream*-power which every night shows thee is thine own; a power transcending all limit and privacy, and by virtue of which a man is the conductor of the whole river of electricity. Nothing walks, or creeps, or grows, or exists, which must not in turn arise and walk before him as exponent of his meaning. Comes he to that power, his genius is no longer exhaustible. All the creatures, by pairs and by tribes, pour into his mind as into a Noah's ark, to come forth again to people a new world. This is like the stock of air, for our respiration, or for the combustion of our fireplace, not a measure of gallons, but the entire atmosphere if wanted. And therefore the rich poets, as Homer, Chaucer, Shakespeare, and Raphael, have obviously no limits to their works, except the limits of their lifetime, and resemble a mirror carried through the street, ready to render an image of every created thing.

O poet! a new nobility is conferred in groves and pastures, and not in castles, or by the sword-blade, any longer. The conditions are hard, but equal. Thou shalt leave the world, and know the muse only. Thou shalt not know any longer the times, customs, graces, politics, or opinions of men, but shalt take all from the muse. For the time of towns is tolled from the world by funereal chimes, but in nature the universal hours are counted by succeeding tribes of animals and plants, and by growth of joy on joy. God wills also that thou abdicate a duplex and manifold life, and that thou be content that others speak for thee. Others shall be thy gentlemen, and shall represent all courtesy and worldly life for thee; others shall do the great and resounding actions also. Thou shalt lie close hid with nature, and canst not be afforded to the Capitol or the Exchange. The world is full of renunciations and apprenticeships, and this is thine; thou must pass for a fool, and a churl for a long season. This is the screen and sheath in which Pan has protected his well-beloved flower, and thou shalt be known only to thine own, and they shall console thee with tenderest love. And thou shalt not be able to rehearse the names of thy friends in thy verse, for an old shame before the holy ideal. And this is the reward: that the ideal shall be real to thee, and the impressions of the actual world shall fall like summer rain, copious, but not troublesome, to thy invulnerable essence. Thou shalt have the whole land for thy park and manor, the sea for thy bath and navigation, without tax and without envy; the woods and the rivers thou shalt own; and thou shalt possess that wherein others are only tenants and boarders. Thou true land-lord! sea-lord! air-lord! Wherever snow falls, or water flows, or birds fly, wherever day and night meet in twilight, wherever the blue heaven is hung by clouds, or sown with stars, wherever are forms with transparent boundaries, wherever are outlets into celestial space, wherever is danger, and awe, and love, there is Beauty, plenteous as rain, shed for thee, and though thou shouldst walk the world over, thou shalt not be able to find a condition inopportune or ignoble.

1844

EXPERIENCE.*

The lords of life, the lords of life,—
I saw them pass,
In their own guise,
Like and unlike,
Portly and grim,
Use and Surprise,
Surface and Dream,
Succession swift, and spectral Wrong,
Temperament without a tongue,
And the inventor of the game
Omnipresent without name;—
Some to see, some to be guessed,
They marched from east to west:
Little man, least of all,
Among the legs of his guardians tall,
Walked about with puzzled look;—
Him by the hand dear Nature took;
Dearest Nature, strong and kind,
Whispered, 'Darling, never mind!
To-morrow they will wear another face,
The founder thou! these are thy race!'

Where do we find ourselves? In a series of which we do not know the extremes, and believe that it has none. We wake and find ourselves on a stair; there are stairs below us which we seem to have ascended; there are stairs above us, many a one, which go upward and out of sight. But the Genius which, according to the old belief, stands at the door by which we enter, and gives us the lethe to drink, that we may tell no tales, mixed the cup too strongly, and we cannot shake off the lethargy now at noonday. Sleep lingers all our lifetime about our eyes, as night hovers all day in the boughs of the fir-tree. All things swim and glitter. Our life is

* From *Essays, Second Series.*

not so much threatened as our perception. Ghostlike we glide through nature, and should not know our place again. Did our birth fall in some fit of indigence and frugality in nature, that she was so sparing of her fire and so liberal of her earth, that it appears to us that we lack the affirmative principle, and though we have health and reason, yet we have no superfluity of spirit for new creation? We have enough to live and bring the year about, but not an ounce to impart or to invest. Ah that our Genius were a little more of a genius! We are like millers on the lower levels of a stream, when the factories above them have exhausted the water. We too fancy that the upper people must have raised their dams.

If any of us knew what we were doing, or where we are going, then when we think we best know! We do not know to-day whether we are busy or idle. In times when we thought ourselves indolent, we have afterwards discovered that much was accomplished, and much was begun in us. All our days are so uncomfortable while they pass, that 't is wonderful where or when we ever got anything of this which we call wisdom, poetry, virtue. We never got it on any dated calendar day. Some heavenly days must have been inter- calated somewhere, like those that Hermes won with dice of the Moon, that Osiris might be born. It is said, all martyr- doms looked mean when they were suffered. Every ship is a romantic object, except that we sail in. Embark, and the ro- mance quits our vessel, and hangs on every other sail in the horizon. Our life looks trivial and we shun to record it. Men seem to have learned of the horizon the art of perpetual retreating and reference. 'Yonder uplands are rich pasturage, and my neighbor has fertile meadow, but my field,' says the querulous farmer, 'only holds the world together.' I quote another man's saying; unluckily, that other withdraws him- self in the same way, and quotes me. 'T is the trick of na- ture thus to degrade to-day; a good deal of buzz, and some- where a result slipped magically in. Every roof is agreeable to the eye, until it is lifted; then we find tragedy and moan- ing women, and hard-eyed husbands, and deluges of lethe, and the men ask, 'What's the news?' as if the old were so bad. How many individuals can we count in society? how many actions? how many opinions? So much of our time is preparation, so much is routine, and so much retrospect, that the pith of each man's genius contracts itself to a very few hours. The history of literature,—take the net result of Tiraboschi, Warton, or Schlegel,—is a sum of very few ideas, and of very few original tales,—all the rest being variation of these. So, in this great society wide lying around us, a critical analysis would find very few spontaneous actions. It is almost all custom and gross sense. There are even few opinions, and these seem organic in the speakers, and do not disturb the universal necessity.

What opium is instilled into all disaster! It shows formidable as we approach it, but there is at last no rough rasping friction, but the most slippery sliding surfaces: we fall soft on a thought: *Ate Dea* is gentle,

> "Over men's heads walking aloft,
>   With tender feet treading so soft."

People grieve and bemoan themselves, but it is not half so bad with them as they say. There are moods in which we court suffering, in the hope that here, at least, we shall find reality, sharp peaks and edges of truth. But it turns out to be scene-painting and counterfeit. The only thing grief has taught me, is to know how shallow it is. That, like all the rest, plays about the surface, and never introduces me into the reality, for contact with which, we would even pay the costly price of sons and lovers. Was it Boscovich who found out that bodies never come in contact? Well, souls never touch their objects. An innavigable sea washes with silent waves between us and the things we aim at and converse with. Grief too will make us idealists. In the death of my son, now more than two years ago, I seem to have lost a beautiful estate,—no more. I cannot get it nearer to me. If to-morrow I should be informed of the bankruptcy of my principal debtors, the loss of my property would be a great inconvenience to me, perhaps, for many years; but it would leave me as it found me,—neither better nor worse. So is it with this calamity: it does not touch me; something which I fancied was a part of me, which could not be torn away without tearing me, nor enlarged without enriching me, falls off from me and leaves no scar. It was caducous. I grieve that grief can teach me nothing, nor carry me one step into real nature. The Indian who was laid under a curse, that the wind should not blow on him, nor water flow to him, nor fire burn him, is a type of us all. The dearest events are summer rain, and we the Para coats that shed every drop. Nothing is left us now but death. We look to that with a grim satisfaction, saying, there at least is reality that will not dodge us.

I take this evanescence and lubricity of all objects, which lets them slip through our fingers then when we clutch hardest, to be the most unhandsome part of our condition. Nature does not like to be observed, and likes that we should be her fools and playmates. We may have the sphere for our cricket-ball, but not a berry for our philosophy. Direct strokes she never gave us power to make; all our blows glance, all our hits are accidents. Our relations to each other are oblique and casual.

Dream delivers us to dream, and there is no end to illusion. Life is a train of moods like a string of beads, and, as we pass through them, they prove to be many-colored lenses which paint the world their own hue, and each shows only what lies in its focus. From the mountain you see the mountain. We animate what we can, and we see only what we animate. Nature and books belong to the eyes that see them. It depends on the mood of the man, whether he shall see the sunset or the fine poem. There are always sunsets, and there is always genius; but only a few hours so serene that we can relish nature or criticism. The more or less depends on structure or temperament. Temperament is the iron wire on which the beads are strung. Of what use is fortune or talent to a cold and defective nature? Who cares what sensibility or discrimination a man has at sometime shown, if he falls asleep in his chair? or if he laugh and giggle? or if he apologize? or is infected with egotism? or thinks of his dollar? or cannot pass by food? or has gotten a child in his boyhood? Of what use is genius, if the organ is too convex or too concave, and cannot find a focal distance within the actual horizon of human life? Of what use, if the brain is too cold or too hot, and the man does not care enough for results, to stimulate him to experiment, and hold him up in it? or if the web is too finely woven, too irritable by pleasure and pain, so that life stagnates from too much reception, without due outlet? Of what use to make heroic vows of amendment, if the same old law-breaker is to keep them? What cheer can the religious sentiment yield, when that is suspected to be secretly dependent on the seasons of the year, and the state of the blood? I knew a witty physician who found the creed in the biliary duct, and used to affirm that if there was disease in the liver, the man became a Calvinist, and if that organ was sound, he became a Unitarian. Very mortifying is the reluctant experience that some unfriendly excess or imbecility neutralizes the promise of genius. We see young men who owe us a new world, so readily and lavishly they promise, but they never acquit the debt; they die young and dodge the account: or if they live, they lose themselves in the crowd.

Temperament also enters fully into the system of illusions, and shuts us in a prison of glass which we cannot see. There is an optical illusion about every person we meet. In truth, they are all creatures of given temperament, which will appear in a given character, whose boundaries they will never pass: but we look at them, they seem alive, and we presume there is impulse in them. In the moment it seems impulse; in the year, in the lifetime, it turns out to be a certain uniform tune which the revolving barrel of the music-box must play. Men resist the conclusion in the morning, but adopt it as the evening wears on, that temper prevails over everything of time, place, and condition, and is inconsumable in the flames of religion. Some modifications the moral sentiment avails to impose, but the individual texture holds its dominion, if not to bias the moral judgments, yet to fix the measure of activity and of enjoyment.

I thus express the law as it is read from the platform of ordinary life, but must not leave it without noticing the capital exception. For temperament is a power which no man willingly hears any one praise but himself. On the platform of physics, we cannot resist the contracting influences of so-called science. Temperament puts all divinity to rout. I know the mental proclivity of physicians. I hear the chuckle of the phrenologists. Theoretic kidnappers and slave-drivers, they esteem each man the victim of another, who winds him round his finger by knowing the law of his being, and by such cheap sign-boards as the color of his beard, or the slope of his occiput, reads the inventory of his fortunes and character. The grossest ignorance does not disgust like this impudent knowingness. The physicians say, they are not materialists: but they are:—Spirit is matter reduced to an extreme thinness: O *so* thin!—But the definition of *spiritual* should be, *that which is its own evidence*. What notions do they attach to love? what to religion? One would not willingly pronounce these words in their hearing, and give them the occasion to profane them. I saw a gracious gentleman who adapts his conversation to the form of the head of the man he talks with! I had fancied that the value of life lay in its inscrutable possibilities; in the fact that I never know, in addressing myself to a new individual, what may befall me. I carry the keys of my castle in my hand, ready to throw them at the feet of my lord, whenever and in what disguise soever he shall appear. I know he is in the neighborhood hidden among vagabonds. Shall I preclude my future, by taking a high seat, and kindly adapting my conversation to the shape of heads? When I come to that, the doctors shall buy me for a cent.—"But, sir, medical history; the report to the Institute; the proven facts!"—I distrust the facts and the inferences. Temperament is the veto or limitation-power in the constitution, very unjustly applied to restrain an opposite excess in the constitution, but absurdly offered as a bar to original equity. When virtue is in presence, all subordinate powers sleep. On its own level, or in view of nature, temperament is final. I see not, if one be once caught in this trap of so-called sciences, any escape for the man from the links of the chain of physical necessity. Given such an embryo, such a history must follow. On this platform, one lives in a sty of sensualism, and would soon come to suicide. But it is impossible that the creative power should exclude itself. Into every intelligence there is a door which is never closed, through which the creator passes. The intellect, seeker of absolute truth, or the heart, lover of absolute good, intervenes for our succor, and at one whisper of these high powers, we awake from ineffectual struggles with this nightmare. We hurl it into its own hell, and cannot again contract ourselves to so base a state.

The secret of the illusoriness is in the necessity of a successor of moods or objects. Gladly we would anchor, but the anchorage is quicksand. This onward trick of nature is too strong for us: *Pero si muove*. When, at night, I look at the moon and stars, I seem stationary, and they to hurry. Our love of the real draws us to permanence, but health of body consists in circulation, and sanity of mind in variety or facility of association. We need change of objects. Dedication to one thought is quickly odious. We house with the insane, and must humor them; then conversation dies out. Once I took such delight in Montaigne, that I thought I should not need any other book; before that, in Shakespeare; then in Plutarch; then in Plotinus; at one time in Bacon; afterwards in Goethe; even in Bettine; but now I turn the pages of either of them languidly, whilst I still cherish their genius. So with pictures; each will bear an emphasis of attention once, which it cannot retain, though we fain would continue to be pleased in that manner. How strongly I have felt of pictures, that when you have seen one well, you must take your leave of it; you shall never see it again. I have had good lessons from pictures, which I have since seen without emotion or remark. A deduction must be made from the opinion, which even the wise express on a new book or occurrence. Their opinion gives me tidings of their mood, and some vague guess at the new fact, but is nowise to be trusted as the lasting relation between that intellect and that thing. The child asks, 'Mamma, why don't I like the story as well as when you told it me yesterday?' Alas, child, it is even so with the oldest cherubim of knowledge. But will it answer thy question to say, Because thou wert born to a whole, and this story is a particular? The reason of the pain this discovery causes us (and we make it late in respect to works of arts and intellect), is the plaint of tragedy which murmurs from it in regard to persons, to friendship and love.

That immobility and absence of elasticity which we find in the arts, we find with more pain in the artist. There is no power of expansion in men. Our friends early appear to us as representatives of certain ideas, which they never pass or exceed. They stand on the brink of the ocean of thought and power, but they never take the single step that would bring them there. A man is like a bit of Labrador spar, which has no lustre as you turn it in your hand, until you come to a particular angle; then it shows deep and beautiful colors. There is no adaptation or universal applicability in men, but each has his special talent, and the mastery of successful men consists in adroitly keeping themselves where and when that turn shall be oftenest to be practised. We do what we must, and call it by the best names we can, and would fain have the praise of having intended the result which ensues. I cannot recall any form of man who is not superfluous sometimes. But is not this pitiful? Life is not worth the taking, to do tricks in.

Of course, it needs the whole society, to give the symmetry we seek. The party-colored wheel must revolve very fast to appear white. Something is learned too by conversing with so much folly and defect. In fine, whoever loses, we are always of the gaining party. Divinity is behind our failures and follies also. The plays of children are nonsense, but very educative nonsense. So it is with the largest and solemnest things, with commerce, government, church, marriage, and so with the history of every man's bread, and the ways by which he is to come by it. Like a bird which alights nowhere, but hops perpetually from bough to bough, is the Power which abides in no man and in no woman, but for a moment speaks from this one, and for another moment from that one.

But what help from these fineries or pedantries? What help from thought? Life is not dialectics. We, I think, in these times, have had lessons enough of the futility of criticism. Our young people have thought and written much on labor and reform, and for all that they have written, neither the world nor themselves have got on a step. Intellectual tasting of life will not supersede muscular activity. If a man should consider the nicety of the passage of a piece of bread down his throat, he would starve. At Education Farm, the noblest theory of life sat on the noblest figures of young men and maidens, quite powerless and melancholy. It would not rake or pitch a ton of hay; it would not rub down a horse; and the men and maidens it left pale and hungry. A political orator wittily compared our party promises to Western roads, which opened stately enough, with planted trees on either side, to tempt the traveller, but soon became narrower and narrower and ended in a squirrel-track, and ran up a tree. So does culture with us; it ends in headache. Unspeakably sad and barren does life look to those, who a few months ago were dazzled with the splendor of the promise of the times. "There is now no longer any right course of action, nor any self-devotion left among the Iranis." Objections and criticism we have had our fill of. There are objections to every course of life and action, and the practical wisdom infers an indifferency, from the omnipresence of objection. The whole frame of things preaches indifferency. Do not craze yourself with thinking, but go about your business anywhere. Life is not intellectual or critical, but sturdy. Its chief good is for well-mixed people who can enjoy what they find, without question. Nature hates peeping, and our mothers speak her very sense when they say, "Children, eat your victuals, and say no more of it." To fill the hour,—that is happiness; to fill the hour, and leave no crevice for a repentance or an approval. We live amid surfaces, and the true art of life is to skate well on them. Under the oldest mouldiest conventions, a man of native force prospers just as well as in the newest world, and that by skill of handling and treatment. He can take hold anywhere. Life itself is a mixture of power and form, and will not bear the least excess of either. To finish the moment, to find the journey's end in every step of the road, to live the greatest number of good hours, is wisdom. It is not the part of men, but of fanatics, or of mathematicians, if you will, to say, that, the shortness of life considered, it is not worth caring whether for so short a duration we were sprawling in want, or sitting high. Since our office is with moments, let us husband them. Five minutes of to-day are worth as much to me as five minutes in the next millennium. Let us be poised, and wise, and our own, to-day. Let us treat the men and women well: treat them as if they were real: perhaps they are. Men live in their fancy, like drunkards whose hands are too soft and tremulous for successful labor. It is a tempest of fancies, and the only ballast I know is a respect to the present hour. Without any shadow of doubt, amidst this vertigo of shows and politics, I settle myself ever the firmer in the creed, that we should not postpone and refer and wish, but do broad justice where we are, by whomsoever we deal with, accepting our actual companions and circumstances, however humble or odious, as the mystic officials to whom the universe has delegated its whole pleasure for us. If these are mean and malignant, their contentment, which is the last victory of justice, is a more satisfying echo to the heart than the voice of poets and the casual sympathy of admirable persons. I think that, however a thoughtful man may suffer from the defects and absurdities of his company, he cannot without affectation deny to any set of men and women a sensibility to extraordinary merit. The coarse and frivolous have an instinct of superiority, if they have not a sympathy, and honor it in their blind capricious way with sincere homage.

The fine young people despise life, but in me, and in such as with me are free from dyspepsia, and to whom a day is a sound and solid good, it is a great excess of politeness to look scornful and to cry for company. I am grown by sympathy a little eager and sentimental, but leave me alone, and I should

relish every hour and what it brought me, the potluck of the
day, as heartily as the oldest gossip in the bar-room. I am
thankful for small mercies. I compared notes with one of my
friends who expects everything of the universe, and is disappointed when anything is less than the best, and I found that
I begin at the other extreme, expecting nothing, and am always full of thanks for moderate goods. I accept the clangor
and jangle of contrary tendencies. I find my account in sots
and bores also. They give a reality to the circumjacent picture, which such a vanishing meteorous appearance can ill
spare. In the morning I awake, and find the old world, wife,
babes, and mother, Concord and Boston, the dear old spiritual
world, and even the dear old devil not far off. If we will take
the good we find, asking no questions, we shall have heaping
measures. The great gifts are not got by analysis. Everything
good is on the highway. The middle region of our being is
the temperate zone. We may climb into the thin and cold
realm of pure geometry and lifeless science, or sink into that
of sensation. Between these extremes is the equator of life, of
thought, of spirit, of poetry,—a narrow belt. Moreover, in
popular experience, everything good is on the highway. A
collector peeps into all the picture-shops of Europe, for a
landscape of Poussin, a crayon sketch of Salvator; but the
Transfiguration, the Last Judgment, the Communion of St.
Jerome, and what are as transcendent as these, are on the
walls of the Vatican, the Uffizii, or the Louvre, where every
footman may see them; to say nothing of nature's pictures in
every street, of sunsets and sunrises every day, and the sculpture of the human body never absent. A collector recently
bought at public auction, in London, for one hundred and
fifty-seven guineas, an autograph of Shakespeare: but for
nothing a school-boy can read Hamlet, and can detect secrets
of highest concernment yet unpublished therein. I think I
will never read any but the commonest books,—the Bible,
Homer, Dante, Shakespeare, and Milton. Then we are impatient of so public a life and planet, and run hither and
thither for nooks and secrets. The imagination delights in the
wood-craft of Indians, trappers, and beehunters. We fancy
that we are strangers, and not so intimately domesticated in
the planet as the wild man, and the wild beast and bird. But
the exclusion reaches them also; reaches the climbing, flying,
gliding, feathered and four-footed man. Fox and woodchuck,
hawk and snipe, and bittern, when nearly seen, have no more

root in the deep world than man, and are just such superficial tenants of the globe. Then the new molecular philosophy shows astronomical interspaces betwixt atom and atom, shows that the world is all outside: it has no inside.

The mid-world is best. Nature, as we know her, is no saint. The lights of the church, the ascetics, Gentoos and corn-eaters, she does not distinguish by any favor. She comes eating and drinking and sinning. Her darlings, the great, the strong, the beautiful, are not children of our law, do not come out of the Sunday school, nor weigh their food, nor punctually keep the commandments. If we will be strong with her strength, we must not harbor such disconsolate consciences, borrowed too from the consciences of other nations. We must set up the strong present tense against all the rumors of wrath, past or to come. So many things are unsettled which it is of the first importance to settle,—and, pending their settlement, we will do as we do. Whilst the debate goes forward on the equity of commerce, and will not be closed for a century or two, New and Old England may keep shop. Law of copyright and international copyright is to be discussed, and, in the interim, we will sell our books for the most we can. Expediency of literature, reason of literature, lawfulness of writing down a thought, is questioned; much is to say on both sides, and, while the fight waxes hot, thou, dearest scholar, stick to thy foolish task, add a line every hour, and between whiles add a line. Right to hold land, right of property, is disputed, and the conventions convene, and before the vote is taken, dig away in your garden, and spend your earnings as a waif or godsend to all serene and beautiful purposes. Life itself is a bubble and a scepticism, and a sleep within a sleep. Grant it, and as much more as they will,—but thou, God's darling! heed thy private dream: thou wilt not be missed in the scorning and scepticism: there are enough of them: stay there in thy closet, and toil, until the rest are agreed what to do about it. Thy sickness, they say, and thy puny habit, require that thou do this or avoid that, but know that thy life is a flitting state, a tent for a night, and do thou, sick or well, finish that stint. Thou art sick, but shalt not be worse, and the universe, which holds thee dear, shall be the better.

Human life is made up of the two elements, power and form, and the proportion must be invariably kept, if we would have it sweet and sound. Each of these elements in excess makes a mischief as hurtful as its defect. Everything runs to excess: every good quality is noxious, if unmixed, and, to carry the danger to the edge of ruin, nature causes each man's peculiarity to superabound. Here, among the farms, we adduce the scholars as examples of this treachery. They are nature's victims of expression. You who see the artist, the orator, and poet, too near, and find their life no more excellent than that of mechanics or farmers, and themselves victims of partiality, very hollow and haggard, and pronounce them failures,—not heroes, but quacks,—conclude very reasonably, that these arts are not for man, but are disease. Yet nature will not bear you out. Irresistible nature made men such, and makes legions more of such, every day. You love the boy reading in a book, gazing at a drawing, or a cast: yet what are these millions who read and behold, but incipient writers and sculptors? Add a little more of that quality which now reads and sees, and they will seize the pen and chisel. And if one remembers how innocently he began to be an artist, he perceives that nature joined with his enemy. A man is a golden impossibility. The line he must walk is a hair's breadth. The wise through excess of wisdom is made a fool.

How easily, if fate would suffer it, we might keep forever these beautiful limits, and adjust ourselves, once for all, to the perfect calculation of the kingdom of known cause and effect. In the street, and in the newspapers, life appears so plain a business, that manly resolution and adherence to the multiplication-table through all weathers, will insure success. But ah! presently comes a day, or is it only a half-hour, with its angel-whispering,—which discomfits the conclusions of nations and of years! To-morrow again, everything looks real and angular, the habitual standards are reinstated, common sense is as rare as genius,—is the basis of genius, and experience is hands and feet to every enterprise;—and yet, he who should do his business on this understanding, would be quickly bankrupt. Power keeps quite another road than the turnpikes of choice and will, namely, the subterranean and invisible tunnels and channels of life. It is ridiculous that we are diplomatists, and doctors, and considerate people; there are no dupes like these. Life is a series of surprises, and would not be worth taking or keeping, if it were not. God delights to isolate us every day, and hide from us the past and the future. We would look about us, but with grand politeness he draws down before us an impenetrable screen of purest sky, and another behind us of purest sky. 'You will not remember,' he seems to say, 'and you will not expect.' All good conversation, manners, and action, come from a spontaneity which forgets usages, and makes the moment great. Nature hates calculators; her methods are saltatory and impulsive. Man lives by pulses; our organic movements are such; and the chemical and ethereal agents are undulatory and alternate; and the mind goes antagonizing on, and never prospers but by fits. We thrive by casualties. Our chief experiences have been casual. The most attractive class of people are those who are powerful obliquely, and not by the direct stroke: men of genius, but not yet accredited: one gets the cheer of their light without paying too great a tax. Theirs is the beauty of the bird, or the morning light, and not of art. In the thought of genius there is always a surprise; and the moral sentiment is well called "the newness," for it is never other; as new to the oldest intelligence as to the young child,—"the kingdom that cometh without observation." In like manner, for practical success, there must not be too much design. A man will not be observed in doing that which he can do best. There is a certain magic about his properest action, which stupefies your powers of observation, so that though it is done before you, you wist not of it. The art of life has a pudency, and will not be exposed. Every man is an impossibility, until he is born; every thing impossible, until we see a success. The ardors of piety agree at last with the coldest scepticism,—that nothing is of us or our works,—that all is of God. Nature will not spare us the smallest leaf of laurel. All writing comes by the grace of God, and all doing and having. I would gladly be moral, and keep due metes and bounds, which I dearly love, and allow the most to the will of man, but I have set my heart on honesty in this chapter, and I can see nothing at last, in success or failure, than more or less of vital force supplied from the Eternal. The results of life are uncalculated and uncalculable. The years teach much which the days never know. The persons who compose our company, converse, and come and go, and design and execute many things, and somewhat comes of it all, but an unlooked-for result. The individual is always mistaken. He designed many things, and drew in other persons as coadjutors, quarrelled with some or all, blundered much, and something is done; all are a little advanced, but the individual is always mistaken. It turns out somewhat new, and very unlike what he promised himself.

The ancients, struck with this irreducibleness of the elements of human life to calculation, exalted Chance into a divinity, but that is to stay too long at the spark,—which glitters truly at one point,—but the universe is warm with the latency of the same fire. The miracle of life which will not be expounded, but will remain a miracle, introduces a new element. In the growth of the embryo, Sir Everard Home, I think, noticed that the evolution was not from one central point, but coactive from three or more points. Life has no memory. That which proceeds in succession might be remembered, but that which is coexistent, or ejaculated from a deeper cause, as yet far from being conscious, knows not its own tendency. So is it with us, now sceptical, or without unity, because immersed in forms and effects all seeming to be of equal yet hostile value, and now religious, whilst in the reception of spiritual law. Bear with these distractions, with this coetaneous growth of the parts; they will one day be *member*s, and obey one will. On that one will, on that secret cause, they nail our attention and hope. Life is hereby melted into an expectation or a religion. Underneath the inharmonious and trivial particulars, is a musical perfection, the Ideal journeying always with us, the heaven without rent or seam. Do but observe the mode of our illumination. When I converse with a profound mind, or if at any time being alone I have good thoughts, I do not at once arrive at satisfactions, as when, being thirsty, I drink water, or go to the fire, being cold: no! but I am at first apprised of my vicinity to a new and excellent region of life. By persisting to read or to think, this region gives further sign of itself, as it were in flashes of light, in sudden discoveries of its profound beauty and repose, as if the clouds that covered it parted at intervals, and showed the approaching traveller the inland mountains, with the tranquil eternal meadows spread at their base, whereon flocks graze, and shepherds pipe and dance. But every insight from this realm of thought is felt as initial, and promises a sequel. I do not make it; I arrive there, and behold what was there already. I make! O no! I clap my hands in infinite joy and amazement, before the first opening to me of this august magnificence, old with the love and homage of innumerable ages, young with the life of life, the sunbright Mecca of the desert. And what a future it opens! I feel a new heart beating with the love of the new beauty. I am ready to die out of nature, and be born again into this new yet unapproachable America I have found in the West.

> "Since neither now nor yesterday began
> These thoughts, which have been ever, nor yet can
> A man be found who their first entrance knew."

If I have described life as a flux of moods, I must now add, that there is that in us which changes not, and which ranks all sensations and states of mind. The consciousness in each man is a sliding scale, which identifies him now with the First Cause, and now with the flesh of his body; life above life, in infinite degrees. The sentiment from which it sprung determines the dignity of any deed, and the question ever is, not, what you have done or forborne, but, at whose command you have done or forborne it.

Fortune, Minerva, Muse, Holy Ghost,—these are quaint names, too narrow to cover this unbounded substance. The baffled intellect must still kneel before this cause, which refuses to be named,—ineffable cause, which every fine genius has essayed to represent by some emphatic symbols, as Thales by water, Anaximenes by air, Anaxagoras by (Noῦs) thought, Zoroaster by fire, Jesus and the moderns by love: and the metaphor of each has become a national religion. The Chinese Mencius has not been the least successful in his generalization. "I fully understand language," he said, "and nourish well my vast-flowing vigor."—"I beg to ask what you call vast-flowing vigor?" said his companion. "The explanation," replied Mencius, "is difficult. This vigor is supremely great, and in the highest degree unbending. Nourish it correctly, and do it no injury, and it will fill up the vacancy between heaven and earth. This vigor accords with and assists justice and reason, and leaves no hunger." In our more correct writing, we give to this generalization the name of Being, and thereby confess that we have arrived as far as we can go. Suffice it for the joy of the universe, that we have not arrived at a wall, but at interminable oceans. Our life seems not present, so much as prospective; not for the affairs on which it is wasted, but as a hint of this vast-flowing vigor. Most of life seems to be mere advertisement of faculty; information is given us not to sell ourselves cheap; that we are very great. So, in particulars, our greatness is always in a tendency or direction, not in an action. It is for us to believe in the rule, not in the exception. The noble are thus known from the ignoble. So in accepting the leading of the sentiments, it is not what we believe concerning the immortality of the soul, or the like, but *the universal impulse to believe,* that is the material circumstance, and is the principal fact in the history of the globe. Shall we describe this cause as that which works directly? The spirit is not helpless or needful of mediate organs. It has plentiful powers and direct effects. I am explained without explaining, I am felt without acting, and where I am not. Therefore all just persons are satisfied with their own praise. They refuse to explain themselves, and are content that new actions should do them that office. They believe that we communicate without speech, and above speech, and that no right action of ours is quite unaffecting to our friends, at whatever distance; for the influence of action is not to be measured by miles. Why should I fret myself, because a circumstance has occurred, which hinders my presence where I was expected? If I am not at the meeting, my presence where I am should be as useful to the commonwealth of friendship and wisdom, as would be my presence in that place. I exert the same quality of power in all places. Thus journeys the mighty Ideal before us; it never was known to fall into the rear. No man ever came to an experience which was satiating, but his good is tidings of a better. Onward and onward! In liberated moments, we know that a new picture of life and duty is already possible; the elements already exist in many minds around you, of a doctrine of life which shall transcend any written record we have. The new statement will comprise the scepticisms, as well as the faiths of society, and out of unbeliefs a creed shall be formed. For, scepticisms are not gratuitous or lawless, but are limitations of the affirmative statement, and the new philosophy must take them in, and make affirmations outside of them, just as much as it must include the oldest beliefs.

It is very unhappy, but too late to be helped, the discovery we have made, that we exist. That discovery is called the Fall of Man. Ever afterwards, we suspect our instruments. We have learned that we do not see directly, but mediately, and that we have no means of correcting these colored and distorting lenses which we are, or of computing the amount of their errors. Perhaps these subject lenses have a creative power; perhaps there are no objects. Once we lived in what we saw; now, the rapaciousness of this new power, which threatens to absorb all things, engages us. Nature, art, persons, letters, religions,—objects, successively tumble in, and God is but one of its ideas. Nature and literature are subjective phenomena; every evil and every good thing is a shadow which we cast. The street is full of humiliations to the proud. As the fop contrived to dress his bailiffs in his livery, and make them wait on his guests at table, so the chagrins which the bad heart gives off as bubbles, at once take form as ladies and gentlemen in the street, shopmen or bar-keepers in hotels, and threaten or insult whatever is threatenable and insultable in us. 'T is the same with our idolatries. People forget that it is the eye which makes the horizon, and the rounding mind's eye which makes this or that man a type or representative of humanity with the name of hero or saint. Jesus, "the providential man," is a good man on whom many people are agreed that these optical laws shall take effect. By love on one part, and by forbearance to press objection on the other part, it is for a time settled, that we will look at him in the centre of the horizon, and ascribe to him the properties that will attach to any man so seen. But the longest love or aversion has a speedy term. The great and crescive self, rooted in absolute nature, supplants all relative existence, and ruins the kingdom of mortal friendship and love. Marriage (in what is called the spiritual world) is impossible, because of the inequality between every subject and every object. The subject is the receiver of Godhead, and at every comparison must feel his being enhanced by that cryptic might. Though not in energy, yet by presence, this magazine of substance cannot be otherwise than felt: nor can any force of intellect attribute to the object the proper deity which sleeps or wakes forever in every subject. Never can love make consciousness and ascription equal in force. There will be the same gulf between every me and thee, as between the original and the picture. The universe is the bride of the soul. All private sympathy is partial. Two human beings are like globes which can touch only in a point, and, whilst they remain in contact, all other points of each of the spheres are inert; their turn must also come, and the longer a particular union lasts, the more energy of appetency the parts not in union acquire. Life will be imaged, but cannot be divided nor doubled.

Any invasion of its unity would be chaos. The soul is not twin-born, but the only begotten, and though revealing itself as child in time, child in appearance, is of a fatal and universal power, admitting no co-life. Every day, every act betrays the ill-concealed deity. We believe in ourselves, as we do not believe in others. We permit all things to ourselves, and that which we call sin in others is experiment for us. It is an instance of our faith in ourselves, that men never speak of crime as lightly as they think: or, every man thinks a latitude safe for himself, which is nowise to be indulged to another. The act looks very differently on the inside, and on the outside; in its quality, and in its consequences. Murder in the murderer is no such ruinous thought as poets and romancers will have it; it does not unsettle him, or fright him from his ordinary notice of trifles: it is an act quite easy to be contemplated, but in its sequel, it turns out to be a horrible jangle and confounding of all relations. Especially the crimes that spring from love, seem right and fair from the actor's point of view, but, when acted, are found destructive of society. No man at last believes that he can be lost, nor that the crime in him is as black as in the felon. Because the intellect qualifies in our own case the moral judgments. For there is no crime to the intellect. That is antinomian or hypernomian, and judges law as well as fact. "It is worse than a crime, it is a blunder," said Napoleon, speaking the language of the intellect. To it, the world is a problem in mathematics or the science of quantity, and it leaves out praise and blame, and all weak emotions. All stealing is comparative. If you come to absolutes, pray who does not steal? Saints are sad, because they behold sin (even when they speculate), from the point of view of the conscience, and not of the intellect; a confusion of thought. Sin seen from the thought is a diminution or *less*: seen from the conscience or will, it is pravity or *bad*. The intellect names it shade, absence of light, and no essence. The conscience must feel it as essence, essential evil. This it is not: it has an objective existence, but no subjective.

Thus inevitably does the universe wear our color, and every object fall successively into the subject itself. The subject exists, the subject enlarges; all things sooner or later fall into place. As I am, so I see; use what language we will, we can never see anything but what we are; Hermes, Cadmus, Columbus, Newton, Bonaparte, are the mind's ministers. Instead of feeling a poverty when we encounter a great man, let us treat the new-comer like a travelling geologist, who passes through our estate, and shows us good slate, or limestone, or anthracite, in our brush pasture. The partial action of each strong mind in one direction, is a telescope for the objects on which it is pointed. But every other part of knowledge is to be pushed to the same extravagance, ere the soul attains her due sphericity. Do you see that kitten chasing so prettily her own tail? If you could look with her eyes, you might see her surrounded with hundreds of figures, performing complex dramas, with tragic and comic issues, long conversations, many characters, many ups and downs of fate,—and meantime it is only puss and her tail. How long before our masquerade will end its noise of tambourines, laughter, and shouting, and we shall find it was a solitary performance?— A subject and an object,—it takes so much to make the galvanic circuit complete, but magnitude adds nothing. What imports it whether it is Kepler and the sphere; Columbus and America; a reader and his book; or puss with her tail?

It is true that all the muses and love and religion hate these developments, and will find a way to punish the chemist, who publishes in the parlor the secrets of the laboratory. And we cannot say too little of our constitutional necessity of seeing things under private aspects, or saturated with our humors. And yet is the God the native of these bleak rocks. That need makes in morals the capital virtue of self-trust. We must hold hard to this poverty, however scandalous, and by more vigorous self-recoveries, after the sallies of action, possess our axis more firmly. The life of truth is cold, and so far mournful; but it is not the slave of tears, contritions, and perturbations. It does not attempt another's work, nor adopt another's facts. It is a main lesson of wisdom to know your own from another's. I have learned that I cannot dispose of other people's facts; but I possess such a key to my own, as persuades me against all their denials, that they also have a key to theirs. A sympathetic person is placed in the dilemma of a swimmer among drowning men, who all catch at him, and if he give so much as a leg or a finger, they will drown him. They wish to be saved from the mischiefs of their vices, but not from their vices. Charity would be wasted on this poor waiting on the symptoms. A wise and hardy physician will say, *Come out of that*, as the first condition of advice.

In this our talking America, we are ruined by our good-nature and listening on all sides. This compliance takes away the power of being greatly useful. A man should not be able to look other than directly and forthright. A preoccupied attention is the only answer to the importunate frivolity of other people; an attention, and to an aim which makes their wants frivolous. This is a divine answer, and leaves no appeal, and no hard thoughts. In Flaxman's drawing of the Eumenides of Æschylus, Orestes supplicates Apollo, whilst the Furies sleep on the threshold. The face of the god expresses a shade of regret and compassion, but calm with the conviction of the irreconcilableness of the two spheres. He is born into other politics, into the eternal and beautiful. The man at his feet asks for his interest in turmoils of the earth, into which his nature cannot enter. And the Eumenides there lying express pictorially this disparity. The god is surcharged with his divine destiny.

Illusion, Temperament, Succession, Surface, Surprise, Reality, Subjectiveness,—these are threads on the loom of time, these are the lords of life. I dare not assume to give their order, but I name them as I find them in my way. I know better than to claim any completeness for my picture. I am a fragment, and this is a fragment of me. I can very confidently announce one or another law, which throws itself into relief and form, but I am too young yet by some ages to compile a code. I gossip for my hour concerning the eternal politics. I have seen many fair pictures not in vain. A wonderful time I have lived in. I am not the novice I was fourteen, nor yet seven years ago. Let who will ask, where is the fruit? I find a private fruit sufficient. This is a fruit,—that I should not ask for a rash effect from meditations, counsels, and the hiving of truths. I should feel it pitiful to demand a result on this town and county, an overt effect on the instant month and year. The effect is deep and secular as the cause. It works on periods in which mortal lifetime is lost. All I know is reception; I am and I have: but I do not get, and when I have fancied I had gotten anything, I found I did not. I worship with wonder the great Fortune. My reception has been so large, that I am not annoyed by receiving this or that superabundantly. I say to the Genius, if he will pardon the proverb, *In for a mill, in for a million*. When I receive a new gift, I do not macerate my body to make the account square, for, if I should die, I could not make the account square. The benefit overran the merit the first day, and has overran the merit ever since. The merit itself, so-called, I reckon part of the receiving.

Also, that hankering after an overt or practical effect seems to me an apostasy. In good earnest, I am willing to spare this most unnecessary deal of doing. Life wears to me a visionary face. Hardest, roughest action is visionary also. It is but a choice between soft and turbulent dreams. People disparage knowing and the intellectual life, and urge doing. I am very content with knowing, if only I could know. That is an august entertainment, and would suffice me a great while. To know a little, would be worth the expense of this world. I hear always the law of Adrastia, "that every soul which had acquired any truth should be safe from harm until another period."

I know that the world I converse with in the city and in the farms is not the world I *think*. I observe that difference, and shall observe it. One day, I shall know the value and law of this discrepance. But I have not found that much was gained by manipular attempts to realize the world of thought. Many eager persons successively make an experiment in this way, and make themselves ridiculous. They acquire democratic manners, they foam at the mouth, they hate and deny. Worse, I observe, that in the history of mankind, there is never a solitary example of success,—taking their own tests of success. I say this polemically, or in reply to the inquiry, why not realize your world? But far be from me the despair which prejudges the law by a paltry empiricism,—since there never was a right endeavor, but it succeeded. Patience and patience, we shall win at the last. We must be very suspicious of the deceptions of the element of time. It takes a good deal of time to eat or to sleep, or to earn a hundred dollars, and a very little time to entertain a hope and an insight which becomes the light of our life. We dress our garden, eat our dinners, discuss the household with our wives, and these things make no impression, are forgotten next week; but in the solitude to which every man is always returning, he has a sanity and revelations, which in his passage into new worlds he will carry with him. Never mind the ridicule, never mind the defeat: up again, old heart!—it seems to say, —there is victory yet for all justice; and the true romance which the world exists to realize will be the transformation of genius into practical power.

1844

POLITICS.*

Gold and iron are good
To buy iron and gold;
All earth's fleece and food
For their like are sold.
Hinted Merlin wise,
Proved Napoleon great,—
Nor kind nor coinage buys
Aught above its rate.
Fear, Craft, and Avarice
Cannot rear a State.
Out of dust to build
What is more than dust,—
Walls Amphion piled
Phœbus stablish must.
When the Muses nine
With the Virtues meet,
Find to their design
An Atlantic seat,
By green orchard boughs
Fended from the heat,
Where the statesman ploughs
Furrow for the wheat;
When the Church is social worth,
When the state-house is the hearth,
Then the perfect State is come,
The republican at home.

In dealing with the State, we ought to remember that its institutions are not aboriginal, though they existed before we were born: that they are not superior to the citizen: that every one of them was once the act of a single man: every law and usage was a man's expedient to meet a particular case: that they all are imitable, all alterable; we may make as good; we may make better. Society is an illusion to the young citizen. It lies before him in rigid repose, with certain names, men, and institutions, rooted like oak-trees to the

* From *Essays, Second Series.*

centre, round which all arrange themselves the best they can. But the old statesman knows that society is fluid; there are no such roots and centres; but any particle may suddenly become the centre of the movement, and compel the system to gyrate round it, as every man of strong will, like Pisistratus, or Cromwell, does for a time, and every man of truth, like Plato, or Paul, does forever. But politics rest on necessary foundations, and cannot be treated with levity. Republics abound in young civilians, who believe that the laws make the city, that grave modifications of the policy and modes of living, and employments of the population, that commerce, education, and religion, may be voted in or out; and that any measure, though it were absurd, may be imposed on a people, if only you can get sufficient voices to make it a law. But the wise know that foolish legislation is a rope of sand, which perishes in the twisting; that the State must follow, and not lead, the character and progress of the citizen; the strongest usurper is quickly got rid of; and they only who build on Ideas, build for eternity; and that the form of government which prevails, is the expression of what cultivation exists in the population which permits it. The law is only a memorandum. We are superstitious, and esteem the statute somewhat: so much life as it has in the character of living men, is its force. The statute stands there to say, yesterday we agreed so and so, but how feel ye this article to-day? Our statute is a currency, which we stamp with our own portrait: it soon becomes unrecognizable, and in process of time will return to the mint. Nature is not democratic, nor limited-monarchical, but despotic, and will not be fooled or abated of any jot of her authority, by the pertest of her sons; and as fast as the public mind is opened to more intelligence, the code is seen to be brute and stammering. It speaks not articulately, and must be made to. Meantime the education of the general mind never stops. The reveries of the true and simple are prophetic. What the tender poetic youth dreams, and prays, and paints to-day, but shuns the ridicule of saying aloud, shall presently be the resolutions of public bodies, then shall be carried as grievance and bill of rights through conflict and war, and then shall be triumphant law and establishment for a hundred years, until it gives place, in turn, to new prayers and pictures. The history of the State sketches in coarse outline the progress of thought, and follows at a distance the delicacy of culture and of aspiration.

The theory of politics, which has possessed the mind of men, and which they have expressed the best they could in their laws and in their revolutions, considers persons and property as the two objects for whose protection government exists. Of persons, all have equal rights, in virtue of being identical in nature. This interest, of course, with its whole power demands a democracy. Whilst the rights of all as persons are equal, in virtue of their access to reason, their rights in property are very unequal. One man owns his clothes, and another owns a county. This accident, depending, primarily, on the skill and virtue of the parties, of which there is every degree, and secondarily, on patrimony, falls unequally, and its rights, of course, are unequal. Personal rights, universally the same, demand a government framed on the ratio of the census: property demands a government framed on the ratio of owners and of owning. Laban, who has flocks and herds, wishes them looked after by an officer on the frontiers, lest the Midianites shall drive them off, and pays a tax to that end. Jacob has no flocks or herds, and no fear of the Midianites, and pays no tax to the officer. It seemed fit that Laban and Jacob should have equal rights to elect the officer, who is to defend their persons, but that Laban, and not Jacob, should elect the officer who is to guard the sheep and cattle. And, if question arise whether additional officers or watch-towers should be provided, must not Laban and Isaac, and those who must sell part of their herds to buy protection for the rest, judge better of this, and with more right, than Jacob, who, because he is a youth and a traveller, eats their bread and not his own?

In the earliest society the proprietors made their own wealth, and so long as it comes to the owners in the direct way, no other opinion would arise in any equitable community, than that property should make the law for property, and persons the law for persons.

But property passes through donation or inheritance to those who do not create it. Gift, in one case, makes it as really the new owner's, as labor made it the first owner's: in the other case, of patrimony, the law makes an ownership, which will be valid in each man's view according to the estimate which he sets on the public tranquillity.

It was not, however, found easy to embody the readily admitted principle, that property should make law for property, and persons for persons: since persons and property mixed themselves in every transaction. At last it seemed settled, that the rightful distinction was, that the proprietors should have more elective franchise than non-proprietors, on the Spartan principle of "calling that which is just, equal; not that which is equal, just."

That principle no longer looks so self-evident as it appeared in former times, partly because doubts have arisen whether too much weight had not been allowed in the laws to property, and such a structure given to our usages, as allowed the rich to encroach on the poor, and to keep them poor; but mainly, because there is an instinctive sense, however obscure and yet inarticulate, that the whole constitution of property, on its present tenures, is injurious, and its influence on persons deteriorating and degrading; that truly, the only interest for the consideration of the State is persons; that property will always follow persons; that the highest end of government is the culture of men: and if men can be educated, the institutions will share their improvement, and the moral sentiment will write the law of the land.

If it be not easy to settle the equity of this question, the peril is less when we take note of our natural defences. We are kept by better guards than the vigilance of such magistrates as we commonly elect. Society always consists, in greatest part, of young and foolish persons. The old, who have seen through the hypocrisy of courts and statesmen, die, and leave no wisdom to their sons. These believe their own newspaper, as their fathers did at their age. With such an ignorant and deceivable majority, States would soon run to ruin, but that there are limitations, beyond which the folly and ambition of governors cannot go. Things have their laws, as well as men; and things refuse to be trifled with. Property will be protected. Corn will not grow, unless it is planted and manured; but the farmer will not plant or hoe it, unless the chances are a hundred to one that he will cut and harvest it. Under any forms, persons and property must and will have their just sway. They exert their power, as steadily as matter its attraction. Cover up a pound of earth never so cunningly, divide and subdivide it; melt it to liquid, convert it to gas; it will always weigh a pound: it will always attract and resist other matter, by the full virtue of one pound weight;—and the attributes of a person, his wit and his moral energy, will exercise, under any law or extinguishing tyranny, their proper force,—if not overtly, then covert-ly; if not for the law, then against it; if not wholesomely, then poisonously; with right, or by might.

The boundaries of personal influence it is impossible to fix, as persons are organs of moral or supernatural force. Under the dominion of an idea, which possesses the minds of multitudes, as civil freedom, or the religious sentiment, the powers of persons are no longer subjects of calculation. A nation of men unanimously bent on freedom, or conquest, can easily confound the arithmetic of statists, and achieve extravagant actions, out of all proportion to their means; as, the Greeks, the Saracens, the Swiss, the Americans, and the French have done.

In like manner, to every particle of property belongs its own attraction. A cent is the representative of a certain quantity of corn or other commodity. Its value is in the necessities of the animal man. It is so much warmth, so much bread, so much water, so much land. The law may do what it will with the owner of property, its just power will still attach to the cent. The law may in a mad freak say, that all shall have power except the owners of property; they shall have no vote. Nevertheless, by a higher law, the property will, year after year, write every statute that respects property. The non-proprietor will be the scribe of the proprietor. What the owners wish to do, the whole power of property will do, either through the law, or else in defiance of it. Of course, I speak of all the property, not merely of the great estates. When the rich are outvoted, as frequently happens, it is the joint treasury of the poor which exceeds their accumulations. Every man owns something, if it is only a cow, or a wheelbarrow, or his arms, and so has that property to dispose of.

The same necessity which secures the rights of person and property against the malignity or folly of the magistrate, determines the form and methods of governing, which are proper to each nation, and to its habit of thought, and nowise transferable to other states of society. In this country, we are very vain of our political institutions, which are singular in this, that they sprung, within the memory of living men, from the character and condition of the people, which they still express with sufficient fidelity,—and we ostentatiously prefer them to any other in history. They are not better, but only fitter for us. We may be wise in asserting the advantage in modern times of the democratic form, but to other states of society, in which religion consecrated the monarchical, that and not this was expedient. Democracy is better for us, because the religious sentiment of the present time accords better with it. Born democrats, we are nowise qualified to judge of monarchy, which, to our fathers living in the monarchical idea, was also relatively right. But our institutions, though in coincidence with the spirit of the age, have not any exemption from the practical defects which have discredited other forms. Every actual State is corrupt. Good men must not obey the laws too well. What satire on government can equal the severity of censure conveyed in the word *politic*, which now for ages has signified *cunning*, intimating that the State is a trick?

The same benign necessity and the same practical abuse appear in the parties into which each State divides itself, of opponents and defenders of the administration of the government. Parties are also founded on instincts, and have better guides to their own humble aims than the sagacity of their leaders. They have nothing perverse in their origin, but rudely mark some real and lasting relation. We must as wisely reprove the east wind, or the frost, as a political party, whose members, for the most part, could give no account of their position, but stand for the defence of those interests in which they find themselves. Our quarrel with them begins, when they quit this deep natural ground at the bidding of some leader, and, obeying personal considerations, throw themselves into the maintenance and defence of points, nowise belonging to their system. A party is perpetually corrupted by personality. Whilst we absolve the association from dishonesty, we cannot extend the same charity to their leaders. They reap the rewards of the docility and zeal of the masses which they direct. Ordinarily, our parties are parties of circumstance, and not of principle; as, the planting interest in conflict with the commercial; the party of capitalists, and that of operatives; parties which are identical in their moral character, and which can easily change ground with each other, in the support of many of their measures. Parties of principle, as, religious sects, or the party of free-trade, of universal suffrage, of abolition of slavery, of abolition of capital punishment, degenerate into personalities, or would inspire enthusiasm. The vice of our leading parties in this country (which may be cited as a fair specimen of these societies of opinion) is, that they do not plant themselves on the deep and necessary grounds to which they are respectively entitled, but lash themselves to fury in the carrying of some local and momentary measure, nowise useful to the commonwealth. Of the two great parties, which, at this hour, almost share the nation between them, I should say, that, one has the best cause, and the other contains the best men. The philosopher, the poet, or the religious man will, of course, wish to cast his vote with the democrat, for free-trade, for wide suffrage, for the abolition of legal cruelties in the penal code, and for facilitating in every manner the access of the young and the poor to the sources of wealth and power. But he can rarely accept the persons whom the so-called popular party propose to him as representatives of these liberalities. They have not at heart the ends which give to the name of democracy what hope and virtue are in it. The spirit of our American radicalism is destructive and aimless; it is not loving; it has no ulterior and divine ends; but is destructive only out of hatred and selfishness. On the other side, the conservative party, composed of the most moderate, able, and cultivated part of the population, is timid, and merely defensive of property. It vindicates no right, it aspires to no real good, it brands no crime, it proposes no generous policy, it does not build nor write, nor cherish the arts, nor foster religion, nor establish schools, nor encourage science, nor emancipate the slave, nor befriend the poor, or the Indian, or the immigrant. From neither party, when in power, has the world any benefit to expect in science, art, or humanity, at all commensurate with the resources of the nation.

I do not for these defects despair of our republic. We are not at the mercy of any waves of chance. In the strife of ferocious parties, human nature always finds itself cherished, as the children of the convicts at Botany Bay are found to have as healthy a moral sentiment as other children. Citizens of feudal states are alarmed at our democratic institutions lapsing into anarchy; and the older and more cautious among ourselves are learning from Europeans to look with some terror at our turbulent freedom. It is said that in our license of construing the Constitution, and in despotism of public opinion, we have no anchor; and one foreign observer thinks he has found the safeguard in the sanctity of Marriage among us; and another thinks he has found it in our Calvinism. Fisher Ames expressed the popular security more wisely, when he compared a monarchy and a republic, saying, "that a monarchy is a merchantman, which sails well, but will sometimes strike on a rock, and go to the bottom, whilst a republic is a raft, which would never sink, but then your feet are always in water." No forms can have any dangerous importance, whilst we are befriended by the laws of things. It makes no difference how many tons' weight of atmosphere presses on our heads, so long as the same pressure resists it within the lungs. Augment the mass a thousand-fold, it cannot begin to crush us, as long as reaction is equal to action. The fact of two poles, of two forces, centripetal and centrifugal, is universal, and each force by its own activity develops the other. Wild liberty develops iron conscience. Want of liberty, by strengthening law and decorum, stupefies conscience. 'Lynch-law' prevails only where there is greater hardihood and self-subsistency in the leaders. A mob cannot be a permanency; everybody's interest requires that it should not exist, and only justice satisfies all.

We must trust infinitely to the beneficent necessity which shines through all laws. Human nature expresses itself in them as characteristically as in statues, or songs, or railroads, and an abstract of the codes of nations would be a transcript of the common conscience. Governments have their origin in the moral identity of men. Reason for one is seen to be reason for another, and for every other. There is a middle measure which satisfies all parties, be they never so many, or so resolute for their own. Every man finds a sanction for his simplest claims and deeds in decisions of his own mind, which he calls Truth and Holiness. In these decisions all the citizens find a perfect agreement, and only in these; not in what is good to eat, good to wear, good use of time, or what amount of land, or of public aid, each is entitled to claim. This truth and justice men presently endeavor to make application of, to the measuring of land, the apportionment of service, the protection of life and property. Their first endeavors, no doubt, are very awkward. Yet absolute right is the first governor; or, every government is an impure theocracy. The idea, after which each community is aiming to make and mend its law, is the will of the wise man. The wise man it cannot find in nature, and it makes awkward but earnest efforts to secure his government by contrivance; as, by causing the entire people to give their voices on every measure; or, by a double choice to get the representation of the whole; or, by a selection of the best citizens; or, to secure the advantages of efficiency and internal peace, by confiding the government to one, who may himself select his agents. All forms of government symbolize an immortal government, common to all dynasties and independent of numbers, perfect where two men exist, perfect where there is only one man.

Every man's nature is a sufficient advertisement to him of the character of his fellows. My right and my wrong is their right and their wrong. Whilst I do what is fit for me, and abstain from what is unfit, my neighbor and I shall often agree in our means, and work together for a time to one end. But whenever I find my dominion over myself not sufficient for me, and undertake the direction of him also, I overstep the truth, and come into false relations to him. I may have so much more skill or strength than he, that he cannot express adequately his sense of wrong, but it is a lie, and hurts like a lie both him and me. Love and nature cannot maintain the assumption: it must be executed by a practical lie, namely, by force. This undertaking for another is the blunder which stands in colossal ugliness in the governments of the world. It is the same thing in numbers, as in a pair, only not quite so intelligible. I can see well enough a great difference between my setting myself down to a self-control, and my going to make somebody else act after my views: but when a quarter of the human race assume to tell me what I must do, I may be too much disturbed by the circumstances to see so clearly the absurdity of their command. Therefore, all public ends look vague and quixotic beside private ones. For, any laws but those which men make for themselves are laughable. If I put myself in the place of my child, and we stand in one thought, and see that things are thus or thus, that perception is law for him and me. We are both there, both act. But if, without carrying him into the thought, I look over into his plot, and, guessing how it is with him, ordain this or that, he will never obey me. This is the history of governments,—one man does something which is to bind another. A man who cannot be acquainted with me taxes me; looking from afar at me, ordains that a part of my labor shall go to this or that whimsical end, not as I, but as he, happens to fancy. Behold the consequence. Of all debts, men are least willing to pay the taxes. What a satire is this on government! Everywhere they think they get their money's worth, except for these.

Hence, the less government we have the better,—the fewer

laws, and the less confided power. The antidote to this abuse of formal government, is, the influence of private character, the growth of the Individual; the appearance of the principal to supersede the proxy; the appearance of the wise man, of whom the existing government is, it must be owned, but a shabby imitation. That which all things tend to educe, which freedom, cultivation, intercourse, revolutions, go to form and deliver, is character; that is the end of nature, to reach unto this coronation of her king. To educate the wise man, the State exists; and with the appearance of the wise man, the State expires. The appearance of character makes the State unnecessary. The wise man is the State. He needs no army, fort, or navy,—he loves men too well; no bribe, or feast, or palace, to draw friends to him; no vantage-ground, no favorable circumstance. He needs no library, for he has not done thinking; no church, for he is a prophet; no statute-book, for he has the lawgiver; no money, for he is value; no road, for he is at home where he is; no experience, for the life of the creator shoots through him, and looks from his eyes. He has no personal friends, for he who has the spell to draw the prayer and piety of all men unto him, needs not husband and educate a few, to share with him a select and poetic life. His relation to men is angelic; his memory is myrrh to them; his presence, frankincense and flowers.

We think our civilization near its meridian, but we are yet only at the cock-crowing and the morning star. In our barbarous society the influence of character is in its infancy. As a political power, as the rightful lord who is to tumble all rulers from their chairs, its presence is hardly yet suspected. Malthus and Ricardo quite omit it; the Annual Register is silent; in the Conversations' Lexicon, it is not set down; the President's Message, the Queen's Speech, have not mentioned it; and yet it is never nothing. Every thought which genius and piety throw into the world, alters the world. The gladiators in the lists of power feel, through all their frocks of force and simulation, the presence of worth. I think the very strife of trade and ambition are confession of this divinity; and successes in those fields are the poor amends, the fig-leaf with which the shamed soul attempts to hide its nakedness. I find the like unwilling homage in all quarters. It is because we know how much is due from us, that we are impatient to show some petty talent as a substitute for worth. We are haunted by a conscience of this right to grandeur of character, and are false to it. But each of us has some talent, can do somewhat useful, or graceful, or formidable, or amusing, or lucrative. That we do, as an apology to others and to ourselves, for not reaching the mark of a good and equal life. But it does not satisfy *us*, whilst we thrust it on the notice of our companions. It may throw dust in their eyes, but does not smooth our own brow, or give us the tranquillity of the strong when we walk abroad. We do penance as we go. Our talent is a sort of expiation, and we are constrained to reflect on our splendid moment, with a certain humiliation, as somewhat too fine, and not as one act of many acts, a fair expression of our permanent energy. Most persons of ability meet in society with a kind of tacit appeal. Each seems to say, 'I am not all here.' Senators and presidents have climbed so high with pain enough, not because they think the place specially agreeable, but as an apology for real worth, and to vindicate their manhood in our eyes. This conspicuous chair is their compensation to themselves for being of a poor, cold, hard nature. They must do what they can. Like one class of forest animals, they have nothing but a prehensile tail: climb they must, or crawl. If a man found himself so richnatured that he could enter into strict relations with the best persons, and make life serene around him by the dignity and sweetness of his behavior, could he afford to circumvent the favor of the caucus and the press, and covet relations so hollow and pompous, as those of a politician? Surely nobody would be a charlatan, who could afford to be sincere.

The tendencies of the times favor the idea of self-government, and leave the individual, for all code, to the rewards and penalties of his own constitution, which work with more energy than we believe, whilst we depend on artificial restraints. The movement in this direction has been very marked in modern history. Much has been blind and discreditable, but the nature of the revolution is not affected by the vices of the revolters; for this is a purely moral force. It was never adopted by any party in history, neither can be. It separates the individual from all party, and unites him, at the same time, to the race. It promises a recognition of higher rights than those of personal freedom, or the security of property. A man has a right to be employed, to be trusted, to be loved, to be revered. The power of love, as the basis of a State, has never been tried. We must not imagine that all things are lapsing into confusion, if every tender protestant be not compelled to bear his part in certain social conventions; nor doubt that roads can be built, letters carried, and the fruit of labor secured, when the government of force is at an end. Are our methods now so excellent that all competition is hopeless? could not a nation of friends even devise better ways? On the other hand, let not the most conservative and timid fear anything from a premature surrender of the bayonet, and the system of force. For, according to the order of nature, which is quite superior to our will, it stands thus; there will always be a government of force, where men are selfish; and when they are pure enough to abjure the code of force, they will be wise enough to see how these public ends of the post-office, of the highway, of commerce, and the exchange of property, of museums and libraries, of institutions of art and science, can be answered.

We live in a very low state of the world, and pay unwilling tribute to governments founded on force. There is not, among the most religious and instructed men of the most religious and civil nations, a reliance on the moral sentiment, and a sufficient belief in the unity of things, to persuade them that society can be maintained without artificial restraints, as well as the solar system; or that the private citizen might be reasonable, and a good neighbor, without the hint of a jail or a confiscation. What is strange too, there never was in any man sufficient faith in the power of rectitude, to inspire him with the broad design of renovating the State on the principle of right and love. All those who have pretended this design have been partial reformers, and have admitted in some manner the supremacy of the bad State. I do not call to mind a single human being who has steadily denied the authority of the laws, on the simple ground of his own moral nature. Such designs, full of genius and full of fate as they are, are not entertained except avowedly as air-pictures. If the individual who exhibits them dare to think them practicable, he disgusts scholars and churchmen; and men of talent, and women of superior sentiments, cannot hide their contempt. Not the less does nature continue to fill the heart of youth with suggestions of this enthusiasm, and there are now men,—if indeed I can speak in the plural number,—more exactly, I will say, I have just been conversing with one man, to whom no weight of adverse experience will make it for a moment appear impossible, that thousands of human beings might exercise towards each other the grandest and simplest sentiments, as well as a knot of friends, or a pair of lovers.

1844

MONTAIGNE; OR, THE SCEPTIC.*

Every fact is related on one side to sensation, and, on the other, to morals. The game of thought is, on the appearance of one of these two sides, to find the other; given the upper, to find the under side. Nothing so thin, but has these two faces; and, when the observer has seen the obverse, he turns it over to see the reverse. Life is a pitching of this penny,—heads or tails. We never tire of this game, because there is still a slight shudder of astonishment at the exhibition of the other face, at the contrast of the two faces. A man is flushed with success, and bethinks himself what this good luck signifies. He drives his bargain in the street; but it occurs, that he also is bought and sold. He sees the beauty of a human face, and searches the cause of that beauty, which must be more beautiful. He builds his fortunes, maintains the laws, cherishes his children; but he asks himself, why? and whereto? This head and this tail are called, in the language of philosophy, Infinite and Finite; Relative and Absolute; Apparent and Real; and many fine names beside.

Each man is born with a predisposition to one or the other of these sides of nature; and it will easily happen that men will be found devoted to one or the other. One class has the perception of difference, and is conversant with facts and surfaces; cities and persons; and the bringing certain things to pass;—the men of talent and action. Another class have the perception of identity, and are men of faith and philosophy, men of genius.

Each of these riders drives too fast. Plotinus believes only in philosophers; Fenelon, in saints; Pindar and Byron, in poets. Read the haughty language in which Plato and the Platonists speak of all men who are not devoted to their own shining abstractions: other men are rats and mice. The lit-

* From *Representative Men.*

erary class is usually proud and exclusive. The correspondence of Pope and Swift describes mankind around them as monsters; and that of Goethe and Schiller, in our own time, is scarcely more kind.

It is easy to see how this arrogance comes. The genius is a genius by the first look he casts on an object. Is his eye creative? Does he not rest in angles and colors, but beholds the design,—he will presently undervalue the actual object. In powerful moments, his thought has dissolved the works of art and nature into their causes, so that the works appear heavy and faulty. He has a conception of beauty which the sculptor cannot embody. Picture, statue, temple, railroad, steam-engine, existed first in an artist's mind, without flaw, mistake, or friction, which impair the executed models. So did the church, the state, college, court, social circle, and all the institutions. It is not strange that these men, remembering what they have seen and hoped of ideas, should affirm disdainfully the superiority of ideas. Having at some time seen that the happy soul will carry all the arts in power, they say, Why cumber ourselves with superfluous realizations? and, like dreaming beggars, they assume to speak and act as if these values were already substantiated.

On the other part, the men of toil and trade and luxury,— the animal world, including the animal in the philosopher and poet also,—and the practical world, including the painful drudgeries which are never excused to philosopher or poet any more than to the rest,—weigh heavily on the other side. The trade in our streets believes in no metaphysical causes, thinks nothing of the force which necessitated traders and a trading planet to exist; no, but sticks to cotton, sugar, wool, and salt. The ward meetings, on election days, are not softened by any misgiving of the value of these ballotings. Hot life is streaming in a single direction. To the men of this world, to the animal strength and spirits, to the men of practical power, while immersed in it, the man of ideas appears out of his reason. They alone have reason.

Things always bring their own philosophy with them, that is, prudence. No man acquires property without acquiring with it a little arithmetic, also. In England, the richest country that ever existed, property stands for more, compared with personal ability, than in any other. After dinner, a man believes less, denies more: verities have lost some charm. After dinner, arithmetic is the only science: ideas are disturbing, incendiary, follies of young men, repudiated by the solid portion of society: and a man comes to be valued by his athletic and animal qualities. Spence relates, that Mr. Pope was with Sir Godfrey Kneller, one day, when his nephew, a Guinea trader, came in. "Nephew," said Sir Godfrey, "you have the honor of seeing the two greatest men in the world." "I don't know how great men you may be," said the Guinea man, "but I don't like your looks. I have often bought a much better than both of you, all muscles and bones, for ten guineas." Thus, the men of the senses revenge themselves on the professors, and repay scorn for scorn. The first had leaped to conclusions not yet ripe, and say more than is true; the others make themselves merry with the philosopher, and weigh man by the pound. They believe that mustard bites the tongue, and pepper is hot, friction-matches are incendiary, revolvers to be avoided, and suspenders hold up pantaloons; that there is much sentiment in a chest of tea; and a man will be eloquent, if you give him good wine. Are you tender and scrupulous,—you must eat more mince-pie. They hold that Luther had milk in him when he said,

> "Wer nicht liebt Wein, Weib, und Gesang,
> Der bleibt ein Narr sein Leben lang";

and when he advised a young scholar, perplexed with fore-ordination and free-will, to get well drunk. "The nerves," says Cabanis, "they are the man." My neighbor, a jolly farmer, in the tavern bar-room, thinks that the use of money is sure and speedy spending: "for his part," he says, "he puts his down his neck, and gets the good of it."

The inconvenience of this way of thinking is, that it runs into indifferentism, and then into disgust. Life is eating us up. We shall be fables presently. Keep cool: it will be all one a hundred years hence. Life's well enough; but we shall be glad to get out of it, and they will all be glad to have us. Why should we fret and drudge? Our meat will taste to-morrow as it did yesterday, and we may at last have had enough of it. "Ah," said my languid gentleman at Oxford, "there's nothing new or true,—and no matter."

With a little more bitterness, the cynic moans: our life is like an ass led to market by a bundle of hay being carried before him: he sees nothing but the bundle of hay. "There is so much trouble in coming into the world," said Lord Bolingbroke, "and so much more, as well as meanness, in going out of it, that 't is hardly worth while to be here at all." I know a philosopher of this kidney, who was accustomed briefly to sum up his experience of human nature in saying, "Mankind is a damned rascal": and the natural corollary is pretty sure to follow,—'The world lives by humbug, and so will I.'

The abstractionist and the materialist thus mutually exasperating each other, and the scoffer expressing the worst of materialism, there arises a third party to occupy the middle ground between these two, the sceptic, namely. He finds both wrong by being in extremes. He labors to plant his feet, to be the beam of the balance. He will not go beyond his card. He sees the one-sidedness of these men of the street; he will not be a Gibeonite; he stands for the intellectual faculties, a cool head, and whatever serves to keep it cool; no unadvised industry, no unrewarded self-devotion, no loss of the brains in toil. Am I an ox, or a dray?—You are both in extremes, he says. You that will have all solid, and a world of pig-lead, deceive yourselves grossly: you believe yourselves rooted and grounded on adamant; and yet, if we uncover the last facts of our knowledge, you are spinning like bubbles in a river, you know not whither or whence, and you are bottomed and capped and wrapped in delusions.

Neither will he be betrayed to a book, and wrapped in a gown. The studious class are their own victims: they are thin and pale, their feet are cold, their heads are hot, the night is without sleep, the day a fear of interruption,—pallor, squalor, hunger, and egotism. If you come near them, and see what conceits they entertain,—they are abstractionists, and spend their days and nights in dreaming some dream; in expecting the homage of society to some precious scheme built on a truth, but destitute of proportion in its presentment, of justness in its application, and of all energy of will in the schemer to embody and vitalize it.

But I see plainly, he says, that I cannot see. I know that human strength is not in extremes, but in avoiding extremes. I, at least, will shun the weakness of philosophizing beyond my depth. What is the use of pretending to powers we have not? What is the use of pretending to assurances we have not, respecting the other life? Why exaggerate the power of virtue? Why be an angel before your time? These strings, wound up too high, will snap. If there is a wish for immortality, and no evidence, why not say just that? If there are conflicting evidences, why not state them? If there is not ground for a candid thinker to make up his mind, yea or nay, —why not suspend the judgment? I weary of these dogmatizers. I tire of these hacks of routine, who deny the dogmas. I neither affirm nor deny. I stand here to try the case. I am here to consider, σκεπτειν, to consider how it is. I will try to keep the balance true. Of what use to take the chair, and glibly rattle off theories of society, religion, and nature, when I know that practical objections lie in the way, insurmountable by me and by my mates? Why so talkative in public, when each of my neighbors can pin me to my seat by arguments I cannot refute? Why pretend that life is so simple a game, when we know how subtle and illusive the Proteus is? Why think to shut up all things in your narrow coop, when we know there are not one or two only, but ten, twenty, a thousand things, and unlike? Why fancy that you have all the truth in your keeping? There is much to say on all sides.

Who shall forbid a wise scepticism, seeing that there is no practical question on which anything more than an approximate solution can be had? Is not marriage an open question, when it is alleged, from the beginning of the world, that such as are in the institution wish to get out, and such as are out wish to get in? And the reply of Socrates, to him who asked whether he should choose a wife, still remains reasonable, "that, whether he should choose one or not, he would repent it." Is not the state a question? All society is divided in opinion on the subject of the state. Nobody loves it; great numbers dislike it, and suffer conscientious scruples to allegiance: and the only defence set up, is the fear of doing worse in disorganizing. Is it otherwise with the church? Or, to put any of the questions which touch mankind nearest,— shall the young man aim at a leading part in law, in politics, in trade? It will not be pretended that a success in either of these kinds is quite coincident with what is best and inmost in his mind. Shall he, then, cutting the stays that hold him fast to the social state, put out to sea with no guidance but his genius? There is much to say on both sides. Remember the open question between the present order of "competition," and the friends of "attractive and associated labor." The generous minds embrace the proposition of labor shared by all; it is the only honesty; nothing else is safe. It is from the poor man's hut alone, that strength and virtue come: and yet, on the other side, it is alleged that labor impairs the form, and breaks the spirit of man, and the laborers cry unan-

imously, 'We have no thoughts.' Culture, how indispensable!
I cannot forgive you the want of accomplishments; and yet,
culture will instantly impair that chiefest beauty of sponta-
neousness. Excellent is culture for a savage; but once let
him read in the book, and he is no longer able not to think of
Plutarch's heroes. In short, since true fortitude of understanding consists "in not letting what we know be embarrassed by what we do not know," we ought to secure those advantages which we can command, and not risk them by
clutching after the airy and unattainable. Come, no chimeras!
Let us go abroad; let us mix in affairs; let us learn, and get,
and have, and climb. "Men are a sort of moving plants, and,
like trees, receive a great part of their nourishment from the
air. If they keep too much at home, they pine." Let us have
a robust, manly life; let us know what we know, for certain;
what we have, let it be solid, and seasonable, and our own. A
world in the hand is worth two in the bush. Let us have to
do with real men and women, and not with skipping ghosts.

This, then, is the right ground of the sceptic,—this of consideration, of self-containing; not at all of unbelief; not at all
of universal denying, nor of universal doubting,—doubting
even that he doubts; least of all, of scoffing and profligate
jeering at all that is stable and good. These are no more his
moods than are those of religion and philosophy. He is the
considerer, the prudent, taking in sail, counting stock, hus-
banding his means, believing that a man has too many enemies, than that he can afford to be his own; that we cannot
give ourselves too many advantages, in this unequal conflict, with powers so vast and unweariable ranged on one
side, and this little, conceited, vulnerable popinjay that a man
is, bobbing up and down into every danger, on the other. It is
a position taken up for better defence, as of more safety,
and one that can be maintained; and it is one of more opportunity and range: as, when we build a house, the rule is to
set it not too high nor too low, under the wind, but out of the
dirt.

The philosophy we want is one of fluxions and mobility.
The Spartan and Stoic schemes are too stark and stiff for our
occasion. A theory of Saint John, and of nonresistance, seems,
on the other hand, too thin and aerial. We want some coat
woven of elastic steel, stout as the first, and limber as the
second. We want a ship in these billows we inhabit. An
angular, dogmatic house would be rent to chips and splinters,

in this storm of many elements. No, it must be tight, and fit to the form of man, to live at all; as a shell must dictate the architecture of a house founded on the sea. The soul of man must be the type of our scheme, just as the body of man is the type after which a dwelling-house is built. Adaptiveness is the peculiarity of human nature. We are golden averages, volitant stabilities, compensated or periodic errors, houses founded on the sea. The wise sceptic wishes to have a near view of the best game, and the chief players; what is best in the planet; art, and nature, places and events, but mainly men. Everything that is excellent in mankind,—a form of grace, an arm of iron, lips of persuasion, a brain of resources, every one skilful to play and win,—he will see and judge.

The terms of admission to this spectacle, are, that he have a certain solid and intelligible way of living of his own; some method of answering the inevitable needs of human life; proof that he has played with skill and success; that he has evinced the temper, stoutness, and the range of qualities which, among his contemporaries and countrymen, entitle him to fellowship and trust. For, the secrets of life are not shown except to sympathy and likeness. Men do not confide themselves to boys, or coxcombs, or pedants, but to their peers. Some wise limitation, as the modern phrase is; some condition between the extremes, and having itself a positive quality; some stark and sufficient man, who is not salt or sugar, but sufficiently related to the world to do justice to Paris or London, and, at the same time, a vigorous and original thinker, whom cities cannot overawe, but who uses them,—is the fit person to occupy this ground of speculation.

These qualities meet in the character of Montaigne. And yet, since the personal regard which I entertain for Montaigne may be unduly great, I will, under the shield of this prince of egotists, offer, as an apology for electing him as the representative of scepticism, a word or two to explain how my love began and grew for this admirable gossip.

A single odd volume of Cotton's translation of the Essays remained to me from my father's library, when a boy. It lay long neglected, until, after many years, when I was newly escaped from college, I read the book, and procured the remaining volumes. I remember the delight and wonder in which I lived with it. It seemed to me as if I had myself written the book, in some former life, so sincerely it spoke to my thought and experience. It happened, when in Paris, in

1833, that, in the cemetery of Père la Chaise, I came to a tomb of Auguste Collignon, who died in 1830, aged sixty-eight years, and who, said the monument, "lived to do right, and had formed himself to virtue on the Essays of Montaigne." Some years later, I became acquainted with an accomplished English poet, John Sterling; and, in prosecuting my correspondence, I found that, from a love of Montaigne, he had made a pilgrimage to his chateau, still standing near Castellan, in Perigord, and, after two hundred and fifty years, had copied from the walls of his library the inscriptions which Montaigne had written there. That Journal of Mr. Sterling's, published in the Westminster Review, Mr. Hazlitt has reprinted in the *Prolegomena* to his edition of the Essays. I heard with pleasure that one of the newly discovered autographs of William Shakespeare was in a copy of Florio's translation of Montaigne. It is the only book which we certainly know to have been in the poet's library. And, oddly enough, the duplicate copy of Florio, which the British Museum purchased, with a view of protecting the Shakespeare autograph, (as I was informed in the Museum,) turned out to have the autograph of Ben Jonson in the flyleaf. Leigh Hunt relates of Lord Byron, that Montaigne was the only great writer of past times whom he read with avowed satisfaction. Other coincidences, not needful to be mentioned here, concurred to make this old Gascon still new and immortal for me.

In 1571, on the death of his father, Montaigne, then thirty-eight years old, retired from the practice of law, at Bordeaux, and settled himself on his estate. Though he had been a man of pleasure, and sometimes a courtier, his studious habits now grew on him, and he loved the compass, staidness, and independence of the country gentleman's life. He took up his economy in good earnest, and made his farms yield the most. Downright and plain dealing, and abhorring to be deceived or to deceive, he was esteemed in the country for his sense and probity. In the civil wars of the League, which converted every house into a fort, Montaigne kept his gates open, and his house without defence. All parties freely came and went, his courage and honor being universally esteemed. The neighboring lords and gentry brought jewels and papers to him for safe-keeping. Gibbon reckons, in these bigoted times, but two men of liberality in France,—Henry IV. and Montaigne.

Montaigne is the frankest and honestest of all writers. His French freedom runs into grossness; but he has anticipated all censure by the bounty of his own confessions. In his times, book were written to one sex only, and almost all were written in Latin; so that, in a humorist, a certain nakedness of statement was permitted, which our manners, of a literature addressed equally to both sexes, do not allow. But, though a Biblical plainness, coupled with a most uncanonical levity, may shut his pages to many sensitive readers, yet the offence is superficial. He parades it: he makes the most of it: nobody can think or say worse of him than he does. He pretends to most of the vices; and, if there be any virtue in him, he says, it got in by stealth. There is no man, in his opinion, who has not deserved hanging five or six times; and he pretends no exception in his own behalf. "Five or six as ridiculous stories," too, he says, "can be told of me, as of any man living." But, with all this really superfluous frankness, the opinion of an invincible probity grows into every reader's mind.

"When I the most strictly and religiously confess myself, I find that the best virtue I have has in it some tincture of vice; and I am afraid that Plato, in his purest virtue, (I, who am as sincere and perfect a lover of virtue of that stamp as any other whatever,) if he had listened, and laid his ear close to himself, would have heard some jarring sound of human mixture; but faint and remote, and only to be perceived by himself."

Here is an impatience and fastidiousness at color or pretence of any kind. He has been in courts so long as to have conceived a furious disgust at appearances; he will indulge himself with a little cursing and swearing; he will talk with sailors and gypsies, use flash and street ballads: he has stayed in-doors till he is deadly sick; he will to the open air, though it rain bullets. He has seen too much of gentlemen of the long robe, until he wishes for cannibals; and is so nervous, by factitious life, that he thinks, the more barbarous man is, the better he is. He likes his saddle. You may read theology, and grammar, and metaphysics elsewhere. Whatever you get here, shall smack of the earth and of real life, sweet, or smart, or stinging. He makes no hesitation to entertain you with the records of his disease; and his journey to Italy is quite full of that matter. He took and kept this position of equilibrium. Over his name, he drew an emblematic pair of scales, and wrote *Que sçais je?* under it. As I look at his effigy opposite the title-page, I seem to hear him say, 'You may play old Poz, if you will; you may rail and exaggerate, —I stand here for truth, and will not, for all the states, and churches, and revenues, and personal reputations of Europe, overstate the dry fact, as I see it; I will rather mumble and prose about what I certainly know,—my house and barns; my father, my wife, and my tenants; my old lean bald pate; my knives and forks; what meats I eat, and what drinks I prefer; and a hundred straws just as ridiculous,—than I will write, with a fine crow-quill, a fine romance. I like gray days, and autumn and winter weather. I am gray and autumnal myself, and think an undress, and old shoes that do not pinch my feet, and old friends who do not constrain me, and plain topics where I do not need to strain myself and pump my brains, the most suitable. Our condition as men is risky and ticklish enough. One cannot be sure of himself and his fortune an hour, but he may be whisked off into some pitiable or ridiculous plight. Why should I vapor and play the philosopher, instead of ballasting, the best I can, this dancing balloon? So, at least, I live within compass, keep myself ready for action, and can shoot the gulf, at last, with decency. If there be anything farcical in such a life, the blame is not mine: let it lie at fate's and nature's door.'

The Essays, therefore, are an entertaining soliloquy on every random topic that comes into his head; treating everything without ceremony, yet with masculine sense. There have been men with deeper insight; but, one would say, never a man with such abundance of thoughts: he is never dull, never insincere, and has the genius to make the reader care for all that he cares for.

The sincerity and marrow of the man reaches to his sentences. I know not anywhere the book that seems less written. It is the language of conversation transferred to a book. Cut these words and they would bleed; they are vascular and alive. One has the same pleasure in it that we have in listening to the necessary speech of men about their work, when any unusual circumstance gives momentary importance to the dialogue. For blacksmiths and teamsters do not trip in their speech; it is a shower of bullets. It is Cambridge men who correct themselves, and begin again at every half-sentence, and, moreover, will pun, and refine too much, and swerve from the matter to the expression. Montaigne talks with shrewdness, knows the world, and books, and himself, and uses the positive degree: never shrieks, or protests, or prays: no weakness, no convulsion, no superlative: does not wish to jump out of his skin, or play any antics, or annihilate space or time; but is stout and solid; tastes every moment of the day; likes pain, because it makes him feel himself, and realize things, as we pinch ourselves to know that we are awake. He keeps the plain; he rarely mounts or sinks; likes to feel solid ground, and the stones underneath. His writing has no enthusiasms, no aspiration; contented, self-respecting, and keeping the middle of the road. There is but one exception,—in his love for Socrates. In speaking of him, for once his cheek flushes, and his style rises to passion.

Montaigne died of a quinsy, at the age of sixty, in 1592. When he came to die, he caused the mass to be celebrated in his chamber. At the age of thirty-three, he had been married. "But," he says, "might I have had my own will, I would not have married Wisdom herself, if she would have had me: but 't is to much purpose to evade it, the common custom and use of life will have it so. Most of my actions are guided by example, not choice." In the hour of death, he gave the same weight to custom. *Que sçais je?* What do I know?

This book of Montaigne the world has indorsed, by translating it into all tongues, and printing seventy-five editions of it in Europe: and that, too, a circulation somewhat chosen, namely, among courtiers, soldiers, princes, men of the world, and men of wit and generosity.

Shall we say that Montaigne has spoken wisely, and given the right and permanent expression of the human mind, on the conduct of life?

We are natural believers. Truth, or the connection between cause and effect, alone interests us. We are persuaded that a thread runs through all things: all worlds are strung on it, as beads: and men, and events, and life, come to us, only because of that thread: they pass and repass, only that we may know the direction and continuity of that line. A book or statement which goes to show that there is no line, but random and chaos, a calamity out of nothing, a prosperity and no account of it, a hero born from a fool, a fool from a hero,—dispirits us. Seen or unseen, we believe the tie exists. Talent makes counterfeit ties; genius finds the real ones. We hearken to the man of science, because we anticipate the sequence in natural phenomena which he uncovers. We love whatever affirms, connects, preserves; and dislike what scatters or pulls down. One man appears whose nature is to all men's eyes conserving and constructive: his presence supposes a well-ordered society, agriculture, trade, large institutions, and empire. If these did not exist, they would begin to exist through his endeavors. Therefore, he cheers and comforts men, who feel all this in him very readily. The nonconformist and the rebel say all manner of unanswerable things against the existing republic, but discover to our sense no plan of house or state of their own. Therefore, though the town, and state, and way of living, which our counsellor contemplated, might be a very modest or musty prosperity, yet men rightly go for him, and reject the reformer, so long as he comes only with axe and crowbar.

But though we are natural conservers and causationists, and reject a sour, dumpish unbelief, the sceptical class, which Montaigne represents, have reason, and every man, at some time, belongs to it. Every superior mind will pass through this domain of equilibration,—I should rather say, will know how to avail himself of the checks and balances in nature, as a natural weapon against the exaggeration and formalism of bigots and blockheads.

Scepticism is the attitude assumed by the student in relation to the particulars which society adores, but which he sees to be reverend only in their tendency and spirit. The ground occupied by the sceptic is the vestibule of the temple. Society does not like to have any breath of question blown on the existing order. But the interrogation of custom at all points is an inevitable stage in the growth of every superior mind, and is the evidence of its perception of the flowing power which remains itself in all changes.

The superior mind will find itself equally at odds with the evils of society, and with the projects that are offered to relieve them. The wise sceptic is a bad citizen; no conservative; he sees the selfishness of property, and the drowsiness of institutions. But neither is he fit to work with any democratic party that ever was constituted; for parties wish every one committed, and he penetrates the popular patriotism. His politics are those of the "Soul's Errand" of Sir Walter Raleigh; or of Krishna, in the Bhagavat, "There is none who is worthy of my love or hatred"; whilst he sentences law, physic, divinity, commerce, and custom. He is a reformer: yet his is no better member of the philanthropic association. It turns out that he is not the champion of the operative, the pauper, the prisoner, the slave. It stands in his mind, that our life in this world is not of quite so easy interpretation as churches and schoolbooks say. He does not wish to take ground against these benevolences, to play the part of devil's attorney, and blazon every doubt and sneer that darkens the sun for him. But he says, There are doubts.

I mean to use the occasion, and celebrate the calendar-day of our Saint Michel de Montaigne, by counting and describing these doubts or negations. I wish to ferret them out of their holes, and sun them a little. We must do with them as the police do with old rogues, who are shown up to the public at the marshal's office. They will never be so formidable, when once they have been identified and registered. But I mean honestly by them,—that justice shall be done to their terrors. I shall not take Sunday objections, made up on purpose to be put down. I shall take the worst I can find, whether I can dispose of them, or they of me.

I do not press the scepticism of the materialist. I know, the quadruped opinion will not prevail. 'T is of no importance what bats and oxen think. The first dangerous symptom I report, is, the levity of intellect; as if it were fatal to earnestness to know much. Knowledge is the knowing that we cannot know. The dull pray; the geniuses are light mockers. How respectable is earnestness on every platform! but intellect kills it. Nay, San Carlo, my subtle and admirable friend, one of the most penetrating of men, finds that all direct ascension, even of lofty piety, leads to this ghastly insight, and sends back the votary orphaned. My astonishing San Carlo thought the lawgivers and saints infected. They found the ark empty; saw, and would not tell; and tried to choke off their approaching followers, by saying, 'Action, action, my dear fellows, is for you!' Bad as was to me this detection by San Carlo, this frost in July, this blow from a bride, there was still a worse, namely, the cloy or satiety of the saints. In the mount of vision, ere they have yet risen from their knees, they say, 'We discover that this our homage and beatitude is partial and deformed: we must fly for relief to the suspected and reviled Intellect, to the Understanding, the Mephistopheles, to the gymnastics of talent.'

This is hobgoblin the first; and, though it has been the subject of much elegy, in our nineteenth century, from Byron, Goethe, and other poets of less fame, not to mention many distinguished private observers,—I confess it is not very affecting to my imagination; for it seems to concern the shattering of baby-houses and crockery-shops. What flutters the church of Rome, or of England, or of Geneva, or of Boston, may yet be very far from touching any principle of faith. I think that the intellect and moral sentiment are unanimous; and that, though philosophy extirpates bugbears, yet it supplies the natural checks of vice, and polarity to the soul. I think that the wiser a man is, the more stupendous he finds the natural and moral economy, and lifts himself to a more absolute reliance.

There is the power of moods, each setting at naught all but its own tissue of facts and beliefs. There is the power of complexions, obviously modifying the dispositions and sentiments. The beliefs and unbeliefs appear to be structural; and, as soon as each man attains the poise and vivacity which allow the whole machinery to play, he will not need extreme examples, but will rapidly alternate all opinions in his own life. Our life is March weather, savage and serene in one hour. We go forth austere, dedicated, believing in the iron links of Destiny, and will not turn on our heel to save our life: but a book or a bust, or only the sound of a name, shoots a spark through the nerves, and we suddenly believe in will: my finger-ring shall be the seal of Solomon: fate is for imbeciles: all is possible to the resolved mind. Presently, a new experience gives a new turn to our thoughts: common sense resumes its tyranny: we say, 'Well, the army, after all, is the gate to fame, manners, and poetry: and, look you,—on the whole, selfishness plants best, prunes best, makes the best commerce, and the best citizen.' Are the opinions of a man on right and wrong, on fate and causation, at the mercy of a broken sleep or an indigestion? Is his belief in God and Duty no deeper than a stomach evidence? And what guaranty for the permanence of his opinions? I like not the French celerity,—a new church and state once a week. This is the second negation; and I shall let it pass for what it will. As far as it asserts rotation of states of mind, I suppose it suggests its own remedy, namely, in the record of larger periods. What is the mean of many states; of all the states? Does the general voice of ages affirm any principle, or is no community of sentiment discoverable in distant times and places? And when it shows the power of self-interest, I accept that as part of the divine law, and must reconcile it with aspiration the best I can.

The word Fate, or Destiny, expresses the sense of mankind, in all ages,—that the laws of the world do not always befriend, but often hurt and crush us. Fate, in the shape of *Kinde* or nature, grows over us like grass. We paint Time with a scythe; Love and Fortune, blind; and Destiny, deaf. We have too little power of resistance against this ferocity which champs us up. What front can we make against these unavoidable, victorious, maleficent forces? What can I do against the influence of Race, in my history? What can I do against hereditary and constitutional habits, against scrofula, lymph, impotence; against climate, against barbarism, in my country? I can reason down or deny everything, except this perpetual Belly: feed he must and will, and I cannot make him respectable.

But the main resistance which the affirmative impulse finds, and one including all others, is in the doctrine of the Illusionists. There is a painful rumor in circulation, that we have been practised upon in all the principal performances of life, and free agency is the emptiest name. We have been sopped and drugged with the air, with food, with woman, with children, with sciences, with events, which leave us exactly where they found us. The mathematics, 't is complained, leave the mind where they find it: so do all sciences; and so do all events and actions. I find a man who has passed through all the sciences, the churl he was; and through all the offices, learned, civil, and social, can detect the child. We are not the less necessitated to dedicate life to them. In fact, we may come to accept it as the fixed rule and theory of our state of education, that God is a substance, and his method is illusion. The Eastern sages owned the goddess Yoganidra, the great illusory energy of Vishnu, by whom, as utter ignorance, the whole world is beguiled.

Or, shall I state it thus?—The astonishment of life, is, the absence of any appearance of reconciliation between the theory and practice of life. Reason, the prized reality, the Law, is apprehended, now and then, for a serene and profound moment, amidst the hubbub of cares and works which have no direct bearing on it;—is then lost, for months or years, and again found, for an interval, to be lost again. If we compute it in time, we may, in fifty years, have half a dozen reasonable hours. But what are these cares and works the better? A method in the world we do not see, but this parallelism of great and little, which never react on each other, nor discover the smallest tendency to converge. Experiences, fortunes, governings, readings, writings, are nothing to the purpose; as when a man comes into the room, it does not appear whether he has been fed on yams or buffalo,—he has contrived to get so much bone and fibre as he wants, out of rice or out of snow. So vast is the disproportion between the sky of law and the pismire of performance under it, that, whether he is a man of worth or a sot, is not so great a matter as we say. Shall I add, as one juggle of this enchantment, the stunning non-intercourse law which makes co-operation impossible? The young spirit pants to enter society. But all the ways of culture and greatness lead to solitary imprisonment. He has been often balked. He did not expect a sympathy with his thought from the village, but he went with it to the chosen and intelligent, and found no entertainment for it, but mere misapprehension, distaste, and scoffing. Men are strangely mistimed and misapplied; and the excellence of each is an inflamed individualism which separates him more.

There are these, and more than these, diseases of thought, which our ordinary teachers do not attempt to remove. Now shall we, because a good nature inclines us to virtue's side, say, There are no doubts,—and lie for the right? Is life to be led in a brave or in a cowardly manner? and is not the satisfaction of the doubts essential to all manliness? Is the name of virtue to be a barrier to that which is virtue? Can you not believe that a man of earnest and burly habit may find small good in tea, essays, and catechism, and want a rougher instruction, want men, labor, trade, farming, war, hunger, plenty, love, hatred, doubt, and terror, to make things plain to him; and has he not a right to insist on being convinced in his own way? When he is convinced, he will be worth the pains.

Belief consists in accepting the affirmations of the soul; unbelief, in denying them. Some minds are capable of scepticism. The doubts they profess to entertain are rather a civility or accommodation to the common discourse of their company. They may well give themselves leave to speculate, for they are secure of a return. Once admitted to the heaven of thought, they see no relapse into night, but infinite invitation to the other side. Heaven is within heaven, and sky over sky, and they are encompassed with divinities. Others there are, to whom the heaven is brass, and it shuts down to the surface of the earth. It is a question of temperament, or of more or less immersion in nature. The last class must needs have a reflex or parasite faith; not a sight of realities, but an instinctive reliance on the seers and believers of realities. The manners and thoughts of believers astonish them, and convince them that these have seen something which is hid from themselves. But their sensual habit would fix the believer to his last position, whilst he as inevitably advances; and presently the unbeliever, for love of belief, burns the believer.

Great believers are always reckoned infidels, impracticable, fantastic, atheistic, and really men of no account. The spiritualist finds himself driven to express his faith by a series of scepticisms. Charitable souls come with their projects, and ask his co-operation. How can he hesitate? It is the rule of mere comity and courtesy to agree where you can, and to turn your sentence with something auspicious, and not freezing and sinister. But he is forced to say: 'O, these things will be as they must be: what can you do? These particular griefs and crimes are the foliage and fruit of such trees as we see growing. It is vain to complain of the leaf or the berry: cut it off; it will bear another just as bad. You must begin your cure lower down.' The generosities of the day prove an intractable element for him. The people's questions are not his; their methods are not his; and, against all the dictates of good-nature, he is driven to say, he has no pleasure in them.

Even the doctrines dear to the hope of man, of the divine Providence, and of the immortality of the soul, his neighbors cannot put the statement so that he shall affirm it. But he denies out of more faith, and not less. He denies out of honesty. He had rather stand charged with the imbecility of scepticism, than the untruth. I believe, he says, in the moral design of the universe; it exists hospitably for the weal of souls; but your dogmas seem to me caricatures: why, should I make believe them? Will any say, this is cold and infidel? The wise and magnanimous will not say so. They will exult in his far-sighted good-will, that can abandon to the adversary all the ground of tradition and common belief, without losing a jot of strength. It sees to the end of all transgression. George Fox saw "that there was an ocean of darkness and death; but withal, an infinite ocean of light and love which flowed over that of darkness."

The final solution in which scepticism is lost, is, in the moral sentiment, which never forfeits its supremacy. All moods may be safely tried, and their weight allowed to all objections: the moral sentiment as easily outweighs them all, as any one. This is the drop which balances the sea. I play with the miscellany of facts, and take those superficial views which we call scepticism; but I know that they will presently appear to me in that order which makes scepticism impossible. A man of thought must feel the thought that is parent of the universe: that the masses of nature do undulate and flow. This faith avails to the whole emergency of life and objects. The world is saturated with deity and with law. He is content with just and unjust, with sots and fools, with the triumph of folly and fraud. He can behold with serenity the yawning gulf between the ambition of man and his power of performance, between the demand and supply of power, which makes the tragedy of all souls.

Charles Fourier announced that "the attractions of man are proportioned to his destinies"; in other words, that every desire predicts its own satisfaction. Yet, all experience exhibits the reverse of this; the incompetency of power is the universal grief of young and ardent minds. They accuse the divine providence of a certain parsimony. It has shown the heaven and earth to every child, and filled him with a desire for the whole; a desire raging, infinite; a hunger, as of space to be filled with planets; a cry of famine, as of devils for souls. Then for the satisfaction,—to each man is administered a single drop, a bead of dew of vital power, *per day*,— a cup as large as space, and one drop of the water of life in it. Each man woke in the morning, with an appetite that could eat the solar system like a cake; a spirit for action and passion without bounds; he could lay his hand on the morning star: he could try conclusions with gravitation or chemistry; but, on the first motion to prove his strength,—hands, feet, senses, gave way, and would not serve him. He was an emperor deserted by his states, and left to whistle by himself, or thrust into a mob of emperors, all whistling: and still the sirens sang, "The attractions are proportioned to the destinies." In every house, in the heart of each maiden, and of each boy, in the soul of the soaring saint, this chasm is found,

—between the largest promise of ideal power, and the shabby experience.

The expansive nature of truth comes to our succor, elastic, not to be surrounded. Man helps himself by larger generalizations. The lesson of life is practically to generalize; to believe what the years and the centuries say against the hours; to resist the usurpation of particulars; to penetrate to their catholic sense. Things seem to say one thing, and say the reverse. The appearance is immoral; the result is moral. Things seem to tend downward, to justify despondency, to promote rogues, to defeat the just; and, by knaves, as by martyrs, the just cause is carried forward. Although knaves win in every political struggle, although society seems to be delivered over from the hands of one set of criminals into the hands of another set of criminals, as fast as the government is changed, and the march of civilization is a train of felonies, yet, general ends are somehow answered. We see, now, events forced on, which seem to retard or retrograde the civility of ages. But the world-spirit is a good swimmer, and storms and waves cannot drown him. He snaps his finger at laws: and so, throughout history, heaven seems to affect low and poor means. Through the years and the centuries, through evil agents, through toys and atoms, a great and beneficent tendency irresistibly streams.

Let a man learn to look for the permanent in the mutable and fleeting; let him learn to bear the disappearance of things he was wont to reverence, without losing his reverence; let him learn that he is here, not to work, but to be worked upon; and that, though abyss open under abyss, and opinion displace opinion, all are at last contained in the Eternal Cause.

"If my bark sink, 't is to another sea."

1850

FATE.*

Delicate omens traced in air
To the lone bard true witness bare;
Birds with auguries on their wings
Chanted undeceiving things

Him to beckon, him to warn;
Well might then the poet scorn
To learn of scribe or courier
Hints writ in vaster character;
And on his mind, at dawn of day,
Soft shadows of the evening lay.
For the prevision is allied
Unto the thing so signified;
Or say, the foresight that awaits
Is the same Genius that creates.

It chanced during one winter, a few years ago, that our cities were bent on discussing the theory of the Age. By an odd coincidence, four or five noted men were each reading a discourse to the citizens of Boston or New York, on the Spirit of the Times. It so happened that the subject had the same prominence in some remarkable pamphlets and journals issued in London in the same season. To me, however, the question of the times resolved itself into a practical question of the conduct of life. How shall I live? We are incompetent to solve the times. Our geometry cannot span the huge orbits of the prevailing ideas, behold their return, and reconcile their opposition. We can only obey our own polarity. 'T is fine for us to speculate and elect our course, if we must accept an irresistible dictation.

In our first steps to gain our wishes, we come upon immovable limitations. We are fired with the hope to reform men. After many experiments, we find that we must begin earlier, —at school. But the boys and girls are not docile; we can make nothing of them. We decide that they are not of good stock. We must begin our reform earlier still,—at generation: that is to say, there is Fate, or laws of the world.

But if there be irresistible dictation, this dictation understands itself. If we must accept Fate, we are not less compelled to affirm liberty, the significance of the individual, the grandeur of duty, the power of character. This is true, and that other is true. But our geometry cannot span these extreme points, and reconcile them. What to do? By obeying each thought frankly, by harping, or, if you will, pounding on each string, we learn at last its power. By the same obedience to other thoughts, we learn theirs, and then comes some reasonable hope of harmonizing them. We are sure, that, though we know not how, necessity does comport with liberty,

* From *Conduct of Life.*

the individual with the world, my polarity with the spirit of the times. The riddle of the age has for each a private solution. If one would study his own time, it must be by this method of taking up in turn each of the leading topics which belong to our scheme of human life, and, by firmly stating all that is agreeable to experience on one, and doing the same justice to the opposing facts in the others, the true limitations will appear. Any excess of emphasis, on one part, would be corrected, and a just balance would be made.

But let us honestly state the facts. Our America has a bad name for superficialness. Great men, great nations, have not been boasters and buffoons, but perceivers of the terror of life, and have manned themselves to face it. The Spartan, embodying his religion in his country, dies before its majesty without a question. The Turk, who believes his doom is written on the iron leaf in the moment when he entered the world, rushes on the enemy's sabre with undivided will. The Turk, the Arab, the Persian, accepts the foreordained fate.

> "On two days, it steads not to run from thy grave,
>   The appointed, and the unappointed day;
> On the first, neither balm nor physician can save,
>   Nor thee, on the second, the Universe slay."

The Hindoo, under the wheel, is as firm. Our Calvinists, in the last generation, had something of the same dignity. They felt that the weight of the Universe held them down to their place. What could *they* do? Wise men feel that there is something which cannot be talked or voted away,—a strap or belt which girds the world.

> "The Destiny, minister general,
>   That executeth in the world o'er all,
> The purveyance which God hath seen beforne,
> So strong it is, that though the world had sworn
> The contrary of a thing by yea or nay,
> Yet sometime it shall fallen on a day
> That falleth not oft in a thousand year;
> For, certainly, our appetités here,
> Be it of war, or peace, or hate, or love,
> All this is ruled by the sight above."
>   CHAUCER: *The Knighte's Tale.*

The Greek Tragedy expressed the same sense: "Whatever is fated, that will take place. The great immense mind of Jove is not to be transgressed."

Savages cling to a local god of one tribe or town. The

broad ethics of Jesus were quickly narrowed to village theologies, which preach an election or favoritism. And, now and then, an amiable parson, like Jung Stilling, or Robert Huntington, believes in a pistareen-Providence, which, whenever the good man wants a dinner, makes that somebody shall knock at his door, and leave a half-dollar. But Nature is no sentimentalist,—does not cosset or pamper us. We must see that the world is rough and surly, and will not mind drowning a man or a woman; but swallows your ship like a grain of dust. The cold, inconsiderate of persons, tingles your blood, benumbs your feet, freezes a man like an apple. The diseases, the elements, fortune, gravity, lightning, respect no persons. The way of Providence is a little rude. The habit of snake and spider, the snap of the tiger, and other leapers and bloody jumpers, the crackle of the bones of his prey in the coil of the anaconda,—these are in the system, and our habits are like theirs. You have just dined, and, however scrupulously the slaughter-house is concealed in the graceful distance of miles, there is complicity,—expensive races,—race living at the expense of race. The planet is liable to shocks from comets, perturbations from planets, rendings from earthquake and volcano, alterations of climate, precessions of equinoxes. Rivers dry up by opening of the forest. The sea changes its bed. Towns and counties fall into it. At Lisbon, an earthquake killed men like flies. At Naples, three years ago, ten thousand persons were crushed in a few minutes. The scurvy at sea; the sword of the climate in the west of Africa, at Cayenne, at Panama, at New Orleans, cut off men like a massacre. Our Western prairie shakes with fever and ague. The cholera, the small-pox, have proved as mortal to some tribes, as a frost to the crickets, which, having filled the summer with noise, are silenced by a fall of the temperature of one night. Without uncovering what does not concern us, or counting how many species of parasites hang on a bombyx; or groping after intestinal parasites, or infusory biters, or the obscurities of alternate generations;—the forms of the shark, the *labrus*, the jaw of the sea-wolf paved with crushing teeth, the weapons of the grampus, and other warriors hidden in the sea,—are hints of ferocity in the interiors of nature. Let us not deny it up and down. Providence has a wild, rough, incalculable road to its end, and it is of no use to try to whitewash its huge, mixed instrumentalities, or to dress up that terrific benefactor in a clean shirt and white neckcloth of a student in divinity.

Will you say, the disasters which threaten mankind are exceptional, and one need not lay his account for cataclysms every day? Ay, but what happens once may happen again, and so long as these strokes are not to be parried by us, they must be feared.

But these shocks and ruins are less destructive to us, than the stealthy power of other laws which act on us daily. An expense of ends to means is fact;—organization tyrannizing over character. The menagerie, or forms and powers of the spine, is a book of fate: the bill of the bird, the skull of the snake, determines tyrannically its limits. So is the scale of races, of temperaments; so is sex; so is climate; so is the reaction of talents imprisoning the vital power in certain directions. Every spirit makes its house; but afterwards the house confines the spirit.

The gross lines are legible to the dull: the cabman is phrenologist so far: he looks in your face to see if his shilling is sure. A dome of brow denotes one thing; a pot-belly another; a squint, a pug-nose, mats of hair, the pigment of the epidermis, betray character. People seem sheathed in their tough organization. Ask Spurzheim, ask the doctors, ask Quetelet, if temperaments decide nothing? or if there be anything they do not decide? Read the description in medical books of the four temperaments, and you will think you are reading your own thoughts which you had not yet told. Find the part which black eyes, and which blue eyes, play severally in the company. How shall a man escape from his ancestors, or draw off from his veins the black drop which he drew from his father's or his mother's life? It often appears in a family, as if all the qualities of the progenitors were plotted in several jars,—some ruling quality in each son or daughter of the house,—and sometimes the unmixed temperament, the rank unmitigated elixir, the family vice, is drawn off in a separate individual, and the others are proportionally relieved. We sometimes see a change of expression in our companion, and say, his father, or his mother, comes to the windows of his eyes, and sometimes a remote relative. In different hours, a man represents each of several of his ancestors, as if there were seven or eight of us rolled up in each man's skin,—seven or eight ancestors at least,—and they constitute the variety of notes for that new piece of music which his life is.

At the corner of the street, you read the possibility of each passenger, in the facial angle, in the complexion, in the depth of his eye. His parentage determines it. Men are what their mothers made them. You may as well ask a loom which weaves huckaback, why it does not make cashmere, as expect poetry from this engineer, or a chemical discovery from that jobber. Ask the digger of the ditch to explain Newton's laws; the fine organs of his brain have been pinched by overwork and squalid poverty from father to son, for a hundred years. When each comes forth from his mother's womb, the gate of gifts closes behind him. Let him value his hands and feet, he has but one pair. So he has but one future, and that is already predetermined in his lobes, and described in that little fatty face, pig-eye, and squat form. All the privilege and all the legislation of the world cannot meddle or help to make a poet or a prince of him.

Jesus said, "When he looketh on her, he hath committed adultery." But he is an adulterer before he has yet looked on the woman, by the superfluity of animal, and the defect of thought in his constitution. Who meets him, or who meets her, in the street, sees that they are ripe to be each other's victim.

In certain men, digestion and sex absorb the vital force, and the stronger these are, the individual is so much weaker. The more of these drones perish, the better for the hive. If, later, they give birth to some superior individual, with force enough to add to this animal a new aim, and a complete apparatus to work it out, all the ancestors are gladly forgotten. Most men and most women are merely one couple more. Now and then, one has a new cell or camarilla opened in his brain,—an architectural, a musical, or a philological knack, some stray taste or talent for flowers, or chemistry, or pigments, or storytelling, a good hand for drawing, a good foot for dancing, an athletic frame for journeying, &c.,—which skill nowise alters rank in the scale of nature, but serves to pass the time, the life of sensation going on as before. At last, these hints and tendencies are fixed in one, or in a succession. Each absorbs so much food and force as to become itself a new centre. The new talent draws off so rapidly the vital force, that not enough remains for the animal functions, hardly enough for health; so that, in the second generation, if the like genius appear, the health is visibly deteriorated, and the generative force impaired.

People are born with the moral or with the material bias; —uterine brothers with this diverging destination: and I suppose, with high magnifiers, Mr. Frauenhofer or Dr. Carpenter might come to distinguish in the embryo at the fourth day, this is a Whig, and that a Free-soiler.

It was a poetic attempt to lift this mountain of Fate, to reconcile this despotism of race with liberty, which led the Hindoos to say, "Fate is nothing but the deeds committed in a prior state of existence." I find the coincidence of the extremes of Eastern and Western speculation in the daring statement of Schelling, "There is in every man a certain feeling, that he has been what he is from all eternity, and by no means became such in time." To say it less sublimely,—in the history of the individual is always an account of his condition, and he knows himself to be a party to his present estate.

A good deal of our politics is physiological. Now and then, a man of wealth in the heyday of youth adopts the tenet of broadest freedom. In England, there is always some man of wealth and large connection planting himself, during all his years of health, on the side of progress, who, as soon as he begins to die, checks his forward play, calls in his troops, and becomes conservative. All conservatives are such from personal defects. They have been effeminated by position or nature, born halt and blind, through luxury of their parents, and can only, like invalids, act on the defensive. But strong natures, backwoodsmen, New Hampshire giants, Napoleons, Burkes, Broughams, Websters, Kossuths, are inevitable patriots, until their life ebbs, and their defects and gout, palsy and money, warp them.

The strongest idea incarnates itself in majorities and nations, in the healthiest and strongest. Probably, the election goes by avoirdupois weight, and, if you could weigh bodily the tonnage of any hundred of the Whig and the Democratic party in a town on the Dearborn balance, as they passed the hayscales, you could predict with certainty which party would carry it. On the whole, it would be rather the speediest way of deciding the vote, to put the selectmen or the mayor and aldermen at the hayscales.

In science, we have to consider two things: power and circumstance. All we know of the egg, from each successive discovery, is, *another vesicle;* and if, after five hundred years, you get a better observer, or a better glass, he finds within the last observed another. In vegetable and animal tissue, it is just alike, and all that the primary power or spasm operates, is, still, vesicles, vesicles. Yes,—but the tyrannical Circumstance! A vesicle in new circumstances, a vesicle lodged in darkness, Oken thought, became animal; in light, a plant. Lodged in the parent animal, it suffers changes, which end in unsheathing miraculous capability in the unaltered vesicle, and it unlocks itself to fish, bird, or quadruped, head and foot, eye and claw. The Circumstance is Nature. Nature is what you may do. There is much you may not. We have two things,—the circumstance and the life. Once we thought, positive power was all. Now we learn, that negative power, or circumstance, is half. Nature is the tyrannous circumstance, the thick skull, the sheathed snake, the ponderous, rock-like jaw; necessitated activity; violent direction; the conditions of a tool, like the locomotive, strong enough on its track, but which can do nothing but mischief off of it; or skates, which are wings on the ice, but fetters on the ground.

The book of Nature is the book of Fate. She turns the gigantic pages,—leaf after leaf,—never re-turning one. One leaf she lays down, a floor of granite; then a thousand ages, and a bed of slate; a thousand ages, and a measure of coal; a thousand ages, and a layer of marl and mud: vegetable forms appear: her first misshapen animals, zoophyte, trilobium, fish; then, saurians,—rude forms, in which she has only blocked her future statue, concealing under these unwieldy monsters the fine type of her coming king. The face of the planet cools and dries, the races meliorate, and man is born. But when a race has lived its term, it comes no more again.

The population of the world is a conditional population; not the best, but the best that could live now; and the scale of tribes, and the steadiness with which victory adheres to one tribe, and defeat to another, is as uniform as the superposition of strata. We know in history what weight belongs to race. We see the English, French, and Germans planting themselves on every shore and market of America and Australia, and monopolizing the commerce of these countries. We like the nervous and victorious habit of our own branch of the family. We follow the step of the Jew, of the Indian, of the Negro. We see how much will has been expended to extinguish the Jew, in vain. Look at the unpalatable conclusions of Knox, in his "Fragment of Races,"—a rash and unsatisfactory writer, but charged with pungent and unforgetable truths. "Nature respects race, and not hybrids." "Every race has its own *habitat*." "Detach a colony from the race, and it deteriorates to the crab." See the shades of the picture. The German and Irish millions, like the Negro, have a great deal of guano in their destiny. They are ferried over the Atlantic, and carted over America, to ditch and to drudge, to make corn cheap, and then to lie down prematurely to make a spot of green grass on the prairie.

One more fagot of these adamantine bandages, is, the new science of Statistics. It is a rule, that the most casual and extraordinary events—if the basis of population is broad enough—become matter of fixed calculation. It would not be safe to say when a captain like Bonaparte, a singer like Jenny Lind, or a navigator like Bowditch, would be born in Boston: but, on a population of twenty or two hundred millions, something like accuracy may be had.*

'T is frivolous to fix pedantically the date of particular inventions. They have all been invented over and over fifty times. Man is the arch machine, of which all these shifts drawn from himself are toy models. He helps himself on each emergency by copying or duplicating his own structure, just so far as the need is. 'T is hard to find the right Homer, Zoroaster, or Menu; harder still to find the Tubal Cain, or Vulcan, or Cadmus, or Copernicus, or Fust, or Fulton, the indisputable inventor. There are scores and centuries of them. "The air is full of men." This kind of talent so abounds, this constructive tool-making efficiency, as if it adhered to the chemic atoms, as if the air he breathes were made of Vaucansons, Franklins, and Watts.

Doubtless, in every million there will be an astronomer, a mathematician, a comic poet, a mystic. No one can read the history of astronomy, without perceiving that Copernicus, Newton, Laplace, are not new men, or a new kind of men, but that Thales, Anaximenes, Hipparchus, Empedocles, Aristarchus, Pythagoras, Œnipodes, had anticipated them: each had the same tense geometrical brain, apt for the same vigorous computation and logic, a mind parallel to the movement

---

* "Everything which pertains to the human species, considered as a whole, belongs to the order of physical facts. The greater the number of individuals, the more does the influence of the individual will disappear, leaving predominance to a series of general facts dependent on causes by which society exists, and is preserved."—QUETELET.

of the world. The Roman mile probably rested on a measure of a degree of the meridian. Mahometan and Chinese know what we know of leap-year, of the Gregorian calendar, and of the precession of the equinoxes. As, in every barrel of cowries, brought to New Bedford, there shall be one *orangia,* so there will, in a dozen millions of Malays and Mahometans, be one or two astronomical skulls. In a large city, the most casual things, and things whose beauty lies in their casualty, are produced as punctually and to order as the baker's muffin for breakfast. Punch makes exactly one capital joke a week; and the journals contrive to furnish one good piece of news every day.

And not less work the laws of repression, the penalties of violated functions. Famine, typhus, frost, war, suicide, and effete races, must be reckoned calculable parts of the system of the world.

These are pebbles from the mountain, hints of the terms by which our life is walled up, and which show a kind of mechanical exactness, as of a loom or mill, in what we call casual or fortuitous events.

The force with which we resist these torrents of tendency looks so ridiculously inadequate, that it amounts to little more than a criticism or a protest made by a minority of one, under compulsion of millions. I seemed, in the height of a tempest, to see men overboard struggling in the waves, and driven about here and there. They glanced intelligently at each other, but 't was little they could do for one another; 't was much as if each could keep afloat alone. Well, they had a right to their eye-beams, and all the rest was Fate.

We cannot trifle with this reality, this cropping-out in our planted gardens of the core of the world. No picture of life can have any veracity that does not admit the odious facts. A man's power is hooped in by a necessity, which, by many experiments, he touches on every side, until he learns its arc.

The element running through entire nature, which we popularly call Fate, is known to us as limitation. Whatever limits us, we call Fate. If we are brute and barbarous, the fate takes a brute and dreadful shape. As we refine, our cheeks become finer. If we rise to spiritual culture, the antagonism takes a spiritual form. In the Hindoo fables, Vishnu follows Maya through all her ascending changes, from insect and craw-fish up to elephant; whatever form she took, he took the male form of that kind, until she became at last woman and goddess, and he a man and a god. The limitations refine as the soul purifies, but the ring of necessity is always perched at the top.

When the gods in the Norse heaven were unable to bind the Fenris Wolf with steel or with weight of mountains,—the one he snapped and the other he spurned with his heel,—they put round his foot a limp band softer than silk or cobweb, and this held him: the more he spurned it, the stiffer it drew. So soft and so stanch is the ring of Fate. Neither brandy, nor nectar, nor sulphuric ether, nor hell-fire, nor ichor, nor poetry, nor genius, can get rid of this limp band. For if we give it the high sense in which the poets use it, even thought itself is not above Fate: that too must act according to eternal laws, and all that is wilful and fantastic in it is in opposition to its fundamental essence.

And last of all, high over thought, in the world of morals, Fate appears as vindicator, levelling the high, lifting the low, requiring justice in man, and always striking soon or late, when justice is not done. What is useful will last; what is hurtful will sink. "The doer must suffer," said the Greeks: "you would soothe a Deity not to be soothed." "God himself cannot procure good for the wicked," said the Welsh triad. "God may consent, but only for a time," said the bard of Spain. The limitation is impassable by any insight of man. In its last and loftiest ascensions, insight itself, and the freedom of the will, is one of its obedient members. But we must not run into generalizations too large, but show the natural bounds or essential distinctions, and seek to do justice to the other elements as well.

Thus we trace Fate, in matter, mind, and morals,—in race, in retardations of strata, and in thought and character as well. It is everywhere bound or limitation. But Fate has its lord; limitation its limits; is different seen from above and from below; from within and from without. For, though fate is immense, so is power, which is the other fact in the dual world, immense. If Fate follows and limits power, power attends and antagonizes Fate. We must respect Fate as natural history, but there is more than natural history. For who and what is this criticism that pries into the matter? Man is not order of nature, sack and sack, belly and members, link in a chain, nor any ignominious baggage, but a stupendous antagonism, a dragging together of the poles of the Universe. He betrays his relation to what is below him,—thick-skulled, small-brained, fishy, quadrumanous,—quadruped ill-disguised, hardly escaped into biped, and has paid for the new powers by loss of some of the old ones. But the lightning which explodes and fashions planets, maker of planet and suns, is in him. On one side, elemental order, sandstone and granite, rock-ledges, peat-bog, forest, sea and shore; and, on the other part, thought, the spirit which composes and decomposes nature,—here they are, side by side, god and devil, mind and matter, king and conspirator, belt and spasm, riding peacefully together in the eye and brain of every man.

Nor can he blink the freewill. To hazard the contradiction, —freedom is necessary. If you please to plant yourself on the side of Fate, and say, Fate is all; then we say, a part of Fate is the freedom of man. Forever wells up the impulse of choosing and acting in the soul. Intellect annuls Fate. So far as a man thinks, he is free. And though nothing is more disgusting than the crowing about liberty by slaves, as most men are, and the flippant mistaking for freedom of some paper preamble like a "Declaration of Independence," or the statute right to vote, by those who have never dared to think or to act, yet it is wholesome to man to look not at Fate, but the other way: the practical view is the other. His sound relation to these facts is to use and command, not to cringe to them. "Look not on nature, for her name is fatal," said the oracle. The too much contemplation of these limits induces meanness. They who talk much of destiny, their birth-star, &c., are in a lower dangerous plane, and invite the evils they fear.

I cited the instinctive and heroic races as proud believers in Destiny. They conspire with it; a loving resignation is with the event. But the dogma makes a different impression, when it is held by the weak and lazy. 'T is weak and vicious people who cast the blame on Fate. The right use of Fate is to bring up our conduct to the loftiness of nature. Rude and invincible except by themselves are the elements. So let man be. Let him empty his breast of his windy conceits, and show his lordship by manners and deeds on the scale of nature. Let him hold his purpose as with the tug of gravitation. No power, no persuasion, no bribe shall make him give up his point. A man ought to compare advantageously with a river, an oak, or a mountain. He shall have not less the flow, the expansion, and the resistance of these.

'T is the best use of Fate to teach a fatal courage. Go face the fire at sea, or the cholera in your friend's house, or the burglar in your own, or what danger lies in the way of duty, knowing you are guarded by the cherubim of Destiny. If you believe in Fate to your harm, believe it, at least, for your good.

For, if Fate is so prevailing, man also is part of it, and can confront fate with fate. If the Universe have these savage accidents, our atoms are as savage in resistance. We should be crushed by the atmosphere, but for the reaction of the air within the body. A tube made of a film of glass can resist the shock of the ocean, if filled with the same water. If there be omnipotence in the stroke, there is omnipotence of recoil.

1. But Fate against Fate is only parrying and defence: there are, also, the noble creative forces. The revelation of Thought takes man out of servitude into freedom. We rightly say of ourselves, we were born, and afterward we were born again, and many times. We have successive experiences so important, that the new forgets the old, and hence the mythology of the seven or the nine heavens. The day of days, the great day of the feast of life, is that in which the inward eye opens to the Unity in things, to the omnipresence of law;— sees that what is must be, and ought to be, or is the best. This beatitude dips from on high down on us, and we see. It is not in us so much as we are in it. If the air come to our lungs, we breathe and live; if not, we die. If the light come to our eyes, we see; else not. And if truth come to our mind, we suddenly expand to its dimensions, as if we grew to worlds. We are as lawgivers; we speak for Nature; we prophesy and divine.

This insight throws us on the party and interest of the Universe, against all and sundry; against ourselves, as much as others. A man speaking from insight affirms of himself what is true of the mind: seeing its immortality, he says, I am immortal; seeing its invincibility, he says, I am strong. It is not in us, but we are in it. It is of the maker, not of what is made. All things are touched and changed by it. This uses, and is not used. It distances those who share it, from those who share it not. Those who share it not are flocks and herds. It dates from itself;—not from former men or better men,— gospel, or constitution, or college, or custom. Where it shines,

Nature is no longer intrusive, but all things make a musical or pictorial impression. The world of men show like a comedy without laughter: populations, interests, government, history; 't is all toy figures in a toy house. It does not overvalue particular truths. We hear eagerly every thought and word quoted from an intellectual man. But, in his presence, our own mind is roused to activity, and we forget very fast what he says, much more interested in the new play of our own thought, than in any thought of his. 'T is the majesty into which we have suddenly mounted, the impersonality, the scorn of egotisms, the sphere of laws, that engage us. Once we were stepping a little this way, and a little that way; now, we are as men in a balloon, and do not think so much of the point we have left, or the point we would make, as of the liberty and glory of the way.

Just as much intellect as you add, so much organic power. He who sees through the design, presides over it, and must will that which must be. We sit and rule, and, though we sleep, our dream will come to pass. Our thought, though it were only an hour old, affirms an oldest necessity, not to be separated from thought, and not to be separated from will. They must always have co-existed. It apprises us of its sovereignty and godhead, which refuse to be severed from it. It is not mine or thine, but the will of all mind. It is poured into the souls of all men, as the soul itself which constitutes them men. I know not whether there be, as is alleged, in the upper region of our atmosphere, a permanent westerly current, which carries with it all atoms which rise to that height, but I see, that when souls reach a certain clearness of perception, they accept a knowledge and motive above selfishness. A breath of will blows eternally through the universe of souls in the direction of the Right and Necessary. It is the air which all intellects inhale and exhale, and it is the wind which blows the worlds into order and orbit.

Thought dissolves the material universe, by carrying the mind up into a sphere where all is plastic. Of two men, each obeying his own thought, he whose thought is deepest will be the strongest character. Always one man more than another represents the will of Divine Providence to the period.

2. If thought makes free, so does the moral sentiment. The mixtures of spiritual chemistry refuse to be analyzed. Yet we can see that with the perception of truth is joined the desire that it shall prevail. That affection is essential to will. More-

over, when a strong will appears, it usually results from a
certain unity of organization, as if the whole energy of body
and mind flowed in one direction. All great force is real and
elemental. There is no manufacturing a strong will. There
must be a pound to balance a pound. Where power is shown
in will, it must rest on the universal force. Alaric and Bonaparte must believe they rest on a truth, or their will can be
bought or bent. There is a bribe possible for any finite will.
But the pure sympathy with universal ends is an infinite
force, and cannot be bribed or bent. Whoever has had experience of the moral sentiment cannot choose but believe in
unlimited power. Each pulse from that heart is an oath from
the Most High. I know not what the word *sublime* means, if it
be not the intimations in this infant of a terrific force. A text
of heroism, a name and anecdote of courage, are not arguments, but sallies of freedom. One of these is the verse of the
Persian Hafiz, " 'T is written on the gate of heaven, 'Woe unto
him who suffers himself to be betrayed by Fate!' " Does the
reading of history make us fatalists? What courage does not
the opposite opinion show! A little whim of will to be free
gallantly contending against the universe of chemistry.

But insight is not will, nor is affection will. Perception is
cold, and goodness dies in wishes; as Voltaire said, 't is the
misfortune of worthy people that they are cowards; *"un des
plus grands malheurs des honnêtes gens c'est qu'ils sont des
lâches."* There must be a fusion of these two to generate the
energy of will. There can be no driving force, except through
the conversion of the man into his will, making him the will,
and the will him. And one may say boldly, that no man has
a right perception of any truth, who has not been reacted on
by it, so as to be ready to be its martyr.

The one serious and formidable thing in nature is a will.
Society is servile from want of will, and therefore the world
wants saviours and religions. One way is right to go: the
hero sees it, and moves on that aim, and has the world under
him for root and support. He is to others as the world. His
approbation is honor; his dissent, infamy. The glance of his
eye has the force of sunbeams. A personal influence towers
up in memory only worthy, and we gladly forget numbers,
money, climate, gravitation, and the rest of Fate.

We can afford to allow the limitation, if we know it is the
meter of the growing man. We stand against Fate, as chil-

dren stand up against the wall in their father's house, and notch their height from year to year. But when the boy grows to man, and is master of the house, he pulls down that wall, and builds a new and bigger. 'T is only a question of time. Every brave youth is in training to ride and rule this dragon. His science is to make weapons and wings of these passions and retarding forces. Now whether, seeing these two things, fate and power, we are permitted to believe in unity? The bulk of mankind believe in two gods. They are under one dominion here in the house, as friend and parent, in social circles, in letters, in art, in love, in religion: but in mechanics, in dealing with steam and climate, in trade, in politics, they think they come under another; and that it would be a practical blunder to transfer the method and way of working of one sphere, into the other. What good, honest, generous men at home, will be wolves and foxes on change! What pious men in the parlor will vote for what reprobates at the polls! To a certain point, they believe themselves the care of a Providence. But, in a steamboat, in an epidemic, in war, they believe a malignant energy rules.

But relation and connection are not somewhere and sometimes, but everywhere and always. The divine order does not stop where their sight stops. The friendly power works on the same rules, in the next farm, and the next planet. But, where they have not experience, they run against it, and hurt themselves. Fate, then, is a name for facts not yet passed under the fire of thought;—for causes which are unpenetrated.

But every jet of chaos which threatens to exterminate us, is convertible by intellect into wholesome force. Fate is unpenetrated causes. The water drowns ship and sailor, like a grain of dust. But learn to swim, trim your bark, and the wave which drowned it will be cloven by it, and carry it, like its own foam, a plume and a power. The cold is inconsiderate of persons, tingles your blood, freezes a man like a dewdrop. But learn to skate, and the ice will give you a graceful, sweet, and poetic motion. The cold will brace your limbs and brain to genius, and make you foremost men of time. Cold and sea will train an imperial Saxon race, which nature cannot bear to lose, and, after cooping it up for a thousand years in yonder England, gives a hundred Englands, a hundred Mexicos. All the bloods it shall absorb and domineer: and more than Mexicos,—the secrets of water and steam, the spasms of electricity, the ductility of metals, the chariot of the air, the ruddered balloon, are awaiting you.

The annual slaughter from typhus far exceeds that of war; but right drainage destroys typhus. The plague in the sea-service from scurvy is healed by lemon-juice and other diets portable or procurable: the depopulation by cholera and small-pox is ended by drainage and vaccination; and every other pest is not less in the chain of cause and effect, and may be fought off. And, whilst art draws out the venom, it commonly extorts some benefit from the vanquished enemy. The mischievous torrent is taught to drudge for man: the wild beasts he makes useful for food, or dress, or labor; the chemic explosions are controlled like his watch. These are now the steeds on which he rides. Man moves in all modes, by legs of horses, by wings of wind, by steam, by gas of balloon, by electricity, and stands on tiptoe threatening to hunt the eagle in his own element. There's nothing he will not make his carrier.

Steam was, till the other day, the devil which we dreaded. Every pot made by any human potter or brazier had a hole in its cover, to let off the enemy, lest he should lift pot and roof, and carry the house away. But the Marquis of Worcester, Watt, and Fulton bethought themselves, that, where was power, was not devil, but was God; that it must be availed of, and not by any means let off and wasted. Could he lift pots and roofs and houses so handily? he was the workman they were in search of. He could be used to lift away, chain, and compel other devils far more reluctant and dangerous, namely, cubic miles of earth, mountains, weight or resistance of water, machinery, and the labors of all men in the world; and time he shall lengthen, and shorten space.

It has not fared much otherwise with higher kinds of steam. The opinion of the million was the terror of the world, and it was attempted, either to dissipate it, by amusing nations, or to pile it over with strata of society,—a layer of soldiers; over that, a layer of lords; and a king on the top; with clamps and hoops of castles, garrisons, and police. But, sometimes, the religious principle would get in, and burst the hoops, and rive every mountain laid on top of it. The Fultons and Watts of politics, believing in unity, saw that it was a power, and, by satisfying it, (as justice satisfies everybody,) through a different disposition of society,—grouping it on a level, instead of piling it into a mountain,—they have contrived to make of this terror the most harmless and energetic form of a State.

Very odious, I confess, are the lessons of Fate. Who likes to have a dapper phrenologist pronouncing on his fortunes? Who likes to believe that he has hidden in his skull, spine, and pelvis, all the vices of a Saxon or Celtic race, which will be sure to pull him down—with what grandeur of hope and resolve he is fired,—into a selfish, huckstering, servile, dodging animal? A learned physician tells us, the fact is invariable with the Neapolitan, that, when mature, he assumes the forms of the unmistakable scoundrel. That is a little overstated,—but may pass.

But these are magazines and arsenals. A man must thank his defects, and stand in some terror of his talents. A transcendent talent draws so largely on his forces, as to lame him; a defect pays him revenues on the other side. The sufferance, which is the badge of the Jew, has made him, in these days, the ruler of the rulers of the earth. If Fate is ore and quarry, if evil is good in the making, if limitation is power that shall be, if calamities, oppositions, and weights are wings and means,—we are reconciled.

Fate involves the melioration. No statement of the Universe can have any soundness, which does not admit its ascending effort. The direction of the whole, and of the parts, is toward benefit, and in proportion to the health. Behind every individual closes organization: before him, opens liberty,—the Better, the Best. The first and worst races are dead. The second and imperfect races are dying out, or remain for the maturing of higher. In the latest race, in man, every generosity, every new perception, the love and praise he extorts from his fellows, are certificates of advance out of fate into freedom. Liberation of the will from the sheaths and clogs of organization which he has outgrown, is the end and aim of this world. Every calamity is a spur and valuable hint; and where his endeavors do not yet fully avail, they tell as tendency. The whole circle of animal life,—tooth against tooth,—devouring war, war for food, a yelp of pain and a grunt of triumph, until, at last, the whole menagerie, the whole chemical mass is mellowed and refined for higher use, —pleases at a sufficient perspective.

But to see how fate slides into freedom, and freedom into fate, observe how far the roots of every creature run, or find, if you can, a point where there is no thread of connection.

Our life is consentaneous and far-related. This knot of nature is so well tied, that nobody was ever cunning enough to find the two ends. Nature is intricate, overlapped, interweaved, and endless. Christopher Wren said of the beautiful King's College chapel, "that, if anybody would tell him where to lay the first stone, he would build such another." But where shall we find the first atom in this house of man, which is all consent, inosculation, and balance of parts?

The web of relation is shown in *habitat*, shown in hybernation. When hybernation was observed, it was found, that, whilst some animals became torpid in winter, others were torpid in summer: hybernation then was a false name. The *long sleep* is not an effect of cold, but is regulated by the supply of food proper to the animal. It becomes torpid when the fruit or prey it lives on is not in season, and regains its activity when its food is ready.

Eyes are found in light; ears in auricular air; feet on land; fins in water; wings in air; and, each creature where it was meant to be, with a mutual fitness. Every zone has its own *Fauna*. There is adjustment between the animal and its food, its parasite, its enemy. Balances are kept. It is not allowed to diminish in numbers, nor to exceed. The like adjustments exist for man. His food is cooked, when he arrives; his coal in the pit; his house ventilated; the mud of the deluge dried; his companions arrived at the same hour, and awaiting him with love, concert, laughter, and tears. These are coarse adjustments, but the invisible are not less. There are more belongings to every creature than his air and his food. His instincts must be met, and he has predisposing power that bends and fits what is near him to his use. He is not possible until the invisible things are right for him, as well as the visible. Of what changes, then, in sky and earth, and in finer skies and earths, does the appearance of some Dante or Columbus apprise us!

How is this effected? Nature is no spendthrift, but takes the shortest way to her ends. As the general says to his soldiers, "If you want a fort, build a fort," so nature makes every creature do its own work and get its living,—is it planet, animal, or tree. The planet makes itself. The animal cell makes itself;—then, what it wants. Every creature—wren or dragon—shall make its own lair. As soon as there is life, there is self-direction, and absorbing and using of material. Life is freedom,—life in the direct ratio of its amount. You may be sure, the new-born man is not inert. Life works both voluntarily and supernaturally in its neighborhood. Do you suppose, he can be estimated by his weight in pounds, or, that he is contained in his skin,—this reaching, radiating, jaculating fellow? The smallest candle fills a mile with its rays, and the papillæ of a man run out to every star.

When there is something to be done, the world knows how to get it done. The vegetable eye makes leaf, pericarp, root, bark, or thorn, as the need is; the first cell converts itself into stomach, mouth, nose, or nail, according to the want: the world throws its life into a hero or a shepherd; and puts him where he is wanted. Dante and Columbus were Italians, in their time: they would be Russians or Americans to-day. Things ripen, new men come. The adaptation is not capricious. The ulterior aim, the purpose beyond itself, the correlation by which planets subside and crystallize, then animate beasts and men, will not stop, but will work into finer particulars, and from finer to finest.

The secret of the world is, the tie between person and event. Person makes event, and event person. The "times," "the age," what is that, but a few profound persons and a few active persons who epitomize the times?—Goethe, Hegel, Metternich, Adams, Calhoun, Guizot, Peel, Cobden, Kossuth, Rothschild, Astor, Brunel, and the rest. The same fitness must be presumed between a man and the time and event, as between the sexes, or between a race of animals and the food it eats, or the inferior races it uses. He thinks his fate alien, because the copula is hidden. But the soul contains the event that shall befall it, for the event is only the actualization of its thoughts; and what we pray to ourselves for is always granted. The event is the print of your form. It fits you like your skin. What each does is proper to him. Events are the children of his body and mind. We learn that the soul of Fate is the soul of us, as Hafiz sings,

> Alas! till now I had not known,
> My guide and fortune's guide are one.

All the toys that infatuate men, and which they play for,— houses, land, money, luxury, power, fame, are the selfsame thing, with a new gauze or two of illusion overlaid. And of all the drums and rattles by which men are made willing to have their heads broke, and are led out solemnly every morning to parade,—the most admirable is this by which we

are brought to believe that events are arbitrary, and independent of actions. At the conjurer's, we detect the hair by
which he moves his puppet, but we have not eyes sharp
enough to descry the thread that ties cause and effect.

Nature magically suits the man to his fortunes, by making
these the fruit of his character. Ducks take to the water,
eagles to the sky, waders to the sea margin, hunters to the
forest, clerks to counting-rooms, soldiers to the frontier. Thus
events grow on the same stem with persons; are sub-persons.
The pleasure of life is according to the man that lives it, and
not according to the work or the place. Life is an ecstasy.
We know what madness belongs to love,—what power to
paint a vile object in hues of heaven. As insane persons are
indifferent to their dress, diet, and other accommodations,
and, as we do in dreams, with equanimity, the most absurd
acts, so, a drop more of wine in our cup of life will reconcile
us to strange company and work. Each creature puts forth
from itself its own condition and sphere, as the slug sweats
out its slimy house on the pear-leaf, and the woolly aphides
on the apple perspire their own bed, and the fish its shell.
In youth, we clothe ourselves with rainbows, and go as brave
as the zodiac. In age, we put out another sort of perspiration,
—gout, fever, rheumatism, caprice, doubt, fretting, and
avarice.

A man's fortunes are the fruit of his character. A man's
friends are his magnetisms. We go to Herodotus and Plutarch
for examples of Fate; but we are examples. *"Quisque suos
patimur manes."* The tendency of every man to enact all that
is in his constitution is expressed in the old belief, that the
efforts which we make to escape from our destiny only serve
to lead us into it: and I have noticed, a man likes better to
be complimented on his position, as the proof of the last or
total excellence, than on his merits.

A man will see his character emitted in the events that
seem to meet, but which exude from and accompany him.
Events expand with the character. As once he found himself
among toys, so now he plays a part in colossal systems, and
his growth is declared in his ambition, his companions, and
his performance. He looks like a piece of luck, but is a piece
of causation; the mosaic, angulated and ground to fit into
the gap he fills. Hence in each town there is some man who
is, in his brain and performance, an explanation of the tillage,
production, factories, banks, churches, ways of living, and

society, of that town. If you do not chance to meet him, all that you see will leave you a little puzzled: if you see him, it will become plain. We know in Massachusetts who built New Bedford, who built Lynn, Lowell, Lawrence, Clinton, Fitchburg, Holyoke, Portland, and many another noisy mart. Each of these men, if they were transparent, would seem to you not so much men, as walking cities, and, wherever you put them, they would build one.

History is the action and reaction of these two,—Nature and Thought; two boys pushing each other on the curbstone of the pavement. Everything is pusher or pushed: and matter and mind are in perpetual tilt and balance, so. Whilst the man is weak, the earth takes up him. He plants his brain and affections. By and by he will take up the earth, and have his gardens and vineyards in the beautiful order and productiveness of his thought. Every solid in the universe is ready to become fluid on the approach of the mind, and the power to flux it is the measure of the mind. If the wall remain adamant, it accuses the want of thought. To a subtler force, it will stream into new forms, expressive of the character of the mind. What is the city in which we sit here, but an aggregate of incongruous materials, which have obeyed the will of some man? The granite was reluctant, but his hands were stronger, and it came. Iron was deep in the ground, and well combined with stone, but could not hide from his fires. Wood, lime, stuffs, fruits, gums, were dispersed over the earth and sea, in vain. Here they are, within reach of every man's day-labor,—what he wants of them. The whole world is the flux of matter over the wires of thought to the poles or points where it would build. The races of men rise out of the ground preoccupied with a thought which rules them, and divided into parties ready armed and angry to fight for this metaphysical abstraction. The quality of the thought differences the Egyptian and the Roman, the Austrian and the American. The men who come on the stage at one period are all found to be related to each other. Certain ideas are in the air. We are all impressionable, for we are made of them; all impressionable, but some more than others, and these first express them. This explains the curious contemporaneousness of inventions and discoveries. The truth is in the air, and the most impressionable brain will announce it first, but all will announce it a few minutes later. So women, as most susceptible, are the best index of the coming hour.

So the great man, that is, the man most imbued with the spirit of the time, is the impressionable man,—of a fibre irritable and delicate, like iodine to light. He feels the infinitesimal attractions. His mind is righter than others, because he yields to a current so feeble as can be felt only by a needle delicately poised.

The correlation is shown in defects. Möller, in his Essay on Architecture, taught that the building which was fitted accurately to answer its end, would turn out to be beautiful, though beauty had not been intended. I find the like unity in human structures rather virulent and pervasive; that a crudity in the blood will appear in the argument; a hump in the shoulder will appear in the speech and handiwork. If his mind could be seen, the hump would be seen. If a man has a seesaw in his voice, it will run into his sentences, into his poem, into the structure of his fable, into his speculation, into his charity. And, as every man is hunted by his own demon, vexed by his own disease, this checks all his activity.

So each man, like each plant, has his parasites. A strong, astringent, bilious nature has more truculent enemies than the slugs and moths that fret my leaves. Such an one has curculios, borers, knife-worms: a swindler ate him first, then a client, then a quack, then smooth, plausible gentlemen, bitter and selfish as Moloch.

This correlation really existing can be divined. If the threads are there, thought can follow and show them. Especially when a soul is quick and docile; as Chaucer sings:—

> "Or if the soul of proper kind
> Be so perfect as men find,
> That it wot what is to come,
> And that he warneth all and some
> Of every of their aventures,
> By previsions or figures;
> But that our flesh hath not might
> It to understand aright
> For it is warned too darkly."

Some people are made up of rhyme, coincidence, omen, periodicity, and presage: they meet the person they seek; what their companion prepares to say to them, they first say to him; and a hundred signs apprise them of what is about to befall.

Wonderful intricacy in the web, wonderful constancy in

the design, this vagabond life admits. We wonder how the fly finds its mate, and yet year after year we find two men, two women, without legal or carnal tie, spend a great part of their best time within a few feet of each other. And the moral is, that what we seek we shall find; what we flee from flees from us; as Goethe said, "what we wish for in youth, comes in heaps on us in old age," too often cursed with the granting of our prayer: and hence the high caution, that, since we are sure of having what we wish, we beware to ask only for high things.

One key, one solution to the mysteries of human condition, one solution to the old knots of fate, freedom and foreknowledge, exists, the propounding, namely, of the double consciousness. A man must ride alternately on the horses of his private and his public nature, as the equestrians in the circus throw themselves nimbly from horse to horse, or plant one foot on the back of one, and the other foot on the back of the other. So when a man is the victim of his fate, has sciatica in his loins, and cramp in his mind; a club-foot and a club in his wit; a sour face, and a selfish temper; a strut in his gait, and a conceit in his affection; or is ground to powder by the vice of his race; he is to rally on his relation to the Universe, which his ruin benefits. Leaving the demon who suffers, he is to take sides with the Deity who secures universal benefit by his pain.

To offset the drag of temperament and race, which pulls down, learn this lesson, namely, that by the cunning co-presence of two elements, which is throughout nature, whatever lames or paralyzes you, draws in with it the divinity, in some form, to repay. A good intention clothes itself with sudden power. When a god wishes to ride, any chip or pebble will bud and shoot out winged feet, and serve him for a horse.

Let us build altars to the Blessed Unity which holds nature and souls in perfect solution, and compels every atom to serve an universal end. I do not wonder at a snow-flake, a shell, a summer landscape, or the glory of the stars; but at the necessity of beauty under which the universe lies; that all is and must be pictorial; that the rainbow, and the curve of the horizon, and the arch of the blue vault, are only results from the organism of the eye. There is no need for foolish amateurs to fetch me to admire a garden of flowers, or a sun-gilt cloud, or a waterfall, when I cannot look without seeing splendor and grace. How idle to choose a random sparkle here or there, when the indwelling necessity plants the rose of beauty on the brow of chaos, and discloses the central intention of Nature to be harmony and joy.

Let us build altars to the Beautiful Necessity. If we thought men were free in the sense, that, in a single exception one fantastical will could prevail over the law of things, it were all one as if a child's hand could pull down the sun. If, in the least particular, one could derange the order of nature,—who would accept the gift of life?

Let us build altars to the Beautiful Necessity, which secures that all is made of one piece; that plaintiff and defendant, friend and enemy, animal and planet, food and eater, are of one kind. In astronomy is vast space, but no foreign system; in geology, vast time, but the same laws as to-day. Why should we be afraid of Nature, which is no other than "philosophy and theology embodied"? Why should we fear to be crushed by savage elements, we who are made up of the same elements? Let us build to the Beautiful Necessity, which makes man brave in believing that he cannot shun a danger that is appointed, nor incur one that is not; to the Necessity which rudely or softly educates him to the perception that there are no contingencies; that Law rules throughout existence, a Law which is not intelligent but intelligence, —not personal nor impersonal,—it disdains words and passes understanding; it dissolves persons; it vivifies nature; yet solicits the pure in heart to draw on all its omnipotence.

1860

ILLUSIONS.*

> Flow, flow the waves hated,
> Accursed, adored,
> The waves of mutation:
> No anchorage is.
> Sleep is not, death is not;
> Who seem to die live.
> House you were born in,
> Friends of your spring-time,
> Old man and young maid,

* From *Conduct of Life.*

Day's toil and its guerdon,
They are all vanishing,
Fleeing to fables,
Cannot be moored.
See the stars through them,
Through treacherous marbles.
Know, the stars yonder,
The stars everlasting,
Are fugitive also,
And emulate, vaulted,
The lambent heat-lightning,
And fire-fly's flight.

When thou dost return
On the wave's circulation,
Beholding the shimmer,
The wild dissipation,
And, out of endeavor
To change and to flow,
The gas becomes solid,
And phantoms and nothings
Return to be things,
And endless imbroglio
Is law and the world,—
Then first shalt thou know,
That in the wild turmoil,
Horsed on the Proteus,
Thou ridest to power,
And to endurance.

Some years ago, in company with an agreeable party, I
spent a long summer day in exploring the Mammoth Cave in
Kentucky. We traversed, through spacious galleries afford-
ing a solid masonry foundation for the town and county
overhead, the six or eight black miles from the mouth of the
cavern to the innermost recess which tourists visit,—a niche
or grotto made of one seamless stalactite, and called, I believe, Serena's Bower. I lost the light of one day. I saw high
domes, and bottomless pits; heard the voice of unseen water-
falls; paddled three quarters of a mile in the deep Echo
River, whose waters are peopled with the blind fish; crossed
the streams "Lethe" and "Styx"; plied with music and guns
the echoes in these alarming galleries; saw every form of
stalagmite and stalactite in the sculptured and fretted chambers,—icicle, orange-flower, acanthus, grapes, and snowball.
We shot Bengal lights into the vaults and groins of the

sparry cathedrals, and examined all the masterpieces which the four combined engineers, water, limestone, gravitation, and time, could make in the dark.

The mysteries and scenery of the cave had the same dignity that belongs to all natural objects, and which shames the fine things to which we foppishly compare them. I remarked, especially, the mimetic habit, with which Nature, on new instruments, hums her old tunes, making night to mimic day, and chemistry to ape vegetation. But I then took notice, and still chiefly remember, that the best thing which the cave had to offer was an illusion. On arriving at what is called the "Star-Chamber," our lamps were taken from us by the guide, and extinguished or put aside, and, on looking upwards, I saw or seemed to see the night heaven thick with stars glimmering more or less brightly over our heads, and even what seemed a comet flaming among them. All the party were touched with astonishment and pleasure. Our musical friends sung with much feeling a pretty song, "The stars are in the quiet sky," &c., and I sat down on the rocky floor to enjoy the serene picture. Some crystal specks in the black ceiling high overhead, reflecting the light of a half-hid lamp, yielded this magnificent effect.

I own, I did not like the cave so well for eking out its sublimities with this theatrical trick. But I have had many experiences like it, before and since; and we must be content to be pleased without too curiously analyzing the occasions. Our conversation with Nature is not just what it seems. The cloud-rack, the sunrise and sunset glories, rainbows and northern lights, are not quite so spheral as our childhood thought them; and the part our organization plays in them is too large. The senses interfere everywhere, and mix their own structure with all they report of. Once, we fancied the earth a plane, and stationary. In admiring the sunset, we do not yet deduct the rounding, co-ordinating, pictorial powers of the eye.

The same interference from our organization creates the most of our pleasure and pain. Our first mistake is the belief that the circumstance gives the joy which we give to the circumstance. Life is an ecstasy. Life is sweet as nitrous oxide; and the fisherman dripping all day over a cold pond, the switchman at the railway intersection, the farmer in the field, the negro in the rice-swamp, the fop in the street, the hunter in the woods, the barrister with the jury, the belle at the ball,

all ascribe a certain pleasure to their employment, which they themselves give it. Health and appetite impart the sweetness to sugar, bread, and meat. We fancy that our civilization has got on far, but we still come back to our primers.

We live by our imaginations, by our admirations, by our sentiments. The child walks amid heaps of illusions, which he does not like to have disturbed. The boy, how sweet to him is his fancy! how dear the story of barons and battles! What a hero he is, whilst he feeds on his heroes! What a debt is his to imaginative books! He has no better friend or influence, than Scott, Shakespeare, Plutarch, and Homer. The man lives to other objects, but who dare affirm that they are more real? Even the prose of the streets is full of refractions. In the life of the dreariest alderman, fancy enters into all details, and colors them with rosy hue. He imitates the air and actions of people whom he admires, and is raised in his own eyes. He pays a debt quicker to a rich man than to a poor man. He wishes the bow and compliment of some leader in the state, or in society; weighs what he says; perhaps he never comes nearer to him for that, but dies at last better contented for this amusement of his eyes and his fancy.

The world rolls, the din of life is never hushed. In London, in Paris, in Boston, in San Francisco, the carnival, the masquerade, is at its height. Nobody drops his domino. The unities, the fictions of the piece, it would be an impertinence to break. The chapter of fascinations is very long. Great is paint; nay, God is the painter; and we rightly accuse the critic who destroys too many illusions. Society does not love its unmaskers. It was wittily, if somewhat bitterly, said by D'Alembert, *"qu'un état de vapeur était un état très fâcheux, parcequ'il nous faisait voir les choses comme elles sont."* I find men victims of illusion in all parts of life. Children, youths, adults, and old men, all are led by one bauble or another. Yoganidra, the goddess of illusion, Proteus, or Momus, or Gylfi's Mocking,—for the Power has many names,—is stronger than the Titans, stronger than Apollo. Few have overheard the gods, or surprised their secret. Life is a succession of lessons which must be lived to be understood. All is riddle, and the key to a riddle is another riddle. There are as many pillows of illusion as flakes in a snow-storm. We wake from one dream into another dream. The toys, to be sure, are various, and are graduated in refinement to the quality of the dupe. The intellectual man requires a fine bait; the sots are easily amused. But everybody is drugged with his own frenzy, and the pageant marches at all hours, with music and banner and badge.

Amid the joyous troop who give in to the charivari comes now and then a sad-eyed boy, whose eyes lack the requisite refractions to clothe the show in due glory, and who is afflicted with a tendency to trace home the glittering miscellany of fruits and flowers to one root. Science is a search after identity, and the scientific whim is lurking in all corners. At the State Fair, a friend of mine complained that all the varieties of fancy pears in our orchards seem to have been selected by somebody who had a whim for a particular kind of pear, and only cultivated such as had that perfume; they were all alike. And I remember the quarrel of another youth with the confectioners, that, when he racked his wit to choose the best comfits in the shops, in all the endless varieties of sweetmeat he could only find three flavors, or two. What then? Pears and cakes are good for something; and because you, unluckily, have an eye or nose too keen, why need you spoil the comfort which the rest of us find in them? I knew a humorist, who, in a good deal of rattle, had a grain or two of sense. He shocked the company by maintaining that the attributes of God were two,—power and risibility; and that it was the duty of every pious man to keep up the comedy. And I have known gentlemen of great stake in the community, but whose sympathies were cold,—presidents of colleges, and governors, and senators,—who held themselves bound to sign every temperance pledge, and act with Bible societies, and missions, and peacemakers, and cry *Hist-a-boy!* to every good dog. We must not carry comity too far, but we all have kind impulses in this direction. When the boys come into my yard for leave to gather horse-chestnuts, I own I enter into Nature's game, and affect to grant the permission reluctantly, fearing that any moment they will find out the imposture of that showy chaff. But this tenderness is quite unnecessary; the enchantments are laid on very thick. Their young life is thatched with them. Bare and grim to tears is the lot of the children in the hovel I saw yesterday; yet not the less they hung it round with frippery romance, like the children of the happiest fortune, and talked of "the dear cottage where so many joyful hours had flown." Well, this thatching of hovels is the custom of the country. Women, more than all, are the element and kingdom of illusion. Being fascinated, they fascinate. They see through Claude-Lorraines. And how dare any one, if he could, pluck away the *coulisses*, stage effects, and ceremonies, by which they live? Too pathetic, too pitiable, is the region of affection, and its atmosphere always liable to *mirage*.

We are not very much to blame for our bad marriages. We live amid hallucinations; and this especial trap is laid to trip up our feet with, and all are tripped up first or last. But the mighty Mother who had been so sly with us, as if she felt that she owed us some indemnity, insinuates into the Pandora-box of marriage some deep and serious benefits, and some great joys. We find a delight in the beauty and happiness of children, that makes the heart too big for the body. In the worst-assorted connections there is ever some mixture of true marriage. Teague and his jade get some relations of mutual respect, kindly observation, and fostering of each other, learn something, and would carry themselves wiselier, if they were now to begin.

'T is fine for us to point at one or another fine madman, as if there were any exempts. The scholar in his library is none. I, who have all my life heard any number of orations and debates, read poems and miscellaneous books, conversed with many geniuses, am still the victim of any new page; and, if Marmaduke, or Hugh, or Moosehead, or any other, invent a new style or mythology, I fancy that the world will be all brave and right, if dressed in these colors, which I had not thought of. Then at once I will daub with this new paint; but it will not stick. 'T is like the cement which the pedler sells at the door; he makes broken crockery hold with it, but you can never buy of him a bit of the cement which will make it hold when he is gone.

Men who make themselves felt in the world avail themselves of a certain fate in their constitution, which they know how to use. But they never deeply interest us, unless they lift a corner of the curtain, or betray never so slightly their penetration of what is behind it. 'T is the charm of practical men, that outside of their practicality are a certain poetry and play, as if they led the good horse Power by the bridle, and preferred to walk, though they can ride so fiercely. Bonaparte is intellectual, as well as Cæsar; and the best soldiers, sea-captains, and railway men, have a gentleness, when off duty; a good-natured admission that there are illusions, and who shall say that he is not their sport? We stigmatize the cast-iron fellows, who cannot so detach themselves, as "dragon-ridden," "thunder-stricken," and fools of fate, with whatever powers endowed.

Since our tuition is through emblems and indirections, 't is well to know that there is method in it, a fixed scale, and rank above rank in the phantasms. We begin low with coarse masks, and rise to the most subtle and beautiful. The red men told Columbus, "they had an herb which took away fatigue"; but he found the illusion of "arriving from the east at the Indies" more composing to his lofty spirit than any tobacco. Is not our faith in the impenetrability of matter more sedative than narcotics? You play with jack-straws, balls, bowls, horse and gun, estates and politics; but there are finer games before you. Is not time a pretty toy? Life will show you masks that are worth all your carnivals. Yonder mountain must migrate into your mind. The fine star-dust and nebulous blur in Orion, "the portentous year of Mizar and Alcor," must come down and be dealt with in your household thought. What if you shall come to discern that the play and playground of all this pompous history are radiations from yourself, and that the sun borrows his beams? What terrible questions we are learning to ask! The former men believed in magic, by which temples, cities, and men were swallowed up, and all trace of them gone. We are coming on the secret of a magic which sweeps out of men's minds all vestige of theism and beliefs which they and their fathers held and were framed upon.

There are deceptions of the senses, deceptions of the passions, and the structural, beneficent illusions of sentiment and of the intellect. There is the illusion of love, which attributes to the beloved person all which that person shares with his or her family, sex, age, or condition, nay with the human mind itself. 'T is these which the lover loves, and Anna Matilda gets the credit of them. As if one shut up always in a tower, with one window, through which the face of heaven and earth could be seen, should fancy that all the marvels he beheld belonged to that window. There is the illusion of time, which is very deep; who has disposed of it? or come to the conviction that what seems the *succession* of thought is only the distribution of wholes into causal series? The intellect sees that every atom carries the whole of Nature; that the mind opens to omnipotence; that, in the endless striving and ascents, the metamorphosis is entire, so that the soul doth not know itself in its own act, when that act is perfected. There is illusion that shall deceive even the elect. There is illusion that shall deceive even the performer of the miracle. Though he make his body, he denies that he makes it. Though the world exist from thought, thought is daunted in presence of the world. One after the other we accept the mental laws, still resisting those which follow, which however must be accepted. But all our concessions only compel us to new profusion. And what avails it that science has come to treat space and time as simply forms of thought, and the material world as hypothetical, and withal our pretension of *property* and even of selfhood are fading with the rest, if, at last, even our thoughts are not finalities; but the incessant flowing and ascension reach these also, and each thought which yesterday was a finality, to-day is yielding to a larger generalization?

With such volatile elements to work in, 't is no wonder if our estimates are loose and floating. We must work and affirm, but we have no guess of the value of what we say or do. The cloud is now as big as your hand, and now it covers a country. That story of Thor, who was set to drain the drinking-horn in Asgard, and to wrestle with the old woman, and to run with the runner Lok, and presently found that he had been drinking up the sea, and wrestling with Time, and racing with Thought, describes us who are contending, amid these seeming trifles, with the supreme energies of Nature. We fancy we have fallen into bad company and squalid condition, low debts, shoe-bills, broken glass to pay for, pots to buy, butcher's meat, sugar, milk, and coal. 'Set me some great task, ye gods! and I will show my spirit.' 'Not so,' says the good Heaven; 'plod and plough, vamp your old coats and hats, weave a shoestring; great affairs and the best wine by and by.' Well, 't is all phantasm; and if we weave a yard of tape in all humility, and as well as we can, long hereafter we shall see it was no cotton tape at all, but some galaxy which we braided, and that the threads were Time and Nature.

We cannot write the order of the variable winds. How can we penetrate the law of our shifting moods and susceptibility? Yet they differ as all and nothing. Instead of the firmament of yesterday, which our eyes require, it is to-day an eggshell which coops us in; we cannot even see what or

where our stars of destiny are. From day to day, the capital
facts of human life are hidden from our eyes. Suddenly the
mist rolls up, and reveals them, and we think how much good
time is gone, that might have been saved, had any hint of
these things been shown. A sudden rise in the road shows us
the system of mountains, and all the summits, which have
been just as near us all the year, but quite out of mind. But
these alternations are not without their order, and we are
parties to our various fortune. If life seem a succession of
dreams, yet poetic justice is done in dreams also. The visions
of good men are good; it is the undisciplined will that is
whipped with bad thoughts and bad fortunes. When we
break the laws, we lose our hold on the central reality. Like
sick men in hospitals, we change only from bed to bed, from
one folly to another; and it cannot signify much what becomes of such castaways,—wailing, stupid, comatose creatures,—lifted from bed to bed, from the nothing of life to
the nothing of death.

In this kingdom of illusions we grope eagerly for stays
and foundations. There is none but a strict and faithful dealing at home, and a severe barring out of all duplicity or
illusion there. Whatever games are played with us, we must
play no games with ourselves, but deal in our privacy with
the last honesty and truth. I look upon the simple and childish virtues of veracity and honesty as the root of all that
is sublime in character. Speak as you think, be what you
are, pay your debts of all kinds. I prefer to be owned as
sound and solvent, and my word as good as my bond, and
to be what cannot be skipped, or dissipated, or undermined,
to all the *éclat* in the universe. This reality is the foundation of friendship, religion, poetry, and art. At the top or at
the bottom of all illusions, I set the cheat which still leads us
to work and live for appearances, in spite of our conviction,
in all sane hours, that it is what we really are that avails
with friends, with strangers, and with fate or fortune.

One would think from the talk of men, that riches and
poverty were a great matter; and our civilization mainly
respects it. But the Indians say, that they do not think the
white man with his brow of care, always toiling, afraid of
heat and cold, and keeping within doors, has any advantage
of them. (The permanent interest of every man is, never to
be in a false position, but to have the weight of Nature to
back him in all that he does.) Riches and poverty are a thick

or thin costume; and our life—the life of all of us—identical. For we transcend the circumstance continually, and taste the real quality of existence; as in our employments, which only differ in the manipulations, but express the same laws; or in our thoughts, which wear no silks, and taste no ice-creams. We see God face to face every hour, and know the savor of Nature.

The early Greek philosophers Heraclitus and Xenophanes measured their force on the problem of identity. Diogenes of Apollonia said, that unless the atoms were made of one stuff, they could never blend and act with one another. But the Hindoos, in their sacred writings, express the liveliest feeling, both of the essential identity, and of that illusion which they conceive variety to be. "The notions, 'I am,' and 'This is mine,' which influence mankind, are but delusions of the mother of the world. Dispel, O Lord of all creatures! the conceit of knowledge which proceeds from ignorance." And the beatitude of man they hold to lie in being freed from fascination.

The intellect is stimulated by the statement of truth in a trope, and the will by clothing the laws of life in illusions. But the unities of Truth and of Right are not broken by the disguise. There need never be any confusion in these. In a crowded life of many parts and performers, on a stage of nations, or in the obscurest hamlet in Maine or California, the same elements offer the same choices to each new-comer, and, according to his election, he fixes his fortune in absolute Nature. It would be hard to put more mental and moral philosophy than the Persians have thrown into a sentence:—

> "Fooled thou must be, though wisest of the wise:
> Then be the fool of virtue, not of vice."

There is no chance, and no anarchy, in the universe. All is system and gradation. Every god is there sitting in his sphere. The young mortal enters the hall of the firmament; there is he alone with them alone, they pouring on him benedictions and gifts, and beckoning him up to their thrones. On the instant, and incessantly, fall snow-storms of illusions. He fancies himself in a vast crowd which sways this way and that, and whose movement and doings he must obey: he fancies himself poor, orphaned, insignificant. The mad crowd drives hither and thither, now furiously commanding this thing to be done, now that. What is he that he should resist their will, and think or act for himself? Every moment, new changes, and new showers of deceptions, to baffle and distract him. And when, by and by, for an instant, the air clears, and the cloud lifts a little, there are the gods still sitting around him on their thrones,—they alone with him alone.

1857

THOREAU.*

Henry David Thoreau was the last male descendant of a French ancestor who came to this country from the Isle of Guernsey. His character exhibited occasional traits drawn from this blood in singular combination with a very strong Saxon genius.

He was born in Concord, Massachusetts, on the 12th of July, 1817. He was graduated at Harvard College in 1837, but without any literary distinction. An iconoclast in literature, he seldom thanked colleges for their service to him, holding them in small esteem, whilst yet his debt to them was important. After leaving the University, he joined his brother in teaching a private school, which he soon renounced. His father was a manufacturer of lead-pencils, and Henry applied himself for a time to this craft, believing he could make a better pencil than was then in use. After completing his experiments, he exhibited his work to chemists and artists in Boston, and having obtained their certificates to its excellence and to its equality with the best London manufacture, he returned home contented. His friends congratulated him that he had now opened his way to fortune. But he replied, that he should never make another pencil. "Why should I? I would not do again what I have done once." He resumed his endless walks and miscellaneous studies, making every day some new acquaintance with Nature, though as yet never speaking of zoölogy or botany, since, though very studious of natural facts, he was incurious of technical and textual science.

At this time, a strong, healthy youth, fresh from college,

* From *Lectures and Biographical Sketches.*

whilst all his companions were choosing their profession, or eager to begin some lucrative employment, it was inevitable that his thoughts should be exercised on the same question, and it required rare decision to refuse all the accustomed paths, and keep his solitary freedom at the cost of disappointing the natural expectations of his family and friends: all the more difficult that he had a perfect probity, was exact in securing his own independence, and in holding every man to the like duty. But Thoreau never faltered. He was a born protestant. He declined to give up his large ambition of knowledge and action for any narrow craft or profession, aiming at a much more comprehensive calling, the art of living well. If he slighted and defied the opinions of others, it was only that he was more intent to reconcile his practice with his own belief. Never idle or self-indulgent, he preferred, when he wanted money, earning it by some piece of manual labor agreeable to him, as building a boat or a fence, planting, grafting, surveying, or other short work, to any long engagements. With his hardy habits and few wants, his skill in wood-craft, and his powerful arithmetic, he was very competent to live in any part of the world. It would cost him less time to supply his wants than another. He was therefore secure of his leisure.

A natural skill for mensuration, growing out of his mathematical knowledge, and his habit of ascertaining the measures and distances of objects which interested him, the size of trees, the depth and extent of ponds and rivers, the height of mountains, and the air-line distance of his favorite summits,—this, and his intimate knowledge of the territory about Concord, made him drift into the profession of land-surveyor. It had the advantage for him that it led him continually into new and secluded grounds, and helped his studies of Nature. His accuracy and skill in this work were readily appreciated, and he found all the employment he wanted.

He could easily solve the problems of the surveyor, but he was daily beset with graver questions, which he manfully confronted. He interrogated every custom, and wished to settle all his practice on an ideal foundation. He was a protestant *à l'outrance*, and few lives contain so many renunciations. He was bred to no profession; he never married; he lived alone; he never went to church; he never voted; he refused to pay a tax to the State; he ate no flesh, he drank no wine, he never knew the use of tobacco; and, though a naturalist, he used neither trap nor gun. He chose, wisely, no doubt, for himself, to be the bachelor of thought and Nature. He had no talent for wealth, and knew how to be poor without the least hint of squalor or inelegance. Perhaps he fell into his way of living without forecasting it much, but approved it with later wisdom. "I am often reminded," he wrote in his journal, "that, if I had bestowed on me the wealth of Crœsus, my aims must be still the same, and my means essentially the same." He had no temptations to fight against,—no appetites, no passions, no taste for elegant trifles. A fine house, dress, the manners and talk of highly cultivated people were all thrown away on him. He much preferred a good Indian, and considered these refinements as impediments to conversation, wishing to meet his companion on the simplest terms. He declined invitations to dinner-parties, because there each was in every one's way, and he could not meet the individuals to any purpose. "They make their pride," he said, "in making their dinner cost much; I make my pride in making my dinner cost little." When asked at table what dish he preferred, he answered, "The nearest." He did not like the taste of wine, and never had a vice in his life. He said,—"I have a faint recollection of pleasure derived from smoking dried lily-stems, before I was a man. I had commonly a supply of these. I have never smoked anything more noxious."

He chose to be rich by making his wants few, and supplying them himself. In his travels, he used the railroad only to get over so much country as was unimportant to the present purpose, walking hundreds of miles, avoiding taverns, buying a lodging in farmers' and fisherman's houses, as cheaper, and more agreeable to him, and because there he could better find the men and the information he wanted.

There was somewhat military in his nature not to be subdued, always manly and able, but rarely tender, as if he did not feel himself except in opposition. He wanted a fallacy to expose, a blunder to pillory, I may say required a little sense of victory, a roll of the drum, to call his powers into full exercise. It cost him nothing to say No; indeed, he found it much easier than to say Yes. It seemed as if his first instinct on hearing a proposition was to controvert it, so impatient was he of the limitations of our daily thought. This habit, of course, is a little chilling to the social affections; and though the companion would in the end acquit him of any malice or untruth, yet it mars conversation. Hence, no equal companion stood in affectionate relations with one so pure and guileless. "I love Henry," said one of his friends, "but I cannot like him; and as for taking his arm, I should as soon think of taking the arm of an elm-tree."

Yet, hermit and stoic as he was, he was really fond of sympathy, and threw himself heartily and childlike into the company of younger people whom he loved, and whom he delighted to entertain, as he only could, with the varied and endless anecdotes of his experiences by field and river. And he was always ready to lead a huckleberry-party or a search for chestnuts or grapes. Talking, one day, of a public discourse, Henry remarked, that whatever succeeded with the audience was bad. I said, "Who would not like to write something which all can read, like 'Robinson Crusoe'? and who does not see with regret that his page is not solid with a right materialistic treatment, which delights everybody?" Henry objected, of course, and vaunted the better lectures which reached only a few persons. But, at supper, a young girl, understanding that he was to lecture at the Lyceum, sharply asked him, "whether his lecture would be a nice, interesting story, such as she wished to hear, or whether it was one of those old philosophical things that she did not care about." Henry turned to her, and bethought himself, and, I saw, was trying to believe that he had matter that might fit her and her brother, who were to sit up and go to the lecture, if it was a good one for them.

He was a speaker and actor of the truth,—born such,—and was ever running into dramatic situations from this cause. In any circumstance, it interested all bystanders to know what part Henry would take, and what he would say; and he did not disappoint expectation, but used an original judgment on each emergency. In 1845 he built himself a small framed house on the shores of Walden Pond, and lived there two years alone, a life of labor and study. This action was quite native and fit for him. No one who knew him would tax him with affection. He was more unlike his neighbors in his thought than in his action. As soon as he had exhausted the advantages of that solitude, he abandoned it. In 1847, not approving some uses to which the public expenditure was applied, he refused to pay his town tax, and was put in jail. A friend paid the tax for him, and he was released.

The like annoyance was threatened the next year. But, as his friends paid the tax, notwithstanding his protest, I believe he ceased to resist. No opposition or ridicule had any weight with him. He coldly and fully stated his opinion without affecting to believe that it was the opinion of the company. It was of no consequence, if every one present held the opposite opinion. On one occasion he went to the University Library to procure some books. The librarian refused to lend them. Mr. Thoreau repaired to the President, who stated to him the rules and usages, which permitted the loan of books to resident graduates, to clergymen who were alumni, and to some others resident within a circle of ten miles' radius from the College. Mr. Thoreau explained to the President that the railroad had destroyed the old scale of distances,—that the library was useless, yes, and President and College useless, on the terms of his rules,—that the one benefit he owed to the College was its library,—that, at this moment, not only his want of books was imperative, but he wanted a large number of books, and assured him that he, Thoreau, and not the librarian, was the proper custodian of these. In short, the President found the petitioner so formidable, and the rules getting to look so ridiculous, that he ended by giving him a privilege which in his hands proved unlimited thereafter.

No truer American existed than Thoreau. His preference of his country and condition was genuine, and his aversation from English and European manners and tastes almost reached contempt. He listened impatiently to news or *bon mots* gleaned from London circles; and though he tried to be civil, these anecdotes fatigued him. The men were all imitating each other, and on a small mould. Why can they not live as far apart as possible, and each be a man by himself? What he sought was the most energetic nature; and he wished to go to Oregon, not to London. "In every part of Great Britain," he wrote in his diary, "are discovered traces of the Romans, their funereal urns, their camps, their roads, their dwellings. But New England, at least, is not based on any Roman ruins. We have not to lay the foundations of our houses on the ashes of a former civilization."

But, idealist as he was, standing for abolition of slavery, abolition of tariffs, almost for abolition of government, it is needless to say he found himself not only unrepresented in actual politics, but almost equally opposed to every class of reformers. Yet he paid the tribute of his uniform respect to the Anti-Slavery party. One man, whose personal acquaintance he had formed, he honored with exceptional regard. Before the first friendly word had been spoken for Captain John Brown, he sent notices to most houses in Concord, that he would speak in a public hall on the condition and character of John Brown, on Sunday evening, and invited all people to come. The Republican Committee, the Abolitionist Committee, sent him word that it was premature and not advisable. He replied,—"I did not send to you for advice, but to announce that I am to speak." The hall was filled at an early hour by people of all parties, and his earnest eulogy of the hero was heard by all respectfully, by many with a sympathy that surprised themselves.

It was said of Plotinus that he was ashamed of his body, and 't is very likely he had good reason for it,—that his body was a bad servant, and he had not skill in dealing with the material world, as happens often to men of abstract intellect. But Mr. Thoreau was equipped with a most adapted and serviceable body. He was of short stature, firmly built, of light complexion, with strong, serious blue eyes, and a grave aspect,—his face covered in the late years with a becoming beard. His senses were acute, his frame well-knit and hard, his hands strong and skilful in the use of tools. And there was a wonderful fitness of body and mind. He could pace sixteen rods more accurately than another man could measure them with rod and chain. He could find his path in the woods at night, he said, better by his feet than his eyes. He could estimate the measure of a tree very well by his eye; he could estimate the weight of a calf or a pig, like a dealer. From a box containing a bushel or more of loose pencils, he could take up with his hands fast enough just a dozen pencils at every grasp. He was a good swimmer, runner, skater, boatman, and would probably outwalk most countrymen in a day's journey. And the relation of body to mind was still finer than we have indicated. He said he wanted every stride his legs made. The length of his walk uniformly made the length of his writing. If shut up in the house, he did not write at all.

He had a strong common sense, like that which Rose Flammock, the weaver's daughter, in Scott's romance, commends in her father, as resembling a yardstick, which, whilst it measures dowlas and diaper, can equally well measure tapestry and cloth of gold. He had always a new resource. When I was planting forest-trees, and had procured half a peck of acorns, he said that only a small portion of them would be sound, and proceeded to examine them, and select the sound ones. But finding this took time, he said, "I think, if you put them all into water, the good ones will sink"; which experiment we tried with success. He could plan a garden, or a house, or a barn; would have been competent to lead a "Pacific Exploring Expedition"; could give judicious counsel in the gravest private or public affairs.

He lived for the day, not cumbered and mortified by his memory. If he brought you yesterday a new proposition, he would bring you to-day another not less revolutionary. A very industrious man, and setting, like all highly organized men, a high value on his time, he seemed the only man of leisure in town, always ready for any excursion that promised well, or for conversation prolonged into late hours. His trenchant sense was never stopped by his rules of daily prudence, but was always up to the new occasion. He liked and used the simplest food, yet, when some one urged a vegetable diet, Thoreau thought all diets a very small matter, saying that "the man who shoots the buffalo lives better than the man who boards at the Graham House." He said,—"You can sleep near the railroad, and never be disturbed: Nature knows very well what sounds are worth attending to, and has made up her mind not to hear the railroad-whistle. But things respect the devout mind, and a mental ecstasy was never interrupted." He noted, what repeatedly befell him, that, after receiving from a distance a rare plant, he would presently find the same in his own haunts. And those pieces of luck which happen only to good players happened to him. One day, walking with a stranger, who inquired where Indian arrow-heads could be found, he replied, "Everywhere," and, stooping forward, picked one on the instant from the ground. At Mount Washington, in Tuckerman's Ravine, Thoreau had a bad fall, and sprained his foot. As he was in the act of getting up from his fall, he saw for the first time the leaves of the *Arnica mollis*.

His robust common sense, armed with stout hands, keen perceptions, and strong will, cannot yet account for the superiority which shone in his simple and hidden life. I must add the cardinal fact, that there was an excellent wisdom in him, proper to a rare class of men, which showed him the material world as a means and symbol. This discovery, which sometimes yields to poets a certain casual and interrupted light, serving for the ornament of their writing, was in him an unsleeping insight; and whatever faults or obstructions of temperament might cloud it, he was not disobedient to the heavenly vision. In his youth, he said, one day, "The other world is all my art: my pencils will draw no other; my jack-knife will cut nothing else; I do not use it as a means." This was the muse and genius that ruled his opinions, conversation, studies, work, and course of life. This made him a searching judge of men. At first glance he measured his companion, and, though insensible to some fine traits of culture, could very well report his weight and calibre. And this made the impression of genius which his conversation sometimes gave.

He understood the matter in hand at a glance, and saw the limitations and poverty of those he talked with, so that nothing seemed concealed from such terrible eyes. I have repeatedly known young men of sensibility converted in a moment to the belief that this was the man they were in search of, the man of men, who could tell them all they should do. His own dealing with them was never affectionate, but superior, didactic,—scorning their petty ways,—very slowly conceding, or not conceding at all, the promise of his society at their houses, or even at his own. "Would he not walk with them?" "He did not know. There was nothing so important to him as his walk; he had no walks to throw away on company." Visits were offered him from respectful parties, but he declined them. Admiring friends offered to carry him at their own cost to the Yellow-Stone River,—to the West Indies,—to South America. But though nothing could be more grave or considered than his refusals, they remind one in quite new relations of that fop Brummel's reply to the gentleman who offered him his carriage in a shower, "But where will *you* ride, then?"—and what accusing silences, and what searching and irresistible speeches, battering down all defences, his companions can remember!

Mr. Thoreau dedicated his genius with such entire love to the fields, hills, and waters of his native town, that he made them known and interesting to all reading Americans, and to people over the sea. The river on whose banks he was born and died he knew from its springs to its confluence with the Merrimack. He had made summer and winter observations on it for many years, and at every hour of the day and the night. The result of the recent survey of the Water Commissioners appointed by the State of Massachusetts he had reached by his private experiments, several years earlier. Every fact which occurs in the bed, on the banks, or in the air over it; the fishes, and their spawning and nests, their manners, their food; the shad-flies which fill the air on a certain evening once a year, and which are snapped at by the fishes so ravenously that many of these die of repletion; the conical heaps of small stones on the river-shallows, one of which heaps will sometimes overfill a cart,—these heaps the huge nests of small fishes; the birds which frequent the stream, heron, duck, sheldrake, loon, osprey; the snake, muskrat, otter, woodchuck, and fox, on the banks; the turtle, frog, hyla, and cricket, which make the banks vocal,—were all known to him, and, as it were, townsmen and fellow-creatures; so that he felt an absurdity or violence in any narrative of one of these by itself apart, and still more of its dimensions on an inch-rule, or in the exhibition of its skeleton, or the specimen of a squirrel or a bird in brandy. He liked to speak of the manners of the river, as itself a lawful creature, yet with exactness, and always to an observed fact. As he knew the river, so the ponds in this region.

One of the weapons he used, more important than microscope or alcohol-receiver to other investigators, was a whim which grew on him by indulgence, yet appeared in gravest statement, namely, of extolling his own town and neighborhood as the most favored centre for natural observation. He remarked that the Flora of Massachusetts embraced almost all the important plants of America,—most of the oaks, most of the willows, the best pines, the ash, the maple, the beech, the nuts. He returned Kane's "Arctic Voyage" to a friend of whom he had borrowed it, with the remark, that "most of the phenomena noted might be observed in Concord." He seemed a little envious of the Pole, for the co-incident sunrise and sunset, or five minutes' day after six months: a splendid fact, which Annursnuc had never afforded him. He found red snow in one of his walks, and told me that he expected to find yet the *Victoria regia* in Concord. He was the attorney of the indigenous plants, and owned to a preference of the weeds to the imported plants, as of the Indian to the civilized man,—and noticed, with pleasure, that the willow bean-poles of his neighbor had grown more than his beans. "See these weeds," he said, "which have been hoed at by a million farmers all spring and summer, and yet have prevailed, and just now come out triumphant over all lanes, pastures, fields, and gardens, such is their vigor. We have insulted them with low names, too,—as Pigweed, Wormwood, Chickweed, Shad-Blossom." He says, "They have brave names, too,—Ambrosia, Stellaria, Amelanchia, Amaranth, etc."

I think his fancy for referring everything to the meridian of Concord did not grow out of any ignorance or depreciation of other longitudes or latitudes, but was rather a playful expression of his conviction of the indifferency of all places, and that the best place for each is where he stands. He expressed it once in this wise:—"I think nothing is to be hoped from you, if this bit of mould under your feet is not sweeter to you to eat than any other in this world, or in any world."

The other weapon with which he conquered all obstacles in science was patience. He knew how to sit immovable, a part of the rock he rested on, until the bird, the reptile, the fish, which had retired from him, should come back, and resume its habits, nay, moved by curiosity, should come to him and watch him.

It was a pleasure and a privilege to walk with him. He knew the country like a fox or a bird, and passed through it as freely by paths of his own. He knew every track in the snow or on the ground, and what creature had taken this path before him. One must submit abjectly to such a guide, and the reward was great. Under his arm he carried an old music-book to press plants; in his pocket, his diary and pencil, a spy-glass for birds, microscope, jack-knife, and twine. He wore straw hat, stout shoes, strong gray trousers, to brave shrub-oaks and smilax, and to climb a tree for a hawk's or a squirrel's nest. He waded into the pool for the water-plants, and his strong legs were no insignificant part of his armor. On the day I speak of he looked for the Menyauthes, detected it across the wide pool, and, on examination of the florets, decided that it had been in flower five days. He drew out of his breast-pocket his diary, and read the names of all the plants that should bloom on this day, whereof he kept account as a banker when his notes fall due. The Cypripedium not due till to-morrow. He thought, that, if waked up from a trance, in this swamp, he could tell by the plants what time of the year it was within two days. The red-start was flying about, and presently the fine grosbeaks, whose brilliant scarlet makes the rash gazer wipe his eye, and whose fine clear note Thoreau compared to that of a tanager which has got rid of its hoarseness. Presently he heard a note which he called that of the night-warbler, a bird he had never identified, had been in search of twelve years, which always, when he saw it, was in the act of diving down into a tree or bush, and which it was vain to seek; the only bird that sings indifferently by night and by day. I told him he must beware of finding and booking it, lest life should have nothing more to show him. He said, "What you seek in vain for, half your life, one day you come full upon, all the family at dinner. You seek it like a dream, and as soon as you find it you become its prey."

His interest in the flower or the bird lay very deep in his mind, was connected with Nature,—and the meaning of Nature was never attempted to be defined by him. He would not offer a memoir of his observations to the Natural History Society. "Why should I? To detach the description from its connections in my mind would make it no longer true or valuable to me: and they do not wish what belongs to it." His power of observation seemed to indicate additional senses. He saw as with microscope, heard as with ear-trumpet, and his memory was a photographic register of all he saw and heard. And yet none knew better than he that it is not the fact that imports, but the impression or effect of the fact on your mind. Every fact lay in glory in his mind, a type of the order and beauty of the whole.

His determination on Natural History was organic. He confessed that he sometimes felt like a hound or a panther, and, if born among Indians, would have been a fell hunter. But, restrained by his Massachusetts culture, he played out the game in this mild form of botany and ichthyology. His intimacy with animals suggested what Thomas Fuller records of Butler the apiologist, that "either he had told the bees things or the bees had told him." Snakes coiled round his leg; the fishes swam into his hand, and he took them out of the water; he pulled the woodchuck out of its hole by the tail, and took the foxes under his protection from the hunters. Our naturalist had perfect magnanimity; he had no secrets: he would carry you to the heron's haunt, or even to his most prized botanical swamp,—possibly knowing that you could never find it again, yet willing to take his risks.

No college ever offered him a diploma, or a professor's chair; no academy made him its corresponding secretary, its discoverer, or even its member. Whether these learned bodies feared the satire of his presence. Yet so much knowledge of Nature's secret and genius few others possessed, none in a more large and religious synthesis. For not a particle of respect had he to the opinions of any man or body of men, but homage solely to the truth itself; and as he discovered everywhere among doctors some leaning of courtesy, it discredited them. He grew to be revered and admired by his townsmen, who had at first known him only as an oddity. The farmers who employed him as a surveyor soon discovered his rare accuracy and skill, his knowledge of their lands, of trees, of birds, of Indian remains, and the like, which enabled him to tell every farmer more than he knew before of his own farm; so that he began to feel a little as if Mr. Thoreau had better rights in his land than he. They felt, too, the superiority of character which addressed all men with a native authority.

Indian relics abound in Concord,—arrow-heads, stone chisels, pestles, and fragments of pottery; and on the river-bank, large heaps of clam-shells and ashes mark spots which the savages frequented. These, and every circumstance touching the Indian, were important in his eyes. His visits to Maine were chiefly for love of the Indian. He had the satisfaction of seeing the manufacture of the bark-canoe, as well as of trying his hand in its management on the rapids. He was inquisitive about the making of the stone arrow-head, and in his last days charged a youth setting out for the Rocky Mountains to find an Indian who could tell him that: "It was well worth a visit to California to learn it." Occasionally, a small party of Penobscot Indians would visit Concord, and pitch their tents for a few weeks in summer on the river-bank. He failed not to make acquaintance with the best of them; though he well knew that asking questions of Indians is like catechizing beavers and rabbits. In his last visit to Maine he had great satisfaction from Joseph Polis, an intelligent Indian of Oldtown, who was his guide for some weeks.

He was equally interested in every natural fact. The depth of his perception found likeness of law throughout Nature, and I know not any genius who so swiftly inferred universal law from the single fact. He was no pedant of a department. His eye was open to beauty, and his ear to music. He found these, not in rare conditions, but wheresoever he went. He thought the best of music was in single strains; and he found poetic suggestion in the humming of the telegraph-wire.

His poetry might be bad or good; he no doubt wanted a lyric facility and technical skill; but he had the source of poetry in his spiritual perception. He was a good reader and critic, and his judgment on poetry was to the ground of it. He could not be deceived as to the presence or absence of the poetic element in any composition, and his thirst for this made him negligent and perhaps scornful of superficial graces. He would pass by many delicate rhythms, but he would have detected every live stanza or line in a volume, and knew very well where to find an equal poetic charm in prose. He was so enamored of the spiritual beauty that he held all actual written poems in very light esteem in the comparison. He admired Æschylus and Pindar; but, when some one was commending them, he said that "Æschylus and the Greeks, in describing Apollo and Orpheus, had given no song, or no good one. They ought not to have moved trees, but to have chanted to the gods such a hymn as would have sung all their old ideas out of their heads, and new ones in." His own verses are often rude and defective. The gold does not yet run pure, is drossy and crude. The thyme and marjoram are not yet honey. But if he want lyric fineness and technical merits, if he have not the poetic temperament, he never lacks the casual thought, showing that his genius was better than his talent. He knew the worth of the Imagination for the uplifting and consolation of human life, and liked to throw every thought into a symbol. The fact you tell is of no value, but only the impression. For this reason his presence was poetic, always piqued the curiosity to know more deeply the secrets of his mind. He had many reserves, an unwillingness to exhibit to profane eyes what was still sacred in his own, and knew well how to throw a poetic veil over his experience. All readers of "Walden" will remember his mythical record of his disappointments:—

"I long ago lost a hound, a bay horse, and a turtle-dove, and am still on their trail. Many are the travellers I have spoken concerning them, describing their tracks, and what calls they answered to. I have met one or two who had heard the hound, and the tramp of the horse, and even seen the dove disappear behind a cloud; and they seemed as anxious to recover them as if they had lost them themselves."

His riddles were worth the reading, and I confide, that, if at any time I do not understand the expression, it is yet just. Such was the wealth of his truth that it was not worth his while to use words in vain. His poem entitled "Sympathy" reveals the tenderness under that triple steel of stoicism, and the intellectual subtilty it could animate. His classic poem on "Smoke" suggests Simonides, but is better than any poem of Simonides. His biography is in his verses. His habitual thought makes all his poetry a hymn to the Cause of causes, the Spirit which vivifies and controls his own:—

> "I hearing get, who had but ears,
>   And sight, who had but eyes before;
> I moments live, who lived but years,
>   And truth discern, who knew but learning's lore."

And still more in these religious lines:—

> "Now chiefly is my natal hour,
>   And only now my prime of life;
> I will not doubt the love untold,
>   Which not my worth or want hath bought,
>   Which wooed me young, and wooes me old,
>   And to this evening hath me brought."

Whilst he used in his writings a certain petulance of remark in reference to churches or churchmen, he was a person of a rare, tender, and absolute religion, a person incapable of any profanation, by act or by thought. Of course, the same isolation which belonged to his original thinking and living detached him from the social religious forms. This is neither to be censured nor regretted. Aristotle long ago explained it, when he said, "One who surpasses his fellow-citizens in virtue is no longer a part of the city. Their law is not for him, since he is a law to himself."

Thoreau was sincerity itself, and might fortify the convictions of prophets in the ethical laws by his holy living. It was an affirmative experience which refused to be set aside. A truth-speaker he, capable of the most deep and strict conversation; a physician to the wounds of any soul; a friend, knowing not only the secret of friendship, but almost worshipped by those few persons who resorted to him as their confessor and prophet, and knew the deep value of his mind and great heart. He thought that without religion or devotion of some kind nothing great was ever accomplished: and he thought that the bigoted sectarian had better bear this in mind.

His virtues, of course, sometimes ran into extremes. It was easy to trace to the inexorable demand on all for exact truth that austerity which made this willing hermit more solitary even than he wished. Himself of a perfect probity, he required not less of others. He had a disgust at crime, and no worldly success would cover it. He detected paltering as readily in dignified and prosperous persons as in beggars, and with equal scorn. Such dangerous frankness was in his dealing that his admirers called him "that terrible Thoreau," as if he spoke when silent, and was still present when he had departed. I think the severity of his ideal interfered to deprive him of a healthy sufficiency of human society.

The habit of a realist to find things the reverse of their appearance inclined him to put every statement in a paradox. A certain habit of antagonism defaced his earlier writings, —a trick of rhetoric not quite outgrown in his later, of substituting for the obvious word and thought its diametrical opposite. He praised wild mountains and winter forests for their domestic air, in snow and ice he would find sultriness, and commended the wilderness for resembling Rome and Paris. "It was so dry, that you might call it wet."

The tendency to magnify the moment, to read all the laws of Nature in the one object or one combination under your eye, is of course comic to those who do not share the philosopher's perception of identity. To him there was no such thing as size. The pond was a small ocean; the Atlantic, a large Walden Pond. He referred every minute fact to cosmical laws. Though he meant to be just, he seemed haunted by a certain chronic assumption that the science of the day pretended completeness, and he had just found out that the *savans* had neglected to discriminate a particular botanical variety, had failed to describe the seeds or count the sepals. "That is to say," we replied, "the blockheads were not born in Concord; but who said they were? It was their unspeakable misfortune to be born in London, or Paris, or Rome; but, poor fellows, they did what they could, considering that they never saw Bateman's Pond, or Nine-Acre Corner, or Becky-Stow's Swamp. Besides, what were you sent into the world for, but to add this observation?"

Had his genius been only contemplative, he had been fitted

to his life, but with his energy and practical ability he seemed born for great enterprise and for command; and I so much regret the loss of his rare powers of action, that I cannot help counting it a fault in him that he had no ambition. Wanting this, instead of engineering for all America, he was the captain of a huckleberry-party. Pounding beans is good to the end of pounding empires one of these days; but if, at the end of years, it is still only beans!

But these foibles, real or apparent, were fast vanishing in the incessant growth of a spirit so robust and wise, and which effaced its defeats with new triumphs. His study of Nature was a perpetual ornament to him, and inspired his friends with curiosity to see the world through his eyes, and to hear his adventures. They possessed every kind of interest.

He had many elegances of his own, whilst he scoffed at conventional elegance. Thus, he could not bear to hear the sound of his own steps, the grit of gravel; and therefore never willingly walked in the road, but in the grass, on mountains and in woods. His senses were acute, and he remarked that by night every dwelling-house gives out bad air, like a slaughter-house. He liked the pure fragrance of melilot. He honored certain plants with special regard, and, over all, the pond-lily,—then, the gentian, and the *Mikania scandens,* and "life-everlasting," and a bass-tree which he visited every year when it bloomed, in the middle of July. He thought the scent a more oracular inquisition than the sight,—more oracular and trustworthy. The scent, of course, reveals what is concealed from the other senses. By it he detected earthiness. He delighted in echoes, and said they were almost the only kind of kindred voices that he heard. He loved Nature so well, was so happy in her solitude, that he became very jealous of cities, and the sad work which their refinements and artifices made with man and his dwelling. The axe was always destroying his forest. "Thank God," he said, "they cannot cut down the clouds!" "All kinds of figures are drawn on the blue ground with his fibrous white paint."

I subjoin a few sentences taken from his unpublished manuscripts, not only as records of his thought and feeling, but for their power of description and literary excellence.

"Some circumstantial evidence is very strong, as when you find a trout in the milk."

"The chub is a soft fish, and tastes like boiled brown paper salted."

"The youth gets together his materials to build a bridge to the moon, or, perchance, a palace or temple on the earth, and at length the middle-aged man concludes to build a wood-shed with them."

"The locust z—ing."

"Devil's-needles zigzagging along the Nut-Meadow brook."

"Sugar is not so sweet to the palate as sound to the healthy ear."

"I put on some hemlock-boughs, and the rich salt crackling of their leaves was like mustard to the ear, the crackling of uncountable regiments. Dead trees love the fire."

"The bluebird carries the sky on his back."

"The tanager flies through the green foliage as if it would ignite the leaves."

"If I wish for a horse-hair for my compass-sight, I must go to the stable; but the hair-bird, with her sharp eyes goes to the road."

"Immortal water, alive even to the superficies."

"Fire is the most tolerable third party."

"Nature made ferns for pure leaves, to show what she could do in that line."

"No tree has so fair a bole and so handsome an instep as the beech."

"How did these beautiful rainbow-tints get into the shell of the fresh-water clam, buried in the mud at the bottom of our dark river?"

"Hard are the times when the infant's shoes are second-foot."

"We are strictly confined to our men to whom we give liberty."

"Nothing is so much to be feared as fear. Atheism may comparatively be popular with God himself."

"Of what significance the things you can forget? A little thought is sexton to all the world."

"How can we expect a harvest of thought who have not had a seed-time of character?"

"Only he can be trusted with gifts who can present a face of bronze to expectations."

"I ask to be melted. You can only ask of the metals that they be tender to the fire that melts them. To nought else can they be tender."

There is a flower known to botanists, one of the same

genus with our summer plant called "Life-Everlasting," a *Gnaphalium* like that, which grows on the most inaccessible cliffs of the Tyrolese mountains, where the chamois dare hardly venture, and which the hunter, tempted by its beauty, and by his love, (for it is immensely valued by the Swiss maidens,) climbs the cliffs to gather, and is sometimes found dead at the foot, with the flower in his hand. It is called by botanists the *Gnaphalium leontopodium*, but by the Swiss *Edelweisse,* which signifies *Noble Purity*. Thoreau seemed to me living in the hope to gather this plant, which belonged to him of right. The scale on which his studies proceeded was so large as to require longevity, and we were the less prepared for his sudden disappearance. The country knows not yet, or in the least part, how great a son it has lost. It seems an injury that he should leave in the midst his broken task, which none else can finish,—a kind of indignity to so noble a soul, that it should depart out of Nature before yet he has been really shown to his peers for what he is. But he, at least, is content. His soul was made for the noblest society; he had in a short life exhausted the capabilities of this world; wherever there is knowledge, wherever there is virtue, wherever there is beauty, he will find a home.

1862

EDUCATION.*

> With the key of the secret he marches faster
> From strength to strength, and for night brings day,
> While classes or tribes too weak to master
> The flowing conditions of life, give way.

. . . . .

There comes the period of the imagination to each, a later youth; the power of beauty, the power of books, of poetry. Culture makes his books realities to him, their characters more brilliant, more effective on his mind, than his actual mates. Do not spare to put novels into the hands of young people as an occasional holiday and experiment; but, above all, good poetry in all kinds, epic, tragedy, lyric. If we can touch the imagination, we serve them, they will never forget

* From *Lectures and Biographical Sketches*.

it. Let him read "Tom Brown at Rugby," read "Tom Brown at Oxford,"—better yet, read "Hodson's Life"—Hodson who took prisoner the king of Delhi. They teach the same truth, —a trust, against all appearances, against all privations, in your own worth, and not in tricks, plotting, or patronage.

I believe that our own experience instructs us that the secret of Education lies in respecting the pupil. It is not for you to choose what he shall know, what he shall do. It is chosen and foreordained, and he only holds the key to his own secret. By your tampering and thwarting and too much governing he may be hindered from his end and kept out of his own. Respect the child. Wait and see the new product of Nature. Nature loves analogies, but not repetitions. Respect the child. Be not too much his parent. Trespass not on his solitude.

But I hear the outcry which replies to this suggestion:— Would you verily throw up the reins of public and private discipline; would you leave the young child to the mad career of his own passions and whimsies, and call this anarchy a respect for the child's nature? I answer,—Respect the child, respect him to the end, but also respect yourself. Be the companion of his thought, the friend of his friendship, the lover of his virtue,—but no kinsman of his sin. Let him find you so true to yourself that you are the irreconcilable hater of his vice and imperturbable slighter of his trifling.

The two points in a boy's training are, to keep his *naturel* and train off all but that:—to keep his *naturel*, but stop off his uproar, fooling and horse-play;—keep his nature and arm it with knowledge in the very direction in which it points. Here are the two capital facts, Genius and Drill. The first is the inspiration in the well-born healthy child, the new perception he has of nature. Somewhat he sees in forms or hears in music or apprehends in mathematics, or believes practicable in mechanics or possible in political society, which no one else sees or hears or believes. This is the perpetual romance of new life, the invasion of God into the old dead world, when he sends into quiet houses a young soul with a thought which is not met, looking for something which is not there, but which ought to be there: the thought is dim but it is sure, and he casts about restless for means and masters to verify it; he makes wild attempts to explain himself and in-voke the aid and consent of the bystanders. Baffled for want of language and methods to convey his meaning, not yet clear to himself, he conceives that though not in this house or town, yet in some other house or town is the wise master who can put him in possession of the rules and instruments to execute his will. Happy this child with a bias, with a thought which entrances him, leads him, now into deserts now into cities, the fool of an idea. Let him follow it in good and in evil report, in good or bad company; it will justify itself; it will lead him at last into the illustrious society of the lovers of truth.

In London, in a private company, I became acquainted with a gentleman, Sir Charles Fellowes, who, being at Xanthus, in the Ægean Sea, had seen a Turk point with his staff to some carved work on the corner of a stone almost buried in the soil. Fellowes scraped away the dirt, was struck with the beauty of the sculptured ornaments, and, looking about him, observed more blocks and fragments like this. He returned to the spot, procured laborers and uncovered many blocks. He went back to England, bought a Greek grammar and learned the language; he read history and studied ancient art to explain his stones; he interested Gibson the sculptor; he invoked the assistance of the English Government; he called in the succor of Sir Humphry Davy to analyze the pigments; of experts in coins, of scholars and connoisseurs; and at last in his third visit brought home to England such statues and marble reliefs and such careful plans that he was able to reconstruct, in the British Museum where it now stands, the perfect model of the Ionic trophy-monument, fifty years older than the Parthenon of Athens, and which had been destroyed by earthquakes, then by iconoclast Christians, then by savage Turks. But mark that in the task he had achieved an excellent education, and become associated with distinguished scholars whom he had interested in his pursuit; in short, had formed a college for himself; the enthusiast had found the master, the masters, whom he sought. Always genius seeks genius, desires nothing so much as to be a pupil and to find those who can lend it aid to perfect itself.

Nor are the two elements, enthusiasm and drill, incompatible. Accuracy is essential to beauty. The very definition of the intellect is Aristotle's: "that by which we know terms or boundaries." Give a boy accurate perceptions. Teach him the difference between the similar and the same. Make him call things by their right names. Pardon in him no blunder.

Then he will give you solid satisfaction as long as he lives. It is better to teach the child arithmetic and Latin grammar than rhetoric or moral philosophy, because they require exactitude of performance; it is made certain that the lesson is mastered, and that power of performance is worth more than the knowledge. He can learn anything which is important to him now that the power to learn is secured: as mechanics say, when one has learned the use of tools, it is easy to work at a new craft.

Letter by letter, syllable by syllable, the child learns to read, and in good time can convey to all the domestic circle the sense of Shakespeare. By many steps each just as short, the stammering boy and the hesitating collegian, in the school debate, in college clubs, in mock court, comes at last to full, secure, triumphant unfolding of his thought in the popular assembly, with a fullness of power that makes all the steps forgotten.

But this function of opening and feeding the human mind is not to be fulfilled by any mechanical or military method; is not to be trusted to any skill less large than Nature itself. You must not neglect the form, but you must secure the essentials. It is curious how perverse and intermeddling we are, and what vast pains and cost we incur to do wrong. Whilst we all know in our own experience and apply natural methods in our own business,—in education our common sense fails us, and we are continually trying costly machinery against nature, in patent schools and academies and in great colleges and universities.

The natural method forever confutes our experiments, and we must still come back to it. The whole theory of the school is on the nurse's or mother's knee. The child is as hot to learn as the mother is to impart. There is mutual delight. The joy of our childhood in hearing beautiful stories from some skilful aunt who loves to tell them, must be repeated in youth. The boy wishes to learn to skate, to coast, to catch a fish in the brook, to hit a mark with a snowball or a stone; and a boy a little older is just as well pleased to teach him these sciences. Not less delightful is the mutual pleasure of teaching and learning the secret of algebra, or of chemistry, or of good reading and good recitation of poetry or of prose, or of chosen facts in history or in biography.

Nature provided for the communication of thought, by planting with it in the receiving mind a fury to impart it. 'T is so in every art, in every science. One burns to tell the new fact, the other burns to hear it. See how far a young doctor will ride or walk to witness a new surgical operation. I have seen a carriage-maker's shop emptied of all its workmen into the street, to scrutinize a new pattern from New York. So in literature, the young man who has taste for poetry, for fine images, for noble thoughts, is insatiable for this nourishment, and forgets all the world for the more learned friend,—who finds equal joy in dealing out his treasures.

Happy the natural college thus self-instituted around every natural teacher; the young men of Athens around Socrates; of Alexandria around Plotinus; of Paris around Abelard; of Germany around Fichte, or Niebuhr, or Goethe: in short the natural sphere of every leading mind. But the moment this is organized, difficulties begin. The college was to be the nurse and home of genius; but, though every young man is born with some determination in his nature, and is a potential genius; is at last to be one; it is, in the most, obstructed and delayed, and, whatever they may hereafter be, their senses are now opened in advance of their minds. They are more sensual than intellectual. Appetite and indolence they have, but no enthusiasm. These come in numbers to the college: few geniuses: and the teaching comes to be arranged for these many, and not for those few. Hence the instruction seems to require skilful tutors, of accurate and systematic mind, rather than ardent and inventive masters. Besides, the youth of genius are eccentric, won't drill, are irritable, uncertain, explosive, solitary, not men of the world, not good for every-day association. You have to work for large classes instead of individuals; you must lower your flag and reef your sails to wait for the dull sailors; you grow departmental, routinary, military almost with your discipline and college police. But what doth such a school to form a great and heroic character? What abiding Hope can it inspire? What Reformer will it nurse? What poet will it breed to sing to the human race? What discoverer of Nature's laws will it prompt to enrich us by disclosing in the mind the statute which all matter must obey? What fiery soul will it send out to warm a nation with his charity? What tranquil mind will it have fortified to walk with meekness in private and obscure duties, to wait and to suffer? Is it not manifest that our academic institutions should have a wider scope; that they should not be timid and keep the ruts of the last generation, but that wise men thinking for themselves and heartily seeking the good of mankind, and counting the cost of innovation, should dare to arouse the young to a just and heroic life; that the moral nature should be addressed in the school-room, and children should be treated as the high-born candidates of truth and virtue?

So to regard the young child, the young man, requires, no doubt, rare patience: a patience that nothing but faith in the remedial forces of the soul can give. You see his sensualism; you see his want of those tastes and perceptions which make the power and safety of your character. Very likely. But he has something else. If he has his own vice, he has its correlative virtue. Every mind should be allowed to make its own statement in action, and its balance will appear. In these judgments one needs that foresight which was attributed to an eminent reformer, of whom it was said "his patience could see in the bud of the aloe the blossom at the end of a hundred years." Alas for the cripple Practice when it seeks to come up with the bird Theory, which flies before it. Try your design on the best school. The scholars are of all ages and temperaments and capacities. It is difficult to class them, some are too young, some are slow, some perverse. Each requires so much consideration, that the morning hope of the teacher, of a day of love and progress, is often closed at evening by despair. Each single case, the more it is considered, shows more to be done; and the strict conditions of the hours, on one side, and the number of tasks, on the other. Whatever becomes of our method, the conditions stand fast,—six hours, and thirty, fifty, or a hundred and fifty pupils. Something must be done, and done speedily, and in this distress the wisest are tempted to adopt violent means, to proclaim martial law, corporal punishment, mechanical arrangement, bribes, spies, wrath, main strength and ignorance, in lieu of that wise genial providential influence they had hoped, and yet hope at some future day to adopt. Of course the devotion to details reacts injuriously on the teacher. He cannot indulge his genius, he cannot delight in personal relations with young friends, when his eye is always on the clock, and twenty classes are to be dealt with before the day is done. Besides, how can he please himself with genius, and foster modest virtue? A sure proportion of rogue and dunce finds its way into every school and requires a cruel share of time, and the gentle teacher, who wished to be a

Providence to youth, is grown a martinet, sore with suspicions; knows as much vice as the judge of a police court, and his love of learning is lost in the routine of grammars and books of elements.

A rule is so easy that it does not need a man to apply it; an automaton, a machine, can be made to keep a school so. It facilitates labor and thought so much that there is always the temptation in large schools to omit the endless task of meeting the wants of each single mind, and to govern by steam. But it is at frightful cost. Our modes of Education aim to expedite, to save labor; to do for masses what cannot be done for masses, what must be done reverently, one by one: say rather, the whole world is needed for the tuition of each pupil. The advantages of this system of emulation and display are so prompt and obvious, it is such a time-saver, it is so energetic on slow and on bad natures, and is of so easy application, needing no sage or poet, but any tutor or schoolmaster in his first term can apply it,—that it is not strange that this calomel of culture should be a popular medicine. On the other hand, total abstinence from this drug, and the adoption of simple discipline and the following of nature, involves at once immense claims on the time, the thoughts, on the life of the teacher. It requires time, use, insight, event, all the great lessons and assistances of God; and only to think of using it implies character and profoundness; to enter on this course of discipline is to be good and great. It is precisely analogous to the difference between the use of corporal punishment and the methods of love. It is so easy to bestow on a bad boy a blow, overpower him, and get obedience without words, that in this world of hurry and distraction, who can wait for the returns of reason and the conquest of self; in the uncertainty too whether that will ever come? And yet the familiar observation of the universal compensations might suggest the fear that so summary a stop of a bad humor was more jeopardous than its continuance.

Now the correction of this quack practice is to import into Education the wisdom of life. Leave this military hurry and adopt the pace of Nature. Her secret is patience. Do you know how the naturalist learns all the secrets of the forest, of plants, of birds, of beasts, of reptiles, of fishes, of the rivers and the sea? When he goes into the woods the birds fly before him and he finds none; when he goes to the river bank, the fish and the reptile swim away and leave him alone.

His secret is patience; he sits down, and sits still; he is a statue; he is a log. These creatures have no value for their time, and he must put as low a rate on his. By dint of obstinate sitting still, reptile, fish, bird and beast, which all wish to return to their haunts, begin to return. He sits still; if they approach, he remains passive as the stone he sits upon. They lose their fear. They have curiosity too about him. By and by the curiosity masters the fear, and they come swimming, creeping and flying towards him; and as he is still immovable, they not only resume their haunts and their ordinary labors and manners, show themselves to him in their work-day trim, but also volunteer some degree of advances towards fellowship and good understanding with a biped who behaves so civilly and well. Can you not baffle the impatience and passion of the child by your tranquillity? Can you not wait for him, as Nature and Providence do? Can you not keep for his mind and ways, for his secret, the same curiosity you give to the squirrel, snake, rabbit, and the sheldrake and the deer? He has a secret; wonderful methods in him; he is,—every child,—a new style of man; give him time and opportunity. Talk of Columbus and Newton! I tell you the child just born in yonder hovel is the beginning of a revolution as great as theirs. But you must have the believing and prophetic eye. Have the self-command you wish to inspire. Your teaching and discipline must have the reserve and taciturnity of Nature. Teach them to hold their tongues by holding your own. Say little; do not snarl; do not chide; but govern by the eye. See what they need, and that the right thing is done.

I confess myself utterly at a loss in suggesting particular reforms in our ways of teaching. No discretion that can be lodged with a school-committee, with the overseers or visitors of an academy, of a college, can at all avail to reach these difficulties and perplexities, but they solve themselves when we leave institutions and address individuals. The will, the male power, organizes, imposes its own thought and wish on others, and makes that military eye which controls boys as it controls men; admirable in its results, a fortune to him who has it, and only dangerous when it leads the workman to overvalue and overuse it and precludes him from finer means. Sympathy, the female force,—which they must use who have not the first,—deficient in instant control and the breaking down of resistance, is more subtle and lasting and creative.

I advise teachers to cherish mother-wit. I assume that you will keep the grammar, reading, writing and arithmetic in order; 't is easy and of course you will. But smuggle in a little contraband wit, fancy, imagination, thought. If you have a taste which you have suppressed because it is not shared by those about you, tell them that. Set this law up, whatever becomes of the rules of the school: they must not whisper, much less talk; but if one of the young people says a wise thing, greet it, and let all the children clap their hands. They shall have no book but school-books in the room; but if one has brought in a Plutarch or Shakespeare or Don Quixote or Goldsmith or any other good book, and understands what he reads, put him at once at the head of the class. Nobody shall be disorderly, or leave his desk without permission, but if a boy runs from his bench, or a girl, because the fire falls, or to check some injury that a little dastard is inflicting behind his desk on some helpless sufferer, take away the medal from the head of the class and give it on the instant to the brave rescuer. If a child happens to show that he knows any fact about astronomy, or plants, or birds, or rocks, or history, that interests him and you, hush all the classes and encourage him to tell it so that all may hear. Then you have made your school-room like the world. Of course you will insist on modesty in the children, and respect to their teachers, but if the boy stops you in your speech, cries out that you are wrong and sets you right, hug him!

To whatsoever upright mind, to whatsoever beating heart I speak, to you it is committed to educate men. By simple living, by an illimitable soul, you inspire, you correct, you instruct, you raise, you embellish all. By your own act you teach the beholder how to do the practicable. According to the depth from which you draw your life, such is the depth not only of your strenuous effort, but of your manners and presence.

The beautiful nature of the world has here blended your happiness with your power. Work straight on in absolute duty, and you lend an arm and an encouragement to all the youth of the universe. Consent yourself to be an organ of your highest thought, and lo! suddenly you put all men in your debt, and are the fountain of an energy that goes pulsing on with waves of benefit to the borders of society, to the circumference of things.

1863, 1864

III. POEMS

GRACE.

How much, preventing God, how much I owe
To the defences thou hast round me set;
Example, custom, fear, occasion slow,—
These scorned bondmen were my parapet.
I dare not peep over this parapet
To gauge with glance the roaring gulf below,
The depths of sin to which I had descended,
Had not these me against myself defended.

1833   1842

THE RHODORA:

ON BEING ASKED, WHENCE IS THE FLOWER?

In May, when sea-winds pierced our solitudes,
I found the fresh Rhodora in the woods,
Spreading its leafless blooms in a damp nook,
To please the desert and the sluggish brook.
The purple petals, fallen in the pool,
Made the black water with their beauty gay;
Here might the red-bird come his plumes to cool,
And court the flower that cheapens his array.
Rhodora! if the sages ask thee why
This charm is wasted on the earth and sky,
Tell them, dear, that if eyes were made for seeing,
Then Beauty is its own excuse for being:
Why thou wert there, O rival of the rose!
I never thought to ask, I never knew:
But, in my simple ignorance, suppose
The self-same Power that brought me there brought you.

1834   1839

EACH AND ALL.

LITTLE thinks, in the field, yon red-cloaked clown
Of thee from the hill-top looking down;
The heifer that lows in the upland farm,
Far-heard, lows not thine ear to charm;
The sexton, tolling his bell at noon,
Deems not that great Napoleon
Stops his horse, and lists with delight,
Whilst his files sweep round yon Alpine height;
Nor knowest thou what argument
Thy life to thy neighbor's creed has lent.
All are needed by each one;
Nothing is fair or good alone.
I thought the sparrow's note from heaven,
Singing at dawn on the alder bough;
I brought him home, in his nest, at even;
He sings the song, but it cheers not now,
For I did not bring home the river and sky;—
He sang to my ear,—they sang to my eye.
The delicate shells lay on the shore;
The bubbles of the latest wave
Fresh pearls to their enamel gave,
And the bellowing of the savage sea
Greeted their safe escape to me.
I wiped away the weeds and foam,
I fetched my sea-born treasures home;
But the poor, unsightly, noisome things
Had left their beauty on the shore
With the sun and the sand and the wild uproar.
The lover watched his graceful maid,
As 'mid the virgin train she strayed,
Nor knew her beauty's best attire
Was woven still by the snow-white choir.
At last she came to his hermitage,
Like the bird from the woodlands to the cage;—
The gay enchantment was undone,
A gentle wife, but fairy none.
Then I said, 'I covet truth;
Beauty is unripe childhood's cheat;

I leave it behind with the games of youth:'—
As I spoke, beneath my feet
The ground-pine curled its pretty wreath,
Running over the club-moss burrs;
I inhaled the violet's breath;
Around me stood the oaks and firs;
Pine-cones and acorns lay on the ground;
Over me soared the eternal sky,
Full of light and of deity;
Again I saw, again I heard,
The rolling river, the morning bird;—
Beauty through my senses stole;
I yielded myself to the perfect whole.
1834(?)   1839

THE SNOW-STORM.

ANNOUNCED by all the trumpets of the sky,
Arrives the snow, and, driving o'er the fields,
Seems nowhere to alight: the whited air
Hides hills and woods, the river, and the heaven,
And veils the farm-house at the garden's end.
The sled and traveller stopped, the courier's feet
Delayed, all friends shut out, the housemates sit
Around the radiant fireplace, enclosed
In a tumultuous privacy of storm.

Come see the north wind's masonry.
Out of an unseen quarry evermore
Furnished with tile, the fierce artificer
Curves his white bastions with projected roof
Round every windward stake, or tree, or door.
Speeding, the myriad-handed, his wild work
So fanciful, so savage, nought cares he
For number or proportion. Mockingly,
On coop or kennel he hangs Parian wreaths;
A swan-like form invests the hidden thorn;
Fills up the farmer's lane from wall to wall,

Maugre the farmer's sighs; and at the gate
A tapering turret overtops the work.
And when his hours are numbered, and the world
Is all his own, retiring, as he were not,
Leaves, when the sun appears, astonished Art
To mimic in slow structures, stone by stone,
Built in an age, the mad wind's night-work,
The frolic architecture of the snow.

1834–1835(?)   1841

THE HUMBLE–BEE.

BURLY, dozing humble-bee,
Where thou art is clime for me.
Let them sail for Porto Rique,
Far-off heats through seas to seek;
I will follow thee alone,
Thou animated torrid-zone!
Zigzag steerer, desert cheerer,
Let me chase thy waving lines;
Keep me nearer, me thy hearer,
Singing over shrubs and vines.

Insect lover of the sun,
Joy of thy dominion!
Sailor of the atmosphere;
Swimmer through the waves of air;
Voyager of light and noon;
Epicurean of June;
Wait, I prithee, till I come
Within earshot of thy hum,—
All without is martyrdom.

When the south wind, in May days,
With a net of shining haze
Silvers the horizon wall,
And with softness touching all,
Tints the human countenance
With a color of romance,

And infusing subtle heats,
Turns the sod to violets,
Thou, in sunny solitudes,
Rover of the underwoods,
The green silence dost displace
With thy mellow, breezy bass.

Hot midsummer's petted crone,
Sweet to me thy drowsy tone
Tells of countless sunny hours,
Long days, and solid banks of flowers;
Of gulfs of sweetness without bound
In Indian wildernesses found;
Of Syrian peace, immortal leisure,
Firmest cheer, and bird-like pleasure.
Aught unsavory or unclean
Hath my insect never seen;
But violets and bilberry bells,
Maple-sap and daffodels,
Grass with green flag half-mast high,
Succory to match the sky,
Columbine with horn of honey,
Scented fern, and agrimony,
Clover, catchfly, adder's-tongue
And brier-roses, dwelt among;
All beside was unknown waste,
All was picture as he passed.

Wiser far than human seer,
Yellow-breeched philosopher!
Seeing only what is fair,
Sipping only what is sweet,
Thou dost mock at fate and care,
Leave the chaff, and take the wheat
When the fierce northwestern blast
Cools sea and land so far and fast,
Thou already slumberest deep;
Woe and want thou canst outsleep;
Want and woe, which torture us,
Thy sleep makes ridiculous.

1837   1839

CONCORD HYMN:

SUNG AT THE COMPLETION OF THE BATTLE MONUMENT, JULY 4, 1837.

By the rude bridge that arched the flood,
  Their flag to April's breeze unfurled,
Here once the embattled farmers stood,
  And fired the shot heard round the world.

The foe long since in silence slept;
  Alike the conqueror silent sleeps;
And Time the ruined bridge has swept
  Down the dark stream which seaward creeps.

On this green bank, by this soft stream,
  We set to-day a votive stone;
That memory may their deed redeem,
  When, like our sires, our sons are gone.

Spirit, that made those heroes dare
  To die, and leave their children free,
Bid Time and Nature gently spare
  The shaft we raise to them and thee.

1837   1837

THE PROBLEM.

I LIKE a church; I like a cowl;
I love a prophet of the soul;
And on my heart monastic aisles
Fall like sweet strains, or pensive smiles:
Yet not for all his faith can see
Would I that cowlèd churchman be.

Why should the vest on him allure,
Which I could not on me endure?

Not from a vain or shallow thought
His awful Jove young Phidias brought;
Never from lips of cunning fell
The thrilling Delphic oracle;
Out from the heart of nature rolled
The burdens of the Bible old;
The litanies of nations came,
Like the volcano's tongue of flame,
Up from the burning core below,—
The canticles of love and woe:
The hand that rounded Peter's dome
And groined the aisles of Christian Rome
Wrought in a sad sincerity;
Himself from God he could not free;
He builded better than he knew;—
The conscious stone to beauty grew.

Know'st thou what wove yon woodbird's nest
Of leaves, and feathers from her breast?
Or how the fish outbuilt her shell,
Painting with morn each annual cell?
Or how the sacred pine-tree adds
To her old leaves new myriads?
Such and so grew these holy piles,
Whilst love and terror laid the tiles.
Earth proudly wears the Parthenon,
As the best gem upon her zone,
And Morning opes with haste her lids
To gaze upon the Pyramids;
O'er England's abbeys bends the sky,
As on its friends, with kindred eye;
For out of Thought's interior sphere
These wonders rose to upper air;
And Nature gladly gave them place,
Adopted them into her race,
And granted them an equal date
With Andes and with Ararat.

These temples grew as grows the grass;
Art might obey, but not surpass.
The passive Master lent his hand
To the vast soul that o'er him planned;
And the same power that reared the shrine

Bestrode the tribes that knelt within.
Ever the fiery Pentecost
Girds with one flame the countless host,
Trances the heart through chanting choirs,
And through the priest the mind inspires.
The word unto the prophet spoken
Was writ on tables yet unbroken;
The word by seers or sibyls told,
In groves of oak, or fanes of gold,
Still floats upon the morning wind,
Still whispers to the willing mind.
One accent of the Holy Ghost
The heedless world hath never lost.
I know what say the fathers wise,—
The Book itself before me lies,
Old *Chrysostom*, best Augustine,
And he who blent both in his line,
The younger *Golden Lips* or mines,
Taylor, the Shakespeare of divines.
His words are music in my ear,
I see his cowlèd portrait dear;
And yet, for all his faith could see,
I would not the good bishop be.

1839   1840

THE SPHINX.

THE Sphinx is drowsy,
    Her wings are furled;
Her ear is heavy,
    She broods on the world.
"Who'll tell me my secret,
    The ages have kept?—
I awaited the seer,
    While they slumbered and slept;—

"The fate of the man-child;
    The meaning of man;
Known fruit of the unknown;
    Dædalian plan;

Out of sleeping a waking,
　　Out of waking a sleep;
Life death overtaking;
　　Deep underneath deep?

"Erect as a sunbeam,
　　Upspringeth the palm;
The elephant browses,
　　Undaunted and calm;
In beautiful motion
　　The thrush plies his wings;
Kind leaves of his covert,
　　Your silence he sings.

"The waves, unashamed,
　　In difference sweet,
Play glad with the breezes,
　　Old playfellows meet;
The journeying atoms,
　　Primordial wholes,
Firmly draw, firmly drive,
　　By their animate poles.

"Sea, earth, air, sound, silence,
　　Plant, quadruped, bird,
By one music enchanted,
　　One deity stirred,—
Each the other adorning,
　　Accompany still;
Night veileth the morning,
　　The vapor the hill.

"The babe by its mother
　　Lies bathed in joy;
Glide its hours uncounted,—
　　The sun is its toy;
Shines the peace of all being,
　　Without cloud, in its eyes;
And the sum of the world
　　In soft miniature lies.

"But man crouches and blushes,
　　Absconds and conceals;

He creepeth and peepeth,
    He palters and steals;
Infirm, melancholy,
    Jealous glancing around,
An oaf, an accomplice,
    He poisons the ground.

"Out spoke the great mother,
    Beholding his fear;—
At the sound of her accents
    Cold shuddered the sphere:—
'Who has drugged my boy's cup?
    Who has mixed my boy's bread?
Who, with sadness and madness,
    Has turned my child's head?' "

I heard a poet answer,
    Aloud and cheerfully,
"Say on, sweet Sphinx! thy dirges
    Are pleasant songs to me.
Deep love lieth under
    These pictures of time;
They fade in the light of
    Their meaning sublime.

"The fiend that man harries
    Is love of the Best;
Yawns the pit of the Dragon,
    Lit by rays from the Blest.
The Lethe of nature
    Can't trance him again,
Whose soul sees the perfect,
    Which his eyes seek in vain.

"To vision profounder,
    Man's spirit must dive;
To his aye-rolling orb
    No goal will arrive;
The heavens that now draw him
    With sweetness untold,

Once found,—for new heavens
   He spurneth the old.

"Pride ruined the angels,
   Their shame them restores;
Lurks the joy that is sweetest
   In stings of remorse.
Have I a lover
   Who is noble and free?—
I would he were nobler
   Than to love me.

"Eterne alternation
   Now follows, now flies;
And under pain, pleasure,—
   Under pleasure, pain lies.
Love works at the centre,
   Heart-heaving alway;
Forth speed the strong pulses
   To the borders of day.

"Dull Sphinx, Jove keep thy five wits;
   Thy sight is growing blear;
Rue, myrrh, and cummin for the Sphinx,
   Her muddy eyes to clear!"
The old Sphinx bit her thick lip,—
   Said, "Who taught thee me to name?
I am thy spirit, yoke-fellow,
   Of thine eye I am eyebeam.

"Thou art the unanswered question;
   Couldst see thy proper eye,
Alway it asketh, asketh;
   And each answer is a lie.
So take thy quest through nature,
   It through thousand natures ply;
Ask on, thou clothed eternity;
   Time is the false reply."

Uprose the merry Sphinx,
   And crouched no more in stone;
She melted into purple cloud,
   She silvered in the moon;

She spired into a yellow flame;
   She flowered in blossoms red;
She flowed into a foaming wave;
   She stood Monadnoc's head.

Thorough a thousand voices
   Spoke the universal dame:
"Who telleth one of my meanings,
   Is master of all I am."

1841

GIVE ALL TO LOVE.

Give all to love:
Obey thy heart;
Friends, kindred, days,
Estate, good-fame,
Plans, credit and the Muse,—
Nothing refuse.

'T is a brave master;
Let it have scope:
Follow it utterly,
Hope beyond hope:
High and more high
It dives into noon,
With wing unspent,
Untold intent;
But it is a god,
Knows its own path
And the outlets of the sky.

It was never for the mean;
It requireth courage stout.
Souls above doubt,
Valor unbending,
It will reward,—
They shall return
More than they were,
And ever ascending.

Leave all for love;
Yet, hear me, yet,
One word more thy heart behoved,
One pulse more of firm endeavor,—
Keep thee to-day,
To-morrow, forever,
Free as an Arab
Of thy beloved.

Cling with life to the maid;
But when the surprise,
First vague shadow of surmise
Flits across her bosom young,
Of a joy apart from thee,
Free be she, fancy-free;
Nor thou detain her vesture's hem,
Nor the palest rose she flung
From her summer diadem.

Though thou loved her as thyself,
As a self of purer clay,
Though her parting dims the day,
Stealing grace from all alive;
Heartily know,
When half-gods go,
The gods arrive.

1846(1847)

URIEL.

It fell in the ancient periods
    Which the brooding soul surveys,
Or ever the wild Time coined itself
    Into calendar months and days.

This was the lapse of Uriel,
Which in Paradise befell.
Once, among the Pleiads walking,
Seyd overheard the young gods talking;
And the treason, too long pent,

To his ears was evident.
The young deities discussed
Laws of form, and metre just,
Orb, quintessence, and sunbeams,
What subsisteth, and what seems.
One, with low tones that decide,
And doubt and reverend use defied,
With a look that solved the sphere,
And stirred the devils everywhere,
Gave his sentiment divine
Against the being of a line.
'Line in nature is not found;
Unit and universe are round;
In vain produced, all rays return;
Evil will bless, and ice will burn.'
As Uriel spoke with piercing eye,
A shudder ran around the sky;
The stern old war-gods shook their heads,
The seraphs frowned from myrtle-beds;
Seemed to the holy festival
The rash word boded ill to all;
The balance-beam of Fate was bent;
The bounds of good and ill were rent;
Strong Hades could not keep his own,
But all slid to confusion.

A sad self-knowledge, withering, fell
On the beauty of Uriel;
In heaven once eminent, the god
Withdrew, that hour, into his cloud;
Whether doomed to long gyration
In the sea of generation,
Or by knowledge grown too bright
To hit the nerve of feebler sight.
Straightway, a forgetting wind
Stole over the celestial kind,
And their lips the secret kept,
If in ashes the fire-seed slept.
But now and then, truth-speaking things
Shamed the angels' veiling wings;
And, shrilling from the solar course,
Or from fruit of chemic force,
Procession of a soul in matter,

Or the speeding change of water,
Or out of the good of evil born,
Came Uriel's voice of cherub scorn,
And a blush tinged the upper sky,
And the gods shook, they knew not why.

1840–1843(?)   1846(1847)

THRENODY.

THE south wind brings
Life, sunshine and desire,
And on every mount and meadow
Breathes aromatic fire;
But over the dead he has no power,
The lost, the lost, he cannot restore;
And, looking over the hills, I mourn
The darling who shall not return.

I see my empty house,
I see my trees repair their boughs;
And he, the wondrous child,
Whose silver warble wild
Outvalued every pulsing sound
Within the air's cerulean round,—
The hyacinthine boy, for whom
Morn well might break and April bloom,—
The gracious boy, who did adorn
The world whereinto he was born,
And by his countenance repay
The favor of the loving Day,—
Has disappeared from the Day's eye;
Far and wide she cannot find him;
My hopes pursue, they cannot bind him.
Returned this day, the south wind searches,
And finds young pines and budding birches;
But finds not the budding man;
Nature, who lost, cannot remake him;
Fate let him fall, Fate can't retake him;
Nature, Fate, men, him seek in vain.

And whither now, my truant wise and sweet,
O, whither tend thy feet?
I had the right, few days ago,
Thy steps to watch, thy place to know:
How have I forfeited the right?
Hast thou forgot me in a new delight?
I hearken for thy household cheer,
O eloquent child!
Whose voice, an equal messenger,
Conveyed thy meaning mild.
What though the pains and joys
Whereof it spoke were toys
Fitting his age and ken,
Yet fairest dames and bearded men,
Who heard the sweet request,
So gentle, wise and grave,
Bended with joy to his behest
And let the world's affairs go by,
A while to share his cordial game,
Or mend his wicker wagon-frame,
Still plotting how their hungry ear
That winsome voice again might hear;
For his lips could well pronounce
Words that were persuasions.

Gentlest guardians marked serene
His early hope, his liberal mien;
Took counsel from his guiding eyes
To make this wisdom earthly wise.
Ah, vainly do these eyes recall
The school-march, each day's festival,
When every morn my bosom glowed
To watch the convoy on the road;
The babe in willow wagon closed,
With rolling eyes and face composed;
With children forward and behind,
Like Cupids studiously inclined;
And he the chieftain paced beside,
The centre of the troop allied,
With sunny face of sweet repose,
To guard the babe from fancied foes.
The little captain innocent
Took the eye with him as he went;

Each village senior paused to scan
And speak the lovely caravan.
From the window I look out
To mark thy beautiful parade,
Stately marching in cap and coat
To some tune by fairies played;—
A music heard by thee alone
To works as noble led thee on.

Now Love and Pride, alas! in vain,
Up and down their glances strain.
The painted sled stands where it stood;
The kennel by the corded wood;
His gathered sticks to stanch the wall
Of the snow-tower, when snow should fall;
The ominous hole he dug in the sand,
And childhood's castles built or planned;
His daily haunts I well discern,—
The poultry-yard, the shed, the barn,—
And every inch of garden ground
Paced by the blessed feet around,
From the roadside to the brook
Whereinto he loved to look.
Step the meek fowls where erst they ranged;
The wintry garden lies unchanged;
The brook into the stream runs on;
But the deep-eyed boy is gone.

On that shaded day,
Dark with more clouds than tempests are,
When thou didst yield thy innocent breath
In birdlike heavings unto death,
Night came, and Nature had not thee;
I said, 'We are mates in misery.'
The morrow dawned with needless glow;
Each snowbird chirped, each fowl must crow;
Each tramper started; but the feet
Of the most beautiful and sweet
Of human youth had left the hill
And garden,—they were bound and still.
There's not a sparrow or a wren,
There's not a blade of autumn grain,
Which the four seasons do not tend

And tides of life and increase lend;
And every chick of every bird,
And weed and rock-moss is preferred.
O ostrich-like forgetfulness!
O loss of larger in the less!
Was there no star that could be sent,
No watcher in the firmament,
No angel from the countless host
That loiters round the crystal coast,
Could stoop to heal that only child,
Nature's sweet marvel undefiled,
And keep the blossom of the earth,
Which all her harvests were not worth?
Not mine,—I never called thee mine,
But Nature's heir,—if I repine,
And seeing rashly torn and moved
Not what I made, but what I loved,
Grow early old with grief that thou
Must to the wastes of Nature go,—
'T is because a general hope
Was quenched, and all must doubt and grope.
For flattering planets seemed to say
This child should ills of ages stay,
By wondrous tongue, and guided pen,
Bring the flown Muses back to men.
Perchance not he but Nature ailed,
The world and not the infant failed.
It was not ripe yet to sustain
A genius of so fine a strain,
Who gazed upon the sun and moon
As if he came unto his own,
And, pregnant with his grander thought,
Brought the old order into doubt.
His beauty once their beauty tried;
They could not feed him, and he died,
And wandered backward as in scorn,
To wait an æon to be born.
Ill day which made this beauty waste,
Plight broken, this high face defaced!
Some went and came about the dead;
And some in books of solace read;
Some to their friends the tidings say;
Some went to write, some went to pray;

One tarried here, there hurried one;
But their heart abode with none.
Covetous death bereaved us all,
To aggrandize one funeral.
The eager fate which carried thee
Took the largest part of me:
For this losing is true dying;
This is lordly man's down-lying,
This his slow but sure reclining,
Star by star his world resigning.

O child of paradise,
Boy who made dear his father's home,
In whose deep eyes
Men read the welfare of the times to come,
I am too much bereft.
The world dishonored thou hast left.
O truth's and nature's costly lie!
O trusted broken prophecy!
O richest fortune sourly crossed!
Born for the future, to the future lost!

The deep Heart answered, 'Weepest thou?
Worthier cause for passion wild
If I had not taken the child.
And deemest thou as those who pore,
With aged eyes, short way before,—
Think'st Beauty vanished from the coast
Of matter, and thy darling lost?
Taught he not thee—the man of eld,
Whose eyes within his eyes beheld
Heaven's numerous hierarchy span
The mystic gulf from God to man?
To be alone wilt thou begin
When worlds of lovers hem thee in?
To-morrow, when the masks shall fall
That dizen Nature's carnival,
The pure shall see by their own will,
Which overflowing Love shall fill,
'T is not within the force of fate
The fate-conjoined to separate.
But thou, my votary, weepest thou?
I gave thee sight—where is it now?

I taught thy heart beyond the reach
Of ritual, bible, or of speech;
Wrote in thy mind's transparent table,
As far as the incommunicable;
Taught thee each private sign to raise
Lit by the supersolar blaze.
Past utterance, and past belief,
And past the blasphemy of grief,
The mysteries of Nature's heart;
And though no Muse can these impart,
Throb thine with Nature's throbbing breast,
And all is clear from east to west.
'I came to thee as to a friend;
Dearest, to thee I did not send
Tutors, but a joyful eye,
Innocence that matched the sky,
Lovely locks, a form of wonder,
Laughter rich as woodland thunder,
That thou might'st entertain apart
The richest flowering of all art:
And, as the great all-loving Day
Through smallest chambers takes its way,
That thou might'st break thy daily bread
With prophet, savior and head;
That thou might'st cherish for thine own
The riches of sweet Mary's Son,
Boy-Rabbi, Israel's paragon.
And thoughtest thou such guest
Would in thy hall take up his rest?
Would rushing life forget her laws,
Fate's glowing revolution pause?
High omens ask diviner guess;
Not to be conned to tediousness.
And know my higher gifts unbind
The zone that girds the incarnate mind.
When the scanty shores are full
With Thought's perilous, whirling pool;
When frail Nature can no more,
Then the Spirit strikes the hour:
My servant Death, with solving rite,
Pours finite into infinite.
Wilt thou freeze love's tidal flow,
Whose streams through nature circling go?

Nail the wild star to its track
On the half-climbed zodiac?
Light is light which radiates,
Blood is blood which circulates,
Life is life which generates,
And many-seeming life is one,—
Wilt thou transfix and make it none?
Its onward force too starkly pent
In figure, bone, and lineament?
Wilt thou, uncalled, interrogate,
Talker! the unreplying Fate?
Nor see the genius of the whole
Ascendant in the private soul,
Beckon it when to go and come,
Self-announced its hour of doom?
Fair the soul's recess and shrine,
Magic-built to last a season;
Masterpiece of love benign,
Fairer that expansive reason
Whose omen 't is, and sign.
Wilt thou not ope thy heart to know
What rainbows teach, and sunsets show?
Verdict which accumulates
From lengthening scroll of human fates,
Voice of earth to earth returned,
Prayers of saints that inly burned,—
Saying, *What is excellent,*
As God lives, is permanent;
Hearts are dust, hearts' loves remain;
Heart's love will meet thee again.
Revere the Maker; fetch thine eye
Up to his style, and manners of the sky.
Not of adamant and gold
Built he heaven stark and cold;
No, but a nest of bending reeds,
Flowering grass and scented weeds;
Or like a traveller's fleeing tent,
Or bow above the tempest bent;
Built of tears and sacred flames,
And virtue reaching to its aims;
Built of furtherance and pursuing,
Not of spent deeds, but of doing.
Silent rushes the swift Lord

Through ruined systems still restored,
Broadsowing, bleak and void to bless,
Plants with worlds the wilderness;
Waters with tears of ancient sorrow
Apples of Eden ripe to-morrow.
House and tenant go to ground,
Lost in God, in Godhead found.'

1842–1843(?)   1846(1847)

MERLIN.

I.

Thy trivial harp will never please
Or fill my craving ear;
Its chords should ring as blows the breeze,
Free, peremptory, clear.
No jingling serenader's art,
Nor tinkle of piano strings,
Can make the wild blood start
In its mystic springs.
The kingly bard
Must smite the chords rudely and hard,
As with hammer or with mace;
That they may render back
Artful thunder, which conveys
Secrets of the solar track,
Sparks of the supersolar blaze.
Merlin's blows are strokes of fate,
Chiming with the forest tone,
When boughs buffet boughs in the wood;
Chiming with the gasp and moan
Of the ice-imprisoned flood;
With the pulse of manly hearts;
With the voice of orators;
With the din of city arts;
With the cannonade of wars;
With the marches of the brave;
And prayers of might from martyrs' cave.

Great is the art,
Great be the manners, of the bard.

He shall not his brain encumber
With the coil of rhythm and number;
But, leaving rule and pale forethought,
He shall aye climb
For his rhyme.
'Pass in, pass in,' the angels say,
'In to the upper doors,
Nor count compartments of the floors,
But mount to paradise
By the stairway of surprise.'

Blameless master of the games,
King of sport that never shames,
He shall daily joy dispense
Hid in song's sweet influence.
Forms more cheerly live and go,
What time the subtle mind
Sings aloud the tune whereto
Their pulses beat,
And march their feet,
And their members are combined.
By Sybarites beguiled,
He shall no task decline;
Merlin's mighty line
Extremes of nature reconciled,—
Bereaved a tyrant of his will,
And made the lion mild.
Songs can the tempest still,
Scattered on the stormy air,
Mould the year to fair increase,
And bring in poetic peace.

He shall not seek to weave,
In weak, unhappy times,
Efficacious rhymes;
Wait his returning strength.
Bird that from the nadir's floor
To the zenith's top can soar,—
The soaring orbit of the muse exceeds that
        journey's length.
Nor profane affect to hit
Or compass that, by meddling wit,
Which only the propitious mind

Publishes when 't is inclined.
There are open hours
When the God's will sallies free,
And the dull idiot might see
The flowing fortunes of a thousand years;—
Sudden, at unawares,
Self-moved, fly-to the doors,
Nor sword of angels could reveal
What they conceal.

II.

THE rhyme of the poet
Modulates the kin's affairs;
Balance-loving Nature
Made all things in pairs.
To every foot its antipode;
Each color with its counter glowed;
To every tone beat answering tones,
Higher or graver;
Flavor gladly blends with flavor;
Leaf answers leaf upon the bough;
And match the paired cotyledons.
Hands to hands, and feet to feet,
In one body grooms and brides;
Eldest rite, two married sides
In every mortal meet.
Light's far furnace shines,
Smelting balls and bars,
Forging double stars,
Glittering twins and trines.
The animals are sick with love,
Lovesick with rhyme;
Each with all propitious Time
Into chorus wove.

Like the dancers' ordered band,
Thoughts come also hand in hand;
In equal couples mated,
Or else alternated;
Adding by their mutual gage,
One to other, health and age.

Solitary fancies go
Short-lived wandering to and fro,
Most like to bachelors,
Or an ungiven maid,
Not ancestors,
With no posterity to make the lie afraid,
Or keep truth undecayed.
Perfect-paired as eagle's wings,
Justice is the rhyme of things;
Trade and counting use
The self-same tuneful muse;
And Nemesis,
Who with even matches odd,
Who athwart space redresses
The partial wrong,
Fills the just period,
And finishes the song.

Subtle rhymes, with ruin rife,
Murmur in the house of life,
Sung by the Sisters as they spin;
In perfect time and measure they
Build and unbuild our echoing clay.
As the two twilights of the day
Fold us music-drunken in.

1845–1846   1846(1847)

HAMATREYA.

BULKELEY, Hunt, Willard, Hosmer, Meriam, Flint,
Possessed the land which rendered to their toil
Hay, corn, roots, hemp, flax, apples, wool and wood.
Each of these landlords walked amidst his farm,
Saying, ' 'T is mine, my children's and my name's.
How sweet the west wind sounds in my own trees!
How graceful climb those shadows on my hill!
I fancy these pure waters and the flags
Know me, as does my dog: we sympathize;
And, I affirm, my actions smack of the soil.'

Where are these men? Asleep beneath their grounds:
And strangers, fond as they, their furrows plough.
Earth laughs in flowers, to see her boastful boys
Earth-proud, proud of the earth which is not theirs;
Who steer the plough, but cannot steer their feet
Clear of the grave.
They added ridge to valley, brook to pond,
And sighed for all that bounded their domain;
'This suits me for a pasture; that's my park;
We must have clay, lime, gravel, granite-ledge,
And misty lowland, where to go for peat.
The land is well,—lies fairly to the south.
'T is good, when you have crossed the sea and back,
To find the sitfast acres where you left them.'
Ah! the hot owner sees not Death, who adds
Him to his land, a lump of mould the more.
Hear what the Earth says:—

EARTH-SONG.

'Mine and yours;
Mine, not yours,
Earth endures;
Stars abide—
Shine down in the old sea;
Old are the shores;
But where are old men?
I who have seen much,
Such have I never seen.

'The lawyer's deed
Ran sure,
In tail,
To them, and to their heirs
Who shall succeed,
Without fail,
Forevermore.

'Here is the land,
Shaggy with wood,
With its old valley,
Mound and flood.
But the heritors?—

Fled like the flood's foam.
The lawyer, and the laws,
And the kingdom,
Clean swept herefrom.

'They called me theirs,
Who so controlled me;
Yet every one
Wished to stay, and is gone,
How am I theirs,
If they cannot hold me,
But I hold them?'

When I heard the Earth-song,
I was no longer brave;
My avarice cooled
Like lust in the chill of the grave.

1845(?) 1846(?)   1846(1847)

ODE.

INSCRIBED TO W. H. CHANNING.

THOUGH loath to grieve
The evil time's sole patriot,
I cannot leave
My honied thought
For the priest's cant,
Or statesman's rant.

If I refuse
My study for their politique,
Which at the best is trick,
The angry Muse
Puts confusion in my brain.

But who is he that prates
Of the culture of mankind,
Of better arts and life?

Go, blindworm, go,
Behold the famous States
Harrying Mexico
With rifle and with knife!

Or who, with accent bolder,
Dare praise the freedom-loving mountaineer?
I found by thee, O rushing Contoocook!
And in thy valleys, Agiochook!
The jackals of the negro-holder.

The God who made New Hampshire
Taunted the lofty land
With little men;—
Small bat and wren
House in the oak:—
If earth-fire cleave
The upheaved land, and bury the folk,
The southern crocodile would grieve.
Virtue palters; Right is hence;
Freedom praised, but hid;
Funeral eloquence
Rattles the coffin-lid.

What boots thy zeal,
O glowing friend,
That would indignant rend
The northland from the south?
Wherefore? to what good end?
Boston Bay and Bunker Hill
Would serve things still;—
Things are of the snake.

The horseman serves the horse,
The neatherd serves the neat,
The merchant serves his meat;
'T is the day of the chattel,
Web to weave, and corn to grind;
Things are in the saddle,
And ride mankind.

There are two laws discrete,
Not reconciled,—

Law for man, and law for thing;
The last builds town and fleet,
But it runs wild,
And doth the man unking.

'T is fit the forest fall,
The steep be graded,
The mountain tunnelled,
The sand shaded,
The orchard planted,
The glebe tilled,
The prairie granted,
The steamer built.

Let man serve law for man;
Live for friendship, live for love,
For truth's and harmony's behoof;
The state may follow how it can,
As Olympus follows Jove.

Yet do not I implore
The wrinkled shopman to my sounding woods,
Nor bid the unwilling senator
Ask votes of thrushes in the solitudes.
Every one to his chosen work;—
Foolish hands may mix and mar;
Wise and sure the issues are.
Round they roll till dark is light,
Sex to sex, and even to odd;—
The over-god
Who marries Right to Might,
Who peoples, unpeoples,—
He who exterminates
Races by stronger races,
Black by white faces,—
Knows to bring honey
Out of the lion;
Grafts gentlest scion
On pirate and Turk.

The Cossack eats Poland,
Like stolen fruit;
Her last noble is ruined,

Her last poet mute:
Straight, into double band
The victors divide;
Half for freedom strike and stand;—
The astonished Muse finds thousands at her side.

1845(?) 1846(?)   1846(1847)

BACCHUS.

BRING me wine, but wine which never grew
In the belly of the grape,
Or grew on vine whose tap-roots, reaching through
Under the Andes to the Cape,
Suffer no savor of the earth to scape.

Let its grapes the morn salute
From a nocturnal root,
Which feels the acrid juice
Of Styx and Erebus;
And turns the woe of Night,
By its own craft, to a more rich delight.

We buy ashes for bread;
We buy diluted wine;
Give me of the true,—
Whose ample leaves and tendrils curled
Among the silver hills of heaven
Draw everlasting dew;
Wine of wine,
Blood of the world,
Form of forms, and mould of statures,
That I intoxicated,
And by the draught assimilated,
May float at pleasure through all natures;
The bird-language rightly spell,
And that which roses say so well.

Wine that is shed
Like the torrents of the sun
Up the horizon walls,

Or like the Atlantic streams, which run
When the South Sea calls.

Water and bread,
Food which needs no transmuting,
Rainbow-flowering, wisdom-fruiting,
Wine which is already man,
Food which teach and reason can.

Wine which Music is,—
Music and wine are one,—
That I, drinking this,
Shall hear far Chaos talk with me;
Kings unborn shall walk with me;
And the poor grass shall plot and plan
What it will do when it is man.
Quickened so, will I unlock
Every crypt of every rock.

I thank the joyful juice
For all I know;—
Winds of remembering
Of the ancient being blow,
And seeming-solid walls of use
Open and flow.

Pour, Bacchus! the remembering wine;
Retrieve the loss of me and mine!
Vine for vine be antidote,
And the grape requite the lote!
Haste to cure the old despair,—
Reason in Nature's lotus drenched,
The memory of ages quenched;
Give them again to shine;
Let wine repair what this undid;
And where the infection slid,
A dazzling memory revive;
Refresh the faded tints,
Recut the aged prints,
And write my old adventures with the pen
Which on the first day drew,
Upon the tablets blue,
The dancing Pleiads and eternal men.

1846   1846(1847)

DAYS.

DAUGHTERS of Time, the hypocritic Days,
Muffled and dumb like barefoot dervishes,
And marching single in an endless file,
Bring diadems and fagots in their hands.
To each they offer gifts after his will,
Bread, kingdoms, stars, and sky that holds them all.
I, in my pleached garden, watched the pomp,
Forgot my morning wishes, hastily
Took a few herbs and apples, and the Day
Turned and departed silent. I, too late,
Under her solemn fillet saw the scorn.

1851   1857

BRAHMA.

IF the red slayer think he slays,
    Or if the slain think he is slain,
They know not well the subtle ways
    I keep, and pass, and turn again.

Far or forgot to me is near;
    Shadow and sunlight are the same;
The vanished gods to me appear;
    And one to me are shame and fame.

They reckon ill who leave me out;
    When me they fly, I am the wings;
I am the doubter and the doubt,
    And I the hymn the Brahmin sings.

The strong gods pine for my abode,
    And pine in vain the sacred Seven;
But thou, meek lover of the good!
    Find me, and turn thy back on heaven.

1856   1857

TWO RIVERS.

THY summer voice, Musketaquit,
Repeats the music of the rain;
But sweeter rivers pulsing flit
Through thee, as thou through Concord Plain.

Thou in thy narrow banks art pent:
The stream I love unbounded goes
Through flood and sea and firmament;
Through light, through life, it forward flows.

I see the inundation sweet,
I hear the spending of the stream
Through years, through men, through nature fleet,
Through love and thought, through power and dream.

Musketaquit, a goblin strong,
Of shard and flint makes jewels gay;
They lose their grief who hear his song,
And where he winds is the day of day.

So forth and brighter fares my stream,—
Who drink it shall not thirst again;
No darkness stains its equal gleam,
And ages drop in it like rain.

1856   1858

WALDEINSAMKEIT.

I DO not count the hours I spend
In wandering by the sea;
The forest is my loyal friend,
Like God it useth me.

In plains that room for shadows make
Of skirting hills to lie,
Bound in by streams which give and take
Their colors from the sky;

Or on the mountain-crest sublime,
Or down the oaken glade,
O what have I to do with time?
For this the day was made.

Cities of mortals woe-begone
Fantastic care derides,
But in the serious landscape lone
Stern benefit abides.

Sheen will tarnish, honey cloy,
And merry is only a mask of sad,
But, sober on a fund of joy,
The woods at heart are glad.

There the great Planter plants
Of fruitful worlds the grain,
And with a million spells enchants
The souls that walk in pain.

Still on the seeds of all he made
The rose of beauty burns;
Through times that wear and forms that fade,
Immortal youth returns.

The black ducks mounting from the lake,
The pigeon in the pines,
The bittern's boom, a desert make
Which no false art refines.

Down in yon watery nook,
Where bearded mists divide,
The gray old gods whom Chaos knew,
The sires of Nature, hide.

Aloft, in secret veins of air,
Blows the sweet breath of song,
O, few to scale those uplands dare,
Though they to all belong!

See thou bring not to field or stone
The fancies found in books;
Leave authors' eyes, and fetch your own,
To brave the landscape's looks.

Oblivion here thy wisdom is,
Thy thrift, the sleep of cares;
For a proud idleness like this
Crowns all thy mean affairs.

1857   1858

BOSTON HYMN.

READ IN MUSIC HALL, JANUARY 1, 1863.

THE word of the Lord by night
To the watching Pilgrims came,
As they sat by the seaside,
And filled their hearts with flame.

God said, I am tired of kings,
I suffer them no more;
Up to my ear the morning brings
The outrage of the poor.

Think ye I made this ball
A field of havoc and war,
Where tyrants great and tyrants small
Might harry the weak and poor?

My angel,—his name is Freedom,—
Choose him to be your king;
He shall cut pathways east and west
And fend you with his wing.

Lo! I uncover the land
Which I hid of old time in the West,
As the sculptor uncovers the statue
When he has wrought his best;

I show Columbia, of the rocks
Which dip their foot in the seas
And soar to the air-borne flocks
Of clouds and the boreal fleece.

I will divide my goods;
Call in the wretch and slave:
None shall rule but the humble,
And none but Toil shall have.

I will have never a noble,
No lineage counted great;
Fishers and choppers and ploughmen
Shall constitute a state.

Go, cut down trees in the forest
And trim the straightest boughs;
Cut down trees in the forest
And build me a wooden house.

Call the people together,
The young men and the sires,
The digger in the harvest field,
Hireling and him that hires;

And here in a pine state-house
They shall choose men to rule
In every needful faculty,
In church and state and school.

Lo, now! if these poor men
Can govern the land and sea
And make just laws below the sun,
As planets faithful be.

And ye shall succor men;
'T is nobleness to serve;
Help them who cannot help again:
Beware from right to swerve.

I break your bonds and masterships,
And I unchain the slave:
Free be his heart and hand henceforth
As wind and wandering wave.

I cause from every creature
His proper good to flow:
As much as he is and doeth,
So much he shall bestow.

But, laying hands on another
To coin his labor and sweat,
He goes in pawn to his victim
For eternal years in debt.

To-day unbind the captive,
So only are ye unbound;
Lift up a people from the dust,
Trump of their rescue, sound!

Pay ransom to the owner
And fill the bag to the brim.
Who is the owner? The slave is owner,
And ever was. Pay him.

O North! give him beauty for rags,
And honor, O South! for his shame;
Nevada! coin thy golden crags
With Freedom's image and name.

Up! and the dusky race
That sat in darkness long,—
Be swift their feet as antelopes,
And as behemoth strong.

Come, East and West and North,
By races, as snow-flakes,
And carry my purpose forth,
Which neither halts nor shakes.

My will fulfilled shall be,
For, in daylight or in dark,
My thunderbolt has eyes to see
His way home to the mark.

1863

TERMINUS.

It is time to be old,
To take in sail:—
The god of bounds,
Who sets to seas a shore,

Came to me in his fatal rounds,
And said: 'No more!
No farther shoot
Thy broad ambitious branches, and thy root.
Fancy departs: no more invent;
Contract thy firmament
To compass of a tent.
There's not enough for this and that,
Make thy option which of two;
Economize the failing river,
Not the less revere the Giver,
Leave the many and hold the few.
Timely wise accept the terms,
Soften the fall with wary foot;
A little while
Still plan and smile,
And,—fault of novel germs,—
Mature the unfallen fruit.
Curse, if thou wilt, thy sires,
Bad husbands of their fires,
Who, when they gave thee breath,
Failed to bequeath
The needful sinew stark as once,
The Baresark marrow to thy bones,
But left a legacy of ebbing veins,
Inconstant heat and nerveless reins,—
Amid the Muses, left thee deaf and dumb,
Amid the gladiators, halt and numb.'

As the bird trims her to the gale,
I trim myself to the storm of time,
I man the rudder, reef the sail,
Obey the voice at eve obeyed at prime:
'Lowly faithful, banish fear,
Right onward drive unharmed;
The port, well worth the cruise, is near,
And every wave is charmed.'

1850–1851, 1866(?)   1867

SELECTED BIBLIOGRAPHY

WORKS BY RALPH WALDO EMERSON

Nature, 1836   Essay
Essays: First Series, 1841
Essays: Second Series, 1844
Poems, 1847
Nature, Addresses, and Lectures (also titled *Miscellanies*), 1849
Representative Men: Seven Lectures, 1850
English Traits, 1856   Essays
Th Conduct of Life, 1860   Essays
May-Day and Other Pieces, 1867   Poems
Society and Solitude, 1870   Essays
Letters and Social Aims, 1876   Essays
Selected Poems, 1876
Complete Works, Centenary Edition, 12 vols., 1903-04
The Letters of Ralph Waldo Emerson, 6 vols., 1939
The Early Lectures of Ralph Waldo Emerson, 3 vols., 1959-72
The Correspondence of Emerson and Carlyle, 1964
The Journals and Miscellaneous Notebooks, 16 vols., 1960-82
Emerson in His Journals, 1982

BIOGRAPHY AND CRITICISM

Allen, Gay Wilson. *Waldo Emerson: A Biography*. New York: Viking, 1981.

Anderson, Quentin. "The Failure of the Fathers." In his *The Imperial Self*. New York: Knopf, 1971, pp. 3-58.

Bercovitch, Sacvan. "The Myth of America." In his *The Puritan Origins of the American Self*. New Haven and London: Yale Univ. Press, 1975, pp. 136-186.

Berthoff, Warner. " 'Building Discourse': The Genesis of Emerson's *Nature*." In his *Fictions and Events: Essays in Criticism and Literary History*. New York: E. P. Dutton, 1971, pp. 182-218.

Bishop, Jonathan. *Emerson on the Soul*. Cambridge: Harvard Univ. Press, 1964.

Buell, Lawrence. *Literary Transcendentalism: Style and Vision in the American Renaissance*. Ithaca and London: Cornell Univ. Press, 1973.

Carpenter, Frederic Ives. *Emerson Handbook*. New York: Hendricks House, 1953.

Cowan, Michael H. *City of the West: Emerson, America, and Urban Metaphor*. New Haven and London: Yale Univ. Press, 1967.

Hopkins, Vivian C. *Spires of Form: A Study of Emerson's Aesthetic Theory*. Cambridge: Harvard Univ. Press, 1951.

Konvitz, Milton R., and Stephen E. Whicher, eds. *Emerson: A Collection of Critical Essays*. Englewood Cliffs, N.J.: Prentice-Hall, 1962.

Levin, David, ed. *Emerson—Prophecy, Metamorphosis, and Influence: Selected Papers from the English Institute*. New York: Columbia Univ. Press, 1975.

Matthiessen, F. O. *American Renaissance: Art and Expression in the Age of Emerson and Whitman*. London and New York: Oxford Univ. Press, 1941.

Miller, Perry. "From Edwards to Emerson." In his *Errand into the Wilderness*. Cambridge: Harvard Univ. Press, 1956, pp. 184-203.

Packer, Barbara L. *Emerson's Fall: A New Interpretation of the Major Essays*. New York: Continuum, 1982.

Paul, Sherman. *Emerson's Angle of Vision: Man and Nature in American Experience*. Cambridge: Harvard Univ. Press, 1952.

Porte, Joel. *Representative Man: Ralph Waldo Emerson in His Time*. New York: Oxford Univ. Press. 1979.

Rusk, Ralph L. *The Life of Ralph Waldo Emerson*. New York: Charles Scribner's Sons, 1949.

Sealts, Merton M., Jr., and Alfred R. Ferguson, eds. *Emerson's Nature: Origin, Growth, Meaning*. 2nd ed., enl. Carbondale: Southern Illinois Univ. Press; London: Feffer, 1979.

Whicher, Stephen E. *Freedom and Fate: An Inner Life of Ralph Waldo Emerson*. Philadelphia: Univ. of Pennsylvania Press, 1953.

Ziff, Larzer. "Sloven Continent: Emerson and an American Idea" and "Right Naming: Emerson, Language, and Literature." In his *Literary Democracy: The Declaration of Cultural Independence in America*. New York: Viking, 1981.